45.00

Silence
and Listening
as Rhetorical Arts

DISCARDED

Silence and Listening as Rhetorical Arts

Edited by Cheryl Glenn and Krista Ratcliffe

Southern Illinois University Press
Carbondale and Edwardsville

14 13 12 11   4 3 2 1

Library of Congress Cataloging-in-Publication Data
Silence and listening as rhetorical arts / edited by Cheryl Glenn and Krista Ratcliffe.
    p. cm.
    Includes bibliographical references and index.
    ISBN-13: 978-0-8093-3017-1 (alk. paper)
    ISBN-10: 0-8093-3017-2 (alk. paper)
    ISBN-13: 978-0-8093-8616-1 (e-book)
    ISBN-10: 0-8093-8616-X (e-book)
    1. English language—Rhetoric—Study and teaching—United States. 2. Report
    writing—Study and teaching (Higher)—United States. 3. Silence—Study and
    teaching (Higher)—United States. 4. Listening—Study and teaching (Higher)—
    United States. I. Glenn, Cheryl. II. Ratcliffe, Krista, date.
PE1405.U6.S55 2011
808'.042'0711—dc22   2010015996

Contents

Silence
and Listening
as Rhetorical Arts

Introduction: Why Silence and Listening Are Important Rhetorical Arts

Cheryl Glenn and Krista Ratcliffe

Throughout Western history, speech has been considered a gift from the gods, the distinguishing characteristic of humans, and, therefore, the authorized medium of culture and power. Little wonder, then, that the positive features of silence and listening have been only briefly mentioned or subtly implied—if not completely ignored. Rarely have they been foregrounded as rhetorical arts vital to our communicative effectiveness.

Westerners have long forgotten (if we ever knew in the first place) the ancient Egyptian[1] and Pythagorean beliefs in the value of silence and listening. The first canon of Egyptian rhetoric was silence,[2] silence as a "moral posture and rhetorical tactic"—not to be confused with "passivity or quietism" (Fox 12). In his maxims, Egyptian vizier Ptahhotep writes that to make a lasting reputation among those who hear you, *listen* (qtd. in Fox 12). Kagemeni, another vizier, encourages silence as a way to establish a good reputation, and Amenemope develops the concept of "'The Truly Silent Man,' the man who succeeds by virtue of his unflagging inner repose and self control," which dictates silence (12). The Pythagoreans,[3] too, advocated silence and listening. Pythagoras, who is believed to have studied with the Egyptians, the Babylonians, and the East Indians (where he was influenced by the teachings of the Supreme Buddha, Gautama), required his initiates to remain silent for five years. Rather than talk and ask questions, the initiates were to listen and learn (Iamblicus 74). Although these early beliefs reference the agency available primarily to royal and educated men, they nevertheless demonstrate a judicious respect not just for the power of silence and listening but also for the spoken word. After all, "speaking is more powerful than any fighting," writes the pharaoh Khety III, to his son Merikare (qtd. in Lichtheim 32), and Ptahhotep records that "eloquence is rarer than emeralds" (qtd. in Fox 12). Preparing the mind through silence and listening was essential preparation for speaking. Spoken eloquence was the aspiration.

Our research in *Unspoken: A Rhetoric of Silence* and in *Rhetorical Listening: Identification, Gender, Whiteness* respects the power of the spoken word at the same time that it challenges the marginalized status of silence and listening. As our research indicates, these rhetorical arts extend beyond Egyptian and Pythagorean beliefs and practices. These arts have been conceptualized and employed in different times and places by many different people—some with power, some without—for purposes as diverse as showing reverence, gathering knowledge, planning action, buying time, and attempting to survive. Yet despite these disparate uses, the rhetorical arts of silence and listening have rarely been articulated within traditional Western rhetorical studies.

The main purpose of this collection, then, is to map such concepts and uses of silence and listening for rhetorical studies. For if serious reconsiderations of silence and listening are to resonate down the corridors of twenty-first-century rhetorical scholarship and language use, then other scholars must extend our initial research and findings. Yet *Silence and Listening as Rhetorical Arts* does much more than simply engage our own research. At the same time that it enriches and complicates our claims about silence and listening, it provides a forum for contributors to articulate multiple ways to historicize, theorize, analyze, and practice both silence and listening as rhetorical arts. And it is worth noting that *practice* signifies the performances of silence and listening in a variety of venues, including but not limited to the classroom. As such, this collection forwards three major arguments:

- Argument one: the arts of silence and listening are as important to rhetoric and composition studies as the traditionally emphasized arts of reading, writing, and speaking.
- Argument two: the arts of silence and listening are particularly effective for historicizing, theorizing, analyzing, and practicing the cultural stances and power of both dominant and nondominant (subaltern) groups.

- Argument three: the arts of silence and listening offer people multiple ways to negotiate and deliberate, whether with themselves or in dyadic, small-group, or large-scale situations.

Individuals, as well as entire political parties, professions, communities, and nations, can more productively discern and implement actions that are more ethical, efficient, and appropriate when all parties agree to engage in rhetorical situations that include not only respectful speaking, reading, and writing but also productive silence and rhetorical listening, all of which help prepare a person for eloquence.

Current Scholarship on Glenn's Silence and Ratcliffe's Listening

This section provides readers a review of scholarship that has evolved from our ideas about silence and listening. As such, it establishes a context for chapters in this collection that engage our research; simultaneously, this section may be read to determine what yet needs to be done in terms of not just extending our research but of moving beyond/outside it, as evidenced by some chapters here that do not directly engage our research but, rather, invoke other grounds for their claims about silence and listening.

Since the publication of Cheryl Glenn's 1997 *Rhetoric Retold*, with its sustained focus on the gendered nature of silence and silencing, her 2002 *JAC* "Silence: A Rhetorical Art for Resisting Discipline(s)," and her 2004 *Unspoken: A Rhetoric of Silence*, there has been a surge in the scholarly attention given to silence. Some of it is anchored in Glenn's work—but not all of it. Much of the sustained concentration on silence as a rhetorical art or purposeful position seems to be the result of morphic resonance.[4] Still, because Glenn's work on silence is multivalent, ranging as it does from the historical silences of women and other subaltern groups to silence as a rhetorical theory and praxis, scholars took from it what could be applied to their own projects.

Initially, recovering women's long-silenced voices was the main industry, with many scholars writing women into the tradition. Arthur E. Walzer and David Beard cite Glenn's foundational question, "What were the silencing mechanisms?" (20), to explain feminist interventions. Beth Burmester credits Glenn with explaining silencing as enclosure: "an enclosed life (domestic confinement)," "a closed body (chastity)," and "a closed mouth (silence)" (312). Nan Johnson argues that, by providing a history of prohibitions against women's participating in public discourse (Logan 157) and then "recovering the silenced voices of women whose contributions . . . have been overlooked" (Johnson 8), Glenn stands "directly in the line of significant canon revisionists" (8). Jessica Enoch encourages scholars to follow Glenn's lead in questioning the seeming silence or diligent obedience of women: "These women still have much to tell us—all we have to do is listen to their voices and their silences" (Glenn qtd. in Enoch 14). Listening to the rhetorical displays of Esther and Sor Juana, Julie K. Bokser invokes Glenn's admonition that "silence is perhaps the most undervalued and *under*-understood traditionally feminine rhetorical site" ("Sor Juana's Rhetoric" 18). As Frank Farmer tells us, "Largely because 'silence and silencing' are 'rhetorical sites most often associated with women,' we have only begun to understand the historical and potential importance of silence as a rhetorical strategy" (2).

Because speaking out has long been the gendered signal of masculinity, silence has long been gendered "feminine," as a lamentable essence of weakness. As a result, then, Glenn's work has been used, according to Wendy S. Hesford, to expand "the rhetorical tradition to include women and minority-group members and [to map] hierarchies of gender, class, race, sexuality, ability," and exclusion ("Global" 793). LuMing Mao and Morris Young credit rhetorical scholars such as Glenn with pointing to the "possibility of much more work to be done in many other communities, including the Asian American community" ("Afterword" 325). Elsewhere, Mao writes that Glenn's efforts help "make what used to be invisible rhetorical experiences visible and consequential, and . . . transform . . . marginalized players into legitimate, viable contenders" (*Reading* 14). In her research on familial agency, Lin-Lee Lee writes, "Glenn reiterates that silence can be as powerful as speech in different contexts and subcultures," especially in cultures which "respect silence and taciturnity" (57). And in rereading Sui Sin Far, Bo Wang responds to Glenn's call to expand the canon, noting that "to do otherwise is to participate in the perpetuating of the values and beliefs that are silencing" (264).

Focusing on the silences and silencing within other cultural-ethnic-political groups, Heidi B. Carlone and Angela Johnson use Glenn's work to explain how successful women-of-color scientists pass the test of their male professors' silences (1205). Patricia O. Covarrubias and Sweeney R. Windchief cite Glenn's ethnographic research to conclude that American Indian college students "actualize silence in the direct service of particularizing, perpetuating, and protecting culture" (333). Covarrubias also builds on Glenn's (and others') "documentation of native appreciation for the vigor and productivity of silence" to demonstrate how "masked silences" in discriminatory race-laden communication takes place (233). Sighted disability-rights advocate Scott Lunsford draws on Glenn's work in deciding how to enter the identity debate within visually impaired and blind culture (2). Finally, Karen I. Fredriksen-Goldsen and her colleagues invoke the "potent 'rhetoric of silence'" to explain why lesbian social workers' intimate relationships have been excluded from public discourses and representations in the history of the profession ("'My Ever Dear'" 326; "Caregiving"). Maria T. Brown calls upon that same rhetoric of silence to explain why LBGT elders have been excluded from queer and gerontological theories as well as from social services (68).

Scholars have also pushed the theoretical possibilities of rhetorical silence. Joyce Irene Middleton writes that Glenn's "argument on silence as a form of rhetorical delivery, is both provocative and useful in fostering honest cultural and personal human engagement" ("Echoes" 367), with Kate Ronald referring to "silence as a rhetorical force" (146). For Lisa Shawn Hogan, Glenn's observation that "the purposeful use of silence . . . can speak volumes" (qtd. in Hogan 76) explains the sustained attention garnered by William Lloyd Garrison's delivery of silence at the 1840 World Anti-Slavery Convention (76), just as that statement explained silence-as-irony for Tarez Samra Graban in her study of sixteenth-century martyr Anne Askew. That silence "can deploy" or "defer to power" energizes David G. Holmes's analysis of the Kennedy-Nixon debates in terms of what the two presidential candidates left unspoken about civil rights ("Affirmative" 29). Michal Ephratt uses Glenn's "constellation of symbolic strategies" to taxonomize "eloquent silence" into six distinctive yet sometimes overlapping functions (Glenn, *Unspoken* 18; Ephratt 1913). Michael-John DePalma, Jeffrey M. Ringer, and Jim Webber advocate a "Burkean anarchic democracy" that includes perspectives that are "non-deliberative and intolerant," such as acts of silence, which, Glenn argues, "have the potential to profoundly disrupt, shift, and deploy power" (332, 331). And Kris Acheson pushes the study of silence into a theory of gesture, citing Glenn's argument that silence functions as a "conspicuous and meaningful" linguistic sign (536).

Studies in silence have also been transported into praxes, most significantly into pedagogy. One of the most powerful implementations of silence as pedagogy comes from Ann Ellen Geller and colleagues, who champion writing center work that "accomplishes its goals by saying less and doing more, in subversive and deliberate ways, as . . . Glenn describes" (118). Lois Agnew argues that teaching propriety can promote "both constructive conversation and the constructive silence that . . . Glenn identifies as offering a special type of rhetorical power" (762). Alyssa J. O'Brien and Christine L. Alfano rely on Glenn's and Ratcliffe's notions of rhetorical silence and rhetorical listening in order to enhance the cross-cultural communication necessary to transform their Swedish, Egyptian, and American online students into global citizens. Gesa E. Kirsch's successful experience connecting spirituality to civic engagement in her writing classroom is, she says, a direct response to "Glenn's invitation" to explore "how contemplative practices can enrich a writing classroom and the intellectual life of students" (W3). Elaine Richardson stresses the importance of educators' understanding how social literacies frame the identity and "sense making" of young Black women whose response to hegemonic forces of violation and hardship is expected to be [Glenn's concept of] "silence" (11). And, finally, in *Between Speaking and Silence: A Study of Quiet Students,* Mary M. Reda redeems the negative reputation of classroom silence, calling on Glenn's argument that silence "can be a deliberative, positive choice," "an invitation into the future, . . . a linguistic art . . . that needs only to be named in order to be understood" (172).

Moving beyond the historiographic, theoretical, and pedagogical realms, recent research on silence is making headway into additional new possibilities for application. In "Gendered War Rhetoric—Rhetoric of Silence," Berit von der Lippe focuses on silence as "a means for survival or a conscious way of resistance," invoking the silent Afghan women, whose "racially and culturally marginalized voices" could "enlarge the field of rhetorical studies" (Glenn, *Unspoken* 4, 2). Brooke Ackerly connects Glenn's interpretations of silence with understanding the difficult-to-interpret absences in universal human rights activism (160). Catherine Hundleby believes "Western science may benefit from considering how silence . . . may . . . signify resistance to current scientific practices, and understanding such resistance would serve the objectivity of science" (4). She also mentions Ratcliffe's listening as "important to science because [it] accounts for silence as well as disclosure, and so maximizes the diversity in recognized perspectives that provide scientific objectivity" (1).

In their study of Houston's Bureau of Air Quality Control, Miriam F. Williams and Daisy D. James write about the elderly African American residents who were silent with regard to potential environmental hazards. Williams and James used Glenn's work to deduce that elderly residents used silence as a means to protect their pride and personal interests from the environmental investigators those residents had deemed untrustworthy (93). Last of all, two teams of medical researchers have conducted studies of silences in surgical theaters. Fauzia Gardezi and colleagues extend Glenn's and Susan Gal's "critical theories in the role of silence in communication for insights into instances of silence and constrained communication in the OR" (1397). And Rhona Flin and Lucy Mitchell conclude that nurses' silences during surgery "can be purposeful and meaningful, a complex mode of communicative participation" (287). Thus, even in fields far removed from rhetoric, the study of silence continues to be productive.

Since the publication of Krista Ratcliffe's 1999 *CCC* "Rhetorical Listening," her 2000 *JAC* "Eavesdropping as Rhetorical Tactic," and her 2005 *Rhetorical Listening: Identification, Gender, Whiteness*, scholars have invoked her writings to engage listening. For instance, scholars have referenced rhetorical listening to identify a scholarly gap in rhetoric and composition studies that their own research may fill. In *Refiguring Rhetorical Education*, Enoch cites Ratcliffe's claim that listening "is consistently overlooked inside rhetoric and composition studies today" to identify a scholarly gap that may be filled by Zitkala-Ša's concept of rhetorical education, a concept that takes listening as a "vital component" (119). In *Rhetoric at the Margins*, David Gold cites Ratcliffe's claim that "'in the 20th-century recovery of rhetoric within composition studies, reading and writing reign as the dominant tropes for interpretive invention; speaking places a respectable third; listening runs a poor, poor fourth'" (195); after identifying with this gap, Gold then argues that writing scholar-teachers should "do a better job of acknowledging and exploring other rhetorical traditions and strategies," such as listening (154–55).

Rhetoric and composition scholars have also woven rhetorical listening into their own disparate interests. When analyzing Angelina Grimké's rhetoric, Pat Arneson juxtaposes Hans-Georg Gadamer's philosophical hermeneutics (that is, its notion of place) alongside Ratcliffe's rhetorical listening (that is, its notion of interpretive invention). D. Diane Davis defines communitarian literacy, in part, by linking the listening for exiled excess in Ratcliffe's theory to the listening for noise frequencies in Avital Ronell's *The Telephone Book*. Kirsch links rhetorical listening to spirituality; Hesford links rhetorical listening to witnessing and testifying ("Documenting"); and Jane E. Hindman links it to personal writing in the academy. When discussing the politics of Indian Country, Ellen Cushman argues that rhetorical listening is imperative for listening to cross-cultural narratives, and Cristina D. Ramirez claims the metonymic moves of rhetorical listening help to explain the mestiza rhetoric of Juana Belén Gutiérrez de Mendoza. Keith Gilyard cites Ratcliffe's and listening to others' discussions of Cornel West as evidence that West's *Race Matters* will be important to rhetoric and composition studies for years to come. When contemplating how to rewrite traditional histories of rhetoric, Phillip P. Marzluf invokes rhetorical listening as well as active silence as methods for hearing what is not seen in these histories (396, 368). And in *Unspoken*, Glenn notes that Anita Hill's silence functions as a kind of rhetorical listening, because Hill's particular silence was a time of "coming to understanding" (53); more generally, Glenn claims that rhetorical listening "opens the silences surrounding codes of cross-cultural conduct" (152).

Ratcliffe's theory of rhetorical listening has been expanded by scholars interested in extending the functions of listening itself. In *Revisionary Rhetoric, Feminist Pedagogy, and Multigenre Texts*, Julie Jung clarifies the relationship between rhetorical listening and Rogerian rhetoric, arguing that the listening posited by Jacqueline Jones Royster, Ratcliffe, and Min-Zhan Lu is not simply a Rogerian "'Yes, I hear what you're saying' response" (17) but rather a response that challenges listeners to engage their emotions and ask questions such as, "Why am I so threatened by this speaker's argument? What is my personal/professional investment in defending that which this speaker challenges? In what ways are the speaker and I alike? In what ways are we different? How do these similarities and differences challenge my comfortable worldview?" (18), the hope being to identify the "'exiled excess'" (59). In "The Perfected Mother," a rhetorical analysis of Munchausen by proxy syndrome, Jung extends Ratcliffe's discussion of disidentification, arguing to "augment our understanding of the relationships among listening, ethos, and identification [by exploring] the limits of using disidentification as a strategy for listening to difference" (345). And Brian Gogan in "Laughing Whiteness" links listening to laughter, arguing that a "responsible rhetoric of laughter seems dependent upon a rhetoric of listening" (79); Gogan's article answers Ratcliffe's call for more tactics for talking about race by offering parody (79) even as it exposes the limits of Ratcliffe's tactic of recognition (82).

Rhetorical listening has also been called into question. Patrocinio Schweickart, in "Understanding an Other," acknowledges Ratcliffe's claim that listeners function differently from readers and argues instead for a method of reading that "take[s] listener and reader to be analogous with regard to their reception" (16). Terese Guinsatao Monberg, in "Listening for Legacies," contemplates the listening advocated by "Jacqueline Jones Royster, Malea Powell, Krista Ratcliffe, and Dorothy Corova herself" as a methodology "to see and hear [Asian American] women who are presumed to be absent . . . [and to] make visible underlying assumptions in feminist historiography that reinforce those presumptions" (86–87); ultimately, though, Monberg selects Royster's and Powell's concepts of listening as the best models for an Asian Pacific American rhetoric (86). And Jill Swiencicki echoes Middleton in "caution[ing] that laying raced text beside raced text may erase the important differences and positions each represents."

Fifth, rhetorical listening has also informed scholar-teachers' pedagogies. Cynthia L. Selfe weaves that unheard dimension of rhetorical listening into her discussion of students' multimodal literacies. Interested in the problematic silences of students, Reda reflects on how her own pedagogy has been informed by Ratcliffe's focus on listening to understand (69), particularly listening across "'different discourse communities'" (159), and she concludes that "Ratcliffe's work challenges us to create a space for listening as a productive, but generally overlooked, rhetorical strategy" (169). Jennifer Seibel Trainor argues that rhetorical listening productively informs (auto)ethnographic classroom studies of racism and whiteness, and Ann E. Green cites rhetorical listening as a tactic for helping teachers negotiate the difficulties in teaching whiteness. Julie Lindquist argues that "teachers can listen to students to know not only how, but who to be with them." To posit a productive means of reading student papers, Andrea Muldoon merges rhetorical listening with Mikhail Bakhtin's dialogism. Jami Carlacio and Alice Gillam advocate rhetorical listening as a tactic for "teaching the craft of virtue"

(160). Pedagogical possibilities of rhetorical listening for teaching close reading and ethos are evident in the work of Zan Meyer Gonçalves (117), which echoes Ratcliffe's injunction to invite students to "'listen with intent, not for it'" (128). And Kathleen J. Ryan and Tarez Samra Graban invoke rhetorical listening as a tactic for training teaching assistants, arguing that trainers need to make space for TAs' identifications and disidentifications with a writing program's established curriculum.

Finally, Ratcliffe's scholarship has been evaluated in terms of its significance for rhetorical studies. In *The SAGE Handbook of Rhetorical Studies*, edited by Andrea Lunsford, Kirt H. Wilson, and Rosa A. Eberly, Middleton likens Ratcliffe's listening to Royster's and Wayne Booth's (364) and notes that Ratcliffe's "acoustic metaphors" (362) of "'harmonies,' 'dissonance,' 'recitatif,' and other (h)earing metaphors . . . extend or overlap rather seamlessly with music as inventive and interpretive" (362–63). Also Ronald argues that Ratcliffe "writes new rhetorical theory here, taking the feminist rhetorical project to new strategies of communication not based on the agonistic rhetorical tradition that Brody, Glenn, Jarratt, and Swearingen critiqued" (147). Though initially linking rhetorical listening to silence, Holmes further discusses the import of rhetorical listening for rhetoric and composition studies, claiming that it "adroitly navigates the theoretical terrain of identity politics, providing an arena where postmodernists and essentialists (regardless of race, ethnicity, nationality, or gender) can be heard. And [it] thereby avoids the social and political landmines manufactured by the excesses of political correctness, on the one hand, and colorblind idealism, on the other" ("Cross-Racial").

Contributors' Engagement with Silence and Listening

Because the above scholarship on silence and listening in rhetoric and composition studies has just begun to appear, the purpose of this collection is to further articulate how silence and listening may enrich this field. Therefore, this collection is organized according to three established research areas within rhetorical studies: history, theory and criticism, and praxes. Obviously, these three research areas blur, yet they remain operative categories in rhetorical studies. As such, they provide scholars a familiar introduction to silence and listening as rhetorical arts and offer multiple ways for contemplating how these arts may engage, redefine, and remap rhetorical studies.

As organizing principles for this collection, the three research areas are defined as follows:

1. The History section captures specific historical moments when concepts of silence and/or listening are (or may be) articulated, contextualizing these moments within rhetorical histories and traditions.
2. The Theory and Criticism section works at the nexus of theory and criticism, demonstrating the ways that theory provides tactics for performing criticism and the ways that criticism provides concepts for building theory.
3. The Praxes section describes performances of silence and/or listening as rhetorical arts in a variety of cultural contexts, including but not restricted to the classroom.

Within this three-part framework, this collection offers an introduction and seventeen chapters. Written by established rhetoric scholars as well as by newcomers to the field, the chapters balance a dual focus on silence *and* listening, reimagine traditional histories and theories of rhetoric, and incorporate issues, such as race, gender, and cross-cultural concerns, into scholarly conversations about rhetorical history, theory, criticism, and praxes.

Overview of the Chapters

Part 1. History

Chapter 1. In "Aspasia's Purloined Letters: Historical Absence, Fictional Presence, and the Rhetoric of Silence," Melissa Ianetta uses Jacques Lacan's "Seminar on 'The Purloined Letter'" to examine how the classical "silence" of Aspasia was appropriated by nineteenth-century writers who created a multitude of Aspasias in their attempt to capture a singular coherent, historically accurate representation of this woman—a representation that this chapter calls into question.

Chapter 2. In "Out of 'Wonderful Silence' Come 'Sweet Words': The Rhetorical Authority of St. Catherine of Siena," Kristie S. Fleckenstein argues that this fourteenth-century mystic and preacher constructed her formidable rhetorical authority through two forms of silence: a generative silence within which she obtained knowledge of God and a performative silence within which she embodied that knowledge.

Chapter 3. In "Purposeful Silence and Perceptive Listening: Rhetorical Agency for Women in Christine de Pizan's *The Treasure of the City of Ladies*," Nancy Myers argues that Pizan's conduct book provides a theory of rhetoric as well as an embodied practice of rhetoric, which offered women rhetorical agency in early-fifteenth-century social and political contexts.

Chapter 4. In "Trying Silence: The Case of Denmark Vesey and the History of African American Rhetoric," Shevaun E. Watson examines the roles of silence and silencing in the Denmark Vesey slave conspiracy trials as well as in historical and contemporary receptions and representations of those trials.

Chapter 5. In "Living Pictures, Living Memory: Women's Rhetorical Silence within the American Delsarte Movement," Lisa Suter offers a historical corrective by resituating the intertextual performative genres of *tableaux vivants* and statue posing within their contemporary framework.

Part 2. Theory and Criticism

Chapter 6. In "Silence: A Politics," Kennan Ferguson investigates the unfamiliar political implications of silence, theorizing how silence can be used not merely to reinforce or resist power but to constitute selves and even communities. That silence can operate in such diverse ways as oppression, resistance, and/or community formation leads to the recognition that its ultimate politics cannot be fixed or determined.

Chapter 7. In "'Down a Road and into an Awful Silence': Graphic Listening in Joe Sacco's Comics Journalism," Andrea A. Lunsford and Adam Rosenblatt explore the functions of listening in the work of graphic arts journalist Joe Sacco. They analyze how Sacco uses his acute self-awareness as a reporter as well as the unique properties of the comics medium to fashion a model of listening that reflects his ethos as a reporter, storyteller, and humanist.

Chapter 8. In "The Ideology of African Philosophy: The Silences and Possibilities of African Rhetorical Knowledge," Omedi Ochieng rereads Odera Oruka's sage philosophy project to argue that the discourse of African sage philosophy emerged from two types of knowledge—forensic and sapiential—whose possibilities may be grounded in two kinds of silences.

Chapter 9. In "Finding Democracy in Our Argument Culture: Listening to Spike Lee's Jazz Funeral on the Levees," Joyce Irene Middleton argues that the aftermath of Hurricane Katrina offers American citizens opportunity to theorize a progressive vision of a reconstituted pluralistic democracy, if we practice strategic uses of rhetorical listening and silence.

Chapter 10. In "Gesturing toward Peace: On Silence, the Society of the Spectacle, and the 'Women in Black' Antiwar Protests," Ashley Elliott Pryor explores silence as a medium of antiwar protest in the context of the Women in Black movement. By reading the women's uses of silence through the rhetorical category of the "gesture," she retrieves and theorizes a meaningful, resistant strategy within the Western rhetorical tradition.

Chapter 11. In "Hearing Women's Silence in Transitional South Africa: Achmat Dangor's *Bitter Fruit*," Katherine Mack analyzes women's silences in a specific historical moment, the South African Truth and Reconciliation Commission's "special hearings on women." Mack also explores Dangor's novelistic response to those hearings, a response that attempts to give voice to the women's silences.

Part 3. Praxes

Chapter 12. In "With Our Ears to the Ground: Compassionate Listening in Israel/Palestine," Joy Arbor introduces the concept of "Compassionate Listening," a model and practice of activist conflict resolution and reconciliation that provides insights into the rhetorical concept of listening-across-differences to all sides of an issue.

Chapter 13. In "A Repertoire of Discernments: Hearing the Unsaid in Oral History Narratives," Frank Farmer and Margaret M. Strain explore the challenges facing oral history scholars during interviews when their subjects respond with silence. Farmer and Strain argue that scholars should pay particular attention to—and ask specific questions about—what is *not* said. To provide scholars tools for engaging such silences, they articulate a "repertoire of discernments" for the interpretation and the uses of oral histories.

Chapter 14. In "Cultivating Listening: Teaching from a Restored Logos," Shari Stenberg examines the pedagogical consequences of a diminished notion of logos that both privileges speech over listening and posits listening and speaking as oppositions. She contends that such a logos perpetuates other dualisms that limit genuine dialogue; then she offers instead a listening logos that makes possible a critical-feminist pedagogy.

Chapter 15. In "Making Ourselves Vulnerable: A Feminist Pedagogy of Listening," Wendy Wolters Hinshaw applies Ratcliffe's model of "listening pedagogically" to negotiate the various types of resistance produced when students *and teachers* attempt to communicate about and across cultural difference, particularly in women's studies courses.

Chapter 16. In "Revaluing Silence and Listening with Second-Language English Users," Jay Jordan argues that theory building about silence and listening in the field of rhetoric can inform studies of second-language use, especially as English continues to evolve locally and globally.

Chapter 17. In "Student Silences in the Deep South: Hearing Unfamiliar Dialects," Suellyn Duffey narrates how the silences of students at her university taught her to familiarize herself with new dialects of silence and with new cultures of listening (or not listening). Duffey's study adds to our emerging awareness that student silences may be powerfully productive—heuristic, active, expressive, and interactive.

The editors and contributors in this collection hope that our conversations about silence and listening—initiated in our books and articles and further articulated in our chapters here—will serve as a springboard for future research on the value and challenges of silence and listening as rhetorical arts.

Acknowledgments

Cheryl and Kris would like to thank Rebecca Wilson Lundin and Heather Brook Adams for their invaluable editorial assistance, Hannah Lewis and Monique Ashly Williams for their clerical assistance, the two outside readers (Maureen Daly Goggin and Roxanne Mountford) for their productive advice, and our contacts at Southern Illinois University Press (especially Karl Kageff, Barb Martin, Kathleen Kageff, and Julie Bush) for their editorial and production assistance.

Notes

1. The Egyptian culture ca. 2200 B.C.E.–1500 B.C.E.; see Fox.

2. Silence, good timing (*kairos*), restraint, fluency, and truthfulness are the five ancient Egyptian canons of eloquence.

3. Fl. 520 B.C.E.

4. Morphic resonance, Rupert Sheldrake says, is "the idea of mysterious telepathy-type interconnections between organisms and of collective memories within species" (117). When collective consciousness encounters contemporary problems, people from all kinds of backgrounds reach similar resolutions: a serious examination of silence seems to have been one such resolution. Productive silence can provide the space for wonder, meditation, attention, care,

independence, anticipation, planning, and empathy. Even resistance, sulking, and punishment can be constructive sites of silence.

Works Cited

Acheson, Kris. "Silence as Gesture: Rethinking the Nature of Communicative Silences." *Communication Theory* 18.4 (2008): 535–55. Print.

Ackerly, Brooke. "Women's Human Rights Activists as Cross-Cultural Theorists." *International Feminist Journal of Politics* 3.3 (2001): 311–46. Print.

Agnew, Lois. "Teaching Propriety: Unlocking the Mysteries of 'Political Correctness.'" *CCC* 60.4 (2009): 746–64. Print.

Arneson, Pat. "A Dialogic Ethic in the Public Rhetoric of Angelina Grimké." *Communication Ethics: Between Cosmopolitan and Provinciality.* Ed. Kathleen Glenister Roberts and Ronald C. Arnett. New York: Peter Lang, 2008. 139–54. Print.

Bizzell, Patricia, ed. *Rhetorical Agendas: Political, Ethical, Spiritual.* Mahwah, NJ: Erlbaum, 2006. Print.

Bokser, Julie K. "The Persuasion of Esther: A Nun's Model of Silent, Seductive, Violent Rhetoric." Bizzell 303–8. Print.

———. "Sor Juana's Rhetoric of Silence." *Rhetoric Review* 25.1 (2006): 5–21. Print.

Brown, Maria T. "LBGT: Aging and Rhetorical Silence." *Sexuality Research and Social Policy: Journal of NSRC* [National Sexuality Research Center] 6.4 (Dec. 2009): 65–78. Print.

Burmester, Beth. "Classical Rhetoric and Nineteenth-Century American Clubwomen: Parallels of Feminist Rhetorics, Civic Reform, and Spiritual Agendas." Bizzell 309–16. Print.

Carlacio, Jami, and Alice Gillam. "Preparing Ethical Citizens for the Twenty-First Century." *Professing Rhetoric: Selected Papers from the 2000 Rhetoric Society of America Conference.* Ed. Frederick J. Antczak, Cinda Coggins, and Geoffrey D. Klinger. Mahwah, NJ: Erlbaum, 2002. 155–62. Print.

Carlone, Heidi B., and Angela Johnson. "Understanding the Science Experiences of Successful Women of Color: Science Identity as an Analytic Lens." *Journal of Research in Science Teaching* 44.8 (2007): 1187–1218. Print.

Covarrubias, Patricia O. "Masked Silence Sequences: Hearing Discrimination in the College Classroom." *Communication, Culture and Critique* 1 (2008): 227–52. Print.

Covarrubias, Patricia O., and Sweeney R. Windchief. "Silences in Stewardship: Some American Indian College Students Examples." *Howard Journal of Communication* 20.3 (2009): 333–53. Print.

Cushman, Ellen. "Toward a Rhetoric of Self-Representation: Identity Politics in Indian Country and Rhetoric and Composition." *CCC* 60.2 (2008): 321–65. *MLA International Bibliography.* Web. Jan. 7, 2010.

Davis, D. Diane. "Finitude's Clamor; or, Notes toward a Communitarian Literacy." *CCC* 53.1 (2001): 119–45. *MLA International Bibliography.* Web. Jan. 7, 2010.

DePalma, Michael-John, Jeffrey M. Ringer, and Jim Webber. "(Re)Charting the (Dis)Courses of Faith and Politics, or Rhetoric and Democracy in the Burkean Barnyard." *Rhetoric Society Quarterly* 38.3 (Summer 2008): 311–34. Print.

Enoch, Jessica. *Refiguring Rhetorical Education: Women Teaching African American, Native American, and Chicano/a Students, 1865–1911.* Carbondale: Southern Illinois UP, 2008. Print.

Ephratt, Michal. "The Functions of Silence." *Journal of Pragmatics* 40.11 (2008): 1909–38. Print.

Farmer, Frank. *Saying and Silence: Listening to Composition with Bakhtin.* Logan: Utah State UP, 2001. Print.

Flin, Rhona, and Lucy Mitchell. *Safer Surgery: Analysing Behavior in the Operating Theatre.* Surrey: Ashgate, 2009. Print.

Fox, Michael V. "Ancient Egyptian Rhetoric." *Rhetorica* 1.1 (Spring 1983): 9–22. Print.

Fredriksen-Goldsen, Karen I., and Charles P. Hoy-Ellis. "Caregiving with Pride." *Journal of Gay and Lesbian Social Services* 18.3–4 (Sept. 2007): 1–13. Print.

Fredriksen-Goldsen, Karen I., Taryn Lindhorst, Susan P. Kemp, and Karina L. Walters. "'My Ever Dear': Social Work's 'Lesbian' Foremothers; A Call for Scholarship." *Affilia* 24.3 (Aug. 2009): 325–36. Print.

Gardezi, Fauzia, Lorelei Lingard, Sherry Espin, Sarah Whyte, Beverley Orser, and G. Ross Baker. "Silence, Power, and Communication in the Operating Room." *JAN: Journal of Advanced Nursing* 65.7 (2009): 1390–99. Print.

Geller, Ann Ellen, Michelle Eodice, Frankie Condon, Meg Carroll, and Elizabeth Bouquet. *The Everyday Writing Center.* Logan: Utah State UP, 2008. Print.

Gilyard, Keith. *Composition and Cornel West: Notes toward a Deep Democracy.* Carbondale: Southern Illinois UP, 2008. Print.

Glenn, Cheryl. *Rhetoric Retold: Regendering the Tradition from Antiquity through the Renaissance.* Carbondale: Southern Illinois UP, 1997. Print.

———. "Silence: A Rhetorical Art for Resisting Discipline(s)." *JAC* 22.2 (Spring 2002): 261–92. Print.

———. *Unspoken: A Rhetoric of Silence.* Carbondale: Southern Illinois UP, 2004. Print.

Gogan, Brian. "Laughing Whiteness: Pixies, Parody, and Perspectives." *The Comedy of Dave Chappelle.* Ed. K. A. Wisniewski. Jefferson, NC: McFarland, 2009. 72–85. Print.

Gold, David. *Rhetoric at the Margins: Revising the History of Writing Instruction in American Colleges, 1873–1947.* Carbondale: Southern Illinois UP, 2008. Print.

Gonçalves, Zan Meyer. *Sexuality and the Politics of Ethos in the Writing Classroom.* Carbondale: Southern Illinois UP, 2005. Print.

Graban, Tarez Samra. "Feminine Irony and the Art of Linguistic Cooperation in Anne Askew's Sixteenth-Century *Examinacyons.*" *Rhetorica* 25.4 (2007): 385–412. Print.

Green, Ann E. "Difficult Stories: Service-Learning, Race, Class, and Whiteness." *CCC* 55.2 (2003): 276–301. *MLA International Bibliography*. Web. Jan. 7, 2010.

Hesford, Wendy S. "Documenting Violations: Rhetorical Witnessing and the Spectacle of Distant Suffering." *Biography: An Interdisciplinary Quarterly* 27.1 (Winter 2004): 104–44. *MLA International Bibliography*. Web. Jan. 7, 2010.

———. "Global Turns and Cautions in Rhetoric and Composition Studies." *PMLA* 121.3 (2006): 787–801. Print.

Hindman, Jane E. "Thoughts on Reading 'The Personal': Toward a Discursive Ethics of Professional Critical Literacy." *College English* 66.1 (Sept. 2003): 9–20. *MLA International Bibliography*. Web. Jan. 7, 2010.

Hogan, Lisa Shawn. "A Time for Silence: William Lloyd Garrison and the 'Woman Question' at the 1840 World Anti-slavery Convention." *Gender Issues* 25.2 (2008): 63–79. Print.

Holmes, David G. "Affirmative Reaction: Kennedy, Nixon, King, and the Evolution of Color-Blind Rhetoric." *Rhetoric Review* 26.1 (2007): 25–41. Print.

———. "Cross-Racial Voicing: Carl Van Vechten's Imagination and the Search for an African American Ethos." *College English* 68.3 (Jan. 2006): 291–307. *MLA International Bibliography*. Web. Jan. 7, 2010.

Hundleby, Catherine. "The Need for Rhetorical Listening to Ground Scientific Objectivity." *Dissensus and the Search for Common Ground*. Ed. H. V. Hansen. 2007. CD-ROM.

Iamblicus. *On the Pythagorean Way of Life*. Trans. Gillian Clark. Liverpool: Liverpool UP, 1989. Print.

Johnson, Nan. *Gender and Rhetorical Space in American Life, 1886–1910*. Carbondale: Southern Illinois UP, 2002. Print.

Jung, Julie. "The Perfected Mother: Listening, Ethos, and Identification in Cases of Munchausen by Proxy Syndrome." Bizzell 345–50. Print.

———. *Revisionary Rhetoric, Feminist Pedagogy, and Multigenre Texts*. Carbondale: Southern Illinois UP, 2005. Print.

Kirsch, Gesa E. "From Introspection to Action: Connecting Spirituality and Civic Engagement." *CCC* 60.4 (2009): W1–W15. *MLA International Bibliography*. Web. Jan. 7, 2010.

Lee, Lin-Lee. "Inventing Familial Agency from Powerlessness: Ban Zhao's *Lessons for Women*." *Western Journal of Communication* 73.1 (2009): 47–66. Print.

Lichtheim, Miriam. *Ancient Egyptian Literature*. Vol. 1. Berkeley: U of California P, 2006. Print.

Lindquist, Julie. "Class Affects, Classroom Affectations: Working through the Paradoxes of Strategic Empathy." *College English* 67.2 (Nov. 2004): 187–209. *MLA International Bibliography*. Web. Jan. 7, 2010.

Lippe, Berit von der. "Gendered War Rhetoric—Rhetoric of Silence." *Rhetorical Citizenship and Public Deliberation*. Ed. Christian Kock and Lisa Villadsen. Under consideration.

Logan, Shirley Wilson. *Liberating Language: Sites of Rhetorical Education in Nineteenth-Century Black America*. Carbondale: Southern Illinois UP, 2009. Print.

Lunsford, Andrea, Kirt H. Wilson, and Rosa A. Eberly, eds. *The SAGE Handbook of Rhetorical Studies*. Los Angeles: SAGE, 2009. Print.

Lunsford, Scott. "The Debate Within: Authority and the Discourse of Blindness." *JVIB* [Journal of Visual Impairment and Blindness] 100.1 (Jan. 2006). Web. Jan. 9, 2010.

Mao, LuMing. *Reading Chinese Fortune Cookie: The Making of Chinese American Rhetoric*. Logan: Utah State UP, 2006. Print.

Mao, LuMing, and Morris Young. "Afterword: Toward a Theory of Asian American Rhetoric: What Is to Be Done?" Mao and Young 323–32. Print.

———, eds. *Representations: Doing Asian American Rhetoric*. Logan: Utah State UP, 2008. Print.

Marzluf, Phillip P. "Originating Difference in Rhetorical Theory: Lord Monboddo's Obsession with Language Origins Theory." *Rhetoric Society Quarterly* 38.4 (Fall 2008): 385–407. Print.

Middleton, Joyce Irene. "Echoes from the Past: Learning How to Listen, Again." Lunsford, Wilson, and Eberly 353–71. Print.

———. "Kris, I Hear You." *JAC* 20 (2000): 433–43. Print.

Monberg, Terese Guinsatao. "Listening for Legacies or, How I Began to Hear Dorothy Laigo Cordova, the Pinay behind the Podium Known as FANHS." Mao and Young 83–105.

Muldoon, Andrea. "Terms of Engagement: A Snapshot of Scholarly Exchange in Rhetoric and Composition Professional Journals." *Reader: Essays in Reader-Oriented Theory, Criticism, and Pedagogy* 56 (Spring 2007): 54–84. *MLA International Bibliography*. Web. Jan. 7, 2010.

O'Brien, Alyssa J., and Christine L. Alfano. "Connecting Students Globally through Video-Conference Pedagogy." *JOLT: Journal of Online Teaching and Learning* 5.4 (2009). Web. Jan. 9, 2010.

Ramirez, Cristina D. "Forging a Mestiza Rhetoric: Mexican Women Journalists' Role in the Construction of a National Identity." *College English* 71.6 (July 2009): 606–29. *MLA International Bibliography*. Web. Jan. 7, 2010.

Ratcliffe, Krista. "Eavesdropping as Rhetorical Tactic: History, Whiteness, and Rhetoric." *JAC* 20 (2000): 87-119. Print.

———. "Rhetorical Listening: A Trope for Interpretive Invention and a 'Code of Cross-Cultural Conduct.'" *CCC* 51.2 (1999): 195-224. Print.

———. *Rhetorical Listening: Identification, Gender, Whiteness*. Carbondale: Southern Illinois UP, 2005. Print.

Reda, Mary M. *Between Speaking and Silence: A Study of Quiet Students*. Albany: State U of New York P, 2009. Print.

Richardson, Elaine. "My *Ill* Literacy Narrative: Growing up Black, Po and a Girl, in the Hood." *Gender and Education* (2009): 1–15. Print.

Ronald, Kate. "Feminist Perspectives on the History of Rhetoric." Lunsford, Wilson, and Eberly 139–52. Print.

Ryan, Kathleen J., and Tarez Samra Graban. "Theorizing Feminist Pragmatic Rhetoric as a Communicative Art for the Composition Practicum." *CCC* 61.1 (2009): W277–W299. *MLA International Bibliography*. Web. Jan. 7, 2010.

Schweickart, Patrocinio. "Understanding an Other: Reading as a Receptive Form of Communicative Action." *New Directions in American Reception Study*. Ed. Philip Goldstein and James L. Malchor. Oxford: Oxford UP, 2008. 3–22. Print.

Selfe, Cynthia L. "The Movement of Air, the Breath of Meaning: Aurality and Multimodal Composing." *CCC* 60.4 (2009): 616–63. *MLA International Bibliography*. Web. Jan. 7, 2010.

Sheldrake, Rupert. *A New Science of Life: A Hypothesis of Formative Causation*. Los Angeles: Tarcher, 1981. Print.

Swiencicki, Jill. "The Rhetoric of Awareness Narratives." *College English* 68.4 (Mar. 2006): 337–55. *MLA International Bibliography*. Web. Jan. 7, 2010.

Trainor, Jennifer Seibel. *Rethinking Racism: Emotion, Persuasion, and Literacy in an All-White High School*. Carbondale: Southern Illinois UP, 2008. Print.

Walzer, Arthur E., and David Beard. "Historiography and the Study of Rhetoric." Lunsford, Wilson, and Eberly 13–33. Print.

Wang, Bo. "Rereading Sui Sin Far: A Rhetoric of Defiance." Mao and Young 244–65. Print.

Williams, Miriam F., and Daisy D. James. "Embracing New Policies, Technologies, and Community Partnerships: A Case Study of the City of Houston's Bureau of Air Quality Control." *Technical Communication Quarterly* 18.1 (2009): 82–98. Print.

Part One

HISTORY

1

Aspasia's Purloined Letters: Historical Absence, Fictional Presence, and the Rhetoric of Silence

Melissa Ianetta

lthough little-known today, Robert Hamerling's nineteenth-century
blockbuster *Aspasia* seems to prophesy the figure's position in contemporary rhetorical studies. In this novel, as in our contemporary
histories, Aspasia is the object of much scrutiny, and this close observation leads to wildly divergent opinions among her spectators:

> One day, during the sultry season, in the city of the Athenians, a
> slender, girlish figure . . . hastily crossed the Agora. A singular result
> of this woman's appearance was, that every man she met on her
> way paused after a glance at her face, and stood as if spellbound,
> following her with his eyes. . . . The faces of those who stared at her
> in passing, or stood rooted to the ground, gazing after her, wore
> every possible expression of astonishment. Some smiled . . . others
> cast a sneering glance at the beautiful woman, and others a shade
> of reverence, as if they beheld a goddess. Some displayed the grave,
> well-satisfied demeanor of connoisseurs, others looked semi-idiotic,
> standing with mouths half-open in amazement. (1)

Hamerling's Aspasia is looked upon with emotions ranging among approval, amusement, veneration, derision, and longing. The variety and
intensity of these responses contrast markedly with Aspasia's silence in
this scene, for she does not speak here—or, indeed, for another hundred

pages. Rather, in this novel she is the silent tabula rasa onto which the male citizens inscribe their emotional, intellectual, and erotic desires, yielding a multitude of Aspasias, each the result of a spectator's gaze rather than her innate qualities.

In like fashion, multiple perspectives on the historical Aspasia have engendered a threefold range of figurations. First, there are depictions of her character and profession, including as rhetor and teacher (Plato), rhetorician (Glenn, *Rhetoric* 36–44), madam (Aristophanes), and colonized other (Jarratt and Ong). A second range of descriptions focuses on characterizing the function and form of her rhetoric—the speech attributed to her in the *Menexenus*, for example, has been read as a Platonic rendering of morally ameliorative discourse, a satiric send-up of rhetoric's pernicious tricks, Plato's social critique of Athenian war-mongering and his propaganda on behalf of orphans.[1] Finally, there is a spectrum of opinion concerning her status as author, for her reported oration in the *Menexenus* has been variously assigned to Pericles, Thucydides, and Plato, as well as to Aspasia herself. With such dissensus, Aspasia's history can seem indefinable, creating a rhetoric based on alluring absence and centuries-old attempts to fill her rhetorical space.

Focusing on meanings assigned to Aspasia and her speech also invites what may seem a surprising comparison with readings of one of the earliest detective stories, Edgar Allan Poe's "The Purloined Letter" (1844). Here, too, we encounter the theft of unknown words belonging to an enigmatic woman, the epistemological machinations their contested ownership creates, and the reoccurring subject positions assumed by those investigating her missing text. Further, Poe's story provided the basis for one of the most provocative analyses of absence and of the ways in which absence creates meaning—Jacques Lacan's "Seminar on 'The Purloined Letter.'" By arguing the enduring impact of unknowable words that nevertheless create meaning, Lacan's analysis suggests new ways of both viewing contemporary historiographical debate and rendering Aspasia's history.[2] For reading responses to Hamerling's novel alongside elements of Lacan's treatment serves as an invitation to rehistoricize these seemingly postmodern debates of Aspasia's historicity and thereby to see her words as influential through their very absence from the historical record. In this essay, then, I first consider the implications of Poe's story and Lacan's analysis for understanding contemporary studies of Aspasia. I then turn to nineteenth-century responses to Hamerling's novel, both to illustrate one potential role for imaginative texts in our historical inquiries and to expand our understanding of the ways in which Aspasia's recreation has masked the power of her absent words. By drawing upon Lacan's essay to read *Aspasia* and its critical reception, this chapter argues for new understandings of the ways in which women's silence has yielded reoccurring responses, demonstrating that women's muted words have been a paradoxically powerful force.

Before moving to Lacan's comments, however, it will be helpful to contextualize his analysis to the story he considers. Imparted by an unnamed narrator, "The Purloined Letter" retells two conversations from the investigative career of C. Auguste Dupin. The story begins when Dupin accepts a commission from the Parisian police to retrieve one of the queen's letters. This letter was stolen, the police chief tells Dupin, in plain view of the king and queen. The queen, however, could not stop the theft without drawing the king's attention to the letter and its scandalous, albeit unknown, contents. At the queen's request, the police have taken apart every item in the thief's rooms in hope of retrieving the letter, with no success. Dupin's famous powers of ratiocination are thus the last resort. The detective determines that, as careful scientific ferreting did not work, the trick to finding the letter is to think and see as the thief. Just as the thief had found the secret letter in plain sight, so too would he hide it in a highly visible locale. Dupin pays him a social call, discovers the letter in open view, and switches it with a simulacrum. The French detective is thus triumphant, the letter is returned to the queen, and, presumably, order is restored.

At first glance, reading "The Purloined Letter" as a historiographic parable might seem most closely allied with understanding Aspasia's silence through the role of Dupin as historian. The parallels suggest themselves readily: Aspasia, like the queen, has lost possession of her words. In both instances, previous investigators—be they the French police of Poe's tale or previous scholars of rhetorical history—have been unable to locate the text. By using revisionist methods—approaches that call for seeing in a new way—the historian-detective locates women's words and "restores" them to their rightful owner. Framing Dupin's tale as a historiographical paradigm would thus appear a fairly straightforward valorization of revisionist methods that use nontraditional means to retrieve past events. Such readings ally closely with feminist studies of Aspasia, such as Cheryl Glenn's *Rhetoric Retold* or Madeleine Henry's

Prisoner of History. Due in large part to these kinds of interventions, scholars have firmly established Aspasia's existence and agreed on biographical details that include her birth on the island of Miletus in the fifth century B.C.E., migration to Athens, partnering with Pericles, and participation in Athenian intellectual life. Such biographical consensus makes the study of Aspasia's absent words possible, for the study of absence I propose here implies prior presence. To speak of Aspasia's seeming silence as a powerful absence in the rhetorical tradition, however, is not just to assume her existence but also to examine the importance of her displacement from this location. As Glenn notes, "Like the zero in mathematics, silence is an absence with a function, a rhetorical one at that" (*Unspoken* 4). To position this absence as a rhetorical silence, then, is to acknowledge not the mere existence of her words but their rhetorical force, even in absentia.

Imagining Woman, Seeing Silence, and Signifying Nothing

While perspectives grounded in revisionist historiography and gender studies reveal women's historical presence, Lacan helps us to unveil the influence of their words' absence. In his "Seminar on 'The Purloined Letter,'" for example, Lacan's discussion of the queen's epistle offers insight into the relationship of Aspasia's lost words to their paradoxical historical impact. Lacan posits the purloined letter as a "pure signifier" (10)—since its contents are unknown to the reader, it is a signifier without a signified. Thus, the letter, in a sense, is "endowed with nullibiety" (16); its contents are irrelevant to its function in the narrative. Lacan emphasizes the need to understand that all signifiers have such "nullibiety." Since language is arbitrary, there is never an insoluble relationship between a word and its referent. As therefore we can never assume that an unbreakable chain connects a word to a concept, so the enigma of the purloined letter is therefore the enigma of language itself.

Both Aspasia's rhetoric and the epistle of Poe's queen are signifiers whose absence draws attention to the innate lack of the signified, whether the signified be a written document or our historical record. In Poe's story, the unreliability of the relationship of the sign and the signified is further underscored by the context in which the reader is made aware of the queen's correspondence. The letter is made known to us via an anonymous narration—we never, in effect, encounter the signifier directly, free of the narrator's perspective. So too, whenever we encounter her in the rhetorical tradition, Aspasia's words are similarly veiled, available only through the accountings of other voices. Here, under the aegis of "Aspasia," collide the lascivious words of the "porne and procuress" of Greek comedy (Henry 28), the erudite eloquence of the rhetor and rhetorician of Plato's dialogue (Glenn, *Rhetoric* 36–44), and the sycophantic syrupiness of Pericles' "intellectual girlfriend" (Stone 134). As with the queen's letter, then, when considering this diversity of Aspasian representation, we have the same sense of frustration at narrative elisions and the same awareness of the ultimate unknowability of those actual words of Aspasia.

Yet, like Lacan's accounting of the circuitous route of the queen's letter, the influence of Aspasia's unknown words circulates widely in rhetorical study, shaping debate and instigating actions. Here, too, Aspasian studies follow Lacan's model. According to Lacan, the signifying power of the letter in Poe's story permits a limited number of potential subject positions to those who come under its influence, for the power of the letter springs from its context rather than its actual contents. Each of these positions is intersubjective—defined by its relationship to the others in the presence of the letter's influence. And as Lacan describes, each position can be summarized in terms of the "glance" the subject position casts upon the signifier:

> The first is based on a glance that sees nothing: the King. . . .

> The second is based on a glance which sees that the first sees nothing and deceives itself into thereby believing to be covered what it hides: the Queen. . . .

> The third is based on a glance which sees the first two glances leave what must be hidden uncovered to whomever would seize it: the [thief]. (10)

In other words, Poe's tale presents us with three distinct yet interrelated perspectives—the blind, the seer, and that actively seeing position, here termed the seeker. In the initial theft of the letter, which Lacan terms the story's "primal scene" (7), we find the archetype for this paradigm. In this moment, the king is the blind, never seeing the letter that is located under his very nose. The queen, occupying the second position of seer, knows what the letter is but erroneously believes this knowledge provides control over the letter. She cannot, however, see the alternate meaning the letter will have for the thief. In turn, the thief, in the third position of seeker, knows what the letter is for the queen (an illicit note) and what it can be for himself (political power via blackmail).

Moreover, Lacan argues, as the story goes on, through the repetition of these roles in the other scenes of the story, the careful reader becomes aware that these positions are fixed but that characters can move among them. Thus, we see these roles reinscribed in the next scene of the story—when Dupin visits the thief in his rooms and steals the letter from underneath his very nose—but now different characters occupy the triadic possibilities. Here, it is Dupin who occupies the role of seeker, as evidenced by his ability to discern the letter, what it means for the thief (power via blackmail), and what it means for the French investigator himself (a commission and the return of order). By contrast, the thief—once the seeker—is now the seer, complacently secure that he alone possesses full knowledge of the letter's contents and location. This repetition of subject positions demonstrates the letter's power as signifier and its ultimate ascendancy over those who would control it. As Lacan points out, mastery over the letter is fleeting. Thus, the thief may have understood the possibilities of the letter when in the presence of the queen, but once he has "detoured" the letter into his own hands (20), Lacan tells us that the thief "become[s] its reflection. By coming into the letter's possession—an admirably ambiguous bit of language—its meaning possesses" him (21).

In marking the thief's own "detour" from seeker to seer, we can better distinguish among the positions of blind, seer, and seeker and better understand the implications of all three positions for perceiving absence. From the perspective of the blind, that which cannot be perceived does not exist. This gaze is built upon "an immutable notion of reality" (Lacan 17) and an inability to understand "that nothing, no matter how deep into the bowels of the world a hand may shove it, will ever be hidden there, since another hand can retrieve it, and that what is hidden is never but what is *not in its place*" (17). In other words, the critical position of blind cannot comprehend that what is unseen nevertheless remains in existence. By contrast, the second position, that of the seer, can understand absence—that the letter can be displaced—but believes an understanding of the signifier yields definitive control over the sign's meaning for others. As Sean Homer describes, an individual in the seer position "sees that the first position is blind and unaware of what is happening and that the third position is fully aware of what is unfolding but . . . [the seer] deludes him/herself that they possess the signifier" (48). This belief in possession—that the meaning the seer has affixed to the signifier is definitive and gives power over the construct—is what differentiates the seer from the seeker. Contrasting the limiting strictures imposed by the seer, the seeker apprehends not only the meaning that the seer has affixed to the letter but also the larger implications of the letter. Seekers can "see what is taking place in front of them, they understand the implication of the [signifier] and moreover know how to act" (48). The seer is thus a passive position that attributes a static meaning to the signifier, while the seeker understands the multiplicity of the signifier's meanings and can determine a course of action in the light of those multiple meanings.

Contemporary historians similarly occupy these three positions when gazing upon Aspasia. Like the policemen of Poe's story who are unable to locate the letter, for instance, there are those unable to perceive that it is their "investigative principles" (Poe 15), those "traditional historical research methods and the traditional notions of truth and evidence" (Gale 363), that do not render Aspasia visible. As Dupin opines, these inquiries may be "good in their kind . . . [but] inapplicable to the case" (Poe 15). In the second position Lacan identified are those historians who, like the seer-queen, circumscribe Aspasia through her insertion into a static history of rhetoric. Barbara Biesecker describes such a position when she considers "female tokenism," the insertion of women into a previously conceptualized definition of rhetoric (142). This category includes those depictions that position Aspasia as an exception shoring up a traditional definition of rhetoric. For example, when James A. Herrick claims that "Aspasia's story underlines both the tremendous rhetorical ability of a remarkable woman, and the stringent limits placed by the ancients on women in the domain of rhetoric" (48), he takes on the perspective of the seer. Unlike the blind, whose maps do not permit a view of this figure, Herrick, like the seer, can see Aspasia, and he defines her by the context into which she is placed and overwrites her enigmatic existence with a belief in the rhetorical tradition. Alternatively, many feminist readings seem to frame their goal from the position of the seeker, a role that both identifies the signifier and is able to take transformative action based on this knowledge. Thus, Glenn actively "wants to challenge the male-dominated history of rhetoric by telling a story of Aspasia" (Glenn,

Rhetoric 5). Like Poe's Dupin, this goal positions Glenn differently from those investigators who came before her, "reading it crookedly and telling it slant" (8), and so creates a map that transforms our understanding of history of rhetoric.

Ironically, whether we adopt the perspective of the blind, the seer, or the seeker when we look upon Aspasia, our arguments nevertheless attempt to assign a meaning to this "floating signifier" (Henry 98). Alternatively, rather than defining Aspasia's rhetoric through evidence of her words, we might instead focus on the repetitions that make up responses to this figure and so take an approach that, like Lacan's analysis, centers on the unknowability of the signified, thereby positioning Aspasia's absent words as possessing a rhetorical power in their own right. Just as the scholarly debate coalescing around Aspasia suggests the ways in which contemporary historiography profits from absence studies, applying Lacan's subject positions to nineteenth-century responses to Hamerling's novel argues that the silencing of Aspasia's voice in the historical record had a powerful and wide-ranging influence long before scholars readily recognized postmodern subject positions or studies of absence. Likening critical responses to this novel to the positions staked in Lacan's seminar not only broadens the value of absence analysis beyond contemporary historiography, then, but also argues its application to the study of literary-rhetorical history.

"Not improbably true": Aspasia's Absence and Fictional Presence

The often-indeterminate line between literary history and historical literature can be seen in novelizations of Aspasia as well as in the responses these imaginative fictions provoke. Although the subtitle of Hamerling's *Aspasia*, for example, reports it to be *A Romance of Art and Love in Ancient Hellas*, the preface makes emphatically clear that its goals are more historical than romantic:

> What I shall relate is the unfalsified, impartial truth. I shall describe human nature and the course of the world. I shall relate the acts and conduct, the struggles and aspirations of men, and the words with which they defend them. I have no tendency in view save that of life, no moral save that of necessity, no logic save that of the fact, which consists of thrust and counter-thrust, as constant and regular as the pine tree in the wind. (ii–iii)

For a sensational romance, such a goal seems an ambitious one. And yet, published reviews of the English translation of his novel apparently affirm his achievement of this lofty ideal. One critic finds that "these characters, as studies of what Aspasia and Pericles really were, are worthy of consideration and not improbably true" ("Rev. of *Aspasia*," *Californian*). Another states that with the rest of his historical accord, Hamerling's Aspasia is found to be accurate: "This Aspasia is found to be less subtle than the Aspasia of Landor,[3] but because of that more faithful to the historic figure. Matchless in the warmth and symmetry of her beauty, matchless in her swift eloquence of wisdom, she wrote her name ineffaceably upon men, women and the State" ("Rev. of *Aspasia*," *San Francisco Bulletin*). Even a reviewer unimpressed with *Aspasia* states that they "do not question the accuracy of the facts" ("Recent Fiction"). Both positive and negative reviews, then, accept Hamerling's figuration as a rendering of historical fact, not romantic fiction. Such responses not only suggest that we can read fictional treatments of Aspasia into her intellectual history but also anticipate Lacan's claim in the "Seminar" that story "is appropriate . . . for shedding light" on truth (7).

This novel's alleged truth will also be familiar to many contemporary historians, for Hamerling's Aspasia largely predicts her figuration in current feminist scholarship. His Aspasia is logographer to Pericles (2.40), an influence on Socrates' philosophy (1.183–86), a teacher of young women (2.171–201), and a proto-feminist activist (2.26–27). Admittedly, Hamerling glosses over those parts of Aspasia's biographical tradition that contradict his "imperialist fantasy in a violet Athens" (Henry 106), such as the son she shared with Pericles or the continuation of her romantic life and public role after the death of the Athenian statesman. Moreover, the rhetorical expertise attributed to Aspasia in Plato's *Menexenus* and Cicero's *De Inventione* is here denied or, at best, diminished to the role of muse, a sort of Woolfian "Angel in the Agora":

> It was even said that Aspasia prepared the speeches that Pericles delivered before the people. Pericles, the Olympian, the famous orator, smilingly allowed it, and confessed that he owed to her the happiest inspirations. Aspasia possessed the charm of ready, fluent speech, sometimes found in women, united to a silvery, musical voice, and thus produced upon men the impression that she was a fine rhetorician, from whom they might learn with advantage. (Hamerling 1.40)

While this Aspasia might give the "impression" that she was a rhetorician, Pericles' patronizing attitude makes it clear that she served as passive object of inspiration, not as an active intellectual collaborator. This Aspasia's legacy therefore is not connected directly to her intellectual or biological progeny but is tied instead to her indirect influence over others. Much of this influence, the reader is told, springs from her physicality rather than her words. As Socrates says, "You, Aspasia, do not require words to express your opinions, I read it in your looks" (Hamerling 2.24). These looks, ironically, last far longer than her verbal influence. According to Hamerling, her image is used as the basis of Alcamenes' renowned statue, *Aphrodite in the Garden*.[4] Her most lasting, most potent rhetorical impact, then, comes from her image: "Rather than creating texts, [this] Aspasia is a text, a Grecian urn of truth and beauty that men can read" (Henry 109). Like Poe's purloined letter, this textual Aspasia's lasting influence stems from her iconic existence, not from the preservation of her words. Even in a novel that bears her name, Aspasia goes down in history quietly.

In *Aspasia*, then, the ultimate silence of the eponymous character lends itself to the study of absence by recollecting both the Aspasia of our contemporary rhetorical study and the letter of Poe's tale. Further, as Hamerling suggests in the passage quoted at the beginning of this chapter, this Aspasia-as-icon is subject to multiple and conflicting readings. Each fictionalized character—Pericles, Protagoras, Socrates, Phidias—views her differently. These conflicting fictional views are reflected in the period's reviews of the book. That is, while the bulk of reviews are united in their complimentary assessment of Hamerling's subject, they nevertheless distinguish themselves from one another and the book itself by creating new and different Aspasias. Akin to those contemporary inquiries that view Aspasia from the position of the blind, for example, are those reviewers who dismiss Aspasia as a subject altogether. Such blindness to Hamerling's Aspasia is perhaps best articulated by distinguished German classicist Ulrich von Wilamowitz-Moellendorff, who not only condemns Hamerling's book as merely suitable for "those who could not find their heroes manly or write history without feminine perfume" (qtd. in Henry 113) but also banishes her from history altogether, claiming "Aspasia's intellect is not a historical question" (qtd. in Henry 171). In contrast to those readers who viewed *Aspasia* as history, von Wilamowitz-Moellendorff erases this woman from the historical narrative as fundamentally and self-evidentially unsuitable material for historical investigation. We can understand such blindness like the failed investigative methods of Poe's police—a fidelity to method that precludes the ability to discern absence.

In contrast to those who did not see Hamerling's Aspasia are also those reviews that accept Hamerling's depiction as illuminating historical reality, attributing to the author a position Lacan would associate with the broad and active gaze of the seeker. In addition to the positive assessments in the *Californian* and the *Dial*, for example, the *San Francisco Bulletin* enthused:

> All the great men and the one great woman of Periclean Athens are drawn here in their historical character. The known incidents of their lives are simply rendered. Whatever must be supplied by the imagination to sustain or correct the glowing picture is as obviously truthful as if it had been actual. . . . You do not always know what Aspasia or Socrates is about to say, but you know that it is what Pericles or Protagoras could not say, and when it is said, you see that Aspasia or Socrates must have said exactly this—more or less. (288)

Hamerling's supporters thus frame this author as the seeker, for he too revisions what he sees and knows how to act in light of his transformed vision. That such an attempt meets with success tells us much about the ways in which historical fiction could be viewed, and the enthusiasm of his reception suggests that the long-standing intellectual tradition associated with Aspasia that Hammering reinscribed, albeit in a gilded fashion, was an accepted placeholder for Aspasia's absent words.

Even as they behold Hamerling's *Aspasia* and laud the author's powers of perception, however, the critics of the period occupy the seer position, for while they praise the historical fullness of his fictionalized heroine, their reviews attempt to capture Aspasia, and their descriptions unwittingly create new versions of this figure. They become, as Lacan would say, possessed by the signifier. Such, at any rate, is the case in the *San Francisco Bulletin*'s assessment of Hamerling's efforts. In the course of praising this Aspasia's historicity, the review yields a new Aspasia, one who not only serves as "the index of great deeds" for men—a claim that is puzzling and difficult to ground in the text—but, more radically, casts her influence "upon women as the mold and teacher of her famous class of girls to become the Aspasias of the next generation." Such a claim seems opposed to the narrative of the novel, where the women of Athens meet Aspasia's liberatory talk with contemptuous derision (2.76–78) and where her short-lived efforts at education are limited to four girls (2.171–201). Starkly contrasting with this reviewer's stainless Aspasia is the *Literary World*'s critique of her "free love" advocacy and "immoral" influence (57), an assessment that would likewise find textual contradiction in Aspasia's proclamations of virginity, her fidelity to Pericles, and the couple's marriage (1.301–23; 2.25–26). Whether lauding *Aspasia* or condemning it, critics are liable to create their own figurations to insert in the place of Hamerling's character and thereby add additional Aspasias to the circulation of the figure.

In their complacent attempts to capture concisely Hamerling's Aspasia, such responses correspond to the category of seeker, for these reviews fix a singular pseudo-historic Aspasia as definitive. As in Hamerling's passage at the beginning of this chapter, such fictional-historical readings endow their subject with characteristics that result from their own critical perspectives—what they represent is not the novel's Aspasia but what they see when they turn a critical gaze upon her. The implications of these reviews for our contemporary debates are particularly aggravated by their advocacy for the historicity of Hamerling's work. By first accepting Hamerling's fiction as history and then substituting in their work a revisioned Aspasia for Hamerling's figure, they further the chain of historic substitution, replacing one simulacrum for another and deferring meaning by mistakenly rooting the historical authority for their own creations in Hamerling's romance. And, like the meandering missive in Poe's story, these facsimiles continue to circulate and disseminate within the space created by Aspasia's absence.

In nineteenth-century literature as in our contemporary debates, then, focusing on responses to Aspasia's silencing reveals repetition across literary and rhetorical criticism, suggesting avenues for further studies and opening investigation into the subject positions her absence affords. For as in Hamerling's novel, so too the representation of Aspasia in such popular nineteenth-century works as Walter Savage Landor's *Pericles and Aspasia* (1836) and Eliza Lynn Linton's *Amymone: A Romance of the Days of Pericles* (1848), as well as in more contemporary revisionings of Aspasia's life, like Gertrude Atherton's *The Immortal Marriage* (1927), Madeline Dimont's *Darling Pericles* (1972), Taylor Caldwell's *Glory and the Lightning* (1976), and Karen Essex's *Stealing Athena* (2008), can tell us much about how authors and readers are able to imagine the history of women's rhetoric. Such books complement biographical studies of Aspasia that work to discern her historical presence. Rather than eroding claims of her existence, the study of absence improves our understanding of her impact on history. By drawing together spectators of Aspasia's historical presence and auditors to her rhetorical silence, the study of absence can help us see not just the influence of the singular historical subject Aspasia but, in fact, the influence of the dozens, perhaps hundreds, of Aspasia-simulacra that have been created in response to her silencing and whose rhetorical influence we have yet to acknowledge.

Notes

1. As representative scholarship that casts Aspasia as a courtesan and denies the accuracy of her representation as a rhetorician, see Collins and Stauffer and Dean-Jones. For considerations of Aspasia that examine her historical impact as rhetor and rhetorician, see Glenn and Jarratt and Ong.

2. Given the space constraints of this chapter and the complexity of Lacan's "Seminar," I here focus on a structural reading, leaving aside for future investigation the psychoanalytic elements inevitable in a full Lacanian analysis. As representative examples of the applications of Lacanian psychoanalysis to woman's role in the ancient tradition, see Ballif and duBois (*Sappho* and *Sowing*). For the application of Lacan to contemporary composition studies, see Wells.

3. Walter Savage Landor's epistolary novel *Pericles and Aspasia* had achieved great commercial and critical success.

4. Now lost, *Aphrodite in the Garden* (ca. 430–420 B.C.E.) is considered to have been one of Alcamenes' finest works.

Works Cited

Aristophanes. *Aristophanes: Acharnians. Knights.* Revised. Loeb Classical Library. Cambridge: Harvard UP, 1998. Print.

"Aspasia." Rev. of *Aspasia: A Romance of Art and Love in Ancient Hellas. Literary World*, Feb. 25, 1882: 57. Print.

Ballif, Michelle. *Seduction, Sophistry, and the Woman with the Rhetorical Figure.* Carbondale: Southern Illinois UP, 2000. Print.

Biesecker, Barbara. "Coming to Terms with Recent Attempts to Write Women into the History of Rhetoric." *Philosophy and Rhetoric* 25.2 (1992): 140–61. Print.

Collins, Susan D., and Devin Stauffer. "The Challenge of Plato's 'Menexenus.'" *Review of Politics* 61.1 (1999): 81–115. Print.

Dean-Jones, Lesley. "Menexenus—Son of Socrates." *Classical Quarterly* 45.1 (1995): 51–57. Print.

duBois, Page. *Sappho Is Burning.* Chicago: U Of Chicago P, 1997. Print.

———. *Sowing the Body: Psychoanalysis and Ancient Representations of Women.* Chicago: U of Chicago P, 1991. Print.

Gale, Xin Liu. "Historical Studies and Postmodernism: Rereading Aspasia of Miletus." *College English* 62.3 (2000): 361–86. Print.

Glenn, Cheryl. *Rhetoric Retold: Regendering the Tradition from Antiquity through the Renaissance.* Carbondale: Southern Illinois UP, 1997. Print.

———. *Unspoken: A Rhetoric of Silence.* Carbondale: Southern Illinois UP, 2004. Print.

Hamerling, Robert. *Aspasia: A Romance of Art and Love in Ancient Hellas.* 2 vols. Trans. Mary J. Safford. New York: Gottsberger, 1885. Print.

Henry, Madeleine M. *Prisoner of History: Aspasia of Miletus and Her Biographical Tradition.* New York: Oxford UP, 1995. Print.

Herrick, James A. *The History and Theory of Rhetoric: An Introduction.* 3rd ed. New York: Pearson, 2004. Print.

Homer, Sean. *Jacques Lacan.* New York: Routledge, 2005. Print.

Jarratt, Susan, and Rory Ong. "Aspasia: Rhetoric, Gender and Colonial Ideology." *Reclaiming Rhetorica.* Ed. Andrea Lunsford. Pittsburgh: U of Pittsburgh P. 9–24. Print.

Lacan, Jacques. "Seminar on 'The Purloined Letter.'" *Écrits: The First Complete Edition in English.* Trans. Bruce Fink. New York: Norton, 2007. 6–48. Print.

Plato. *The Dialogues of Plato.* Trans. Benjamin Jowett. New York: Scribner, 1902. Print.

Poe, Edgar Allan. "The Purloined Letter." *The Purloined Poe: Lacan, Derrida, and Psychoanalytic Reading.* Ed. William J. Richardson and John P. Muller. 4th ed. Baltimore: Johns Hopkins UP, 1987. 3–27. Print.

"Recent Fiction." *Critic*, July 29, 1882: 200. Print.

"Rev. of *Aspasia: A Romance of Art and Love in Ancient Hellas.*" *Californian*, Sept. 1822: 288. Print.

"Rev. of *Aspasia: A Romance of Art and Love in Ancient Hellas.*" *San Francisco Bulletin*, Apr. 15, 1882: 1. Print.

Stone, I. F. *The Trial of Socrates.* New York: Anchor, 1989. Print.

Wells, Susan. *Sweet Reason: Rhetoric and the Discourses of Modernity.* Chicago: U of Chicago P, 1996. Print.

2

Out of "Wonderful Silence" Come "Sweet Words": The Rhetorical Authority of St. Catherine of Siena

Kristie S. Fleckenstein

Although resistance to women's participating in the economic sphere and speaking in the public sphere waxed and waned throughout the Middle Ages, the patristic prohibitions to women's speaking in the name of the church, either formally or informally, were consistently imposed, especially in the late Middle Ages. The Fourth Lateran Council (1215) explicitly suppressed lay preaching by women, naming it as a threat to the social order and church hierarchy. Spontaneous preaching by women (the Beguines, for instance) had likewise been condemned by the Council of Vienne (1311–12) as a usurpation of church authority (Hilkert 28–29). In this late medieval era, Catherine of Siena (1347–80), the illiterate daughter of a prosperous cloth dyer, became God's *apostola*, proclaiming the truth on her tongue to laypersons, aristocrats, and church fathers. From her early twenties until her death at thirty-three, this fourteenth-century mystic and church reformer traveled as an itinerant preacher, served as an interlocutor to Pope Gregory XI, advised Pope Urban VI, lobbied for the return of the papal seat to Rome, and mediated conflicts among the Italian city-states. According to Pope Paul VI, Catherine was a "singular woman politician" who had at the heart of her politics a belief in the moral accountability of both secular and sacred authorities (qtd. in Cavallini 108). Canonized in 1461 and declared Patron of Rome in 1866, Patron of Italy in 1939, Doctor of the Church in 1970, and Patron of Europe in 1999, Catherine wielded an amazing amount of power (Underhill, *Essentials* 33). Despite strong secular prohibitions against women's public speaking and despite strong religious prohibitions against women's public preaching, she changed the face of Italian politics. Catherine demanded "no more silence," urging the faithful "to shout out with a hundred thousand tongues," a call she answered in her own life with words that carried religious and political weight (*Letters* 117).

Catherine's rhetorical authority constitutes the subject of this chapter. How did this dyer's daughter break the silence imposed on women to become a "singular woman politician"? Drawing on Cheryl Glenn's contention that silence is "an absence with a function, and a rhetorical one at that" (4), I argue that the ability of Catherine's "sweet words" to sway popes, prelates, and city-state rulers paradoxically derived from her "wonderful kind of silence" (Raymond, *Blessed* 16). As Glenn points out, "speech and silence are not mutually exclusive; they are inextricably linked and often interchangeably, simultaneously, meaningful" (7). More specifically, Catherine's rhetorical authority, defined as the capacity of her words to affect beliefs, policies, and actions, arose from the matrix of generative and performative silences. Catherine's rhetorical authority illustrates both linkages and interchangeability. This fourteenth-century uneducated laywoman took her persuasive power from a generative silence within which she contemplated God, who is the source of all words, and from a performative silence through which she enacted God's words. Both silences provided Catherine with a formidable rhetorical provenance, enabling her to speak with a salient and revelatory tongue.

To illustrate the integral role of generative and performative silences in Catherine's rhetorical authority, I begin with a brief description of Catherine's life and the complex network of orality and silence within which Catherine's words acquired their gravitas. Then, focusing on God's generative silence in Catherine's *Dialogue*, her mystical conversation with God, I analyze Catherine's reliance on knowledge of God acquired through a contemplation that both propelled and endorsed the saint's words. Performative silence, the subject of my third section, reinforces the authority Catherine acquired through generative silence by making physically manifest her intimate knowledge of God through two strategies: a rhetoric *on* the body (extreme asceticism) and a rhetoric *with* the body (charity). By becoming an embodied word, Catherine aligned her ethos with that of Jesus, who, as "wholly God and wholly human," was the ultimate Word Incarnate (Catherine, *Dialogue* 66). His authority affirmed her authority.

A Life of Contemplation and Action

By 1717, Girolamo Gigli had completed *A* through *R* of his *Vocabolario Cateriniano*, a dictionary of several hundred of the words used by Catherine in her letters, prayers, and *Dialogo della divina providenza*, the long dialogue with God that Catherine referred to as her *Libro* (Tylus 2). His dictionary contains entries and entire essays on the words of "the first woman to write in the Tuscan vernacular and the first Sienese to leave a significant body of written work" (2). Gigli argues for recognition of Catherine's contribution to the Italian language, pointing to the fourteenth-century Florentines who "respected her, deeming her worthy to speak publicly" because of the saint's "*pulcherrimos sermones*," which moved an entire city (qtd. in Tylus 4). In addition, he reminds his readers that Catherine was acclaimed for her wisdom and for her oratorical powers, defending her apostolic ministry so fervently that he implicitly highlights the rarity of such a calling in the eighteenth, as well as the fourteenth, century (5).

This woman who, more than three centuries after her death, inspired a dictionary and a claim to authorial stature superior to that of Dante, Petrarch, and Boccaccio lived a life that "dramatically crossed boundaries and transgressed inherited categories" (Luongo 4). Born the twenty-fourth child of Iacopo di Benincasa, a wool master and cloth dyer, and Lapa di Piacente, the daughter of a successful Sienese poet, Catherine balanced her life between contemplation and action, silence and words. F. Thomas Luongo argues that "Catherine's involvement in the politics of the 1370s was not a secondary part of her career, an ancillary relation to some essential core of saintly or spiritual identity. Catherine's sanctity and her involvement in worldly affairs were fully interrelated" (206). Suzanne Noffke concurs, calling this dyer's daughter a "social mystic" and a "mystic activist" ("Introduction" 9). Contemplation for Catherine did not serve only as an oasis or a means to refuel. Rather, contemplation threaded through her activism: she "pursued the kind of activism her mystical experience demanded and the kind her writings set before us" (9). God makes this point clear to Catherine: "[T]he soul in love with my truth never ceases doing service for all the world" (*Dialogue* 37). That interrelation between contemplation and action structured Catherine's life and infused her words with rhetorical authority.

According to Raymond of Capua, Catherine's fourteenth-century biographer and confessor, Catherine's early life focused on contemplation, not action.[1] Less than a year after her first vision, the seven-year-old Catherine "withdrew herself from all company" to gain a "freer and more familiar access to God in holy meditations and prayer," describes Raymond. "She bound herself to a wonderful kind of silence" (*Blessed* 16), promising herself to Jesus as his bride, a commitment she revealed to her family only in her mid-teens when they sought to arrange a marriage for her. After acquiring her family's support for her vocation, Catherine gained admittance to the Sisters of Penance of St. Dominic, a Dominican tertiary, or lay order. Also called "Mantellate" because of their uniform of black cloak over a white tunic, the Sisters of Penance consisted almost entirely of widows or matrons who followed the rule of St. Dominic without cloistering. Instead, they lived and served in the community. However, rather than joining the sisters in their charitable work after her investiture, Catherine instead self-cloistered in a small bare room at her home, pursuing complete silence (except for confession) and a strict regimen of self-mortification for more than three years.

If Catherine had lived her life circumscribed by the walls of her small bedroom, Gigli would have had no need to create a dictionary of her words. But Catherine's self-imposed solitude ended with a vision in 1368, one known as her mystical marriage to Jesus, in which God called Catherine to service in the world. This experience sharply divided Catherine's life, turning her from a personal to an altruistic mysticism and propelling her to navigate a course between contemplation and action. During the next twelve years, Catherine served her family, her sisterhood, her city-state, and the world. She gathered around her followers and disciples, referred to as *la bella brigata* of the *docissima mama* (Lagorio 184). Consisting of women, friars and priests, and young, sometimes unruly, aristocrats, this group served as Catherine's *famiglia*, whom Catherine trained "in the spiritual life, and herself did penance for their sins" (Underhill, *Mystics* 155). Then, with and without her *bella brigata*, Catherine engaged in itinerant preaching, traveled as a religious ambassador to two popes, and served as a political mediator among squabbling Italian city-states. Her reach extended beyond her physical journeys, as well, for she wrote more than 380 letters to support her various missions for both church and state. In addition, in 1377 she began composing what she called her *Libro*, setting out the framework in a letter to Raymond, working on it during a six-month stay at Rocca d'Orcia, near Siena, and then intermittently revising it throughout the next year as she moved from Siena to Florence and back to Siena on ministerial work (Noffke, "Introduction" 6). Finally, heeding a summons from Pope Urban VI, Catherine journeyed to Rome with a few of her *bella brigata*. There, Catherine spent the last eighteen months of her life, supporting the irascible Pope Urban VI and urging him to moderate his dealings with the Italian city-states. She succumbed to heart failure in April 1380, her body exhausted by her years of extreme asceticism and indefatigable charity.

The devotion of Catherine's *bella brigata*, the importance of her various spiritual and secular missions, her popularity as an *apostola*, and her work as a political mediator all illustrate a life situated between contemplation and action. In addition, devotion, missions, preaching, and mediation embody a rhetorical authority balanced between the silence of contemplation and the orality of action. Motivated to redeem the importance of spoken words in creating written, literary language, Gigli sought through his *Vocabolario Cateriniano* to put writing and speaking back together without making speaking inferior to writing. For Gigli, Catherine provided an exemplar of a national language based on living, spoken language rather than on "dead words" found only in books, a connection that Jane Tylus subsequently explores in her extraordinary reclamation of Catherine (7). Without discounting either the saliency of Gigli's argument or the merit of Tylus's work, I want to emphasize the intimate connections between silence and orality characteristic of the late Middle Ages and central to Catherine's rhetorical provenance. From the ineffability of God's nature and the regimented silence of monastic orders to the wild popularity of itinerant preachers and communal reading, major religious and secular institutions existed as a result of the interplay between silence and speaking. A mark of Catherine's rhetorical achievement consisted of her ability to tap into and derive persuasive power from both, a remarkable feat at a time when state and canonical systems restricted women's public participation, especially public preaching.

Catherine developed her persuasive power in part from the rich oral cultural scene where words functioned as a living presence. An oral-aural orientation organizes knowledge according to the heartbeat of the life world, Walter J. Ong explains, ensuring that a culture "can never get far away from the word as a vocalization, a happening. The expression of truth is felt as itself always as event" (33). Thus, regardless of the exploding rates of what Harvey J. Graff calls "pragmatic literacy" in the fourteenth and fifteenth centuries, particularly signaled by the increase in vernacular (rather than Latin) texts, late medieval daily life remained largely oral (54). Historian Johan Huizinga claims that "we, readers of newspaper, can hardly imagine anymore the impact of the spoken word" on medieval community members (4). In a culture largely bereft of the written word, the spoken word served as the site of pleasure, education, and faith. To illustrate, Huizinga describes the almost frenetic enthusiasm with which people in the late Middle Ages turned out to listen to itinerant preachers, those with and without church credentials (4–5), an enthusiasm reflected in Catherine's own ministry. Raymond attests that "I myself have seen a crowd of a thousand or more men and women . . . coming to see her and hear her" (qtd. in Tylus 76). Thus, while the proliferation of medieval scriptoria (including Catherine's own) and the circulation of the *ars dictaminis* from Monte Cassino in eleventh-century Italy throughout continental Europe ensured the distribution of written literacy, the habit of reading those texts and letters aloud in oral performances underscores the tenacity of orality.[2] At this point in history, written texts resonated with attitudes toward meaning fostered by orality. For a citizen of western Europe's late Middle Ages, then, the word (spoken and written) existed not as an inert record but as a living force woven into the fabric of daily life (Ong 12).

The vigorous oral culture of late-fourteenth-century Italy acted as both invitation and deterrent for Catherine. Born and bred in this oral-aural milieu, Catherine grew up in an environment where words were alive. With no formal training in reading and writing, she relied in her youth on verbal homilies and biblical exegeses provided by males authorized to speak in her culture. As she listened attentively, she absorbed the attitude to word-as-a-happening and to truth-as-an-event. By relating to sacred texts during her formative years exclusively through the spoken interface, she grew up interweaving corporeality, belief, and texts into a single fabric, a theme that emerges repeatedly in the *Dialogue* where God's son is food (177) and wet nurse to the faithful (178–79), who dwell in his mouth where they taste peace (64–65). However, the orality that inspirited sacred texts, inviting Catherine to speak and live her faith, also acted as a curb because it was marked male. It was the male "apostles and evangelists, the martyrs and confessors and holy doctors who have been set like lamps in the holy church" (71); the Holy Spirit perched on their tongues, not the tongues of women. Canon and statute law denied Catherine, as it did other women during the Middle Ages, the right to be an active part of the event as speaker rather than listener, for speaking constituted the domain of men and listening that of women, a social division that intensified as the Middle Ages waned. While orality characterized daily medieval life, orality in the public sphere was considered by both church and state law to be the sole province of men. As a result, women, especially women like Catherine, with neither education nor family connections, had little choice in the course of their lives and little opportunity to contribute to the larger religious or political public arena.

Against this backdrop of rich orality, where word and truth existed as happenings or living events, and imposed silence, where women were excluded from public engagement with that orality, Catherine grew to religious and political power, swaying prelates, popes, and peasants. The alchemy by which this dyer's daughter transformed the strictures on women preaching lies within the silence-orality interface, for Catherine secured her right to speak and be heard by drawing on generative silence, within which she found God's truth, and on performative silence, whereby she embodied that truth.

Generative Silence and Rhetorical Authority

Like other women of her era who found in the ardently pursued silences of faith a means to challenge their cultural roles, Catherine rooted the rhetorical authority of her words and her belief in her right to speak them in the fertile silences of the church. "'Liberated' from their ascribed social identities," women found that the church provided a "safe refuge" and new avenues for "exploring their individuality," Rebecca J. Lester explains (196). Even in the late *trecento*, when the church was rife with corruption, divisiveness, and chaos, Roman Catholicism functioned as the major organizing force for spiritual and material life. Religious faith served as the glue by which the medieval community cohered, and the paradox of truth in silence constitutes a crucial ingredient of that glue. As in the larger culture, silence and words intertwined in the church, an integration vital to the church's characterization of God and to Catherine's rhetorical agency.

The power of generative silence stems from the identity of the medieval Christian God, who existed as both the absence and the promise of language. As an infinite being, God resisted conceptualization through the finite limitations of language. One cannot even call God "ineffable," St. Augustine points out in the first chapter of *De Doctrina Christiana*, because doing so already speaks the unspeakable. This conundrum, Augustine says, "is to be passed over in silence rather than resolved verbally" (11). God, then, could be comprehended only in silence as a silence. Catherine reached this same conclusion, for, as she confesses, finite words cannot express infinity, including her infinite longing to join with God (*Dialogue* 325). But God as silence was neither empty nor arid. Instead, he was generative, the starting point for everything, including words.

As silence, God functioned as the source of meaning, a highly potent presence that constituted the font of life and words. The disciples spoke God's truth, Catherine claims in her *Dialogue*, because God, through the silence of the Holy Spirit, perched on their tongues (77). Graham Ward elucidates this seemingly paradoxical linkage between silence and language in God. Correcting the mistaken belief that language and silence are incommensurate, Ward unlocks "other possibilities for the nature and operation of language" through silence (162). Drawing, in turn, on Jacques Derrida and then Michel Serres, Ward contends that the inevitable gaps in meaning require that silence be recognized as "integral to communication; silence *as* a form of communication" (179). Silence, in fact, exists in tension with arrangements of language, a tension essential for communication. "It [silence] is a space for/of breathing," Ward asserts, a rest "written into the fabric of creation" (179). The author of that silence and the origin of that breath is God. Ward argues that God as silence is neither unspeakable nor unspoken. Instead, God constitutes the fountainhead from which all creation, including words, springs. The silence that preceded creation in Genesis consists of the creative, pulsing silence of God, not the emptiness of the blank page or of nonexistence. Without silence, then, there are no words; without God *as* silence there are no true words. Thus, God is the ultimate warrant for one's words and the ultimate warrant for one's authority.

Immersing herself in God's silence provided Catherine with an unassailable rhetorical authority because it provided her with unassailable knowledge. Rhetorical authority and generative silence join in the *Dialogue*, Catherine's ecstatic conversation with God. Written and revised near the end of her life, the *Dialogue* provides a justification and rationale for her apostolic mission anchored in contemplation. It is a testament to the necessity of silence as a wellspring of—a prelude to—true rhetoric because it is the wellspring of true knowledge. As Catherine notes in a letter to her niece, "By the light of her intellect she [the soul] sees and knows, and she clothes herself in truth" (qtd. in O'Driscoll 23). God reinforces this in the *Dialogue*, telling Catherine that "you cannot arrive at virtue except through knowing yourself and knowing me," where knowing God becomes knowing self (88). Thus, the faithful soul, God says, "should not rest in her union with me" but rather actively explore "the valley of self-knowledge" (166), which is intimately connected to knowledge of God. "Do you know, daughter, who you are and who I am?" God asks Catherine in a vision. "You are the one who is not, whereas I am the one who is" (Raymond, *Life* 79). Knowledge of self can be found only through knowledge of God in "the light of discernment": "For I told you in the beginning that one comes to knowledge of truth through self-knowledge. But self-knowledge alone is not enough: It must be seasoned by and joined with knowledge of me within you" (Catherine, *Dialogue* 158). The road to discernment runs through silence, through contemplation when the attention turns toward and focuses on the gaze of the inner eye. "Open your mind's eye," God tells Catherine repeatedly in the *Dialogue*, and through such silent contemplation will the soul know God. This image reinforces Catherine's rhetorical authority because God is the source of her knowledge and thus her words.

The key image of *mind's eye*, the dominant metaphor for knowledge through silence throughout the *Dialogue*, highlights the intertwining of silence and knowledge, a necessary foundation for rhetorical authority. While Catherine refers to discernment by a variety of metaphors throughout the *Dialogue*—a lamp, a knife, a light, a tree—the metaphor of the eye constitutes the central trope. As God explains to Catherine, the soul's chief happiness evolves out of "seeing and knowing—the mind's eye is the eye of understanding . . . the soul's eye. The pupil of the eye is the holy faith" (92). After "baptism, the pupil of faith was put into the eye of their understanding" (94) so that the faithful can seek and find knowledge of God and self. Thus, God tells Catherine that "no one can walk in the way of truth without . . . the eye of your understanding" (184). Because of this, the eye of the faithful opens wide, but the eye of the sinner is blind: with "eyes of the damned," with "sick eyes," the sinner can see only through a "terribly darkened vision" (82). Sinners are incapable of seeing with that inner eye because the devil "blinds them" (89–90), or they blind themselves through disordered love (91). In silent contemplation, then, the faithful will open the mind's eye to discover God and his knowledge within a secret inner cell that all possess.

Here, in this secret cell, resides the presence of God who provides for the faithful a "gentle mirror of God" (*Dialogue* 44), the second image central to Catherine's rhetorical authority. The metaphor of God's mirror emphasizes Catherine's call to act on her self-knowledge. While used far less frequently than the image of the inner eye, the concept of God as a mirror within which the soul finds its own ideal reflection permeates the *Dialogue* on an implicit level. The soul, God tells Catherine, through the inner eye of faith will see herself reflected in the mirror that is God: she will gain self-knowledge, knowledge of self as the image of God. As a result of this knowledge, then, she is called to live, act, and speak in ways that align with that image: "In the gentle mirror of God she sees her own dignity: that through no merit of hers but by his creation she is the image of God" (48).

Catherine was herself conscious of the power she derived from the image of God perceived within generative silence. The visions she experienced during moments of intense contemplation drove her to act in the world and simultaneously justified those actions. She explains just such logic in a letter to Raymond, describing a vision involving Jesus, who put a cross around her neck and placed an olive branch in her hand, explicitly telling her to carry his message to the people. She recounts to Raymond, in an echo of God's words to Mary Magdalene: "And he said to me: 'Tell them, "I announce to you a great joy"'" (qtd. in Scott 37). Thus, a revelation, a discernment available to her through her mind's eye, dictated that she go out into the world to speak to the world as one chosen by God, the ultimate rhetorical authority. Her rhetorical authority became a mirror, a reflection, of his rhetorical authority. Karen Scott explains: "[R]ather than sit in her cell, pray, do penance, and at most communicate with people orally or by letter, Catherine recalls that she was told to *carry* the olive branch and the cross *to* the Christian peoples and the infidels" (38, emphasis in original). Catherine received her charge directly from God out of his generative silence.

Whether she was speaking through her prayers, in her letters, or as God's partner in conversation, Catherine discovered her rhetorical authority in silence and nurtured it by a continual dwelling in silence even as she participated in the world. Catherine believed that, through contemplation with the mind's eye, the devout would acquire the discernment necessary for knowledge of God and self-knowledge. This doubled knowledge was the piston that drove Catherine's rhetorical authority. Thus, God as generative silence constituted the first authorizing agent for Catherine's rhetorical power because that power swelled up not from the credentialing authority of secular or church law but from God himself. With God as her provenance, Catherine believed her words bore the weight of God's truth. However, generative silence constituted only the first element of Catherine's rhetorical authority. The second component of her agency derived from performative silence, for Catherine, like her God, made her body into a word that acted in the world.

Performative Silence and Rhetorical Authority

God as generative silence provided a foundation for Catherine's rhetorical authority. The words she spoke were persuasive because the knowledge from which the words emerged was true. Insights that Catherine gained from her mind's eye were infinite because God is infinite, but language, unfortunately, is human and therefore limited. Catherine herself notes this frustration: "And what shall I say? I will stutter, 'A-a,' because there is nothing else I know how to say" (*Dialogue* 325). Performative silence, the physical manifestation of God's knowledge by means of the body, provides the answer. Catherine constructed her rhetorical bridge out of two linked physical choices: her private ascetic lifestyle, which produced a rhetoric *on* the body, and her public acts of mercy, which constituted a rhetoric *with* the body. The identity of Jesus as Word Incarnate, an identity lodged within the interplay of silence and orality in the Middle Ages, secured the effectiveness of these two strategies. A visible and corporeal sign of God's true knowledge, Jesus himself existed as a performative silence, one who built the way to salvation through his actions first and his words second (*Dialogue* 69).

Conceived in profoundly oral terms during the Middle Ages, Jesus as Word Incarnate took on all the trappings of the medieval oral word: he was an event, a happening, a living rather than inert truth. He positioned himself between verbal language and embodied language, enacting in his body the knowledge that he shared through his words. Thus, *Word* in this context, Ong explains, is the proper name of the Son (13). When

John the Evangelist announces in the first verse of his gospel that "in the beginning was the Word," his assertion encompasses both *logos* and Jesus as each intertwines through the rhythms of a silently speaking God. Ong highlights that material orality in Jesus: "When the Son is conceived as the word of God, he is certainly not conceived of as a written word, either in the Father's thought or in our own" (188). Although shrouded in silence, God becomes sound through the Son, a point the apostle Paul makes in Romans 10:17: "So then faith cometh by hearing, and hearing by the word of God." The Word of God (Jesus) and the word of God (*logos*) live in the world through a somatic identity that Caroline Walker Bynum claims is "profoundly alien to modern sensibilities" ("Female Body" 182). As a result, medieval piety, especially female medieval piety, was also deeply somatic, Bynum argues, with the body serving as a conduit and opportunity for the soul's ascent. The believer's faith in God manifested itself in his or her physical being: the word becomes incarnate through the silent performance of the flesh. God highlights this explicitly for Catherine in the *Dialogue*: "If a woman has conceived a child but never brings it to birth for people to see, her husband will consider himself childless. Just so, I am the spouse of the soul, and unless she gives birth to the virtue she had conceived [by showing it] in her charity to her neighbors . . . then I insist that she has never in truth even conceived of virtue within her" (45). Without action through charity, virtue is still-born. Action becomes an expression of the devout's knowledge of God. The devout of the Middle Ages obtained the truth of God through his generative silence and then enacted that truth through the performative silence of the body by working in the world and by imitating Jesus' corporeal suffering.

Catherine, too, used her body as a sign of and tool for affective piety, therein gaining the second source of her rhetorical authority. Here, at the nexus of silence, word, body, and faith, she found the inspiration and the conviction to defy social strictures on women's public preaching and to speak through her actions the truth derived from her mind's eye. God in the *Dialogue* repeatedly urges Catherine to speak not in words alone but also in actions: "I am one who is pleased by few words and many works" because, as "virtue [proves] itself in response to need," works become words (42). When action is inspirited with grace, the body persuades through its performative silence. God reminds Catherine that Jesus "taught you more by example than with words, always doing first what he talked about" (69). He calls her to act in the world because, without action, faith is "dead" (95). Therefore, the faithful cannot remain ensconced within an inner mental cell immersed in God's generative silence and basking in the glow of his gentle image. Instead, they are called to act, to work, to speak in the world. They are called to cross the threshold of the cell. "The light of discernment, which is born of charity, gives order to your love for your neighbors" (44). True knowledge of self is incomplete without "constant charity for her [the soul's] neighbors" (164). It is within this space of performative silence that Catherine's rhetoric displays God's imprimatur. Catherine followed in the footsteps of her Christ to enact externally the knowledge that she discerned internally. By reflecting in her body the fruits of labor (*Dialogue* 86), by melding the infinity (and authority) of God with the humanity of Jesus, Catherine made her body into a highly effective rhetorical bridge between the silence of God and the language of human beings through two strategies: crafting a rhetoric on the body and a rhetoric with the body.

Catherine's rhetoric *on* the body emerged from the decision to follow in the footsteps of other mystics who practiced *imitatio Christi*. Catherine was chastised and criticized throughout her adult life for her extreme practices of self-abnegation, which, although performed in private, left visible evidence on her increasingly frail body. Catherine began her asceticism in her childhood and practiced it rigorously until her death. Raymond records an early instance of physical penance. Following her first vision at six, Catherine began to discipline her body. And, as Raymond recounts, her physical being—her rhetoric on the body—was so persuasive that other young children around her begged her instruction. So she taught them to fray the ends of a rope in order that they, too, might shrive the body. In addition, Catherine created a monastic cell out of her bedroom where she engaged in severe and regular austerities, particularly regarding food. As Bynum points out, obsessive fasting formed a key element of Catherine's religious practices, a habit that followed her into adulthood and ultimately contributed to her death (*Holy Feast* 165). By renouncing food and, in "eucharistic piety," consuming only the consecrated wafer and wine of Holy Communion, Catherine demonstrated the "kind of courage and holy foolishness that marked the saints" (2). Deliberate starvation in conjunction with other bodily asceticism, such as wearing a hair shirt under her clothes and chaining her hips and breasts at the onset of puberty, was particularly severe during her three years of self-cloistering but continued throughout her ministering in the world.

Performed privately but marking the body in highly visible ways, this rhetoric on the body served two different audiences—God and human— at the same time. First, austerities constituted a plea to God. Penances pursued as ends in themselves lead to spiritual self-will, God warns Catherine. Instead, these acts undertaken in silence must benefit others. Thus, Catherine disciplined her body so that she could pay the toll of sin for her loved ones, from family to neighbors to the Dominican order itself. "Since I in my sins am the cause of the sufferings my neighbors must endure, I beg you in mercy to punish me for them," Catherine pleads with God in the early pages of her *Dialogue* (27), enacting that petition through the rhetoric on her body. Second, her rhetoric on the body served as an implicit testament of her right to plead with God in the name of her neighbors. Aimed implicitly at those neighbors, Catherine's rhetoric on the body connected her visibly suffering flesh to the flesh of humanity and, through that linkage, to God's power to forgive and bless. To her, physical suffering was not the ultimate goal of her bodily austerities, which, Catherine says, God dismisses as a sin in the making: "works of penance and other bodily practices are to be undertaken as means, not as your chief goal" (42). Otherwise, physical shriving transmutes into the sin of pride, a sin compounded when practitioners, tempted by hubris to set themselves up as judges, condemn those whose path to God differs from their own (187). Instead of expressions of spiritual self-will, Catherine's penances were practiced as expiation for neighbors' sins. As a result, her rhetoric on her body constituted an entreaty to her neighbors to heed her commitment to their spiritual wellbeing and to acknowledge her ability to communicate with God through the medium of her flesh. Written in visible signs on the body, these private acts of asceticism were salient to Catherine's secular authority because they demonstrated her intimate relationship with God's spiritual authority. Furthermore, Catherine's rhetoric on the body secured her persuasive power because it was conceived and pursued as a part of a larger corporeal agenda carried out explicitly in public: ongoing acts of mercy, or a rhetoric with the body.

Manifested in the public flesh, private asceticism carved a rhetoric on Catherine's body, serving as one aspect of her performative silence and contributing one strand to her intricately woven rhetorical author-ity. Equally important in reinforcing Catherine's right to speak was her rhetoric *with* the body: physical and public acts of mercy that gave "birth to virtue through your neighbors" (*Dialogue* 159). The significance of deeds and words are emphasized repeatedly throughout the *Dialogue*, particularly in terms of Jesus, who is the quintessential practitioner of performative silence. "First he [Jesus] acted," God reminds, "and from his actions he built the way" (69). Through his crucifixion, he became the ultimate rhetorical act and ransomed via performative silence hu-manity from damnation. Catherine patterned herself after Jesus, seeking to ransom souls by deploying a rhetoric *with* the body in which flesh became the means of performing, or delivering, persuasion. The perfor-mative silence enacted by Catherine's rhetoric with her body warranted her political advocacy by intertwining that advocacy inextricably with her charities.

Called from her self-cloistering in 1368 by God's command, Catherine began practicing her rhetoric with the body outside of the home and in the world, first on a Sienese, then an Italian, and finally a European stage. From the moment of her mystical marriage to Jesus, Catherine enacted a rhetoric with the body by "burning incessantly with the fires of compassion" (Raymond, *Life* 126).[3] With her father's permission, she distributed secret alms to those in need, supplying food, clothing, and other supplies out of the family coffers. She violated social prohibitions by nursing the lepers in Siena's San Lazzaro, laboring particularly for the comfort of impoverished sufferers. In addition, Catherine joined the other *mantellatae*, spending twelve to fourteen hours a day at Casa della Misericordia, a hospital and charitable institution. With the resurgence of the plague in 1374, she redoubled her efforts, scolding those of her followers who failed to follow her example of service because of fear. Furthermore, Catherine extended her charitable attentions beyond the respectable ill. She found no task too menial, no person unworthy of her attention, from condemned prisoners to prostitutes (Underhill, *Mystics* 154–55). Despite the recipient's response or status, God called Catherine to give lavishly of herself and "to love them [neighbors] without being loved by them" (*Dialogue* 165). Finally, her rhetoric with the body poured forth and continued with her rise to power within the halls of church and state. Regardless of her growing prominence, she maintained her service to her neighbors, whoever and wherever those neighbors might be. Thus, her political activities constituted an expression of her charitable activities as both were integrated into her rhetoric with the body.

From the generative silence of inner discernment sprang the performative silence of acting in the world; rhetorics on the body and with the body linked the infinity of God with the finitude of humanity through the medium of Catherine's flesh. This matrix of spiritual and physical silences authorized Catherine's sweet words, words that had the strength to persuade sacred and secular powers because they provided evidence of her union with God. "You will all be made like him in joy and gladness: eye for eye, hand for hand, your whole bodies will be made like the body of the Word my son," God promises Catherine (*Dialogue* 85); in that becoming Catherine spoke and wrote.

Sweet Agency in Sweet Words

Generative silence warranted Catherine's rhetorical authority, and performative silence bridged the spiritual and material dimensions in visible, persuasive ways. Both silences were central to the rhetorical weight the mystic's words carried. Both were also central to the saint's own belief in her right to speak the sweet word itself. Even though God warns Catherine that "the good of these souls is beyond what your mind's eye can see or your ear hear or your tongue describe or your heart imagine" (*Dialogue* 84), God also anoints this medieval mystic to speak on his behalf: she believes and in that belief becomes his *apostola*. Catherine's own words reveal that she perceived these double silences as the source of her rhetorical authority, particularly in her identification with the male disciples.

The apostles spoke because the Holy Spirit was on their tongues. The gender of the tongue was not important; the presence of the Holy Spirit was. God makes this dismissal of gender explicit in the *Dialogue* when he establishes a direct connection between the soul and the disciples: "Now the soul who would rise up from imperfection by awaiting my providence in the house of self-knowledge with the lamp of faith ought to do and does just as the disciples did. They waited in the house and did not move from there, but persevered in watching and in constant humble prayer until the coming of the Holy Spirit" (136). And so, like the disciples, the soul "remains watching, gazing with her mind's eye into the teaching of my Truth" (136). Furthermore, just as the disciples, who, once inspirited by the truth, resided in God's house (his generative silence) and then left his house to enact and proclaim his truth (performative silence), so, too, must the soul. Again, the gender of the soul is unimportant; the presence of the truth is. God tells Catherine:

> They [the disciples] left the house and fearlessly preached my message by proclaiming the teaching of the Word, my only-begotten Son. . . . So it is with the soul who has waited for me in self-knowledge. . . . I gave her a share in this love, which is the Holy Spirit, within her will by making her will strong to endure suffering and to leave her house in my name to give birth to the virtues for her neighbors. (*Dialogue* 136–37)

The essential criterion for Catherine consisted neither of the gender of the soul nor of the tongue; rather, the key was the presence of the Holy Spirit, which authorized the soul to speak and affirmed the soul's belief in the rightness of that speaking. When God tells Catherine, "And if anyone should ask me, what this soul is, I would say: She is another me, made so by the union of love" (181), he endows her words with authority out of generative silence. That generative silence fuels performative silence, which, in turn, aligns Catherine with Jesus. By walking in the way of the Incarnate Word, Catherine warrants her speaking as a gift from God. Sanctioned by God and inspired by the Son's example, she, too, becomes "sweet Truth."

Catherine's words arise, heavy with rhetorical authority and agency, from this matrix of generative and performative silences. Tracing these textual and material paths provides insight into the interplay between silence and words characterizing the late Middle Ages. It reveals that one woman in an age that disdained both women and women preaching was able to develop persuasive language practices in response to the unique demands of subject matter, situation, and audience. It confirms the possibility of rhetorical authority and agency at a time when Catherine was marginalized by her gender, her lay status, and her lack of formal religious training and education. It demonstrates that silence is not bereft of meaning; rather, it is the beginning of meaning and a conduit for meaning. Springing forth from a wonderful silence, Catherine's sweet words were warranted by that silence.

Notes

1. Raymond's hagiography provides the essential details of this biographical sketch. However, see Luongo for an alternative account, one that focuses in meticulous detail on Catherine's deep engagement with the politics and cultural upheavals of the late *trecento*, an aspect of her life that Raymond elides.

2. See Fleckenstein, "Decorous Spectacle," for the importance of orality in the *ars dictaminis*; see Fleckenstein, "Incarnate Word," for the participatory, lived quality of late medieval rhetorical and visual cultures within which the arts of letter writing emerged. Finally, see Tylus, who emphasizes both the spoken, collaborative nature of medieval epistles and the degree to which Catherine's letters entered into this tradition (127).

3. See, especially, Noffke, "Physical," and Papka for the role of the body in Catherine's ministry and mysticism.

Works Cited

Augustine. *On Christian Doctrine*. Trans. D. W. Robertson Jr. Indianapolis: Bobbs-Merrill, 1958. Print.

Bynum, Caroline Walker. "The Female Body and Religious Practice in the Later Middle Ages." *Fragmentation and Redemption: Essays on Gender and the Human Body in Medieval Religion*. New York: Zone Books, 1992. 181–238. Print.

———. *Holy Feast and Holy Fast: The Religious Significance of Food to Medieval Women*. Berkeley: U of California P, 1987. Print.

Catherine of Siena. *The Dialogue*. Trans. Suzanne Noffke. New York: Paulist, 1980. Print.

———. *The Letters of Catherine of Siena*. Vol. 2. Trans. Suzanne Noffke. Tempe: Arizona Center for Medieval and Renaissance Studies, 2001. Print.

Cavallini, Guiliana. *Catherine of Siena*. London: Continuum, 1998. Print.

Fleckenstein, Kristie S. "Decorous Spectacle: Mirrors, Manners, and the *Ars Dictaminis* in Late Medieval Civic Engagement." *Rhetoric Review* 28 (2009): 111–27. Print.

———. "Incarnate Word: Verbal Image, Body Image, and the Rhetorical Authority of Saint Catherine of Siena." *Enculturation: A Journal of Rhetoric, Writing, and Culture* 6.2 (2009). Web. Oct. 10, 2009.

Glenn, Cheryl. *Unspoken: A Rhetoric of Silence*. Carbondale: Southern Illinois UP, 2004. Print.

Graff, Harvey J. *The Legacies of Literacy: Continuities and Contradictions in Western Culture and Society*. Bloomington: Indiana UP, 1987. Print.

Hilkert, Mary Catherine. *Speaking with Authority: Catherine of Siena and the Voices of Women Today*. New York: Paulist, 2008. Print.

Huizinga, Johan. *The Autumn of the Middle Ages*. Trans. Rodney J. Payton and Ulrich Mammitzsch. Chicago: U of Chicago P, 1996. Print.

Lagorio, Valerie M. "The Medieval Continental Women Mystics: An Introduction." *An Introduction to the Medieval Mystics of Europe*. Ed. Paul Szarmach. Albany: State U of New York P, 1984. 161–94. Print.

Lester, Rebecca J. "Embodied Voices: Women's Food Asceticism and the Negotiation of Identity." *Ethos* 23.2 (1995): 187–222. Print.

Luongo, F. Thomas. *The Saintly Politics of Catherine of Siena.* Ithaca, NY: Cornell UP, 2006. Print.

Noffke, Suzanne. "Introduction." Catherine of Siena, *Dialogue* 1–22.

———. "The Physical in the Mystical Writing of Catherine of Siena." *Annali D'Italianistica* 13 (1995): 109–30. Print.

O'Driscoll, Mary, ed. *Catherine of Siena, Passion for Truth, Compassion for Humanity: Selected Spiritual Writings.* Hyde Park, NY: New City, 1993. Print.

Ong, Walter J. *The Presence of the Word: Some Prolegomena for Cultural and Religious History.* Minneapolis: U of Minnesota P, 1967. Print.

Papka, Claudia Rattazzi. "The Written Woman Writes: Caterina de Siena between History and Hagiography, Body and Text." *Annali D'Italianistica* 13 (1995): 131–50. Print.

Raymond of Capua. *The Life of St. Catherine of Siena.* Trans. George Lamb. New York: P. J. Kennedy, 1960. Print.

———. *The Life of the Blessed Virgin, Saint Catherine of Siena.* Trans. Iohn Fen. 1609. *EEBO* (Early English Books Online). Web. Jan. 8, 2008.

Scott, Karen. "St. Catherine of Siena, 'Apostola.'" *Church History* 61.1 (1992): 34–46. Print.

Tylus, Jane. *Reclaiming Catherine of Siena: Literacy, Literature, and the Signs of Others.* Chicago: U of Chicago P, 2009. Print.

Underhill, Evelyn. *The Essentials of Mysticism.* New York: E. P. Dutton, 1960. Print.

———. *Mystics of the Church.* Harrisburg, PA: Morehouse, 1925. Print.

Ward, Graham. "In the Daylight Forever? Language and Silence." *Silence and the Word: Negative Theology and Incarnation.* Ed. Oliver Davies and Denys Turner. Cambridge: Cambridge UP, 2004. 159–84. Print.

Purposeful Silence and Perceptive Listening: Rhetorical Agency for Women in Christine de Pizan's *The Treasure of the City of Ladies*

Nancy Myers

The misogynistic attitudes documented in the religious doctrines, social laws, and cultural practices of the late Middle Ages restricted European women's lives and held them captive in subordinate roles. While women could embrace a religious life, canon law prohibited them from attending "the cathedral schools and universities through which male clergy gained both education and professional opportunities" (Mitchell 152). For laywomen, canon law dictated legitimacy of marriages and progeny, making accusations of rape within marriage impossible (149–50). Civil laws concerning inheritance, marriage (including a woman's dowry), and restrictions on dress (sumptuary laws) varied across Europe but tended to privilege men over women: "Legal historians agree that women in medieval France were considered to be inferior to men under the law" (Reyerson and Kuehn 131). As Jennifer Ward explains, the medieval society's view was that "women were weak, extravagant and pleasure-loving, and that their vices, unless checked, would undermine both family and state" (9). To keep women and the society stable, men—husbands and male relatives, religious leaders, rulers—regulated women because custom dictated that men had the ability to reason and often were better educated. During the fourteenth and fifteenth centuries, conduct books of religious and social instruction for European laywomen appeared, admonishing women to be "chaste, modest, silent, submissive, hardworking, soberly dressed, pious, and long-suffering" (Jewell 153). Thus, women's acts of silence were what Cheryl Glenn refers to as "expected silences," acts that reinforced women's subordination and submission, and women's acts of listening were unquestioning and accepting of what was heard (11).

Within that European social context, in Paris during 1405 Christine de Pizan wrote two books that spoke back to these misogynistic attitudes and practices. *The Book of the City of Ladies* (*The Book*) systematically addresses women's abilities to learn, to reason, and to act morally, constructing an allegorical city for women that highlights all of their virtues. The sequel to the allegory is *The Treasure of the City of Ladies* (*The Treasure*), a conduct book that offers practical strategies to the French women of Christine's time in order for them to develop the necessary virtues for admittance to the City. In this chapter, I argue that these strategies are integral to what Jenny R. Redfern describes as Christine's rhetorical system for women. While Christine never identifies *The Treasure* as a rhetoric for women, Redfern contends that this fifteenth-century conduct book constitutes a rhetoric because the "instruction has the potential to empower women's speech acts in both public and private matters" (74). I extend Redfern's argument here, claiming that *The Treasure* functions as a systematic set of theories and strategies to induce cooperation and persuasion. Moreover, it operates as an embodied rhetoric that includes both discursive and material components. This system of rhetoric for women works within and reflects the traditional and accepted social and cultural institutions of Christine's time yet pushes against those norms and expectations.

Christine lived what she preached in *The Treasure*, for both *The Book* and *The Treasure* further strengthened Christine's literary reputation in the French court, which began with her poetry in the 1390s, and built on her arguments contained in three letters, written between 1401 and 1402, that engaged in the celebrated debate on Jean de Meun's portion of *The Romance of the Rose*.[1] By 1400, her verse and prose were being read and circulated outside of France, particularly in England and Italy (Willard, *Christine* 51). To develop her reputation quickly as a writer was important for Christine, for, even with access to the French court and friends among the royalty, she needed patronage. After the deaths of her father in 1387 and husband in 1390, she became responsible for five family members in addition to herself and dealt with financial loss and multiple lawsuits: "With small inheritance and only a little land, Christine eventually turned to writing as her profession, maneuvering skillfully among the murderous rivalries that plagued the French ruling houses" (Delany 182).[2]

The Book and The Treasure arose from a complex set of forces driven by Christine's financial need and by what Rosalind Brown-Grant refers to as her "moral vision" in which virtue is no longer "an exclusively male preserve" (3). As allegory, The Book offers exemplary and unique illustrations of historical, biblical, and literary women who transcended or operated outside of the social codes and norms and whose rhetorical, religious, and political agency influenced others. Based on Boccaccio's Famous Women, it creates an allegorical city through the stories of former pagan and religious women who represent female achievement, bringing together such disparate figures as the Amazons, Medea, and the Virgin Mary. It refutes misogynistic claims through the advice, aid, and teachings of the personified virtues Reason, Rectitude, and Justice and offers the city as a safe haven to virtuous women. In contrast, The Treasure's advice works within the restrictive confines of the social and cultural codes and norms. Instead of focusing on female achievement, the conduct book condemns contemporary practices of gossip, frivolity, and extravagance and outlines appropriate behavior, language, and dress for women representing each class of the French social hierarchy, from princess to prostitute. Christine's goal in these two texts is not to present women with a paradox impossible to reconcile in that The Book offers social transgression and The Treasure social conformity. Rather, her goal is to reconcile transgression and conformity because in that reconciliation lies agency. In Gendering the Master Narrative, Mary C. Erler and Maryanne Kowaleski define female agency in women's history both "as individual or group agency" and "as an effect produced by social forces acting on social conceptions of female nature" (6). Over a period of time and due to specific circumstances, repeated individual acts and/or group acts operate within and against the social practices, resulting in a network of forces that creates a process of change through discursive and material means. As such, this process is a type of rhetorical agency. Within a misogynistic society that required women to be silent, submissive, and accepting of others' edicts, Christine's conduct book offered women of the Middle Ages agency, a means of chosen action, empowering them to be heard and to influence those around them on a daily basis. She did this by reconceptualizing the acts of silence and listening as calculated and determined activities within a larger rhetorical system for women. She advocated what I refer to as purposeful silence and perceptive listening.

Purposeful silence (based on a woman's deliberate restraint and choice) and perceptive listening (based on a woman's processes of reasoning and reflecting) are ongoing acts of learning. Contingent and negotiated, purposeful silence and perceptive listening ensure the possibility of cooperation and influence when a woman chooses to speak or write. As elements of Christine's rhetoric, purposeful silence and perceptive listening provided the social perception of conformity and submission while offering women the opportunity to make deliberate choices about when to be silent and when to speak in order to maintain the balance between a devotion to God and a respectable reputation in society. In the next section, I outline Christine's material rhetoric, which simultaneously delineates strategies for maintaining a woman's spiritual honor and for creating and sustaining a woman's social reputation. Then, the following sections demonstrate how Christine as writer employs the strategies of purposeful silence and perceptive listening in this rhetorical system through two textual domains, precepts offering guidance and personae demonstrating enactment. Both Christine's precepts and personae in *The Treasure* explain and model purposeful silence and perceptive listening, strategies that subtly transgressed social codes in order to forward a woman's influence and to aid her in protecting her fragile reputation.

The Treasure as a Material Rhetoric for Women

An effective rhetorical system must offer women strategies that negotiate thinking, speaking, and acting in specific contexts for the benefit of the self and others. According to Cheryl Geisler in her report on the 2003 Alliance of Rhetoric Societies' discussions on rhetorical agency, rhetorical agency operates as a capacity for the individual to act, arises as "a resource constructed in particular contexts and particular ways," and is a negotiated process that "materializes out of a combination of individual will and social circumstances" (12, 14). Moreover, as a construction, rhetorical agency operates performatively and dynamically, including not only language but also behavior/action and manner/dress. Throughout this conduct book, Christine provides the women of the late Middle Ages with strategies for rhetorical agency regarding not only language but also their behavior and actions and their manner and dress. This discursive-material approach opens the way to see rhetorical agency for Christine's contemporary female readers as contingent and negotiated, as possibility and potential, rather than as mere result or static representational model for feminine behavior. Thus, *The Treasure* as a rhetoric consists of inventive strategies rather than confining rules of decorum for speech and action.

Christine's rhetorical system resolves two culturally established challenges that she confronts in writing a conduct book that reconciles the female agency in *The Book*, demonstrated through women whose remarkable lives exceed social expectations, with the precepts in *The Treasure* for women whose lives must work within those restrictive doctrines. The first is the social understanding that a good rhetor, as argued by Cicero and Quintilian, is a man of good and knowledgeable character; therefore, logical and persuasive reasoning comes from an intelligent, moral, and upright male. The second is that the Christian societies of the late Middle Ages believed that God ordained the hierarchical societal structure, so, if one was born a princess or a prostitute, she was intended for that station in life. Both principles reinforce a woman's powerlessness: she is not moral, so she cannot reason, and her station in society is God-given, so she has no right to question God, only honor Him. She is silent in the face of men and God.

Christine recasts both of these assumptions in terms of appropriate female action within that social hierarchy: "She will arrange her life principally in two areas. The first will be concerned with the manners and behaviour that she wishes to practice, and the second with the manner and order of living that she will wish to establish" (*Treasure* 29).[3] Within the confines of the social strictures, a woman could deliberately make decisions about her speech, acts, and dress, could enact those decisions daily, and could influence to some extent her immediate circumstances. Because of that potential influence, the decisions and actions that regulated the self were rhetorical and supported a woman's agency. Moreover, a woman was to reflect her devotion to God by developing the virtues of discretion, humility, patience, and charity, for, as Christine counsels, "'it does not displease God for a person to live in this world morally, and if she lives morally she will love the blessing of a good reputation, which is honour'" (28). A woman's earthly moral behavior generated favor with God and with society. This relationship between responsibility and devotion to God and the creation and maintenance of an honorable reputation was a negotiated series of actions for women. Christine acknowledges that the two are related, yet she also understands that social reputation is about human perception, while God's omniscience judges devotion: "A woman is of excellent character and without any bad deed or thought in her head: but no one will believe it, for she is seen wearing clothing above her station" (133). Appearances in the world may not have coincided with a woman's true character, so a woman needed to be cautious.

The relationship between God and woman, based on her love and fear, was the foundation for a woman's rhetorical agency in the world, for Christine privileges the woman's relationship with God over that of those mortal associations. This bifurcated approach to rhetorical agency offered a woman control over her spirituality and her worldly reputation, two related but distinct types of rhetorical agency, and allowed a woman to deliberately manipulate linguistic, social, and cultural codes in human relationships for the sake of appearance rather than honesty in order to be true to God. The rhetorical agency affecting human relationships provided a woman with a defense against the injustices and cruelties of the earthly world, because leading a virtuous life did not necessarily result in an honorable reputation. The latter had to be developed and maintained. In response to a question concerning the elements of "genuine honour," Worldly Prudence answers, "'In truth they are good manners and behaviour'" (28). Honor in the world was a good reputation and name that could be acquired through a woman's use of linguistic and material symbols, but a virtuous life reflected a woman's choices about God.

From the beginning of the conduct book, women are given a choice that provides rhetorical agency: they love and fear God or they do not, and in either choice linguistic and physical action and agency are involved. Christine's emphasis on spiritual devotion begins *The Treasure*. In book 1, chapter 2, she provides the rationale for this love and fear and explains its outcome or reward for all women, insight and access to the virtues: "Why love Him? For His infinite goodness and for the very great blessings that you receive from Him. Fear Him for His divine and holy justice, which leaves nothing unpunished. If you have this love and fear constantly in view, you will infallibly be on the way to the goal where your instruction will lead you, that is, to the virtues" (5–6). If a woman chooses not to love and fear, Christine explains in chapter 5 that she will be damned. But if she is steadfast and consistently chooses God over the temptations of the world, her life will lead to a "face to face" encounter with "God and the Holy Trinity" (13). In order to achieve this moment of spiritual ecstasy, a woman must cultivate and practice the virtues of discretion, humility, patience, and charity. In this spiritual rapture after death, the woman becomes one with God. While this spiritual rapture matched the religious doctrines and beliefs of the time, particularly for female mystics and religious orders, Christine's advocacy of it for lay-women was not the norm and established a distinction between what a woman thought, said, and did and how society perceived her.

A brief and abrupt transition in chapter 11 distinguishes the relationship of woman with God from the one of woman with society. Christine shifts from the spiritual to the material to establish the distinct aims and means of rhetorical agency for both types of relationships. She plays on the terms of love and fear to authorize the two now separate relationships: "We have sufficiently described the teachings and admonitions that the love and fear of God give the good princess or high-born lady. From now on we must speak of the lessons Worldly Prudence gives her. These teachings and admonitions are not separate from those of God but come from them and are based on them" (28). Christine works within the expected generalizations of social conventions and religious doctrines that define an honorable woman. However, the point that human associations are "based on" this relationship with God does not mean that human ones are the same as or even parallel to the one with God; rather, this membership in society is guided by the teachings of "Worldly Prudence." She is quite explicit about the differences in the two relationships and the important role that behavior and manners hold in maintaining a good reputation in social ones.

Since there is no one-to-one correlation between the world's understanding of a woman's linguistic and material actions and God's judgment of them, the canny bifurcated nature of this rhetoric for women manifests itself in Christine's discussion concerning the appropriate rhetorical approach for dealing with enemies: "She will pretend that she wishes to defer to them and their advice, and she will summon them to confidential meetings (as she will pretend them to be), where she will tell them ordinary things with a great show of secrecy and confidence and keep her real thoughts to herself" (44–45). A woman's rhetorical approach and her rhetorical agency, as proposed by Christine, emphasize a deceitful style over moral and charitable substance. In the association of a woman with the world, the goal is for the woman to separate herself from her enemies through her linguistic and behavioral pretense; however, the virtues of this type of relationship are that "good manners and behaviour" are maintained (28). If applied skillfully, a woman's rhetorical approach persuades the enemies into believing that the rapport is cordial and productive. Because the woman in this circumstance could be deemed uncharitable by not being truthful with her enemies, her deceit could be argued as a break in her association with God, but it is just the opposite. By choosing discretion, "the mother" and first of the virtues, over charity, the woman has maintained a continuous relationship with God, for as Christine writes, "Thus the wise lady will use this discreet pretense and prudent caution, which is not to be thought a vice, but is a great virtue" (16, 45).

The Treasure establishes a rhetorical system of dual relationships for women, one arising from the unique one-to-one relationship between a woman and God that is privileged and private and one arising from sociocultural affiliations. This separation of relationships allows women rhetorical agency in both. Christine argues that manner, deeds, and words all work together to present the appearance of a constant and positive reputation; within individual circumstances, a female voice can be heard and can be influential. Underlying this, of course, is a reverence and devotion to God based on enacting the virtues of discretion, humility, patience, and charity, with discretion being paramount. Embracing the virtue of discretion, a woman is devout even when the appearances of her actions and words in the world do not reflect her beliefs. A woman's honesty and constancy to God, her "love and fear," matter most, not the practices or products of her social interactions.

Purposeful Silence, Perceptive Listening, and the Virtue of Discretion

As it is constructed in *The Treasure*, rhetorical agency operating from the virtue of discretion opens the way for women to negotiate the possible and to envision the potential, rather than live with the inevitable. Christine's emphasis on discretion as the mother of virtues further supports a bifurcated rhetorical system for women, for discretion "guides and sustains the others [virtues]" that please God (16). If a woman does not "work by discretion," her action or word "comes to nothing and is of no effect" (16). Discretion includes the quality of being cautious as well as the ability to make responsible decisions, whether these choices are enacted in manner, dress, or speech. It is a mental activity of appraising the situation, weighing options, and taking the best course of action. Moreover, discretion as the primary virtue that pleases God suggests a habitual moral excellence of character, so the rhetorical strategies that enable a woman to enact the virtue of discretion on a daily basis should also support her efforts to gain "an honourable reputation" (29).

As components of Christine's rhetorical system, the strategies of purposeful silence and perceptive listening support a woman's development of the virtue of discretion. While these acts make a woman appear compliant and well trained in the social norms and expectations, purposeful silence and perceptive listening push against those strictures of a woman's silence as enforced and of listening as passive. As a dynamic set of strategies, they cultivate discretion through a woman's mindful use of self-restraint, demonstration of modesty, and responsibility for her speech and behavior. In any given situation, a woman enacts the virtue's quality and demonstrates her ability, even when the appearance of her actions and speech toward others does not reveal her true intent.

Purposeful silence, as restraint and choice, includes deciding when to speak, to whom, and about what; it is self-enforced even though socially sanctioned. Employing purposeful silence increases the probability of others' listening when one speaks and of influencing others' perceptions of the speaker's character. As a strategy enabling rhetorical agency, purposeful silence is calculated; it is to a woman's advantage to practice restraint rather than react and to choose her words before she speaks rather than to be spontaneous. Just as Glenn argues, silence, "as a means of rhetorical delivery, can be empowered action, both resistant and creative" (155). The restraint and choice of purposeful silence works with perceptive listening for Christine.

Perceptive listening focuses on the processes of reasoning and reflection, and its strategies allow the hearer to assess the credibility of the speech and the reliability of the speaker's character in order to make critical judgments about self, others, and future actions. For Christine, reasoning and reflection work together, but reasoning involves social and political logics, while reflection entails spiritual insight, what she refers to as "divine inspiration" (*Treasure* 18). The strategies of perceptive listening operate as a type of "interpretive invention" that allows women to be devout to God and to be accountable for their words and deeds; it provides them the agency to protect themselves from others' harmful speech and actions (Ratcliffe 25–34). *The Treasure* displays the strategies of purposeful silence and perceptive listening through the textual domains of precepts and personae and demonstrates that, when used, these strategies enact the virtue of discretion, one that pleases God and safeguards women.

Christine's Precepts on Silence and Listening in Creating a Woman's Reputation

In *The Treasure*, purposeful silence (restraint and choice) and perceptive listening (reasoning and reflection) demonstrate a rhetorical agency based on the virtue of discretion, an agency by which socially a woman may appear one way while operating and thinking another. To establish and maintain a good reputation and to gain influence over men and women in her sphere—in other words, to have rhetorical agency—a woman must be intentional in her silence, and she must actively listen as a primary means of learning and discovering. As lifelong processes and practices of restraint, reasoning, and reflection on others' language and actions, purposeful silence in conjunction with perceptive listening is contingent and negotiated so that, when a woman speaks or writes, cooperation and influence are possible outcomes. This agency may appear to others as docility, but so much the better for the woman's reputation. Christine writes of this appearance/reality maneuver when counseling the princess on her conduct toward her enemies: "They [her enemies] will think that she has more trust in them than in anyone else. But she should be so wise and circumspect that no one can perceive that she does it calculatingly" (44). The woman's relationship with society in any one circumstance is a bringing together of people yet making distinctions among them. As enactments of discretion, negotiating who she is and who she appears to be within the social forces constitutes the rhetorical agency of the relationship between a woman and those around her without compromising her devotion to God. Offered as precepts, these strategies allow women to analyze their circumstances and make decisions based on that analysis. Christine intends these guidelines for all women of every social rank, for as the three ladies state at the beginning of book 3, "We intend everything that we have laid down for other ladies and young women concerning both virtues and the management of one's life to apply to every woman of whatever class she may be" (127).

Through the use of restraint and choice, a woman uses purposeful silence in two ways: to protect her reputation and to determine in what rhetorical contexts her speech will be heard, but both have to be accomplished without harming her devotion to God. Christine explains how decisions about intentional silence and speaking can establish and reinforce an honorable social reputation. One way is by remaining silent, particularly when a woman is angry: "With a heart that is large and full, a lady cannot always keep quiet about what displeases her, but if she let slip a wrong word she might ruin her whole project" (45). For Christine, "whole project" means the woman's role in resolving the immediate issue or problem, her ability to work with men and women she may not respect, and her need and desire to maintain a sterling reputation. This intentional silence is pleasing to God because the woman is also developing her virtue of discretion.

To create and maintain an honorable reputation, a woman needs to actively monitor her speech and silence in all social situations, particularly to prevent the gossip of others and to prevent herself from appearing an idle talker. Being silent in the face of gossip is a strategy of self-protection. Christine advises that sobriety will help in this endeavor of purposeful silence: "In addition this Sobriety will so correct, chastise and control the mouth and the speech of the wise lady, whom she will keep principally from talking too much (which is a most unseemly thing in a noble lady, or in any woman of quality)" (30). If a woman talks too much and in certain ways, she puts her reputation at risk for others to attack or to gossip about. Thus, she needs to inhibit herself in public and private "from saying any word, especially in a place where it could be passed on and reported, that she has not well examined" (31). Calculated silence and speech through the practice of restraint also keeps her from engaging in gossip because "it is no hardship to keep quiet about the thing when mentioning it would accomplish nothing" (135). A woman deliberately chooses not to gossip even when slandered by others in order to appear honorable. Christine claims that the outcome of this restraint builds a woman's reputation: "Everyone who sees you thus graciously put up with the pride and presumption of someone else without talking about it or showing your irritation will esteem you for it and love you more" (101).

Purposeful silence regularly practiced gives the appearance of a model feminine character; it is from this self-generated and established model that a woman's speech has the possibility of being heard. Such silence, while an enactment of restraint, is also a matter of choice, so a woman may decide to speak to help resolve the issues of her husband or of those less fortunate than herself. Christine advises that when a noble lady listens to her subjects' grievances, she must act as a mediator between the petitioners and her husband. Dealing with two audiences, she must choose her words carefully and thoughtfully for each, and she must present her case to her husband "so thoroughly that she will have all or part of her request" so that her subjects "will feel satisfied" (22). Thus, purposeful silence cannot be enacted unless a woman also practices perceptive listening.

The skills of perceptive listening are based on her relationship with God but distinct from her associations with society. Through reflection, a process that involves asking for guidance and listening to it, God enlightens her: "Holy Inspiration comes to the good princess and speaks to her in this manner: 'Now here is what you must do'" (17). These spiritual lessons are combined with a woman's logical reasoning: "She will ponder long and hard whether she can do something" (22). Together, reflection and reasoning, as perceptive listening, offer a woman a better understanding of the issue, the options, and the best solution. As Christine explains, "She will conscientiously hear. . . . She will be so attentive that she will grasp the principal points and conclusions of matters" (34). This type of engaged listening is based on a judicious understanding of men's characters, their intelligences, and their uses of rhetoric. It also supports a woman's use of purposeful silence in her protection of her family and in her charity toward others.

To protect herself, her family, and others, a woman listens to God's lessons and supports them with earthly moral counsel and learning: "The good princess will have these or similar ideas by divine inspiration, and in order to put them into effect, she will see that she needs to be well informed by good and wise people about what is right and what is wrong, so that she can choose the one and avoid the other" (18). The ongoing act of learning through hearing is to develop both her religious beliefs and her secular responsibilities, for Christine advises that a princess should "often hear sermons" and "inspirational readings" as well as informed talk of "worldly affairs" (32). By deepening her knowledge, she will develop both her skills of reflection and reasoning so that she will be better able to protect her family, particularly if she is a princess and has the responsibility of government: "She will conscientiously hear the proposals that are put forward and listen to everyone's opinion. She . . . will note carefully which of her counsellors speak better and with the best deliberation and advice, and which seem to her the most prudent and intelligent" (34). As a woman who reasons and reflects on what she has heard, she is a better mediator between her husband and subjects or between her husband and laborers, depending on her rank. A woman's astute listening skills allow her to make conscious decisions about the best course of speech and action while showing restraint. For those in worse circumstances than herself, a woman, whether princess or merchant's wife, needs to be "full of pity, goodness, and charity," and she needs to act in their best interests (21). She accomplishes this not only through what she observes in silence but also in what she hears in their petitions. In this way, she can advocate for them with the men who can change their circumstances. Thus, her charity for others is based on her advocacy. Because of her developed listening and thinking skills, she chooses which petitions to champion with those in power.

Christine's precepts comprise strategies of silence and listening that require a woman to be purposeful and perceptive in order to influence the decisions made around her. Through Christine's advice about purposeful silence and perceptive listening in *The Treasure*, she outlines the benefits of those strategies for maintaining an honorable reputation, one anchored in her association with God, particularly the virtue of discretion, but based on social expectations and human fallibility. These religious and social agendas may work together; however, a woman's rhetorical agency does not rely on that. It happens more on a daily basis when she is making deliberate choices about her acts of silence and calculated decisions based on her listening practices.

Christine's Personae Modeling Silence and Listening in Creating Rhetorical Authority

Along with precepts, *The Treasure* offers female personae as textual models to demonstrate purposeful silence and perceptive listening as a means for woman's rhetorical agency and authority. The three Ladies of Virtue and Christine the narrator illustrate specific aspects of the virtue of discretion. Authorized by God, the three ladies, as virtues, embody habitual moral excellence and model restraint and reasoning for Christine the narrator through their dress, manner, and speech. Christine the narrator learns that silence and listening are not just social expectations but practical and calculated skills. Moreover, through *The Treasure*'s rhetorical moves, Christine the writer transgresses the socially accepted standards of the time by claiming authority as writer of a conduct book for women. As Gwendolyn Audrey Foster contends about Christine's conduct books for men, she gains her authority "as an appropriator and compiler of the male word" (20).

Christine the writer's authority arises from her employment of a weak, vain, and mostly silent woman persona, Christine the narrator, who is the mere scribe for the three ladies' teachings, juxtaposed with the voices of Reason, Rectitude, and Justice, the Ladies of Virtue sent by God. *The Book* lays the foundation for Christine the narrator's learning processes in *The Treasure* that are vital to both purposeful silence and perceptive listening, because *The Book* illustrates the importance of women, even if allegorical figures, modeling the appropriate actions of reasoning, reflection, restraint, and choice for other women. At the beginning of *The Book*, Christine as narrator is troubled and saddened by "the treatises of all philosophers and poets and from all the orators" because they all make the same argument "that the behavior of women is inclined to and full of every vice" (4). This results in her hating herself and "the entire feminine sex" (5). She falls asleep and is visited by three ladies—Reason, Rectitude, and Justice—who have come to help her build a city for "ladies of fame and women worthy of praise" (11). Upon hearing the news, Christine as narrator exclaims: "When the speeches of all three ladies were over—to which I had listened intently and which had completely taken away the unhappiness which I had felt before their coming—I threw myself at their feet, not just on my knees but completely prostrate because of their great excellence" (15).

The juxtaposition of these first two scenes, the men's treatises and speeches and the three ladies' speeches, demonstrates the importance of perceptive listening. Christine as narrator takes the men's arguments as true even though she questions their validity, but she learns that the men's arguments are false through a dialectic exchange of question-and-answer with the three allegorical female figures. Because the three ladies consistently model logical and balanced rebuttals to each attack on women, Christine the narrator comes to value herself and all women more. Through her attentive listening, she has learned through the ladies' teaching and speaking how to reason and reflect for herself. Moreover, God has sent the three ladies to instruct and guide Christine in the city's construction, which Justice populates "with worthy ladies" (*Book* 14), so their sacred charge and holy instruction make them more trustworthy than mere mortal men. Christine's purposeful silence and perceptive listening demonstrated in *The Book* is the backdrop for *The Treasure*.

Rhetorically, in both *The Book* and *The Treasure*, Christine the writer's authority evolves through her personae of the three ladies and of Christine the narrator. This combination of the wise ladies sent by God and the weak woman Christine the narrator establishes a textual barrier between the writer and the reader that allows for the authority of the ladies' teachings and for the reader's association with the narrator. In *The Treasure*, Christine's deliberate effacement of herself as writer allows her arguments to be heard through the combined voice of Reason, Rectitude, and Justice. Unlike *The Book*, in which each lady explains her individual role and speaks for an entire section, in *The Treasure* the three ladies speak as one voice, in the first person plural *we*. This combined voice of multiple virtues reinforces the teachings of the prequel that God has given women minds that "can conceive, know, and retain all perceptible things" (*Book* 86–87). As virtues chosen by God "to bring order and maintain in balance" the world, their one voice provides the lessons with explanations for a woman's worldly conduct (9). The authority of the allegorical virtues in *The Treasure* is directly connected to their teachings in *The Book*, to their collective voice, and to their ordained objective. While these are Christine the writer's words, they appear to be "divine inspiration" and instruction so that the writer is distanced from the teachings, silenced by them (*Treasure* 18).

The personae of the three ladies in *The Treasure* are contrasted to Christine the weak and vain narrator to build Christine the writer's authority through their juxtaposition. The disparity between the celestial beings and the frail human narrator highlights the authority of the former and the educational needs of the latter, thus demonstrating a process of teaching and learning. As scribe, Christine the narrator is recapitulating the three ladies' "worthy lessons" and thus modeling listening and silence, for she does not speak these precepts but merely records them (167). After all, perceptive listening is a prerequisite for divine inspiration. In the first chapter, the narrator Christine, as weak writing woman, reacts to the ladies' demands and the scribal work with silence and emotion: "exhausted," "joy," "trembling" (3, 4). This is in direct contrast to the wise and reasoned commands of the ladies. Christine the narrator reinforces the ladies' lessons through her desire and her decision to learn and practice them for herself in order to be a more virtuous woman.

In her intentional silence and listening, Christine the narrator enacts the virtue of discretion, which pleases God and serves her well in the world. The narrator's transformation from weak and vain female to reasoned and reflective woman frames *The Treasure*. For most of the treatise, she is listening in silence while she records the three ladies' words. It begins with Christine the narrator praising her past work of building the "City of Ladies" under the direction of "the three Ladies of Virtue, Reason, Rectitude and Justice" (3). Her pride grows with her declaration that she, "more than anyone else, had worked so hard to finish the project," and because of that work, she planned to "be idle for a while" (3). The three ladies appear and chastise her for her pride and laziness and command her to "get up out of the ashes of indolence" so that she can continue the "good work" of the teachings in *The Book* (3). Emotionally, Christine obeys the ladies' command to "'take your pen and write'" and listens to their worthy lessons until the last chapter (4).[4] Christine the narrator at the end of the conduct book is quite different from the vain and lazy one in the first chapter, for when the ladies "stopped speaking and suddenly disappeared," Christine, although tired, is pleased, excited, and humbled by the ladies' teachings that she had "recapitulated" (167). Not only does Christine the narrator learn through her listening and silence, but also she chooses to distribute the instruction that she has recorded, an act that provides the potential for the ladies' words to be heard by others.

Christine the narrator's transformation of character from the beginning to the end of the conduct book provides the proof of this active and participatory learning through silence and listening as she deliberately chooses to disperse copies so that these lessons are "spread among other women" now and in the future "without falling into disuse" (168). With this act of distribution, of choosing to speak, the transformed Christine the narrator merges with Christine the writer, for she directly addresses the reader, asking her to pray for Christine so that she will have the "light of knowledge and true wisdom" to use "in the noble labour of study and the exaltation of virtue in good examples to every human being" (168). The references to multiple copies, to her ongoing education, and to her good literary models draw attention to her continuing work as Christine the writer. In this rhetorical moment, both the female narrator and the woman writer, as women in a patriarchal society, transgress the social codes of the time, for both choose to speak/write out of their purposeful silence and because of their perceptive listening. These rhetorical techniques further Christine's dual agenda in the conduct book as the ladies are God's representatives and Christine the narrator is of the world. Christine's duality of writer and narrator models a woman's rhetorical agency through the female writer's subversion of the misogynistic system's acceptance of the word as male and also through the narrator's transgression of distributing the ladies' teachings "throughout the world" so that their words "might be more honoured and exalted" (168).

As a dynamic set of strategies in *The Treasure*, purposeful silence and perceptive listening push against those expectations of women's silence as enforced and of listening as passive. Purposeful silence and perceptive listening are integral elements of Christine's rhetoric for women, for without the strategies of restraint, choice, reflection, and reasoning, women's speech, actions, and manners are suspect and their reputations at risk. These are lifelong skills that are continually developed so that a woman may have the authority not only to speak but also to be heard. Based on devotion to God and social reputation, related but distinct agendas, Christine's conduct book, as a secular rhetoric, redefines silence and listening as deliberate and chosen skills and strategies so that women have the possibility to enact a positive and productive influence on society. The possibility to influence through writing/speech, acts, and manner is integrally related to a woman's ability to employ purposeful silence and perceptive listening within a constrictive and oppressive social code in order to maintain her devotion to God and to maintain an honorable social reputation. This study of Christine's conduct book demonstrates the opportunity for examining the ways silence and listening are represented in other conduct books and educational treatises by and for women in order to "locate, discover, stumble over, and then open up" the potential and possibility of rhetorical agency (Glenn, *Unspoken* 151).

Notes

1. Known as the *Querelle de la Rose*, Christine's letters, which argue against the misogyny promoted in de Meun's text, are novel in two ways: as a woman she enters a public male debate between Jean de Montreuil, provost of Lille, and Jean Gerson, chancellor of the University of Paris, and she argues against statements within a popular and authoritative text of the time period.

2. Unlike many women of her time, Christine was born to privilege, had access to the French court, and benefited from a father and husband who supported her passion for learning. However, even with these economic, political, and social advantages, once widowed, she wrote for the next twenty years to provide a regular income for her family until at least 1409, when her son became a "secretary in the royal chancellery" (Willard, *Christine* 196).

3. While I am using Lawson's revised translation of *The Treasure* from 2003, in 1989 Willard translated and published MS 1528, a 1405 copy of *The Treasure* that resides in the Boston Public Library (*A Medieval Woman's Mirror of Honor*).

4. Christine appears in *The Treasure* at one other point. In book 2, chapter 12, Christine as writer announces herself as narrator/character. She is only apparent in the title of the section and in the first sentence before the style reverts back to the three Virtues. It is not clear why Christine, rather than the three Virtues, is criticizing the women at Mass.

Works Cited

Brown-Grant, Rosalind. *Christine de Pizan and the Moral Defence of Women: Reading Beyond Gender*. New York: Cambridge UP, 1999. Print.

Delany, Sheila. "'Mothers to Think Back Through': Who Are They? The Ambiguous Example of Christine de Pizan." *Medieval Texts and Contemporary Readers*. Ed. Laurie A. Finke and Martin B. Shichtman. Ithaca: Cornell UP, 1987. 177–97. Print.

de Pizan, Christine. *The Book of the City of Ladies*. Trans. Earl Jeffrey Richards. Rev. ed. New York: Persea, 1998. Print.

———. *The Treasure of the City of Ladies*. Trans. Sarah Lawson. Rev. ed. New York: Penguin, 2003. Print.

Erler, Mary C., and Maryanne Kowaleski. "A New Economy of Power Relations: Female Agency in the Middle Ages." *Gendering the Master Narrative: Women and Power in the Middle Ages*. Ed. Erler and Kowaleski. Ithaca: Cornell UP, 2003. 1–16. Print.

Foster, Gwendolyn Audrey. *Troping the Body: Gender, Etiquette, and Performance*. Carbondale: Southern Illinois UP, 2000. Print.

Geisler, Cheryl. "How Ought We to Understand the Concept of Rhetorical Agency?" *Rhetoric Society Quarterly* 34.3 (2004): 9–17. Print.

Glenn, Cheryl. *Unspoken: A Rhetoric of Silence*. Carbondale: Southern Illinois UP, 2004. Print.

Jewell, Helen M. *Women in Late Medieval and Reformation Europe, 1200–1550*. New York: Palgrave, 2007. Print.

Mitchell, Linda E. "Women and Medieval Canon Law." *Women in Medieval Western European Culture*. Ed. Linda E. Mitchell. New York: Garland, 1999. 143–53. Print.

Ratcliffe, Krista. *Rhetorical Listening: Identification, Gender, Whiteness*. Carbondale: Southern Illinois UP, 2005. Print.

Redfern, Jenny R. "Christine de Pisan and *The Treasure of the City of Ladies*: A Medieval Rhetorician and Her Rhetoric." *Reclaiming Rhetorica*. Ed. Andrea A. Lunsford. Pittsburgh: U of Pittsburgh P, 1995. 73–92. Print.

Reyerson, Kathryn, and Thomas Kuehn. "Women and Law in France and Italy." Mitchell 131–41. Print.

Ward, Jennifer. *Women in Medieval Europe, 1200–1500*. New York: Longman, 2002. Print.

Willard, Charity Cannon. *Christine de Pizan: Her Life and Works*. New York: Persea, 1984. Print.

———, trans. *A Medieval Woman's Mirror of Honor: The Treasury of the City of Ladies*. By Christine de Pizan. New York: Persea, 1989. Print.

Trying Silence: The Case of Denmark Vesey and the History of African American Rhetoric

Shevaun E. Watson

In 1822, Denmark Vesey was accused of masterminding a massive slave conspiracy in Charleston, South Carolina. Since then, he has become the subject of myriad cultural representations and interpretations, including monographs and memorials, novels and plays, TV specials and documentaries, dissertations and Web sites, historiographical debates and public controversies.[1] If one knows of Vesey at all, it is likely for his bold criticism of slavery in the early American South. In the acclaimed book *This Far by Faith*, for example, radio personality Juan Williams rehearses the familiar description of Vesey as "the most outspoken black man in the city [of Charleston]" (15). The suasory power necessary to launch the greatest slave threat to any American city certainly compels the attention of rhetoric scholars, too, especially given the growing interest in cultural rhetorics and histories thereof.

Vesey was a free black man of some wealth who, by most accounts, possessed a candid disdain of racial prejudice and devoted several years to plotting the liberation of Charleston-area slaves.[2] He allegedly recruited several co-conspirators to organize large groups of slaves, perhaps as many as several thousand, to attack Charleston from different locations on July 14, 1822. Many believe Vesey was a charismatic leader whose commanding voice and forbidding stature instilled admiration among slaves and fear among whites. He is thought to be have been fluent in several languages, worldly in experience, well versed in liberatory Christianity, and knowledgeable about antislavery efforts in America and the transatlantic world. A lay preacher at a local African church, Vesey purportedly converted religious meetings into secret recruiting and planning sessions, strategies that were ultimately betrayed by a slave. It is believed that Vesey responded to this treachery by moving the date of the revolt up several weeks in an effort to preserve the crucial element of surprise, but this preemptive move was also apparently leaked to white authorities. Finding the city vigilantly guarded on the evening of the newly appointed attack, June 16, Vesey and his ringleaders ostensibly aborted the plan. Charleston officials hunted down all of the known conspirators and convened a special Court of Magistrates and Freeholders, which by summer's end had tried ninety-three slaves and free blacks on conspiracy charges. Many were found guilty and exiled; others were acquitted or released for lack of evidence. Thirty-five, including Vesey, were hanged, making 1822 one of the deadliest years for blacks in South Carolina history.

By most reports, Vesey's legacy as an early black leader is defined by his remarkable oratorical skill. The judges presiding over his trial describe his rhetorical prowess as including, among other things, the ability to quote "Scripture to prove that slavery was contrary to the laws of God," the propensity to argue "that slaves were bound to attempt their emancipation, however shocking and bloody might be the consequences," and the willingness to "rebuke any companion [who] bowed to a white person" (Kennedy and Parker 17–19). They continue: Vesey "sought every opportunity of entering into conversation with white persons . . . during which he would artfully introduce some bold remark on slavery," and in this way he "obtained incredible influence amongst persons of color" (19, 20).

Interestingly enough, not one of Vesey's actual words survives; he does not appear as a speaking subject in any of the extant sources. All phrases, sentiments, and persuasive powers attributed to him come down secondhand. This lack of primary sources certainly does not mean that Vesey was not an important black figure, well deserving of a place within American rhetorical history. The rhetorical achievements of Socrates and Aspasia, also recounted through secondary sources, provide but two examples of figures known through such palimpsests. Yet, this historical silence—because it is in this particular case inextricably linked to both slavery and conspiracy—deserves much more attention than it has received. Perhaps it is silence, and not eloquent speech, that one is supposed to hear in the Vesey archives.

At least one source points clearly in this direction. On Tuesday morning, July 2, 1822, Vesey and five alleged co-conspirators were secretly hanged outside of town in front of only a few onlookers. Charleston authorities worried that Vesey would use the scaffold as a final stage for his polemical talk and insurrectionary rhetoric. To everyone's surprise, Vesey was silent. This remarkable act was recounted by one local woman named Mary Beach in a letter to her sister, dated July 5, 1822:

> The execution is over to us at least for the present and has not been attended with tumult or assistance as was feared by some. . . . You will doubtless feel as I did, desirous of knowing how the criminals behaved at the execution, for I greatly feared they would have made some address to excite further rebellion; but they did not attempt it. . . . Mr. T. Legare says he heard from a white person, a gentleman I believe, but one who was near enough to touch him that he [Vesey] did not make a single remark but appeared like one "collecting his thoughts for the scene before him."

I want to pause at this scene of Vesey's quiet contemplation to consider the significance of this silence for the history and the historiography of African American rhetoric. The fact that this mighty rhetor did not speak at the moment of his death—he who had apparently been speaking incessantly and irreverently for years, he who allegedly brought Charleston to a terrified standstill only weeks earlier—suggests that silence functions here in unique and complex ways. Both academic and popular accounts fail to acknowledge the role that both silence and silencing played in the Vesey conspiracy affair.

As scholars begin to examine seriously the meanings and implications of silence and listening as rhetorical arts, especially as those arts apply to historical figures on the margins of the rhetorical tradition, it is important to maintain a critical awareness of historiography. For African American rhetoric, the construction of that history is necessarily tied to issues of silence. As Alex Bontemps argues in *The Punished Self*, the history of African Americans is characterized foremost by "the double silence of slavery": the relative absence of "authentic" or unmediated black voices in the archives and the absence of blacks' own subjectivity in the historical records of whites (4). "So deafening has the silence (and silencing) of black voices been to historians of slavery in America," Bontemps continues, "that it has virtually drowned out [blacks' own] silence in extant sources" (5). Slavery then creates an array of vexing problems for the historian of early African American rhetoric. How can silence be appreciated as one of the many rhetorical arts deployed by blacks if the archives are generally silent about African American rhetoric in the first place? How can historical instances of strategic silence be accounted for when that very rhetoric is, in effect, erased (or not heard or understood) by those doing the documenting?

Out of this conundrum, scholars of African American rhetoric have been working to elaborate the history of a distinctive rhetorical tradition created by black Americans. Much of this important work focuses on the mid-nineteenth century or later, drawing upon accessible source materials: newspapers pamphlets, petitions, speeches, sermons, essays, autobiographies, journals, letters, and such (see, for example, Bacon; Bacon and McClish; Gilyard; Richardson and Jackson; Logan; Royster; and Simpkins). An examination of Denmark Vesey expands current discussions about African American rhetoric to include earlier periods in history, as well as a wider range of figures and events that may have rhetorical import. As we discover more voices from the past, we confront the challenge of understanding deliberate silences and affective caesurae. Since Vesey's silence is recorded in a few extant accounts, such as Mary Beach's letter, the Vesey conspiracy case offers one way to begin to recuperate silence as a viable rhetorical strategy for those who have been silenced themselves within the history of American slavery.

I am not, however, solely interested in recovering Vesey's silence; there is something more interesting at work here, something at the intersection of silence and silencing. I seek instead to examine why Vesey's silence has not been heard, why it does not figure more prominently in the official documents about the conspiracy and all discussions thereafter. Since that frightful summer when the tremors of a threatened slave revolt shook Charleston's very foundations, competing narratives have sought to explain the conspiracy and Vesey's role in it. Whether Vesey is characterized as a vicious black man or a visionary leader, the majority of records and retellings suggest that his deliberate silences were replaced with courtroom eloquence and churchyard jeremiads, as if silence itself was not a meaningful intervention within the difficult rhetorical situation Vesey found himself. As I will demonstrate, Vesey's silence was itself effectively silenced by the whites who were convicting and executing him. They did so, I argue, because the city authorities needed to cast Vesey as a dangerous rhetor who had to be vanquished. Since then, what was once considered to be Vesey's menacing bombast is recast in more sympathetic treatments as articulateness, his threat as inspiration, his nefarious design as liberation struggle. In either case, both then and now, there seems to be the need for a kind of Ciceronian or Demosthenian Vesey, rather than a silent one, driving the telling of this slave conspiracy tale.

Failure to acknowledge Vesey's silence in all of this is to miss the real ingenuity of his strategy for dealing with white authorities within a legal system that afforded him no rights and a conspiracy charge that allowed him no options. Similar to Kathleen Hall Jamieson's idea of a "double bind" wherein a certain level of rhetorical failure is inevitable due to the constraints of the situation, Vesey's rhetorical problem was confounding: silence would make him look guilty, but so would eloquence, since reports of his impassioned appeals among Charleston's slaves were used as some of the most damning evidence against him. It cannot be known for certain whether Vesey's silence was deliberate, but its effects can be identified. If he used silence strategically, perhaps as a kind of "rhetorical refusal" to engage in the legal process (Schilb), the court was forced to try that silence, which created a unique set of problems for a conspiracy charge specifically. Vesey's was also a trying silence for the other black defendants, many of whom were made to bear additional burdens as witnesses against him. His silence also creates new possibilities of interpretation today, which pertain directly to the historiography of early African American rhetoric.

All descriptions of Vesey's flair for speech can ultimately be traced back to Charleston mayor James Hamilton's 1822 pamphlet, *An Account of the Late Intended Insurrection Among a Portion of the Blacks of the City of Charleston, South Carolina*, which sought to explain to a fearful population the exact nature of the slave conspiracy and to reassure citizens that authorities handled the threat with due diligence. Hamilton assumes an air of objectivity as he outlines the "facts" that prove "the atrocious guilt of Denmark Vesey," and he takes pain to exemplify the "generous devotion and unremitting assiduity to the publick [sic] interests and safety" of himself and other authorities (16-18), though his private correspondence reveals a more calculating attitude: "In either alternative [that is, whether or not the conspiracy was real]," Hamilton informs a fellow politico, "we are safe, as the measures to be adopted [for example, court proceedings, hangings] assure to us immediate security and ample triumph."[3] Regardless of how biased Hamilton's account may be, his pamphlet has been used as the definitive source on Vesey, whom Hamilton describes in a lengthy footnote: "As Denmark Vesey has occupied so large a place in the conspiracy, a brief notice of him will, perhaps, be not devoid of interest" (17). Hamilton goes on to explain Vesey's life as a slave and then as a free black man who gained some prominence as a local carpenter. Most salient here are the descriptions of Vesey's influence: "Among his colour," Hamilton asserts, "he [Vesey] was always looked up to with awe and respect. His temper was impetuous and domineering in the extreme, qualifying him for the despotick [sic] rule, of which he was ambitious. All his passions were ungovernable and savage" (18). As for Vesey's rhetorical power, Hamilton portrays him as the primary "channel of communication and intelligence" for the slave plot:

> [At] the secret meetings of the conspirators, he [Vesey] was invariably a leading and influential member; animating and encouraging the timid, by the hopes and prospects of success; removing the scruples of the religious, by the grossest prostitution and perversion of the sacred oracles, and inflaming and confirming the resolute, by all the savage fascinations of blood and booty. (17)

The courtroom was, most believe, where Vesey shined. The forensic drama is first described by the court magistrates, Lionel H. Kennedy and Thomas Parker, in their publication about the conspiracy, *An Official Report of the Trials of Sundry Negroes*. Their numerous details about Vesey's demeanor are worth quoting at length:

> When Vesey was tried, he folded his arms and seemed to pay great attention to the testimony given against him, but with his eyes fixed on the floor. In this situation he remained immoveable, until the witnesses had been examined by the Court and cross-examined

by his counsel, when he requested to be allowed to examine the witnesses himself. He at first questioned them in the dictatorial, despotic manner in which he was accustomed to address them; but this was not producing the desired effect, [so] he questioned them with affected surprise and concern for bearing false witness against him; still failing in his purpose, he then examined them strictly as to dates, but could not make them contradict themselves. The evidence being closed, he addressed the Court at considerable length, in which his principle endeavor was to impress them with the idea, that as his situation in life had been such that he could have no inducement to join in such an attempt [that is, that he had no motivation to revolt since he was a free black], that the charge against him must be false; and he attributed it to the great hatred which he alleged the blacks had against him; but his allegations were unsupported by proof. (45)[4]

What seems most interesting about these accounts of Vesey's rhetoric is the attention given to his orotund style and measured strategies without any examples of what he may actually have said. In their sentencing of Vesey, Kennedy and Parker assert: "You were also heard in your own defence [sic], in which you endeavored, with great art and plausibility, to impress a belief of your innocence" (177). But why speak only to the form and not the content? Why refer to his "art" rather than offer choice excerpts of it? There may have been many reasons for not quoting the hated conspirator in official records: to give Vesey voice would be to assign him agency. But to not provide the content of his speech has also presented opportunities for critical speculation about that artfulness.

Since other sources, aside from those by white officials and politicians, suggest that Vesey never got his day in court or that he was silent during his court appearances, it may be worth considering alternative interpretations of his rhetorical strategy. In the same letter to her sister, for example, Mary Beach writes that "Vesey asserted in Jail that he had not had a fair trial, [and] that his accusers had not been brought before him." More troubling is the discrepancy between the "official" reports and the trial records. Oddly, Kennedy and Parker do not identify the date of Vesey's trial. John Lofton and other contemporary researchers place it on June 23, 1822, but the most definitive trial transcript ("Evidence Document B") shows that the court was recessed on June 23, a Sunday, and, further, that the only time Vesey may have appeared in the courtroom is June 26 (see Kennedy and Parker 85; Hamilton, *Account* 16; Lofton 159). Even on June 26, it is unclear whether Vesey was actually present and, if so, whether he or his lawyer spoke. The record states: "William [Paul] and Joe [LaRoche] were again examined against Denmark Vesey and X [cross-]examined by Mr. Cross—their testimony was nearly the same as before—Rolla was also re-examined and X examined by Mr. Cross and testified much as before" ("Evidence Document B" 166). Vesey never took the stand himself. "If a trial of Denmark Vesey was held," historian Michael P. Johnson concludes, "no sign of it appears in the original manuscript of the court proceedings" ("Denmark Vesey" 934). Though assurances were provided that all defendants would face their accusers and be fairly represented by counsel (Kennedy and Parker vi), the actual procedures of the court were inconsistent at best and blatantly unfair when it came to Vesey himself. Vesey's lawyer was the owner of a slave who testified against him, and most of the evidence used to convict Vesey was actually gathered in trials that postdate Vesey's execution.[5]

One of the primary indications of Vesey's strategy of silence, in addition to his contemplative silence on the scaffold, is that Vesey never confessed. Whether willfully or under duress, every other witness either confessed to participating in the conspiracy or provided corroborating testimony for Vesey's masterminding of it. In his pamphlet, Hamilton opines: "It is much to be lamented that . . . Vesey could not have been subjected to the gloom and silence of a solitary cell. He might have softened, and afforded the most precious confessions, as his knowledge and agency in the nefarious scheme very far exceeded the information of others" (*Account* 19). While not confessing does not in and of itself constitute silence, the authorities seemed to have thought it did. Hamilton attributes Vesey's silence to a pact the ringleaders were thought to have made with one another in jail: "*Do not open your lips! Die silent, as you shall see me do!*" Vesey's "comrade," Peter Poyas, supposedly demanded of his cellmates (19). But even Poyas confessed in the end, hoping to save his own life but not succeeding. Refusing to provide crucial evidence or testimony, particularly a confession, can be understood as a form of strategic silence within the context of a conspiracy.

Conspiracy is a crime of illicit speech and dangerous persuasion aimed to orchestrate unlawful acts. The leader of a conspiracy may enjoin participants to silence about the scheme, but the crime itself is one of speech. Prosecuting a slave conspiracy in the South of 1822, let alone Charleston—the major entrepôt for America's slave trade—placed the court in a difficult rhetorical position. Magistrates Kennedy and Parker needed to exemplify the persuasive powers of the alleged conspirators without overstating the defendants' abilities. When blacks were tried for violence or pillage, for example, their brutish "nature" needed only be exposed and verified. Conspiracy, however, suggests a higher order of being, involving a special ability or "dynamis," as Aristotle describes rhetoric: it is an intellectual virtue, a faculty of seeing how persuasion can be effected, a "reasoned state of capacity to make [things happen]" (*On Rhetoric* 1355b29–30; *Nicomachean Ethics* VI.4). The magistrates had to negotiate between Vesey's rhetorical mastery and their mastery over him, knowing that the legitimacy of the trials depended upon the public's belief in a formidable foe who was vanquished by the acumen of white authorities.

The lengthy preface to the court's *Official Report* is an explicit indictment of the alleged conspirators' crimes of rhetoric. All that needed to be established was Vesey's ability to persuade, evidence that he had "obtained incredible influence amongst persons of color" (Kennedy and Parker 20). Specifically, the magistrates maintain, Vesey "constantly and assiduously engaged in endeavoring to embitter the minds of the colored population against the white" (17). They follow Hamilton closely in describing Vesey's skill and conclude that "to induce the colored population to join [him], every principle which could operate upon the mind of man was artfully employed: Religion, Hope, Fear, Deception were resorted to as occasion required" (21). They note Vesey chose equally effective rhetoricians as his associates. The ringleaders were "plausible," "bold," "ardent," "intrepid and resolute," "cautious" but "not daunted," "discreet and intelligent," "artful [and] cruel" (24). Kennedy and Parker wanted the public to believe that the personal traits of these slaves found their most cogent and "diabolical" expression in the rhetorical act of plotting an elaborate conspiracy.

The magistrates establish the malice of Vesey and the others by demonstrating their ability to win over converts and followers through misguided persuasion. Blacks' rhetoric, they suggest, is not true or virtuous but decidedly "evil and deceitful, ignoble and illiberal, performing its deceptions by means of forms and colors, polish and fine garments," recalling Plato's indictment of rhetoric in *Gorgias* (465b). According to these white authorities, Vesey is not a true orator but a kind of rhetorical tyrant who often intimidated Charleston slaves:

> Even whilst walking through the streets in company with another, he [Vesey] was not idle, for if his companion bowed to a white person he would rebuke him, and observe that all men were born equal, and that he was surprised that any one would degrade himself by such conduct; that he would never cringe to the whites, not ought any one who had the feelings of a man. (Kennedy and Parker 19)

The court amplifies the sense of Vesey's rhetorical treachery by suggesting an additional malevolent dimension of Vesey's "crime": he preyed upon the presumed mental "weaknesses" and emotional "vulnerabilities" of local slaves. By convincing these blacks to join the insurrection, Vesey gained persuasive control over his followers, the authorities imply, thus committing a crime of even greater rhetorical magnitude, going beyond just conspiratorial talk itself. Vesey "poisoned" the minds of slaves and "embittered [them] against the white population" (Kennedy and Parker 24). In a bizarre twist of logic, a black rhetor who may have tried to convince slaves to revolt against their unjust bondage becomes a worse offender of slavery than the slave owners themselves: no "person of color [could] withhold his assent" (21–22). The court takes pains to establish that though Vesey may have effectively persuaded many blacks, his rhetoric is completely disassociated from all that is truthful and just.

Whereas slaves were "naturally" unable to penetrate the intricate web of Vesey's rhetorical designs, the white authorities present themselves as capable of discerning quite easily between "true" and "false" rhetoric. In the preface to his pamphlet, Hamilton asserts "the salutary inculcation of one lesson, [that] among a certain portion of our population, there is nothing they are bad enough to do that we are not powerful enough to punish" (*Account*, n. pag.). It is as though authorities conjured a greater rhetorical foe in Vesey than what may have actually existed for the purpose of embellishing their own significance. As one federal judge later commented on the conspiracy trials, "Be assured it [the conspiracy] was nothing in comparison with what it was magnified to be.... To magnify danger is to magnify the claims of those who arrest it" (qtd. in Morgan 138). In a case where talk constitutes the crime, the rhetorical prowess of both the accused and the court must be firmly established: the greater the rhetorical skills of the conspirator, the greater the threat, the greater the punishment, and the greater the powers of discrimination necessary to expose such malevolence.

In this situation, Vesey was faced with few options, none of them good ones. He could have confessed or told the authorities the horrific "truths" they wanted to hear. He could have defended himself, as the magistrates maintain he did. Or he could have remained silent. Since the other defendants opted for either of the first two strategies, most to no avail, Vesey likely charted a different course through the rhetorical minefield of his criminal trial. There were no assurances that any kinds of words—whether guilty, conciliatory, corroborating, eloquent, truthful, or malicious—would save one's life. Some who indicted Vesey here hanged; others were spared. Some who confessed were sentenced to death; others were forgiven. But for the accused mastermind of the slave plot, silence was a masterful tactic. Vesey was so skilled a rhetorician as to understand that not only would his words not be believed but would, more importantly, prove his guilt. Self-defense was, I believe, out of the question. For Vesey to demonstrate any suasory power in this situation would, ironically, only provide authorities with evidence of the very thing he needed to disprove: his ability to speak artfully. To attempt persuasion, Vesey realized, was to provide fodder for the authorities' case against him. A conspirator talks—incessantly, passionately, indignantly; an innocent man (or a guilty man refusing to cooperate) does not have anything to say. Remaining silent may not have proved his innocence (or his guilt), but it did create problems for some and possibilities for others.

We can understand Vesey's silence, or rhetorical refusals, as an attempt to short-circuit the white legal system. Within slavery and other systems of oppression, the one exerting control typically demonstrates mastery through silence: "The agency of domination does not reside in the one who speaks (for it is he who is constrained)," Michel Foucault explains, "but in the one who listens and says nothing" (*History* 62). I contend Vesey met his examiners' silence with his own. "Justices were called upon to defend their rulings," notes Carolina historian Robert Olwell, "when slaves [or blacks] managed to throw a wrench into the their lives" (82). The magistrates' *Official Report* is clearly a defense of their jurisprudence, which was implicitly called into question without Vesey's confession, testimony, or words of any kind. The slave court's routine of unspoken judicial procedures and practices (such as slave testimony taken without oaths) could not be maintained without evidence of Vesey's dangerous talk. A prisoner who resists regular judicial mandates or remains silent seriously jeopardizes the judicial authority (Foucault, *Discipline* 41).

One of the major and immediate effects of Vesey's silence, then, was to compel the authorities to speak publicly and copiously about the case. They needed to fill the numerous gaps Vesey created by withholding evidence of his artful speech. The city council charged Hamilton with "preparing a publication . . . of facts in connexion [*sic*] with the same [slave plot] as may be deemed of publick interest," and the court's report, usually a pro forma document, took months to prepare and finally exceeded two hundred pages.[6] In a public statement prefacing his *Account*, Hamilton admits "not being insensible to the difficulties and embarrassments necessarily incident to the subject, as to what it might be politick either to publish or suppress" (n. pag.). While he acknowledges that "suppression might assume the appearance of timidity or injustice," it was the authorities' own strategy of suppression and secrecy about the investigation and trials that prompted the council's request for a public declaration of known facts. Such secrecy was necessary in part because they lacked Vesey's crucial, incriminating words: if he had talked, authorities would not have needed to withhold information about the status of the investigation or root out more evidence against Vesey from nearly one hundred slaves.

As the presiding judges of the trials and sentencing, Kennedy and Parker faced similar challenges in presenting the pieces of the conspiracy puzzle to the public. They go to unusual lengths to establish their judicial and moral rectitude, devoting nearly half of their report to legal guidelines and professional opinions. Relatively little of the document actually discusses the ninety-three individual trials held that summer. "It was thought advisable," they conclude, "to lay before the public, the whole narrative, as it was given by the witnesses, and not to suppress any part if it" (iv). Yet the legalistic intricacies of who could say what under which circumstances and what kind of information was "officially" recorded not only undermine their assurances of a comprehensive and definitive account but ultimately undercut their integrity, too. So many defenses of their honor and claims of veracity in the first sixty pages have the rhetorical effect of provoking suspicion. Without Vesey's self-incriminating speech, the magistrates seem to scramble to bring the trials to a plausible conclusion. As Olwell recounts, some cases against slaves in South Carolina completely unraveled without their testimony: to maintain one's innocence or silence "appeared to defy the law's right to have brought the charge in the first place" (88–89). In this way, we can understand the mayor's and the magistrates' descriptions of Vesey's rhetorical power as part of their own self-defense, as a publicly mandated justification of their findings and judgments, which, despite their greatest efforts of presentation and persuasion, have continued to be scrutinized for almost two centuries.

If Vesey's silence created problems for the court, it also had the unfortunate effect of forcing other blacks to fill in the gaps of the conspiracy narrative. Other slave defendants maintained their innocence, as Vesey did, but none other preserved such stalwart silence. They were forced to provide incriminating testimony in the absence of Vesey's confession. As slaves were rounded up, they were kept in "the hole," the local workhouse that featured such contraptions as the "Crane" to correct indolent slaves. Public floggings and the torture of slaves on a "treadmill" outside of the workhouse or guardhouse were other methods to persuade blacks to confess.[7] Native Charlestonian Angelina Grimké describes living in the city that summer as "walking on the very confines of hell" due to the frequency of such gruesome public spectacles and screams emanating from the jail (qtd. in Lerner 77–78).

One slave witness, William Paul, for example, initially "flatly denied" the existence of a slave plot and other accusations connecting him to a conspiracy (Hamilton, *Account* 5). Instead of listening to Paul's speech, however, authorities read his body, which they believed communicated "so many obvious indications of guilt," Hamilton recounts. "It was [therefore] deemed unwise to discharge him. He was remanded, for the night, to the guardhouse" (5). Slowly, over the course of a week in the "black-hole," and likely "beginning to fear that he would soon be led forth to the scaffold for summary execution," Paul confessed, among other things, that the plot "was very extensive, embracing an indiscriminate massacre of whites" (7). Slaves like Paul were placed in an impossible situation, one "fraught with deadly consequences if they misspoke [since] it was not always clear what sort of testimony would lead them to safety," Olwell explains (92). Paul's court confession, given more than a week after his release from the workhouse, conflicts in several key ways with his initial ones, the most significant discrepancy being that Paul shifted the blame from Gullah Jack to Vesey as the head of the alleged conspiratorial network only after Vesey had become the court's main suspect (see Hamilton, *Account* 7; "Evidence Document B" 151).

Another slave named Frank became implicated in the plot by a suspect being held at the workhouse. His owner, James Ferguson, became frantic when Frank refused to confess "what had so fully been proved against him" (Kennedy and Parker 30). The coerced testimony of the jailed slave was much more credible than Frank's denials and protestations, so Ferguson ordered his slave driver to "press on him" (30). But Frank did not capitulate for four weeks, and the ineffectual driver was then implicated in the scheme himself and sent to the workhouse. When Frank finally became "ready to confess all," it is little wonder that his testimony nicely confirmed officials' reports (Hamilton, *Account* 30–31), and Frank was then used as a star witness against Vesey, even though his testimony postdated Vesey's execution by several weeks ("Evidence Document B" 166–67). Though the slave defendants may have been coerced anyway, Vesey's silence in the jail, in the courtroom, and on the scaffold certainly made those confessions all the more necessary and the interrogations perhaps all the more brutal. While silence provided Vesey some tactical agency and complicated the prosecution of his case, it also shifted the burden of proof to the slaves, who literally felt the effect of his silence on their bodies.

In the absence of his words, others—black and white alike—created an outpouring of words to construct Vesey as a masterful rhetor, a slave leader, and an enemy of the state. But if the court capitalized on Vesey's silence to justify his hanging and consolidate white power in the process, others—such as abolitionists—would later portray Vesey as a martyr for the cause. After shots rang out from Fort Sumter, Thomas Wentworth Higginson, for example, published a moving portrait of Vesey as a freedom fighter before his time. William Wells Brown used Vesey as one of the best examples of blacks' "genius" and "achievements." Black nationalists a century later took up Vesey as an early emblem of "Black revolutionaries ready to lay their lives on the line for the cause of Black liberation." John Oliver Killens continues, "Denmark . . . dreamed of an end to slavery everywhere. And he was the kind of dreamer whose dreams led to action. There is a tradition amongst Black folk for that kind of dreamer, one whose dreams do not drug him into idleness. . . . He was a patriot of liberation" (ix, xi–xii). Today, Vesey lives on in liberatory narratives about the power of rhetoric in a democratic America.

I am not arguing that such narratives are wrong. That Vesey has become a major figure in the history of American slavery and deserves to be recognized in American rhetorical history should not be disputed. In fact, as I have tried to show, there is much here that pertains to rhetorical history and African American rhetoric. My primary interest, however, is to shed new light on the case as a whole rather than rehearse familiar, heroic refrains about Vesey. Attending to the complex layers of silence and silencing in the Vesey conspiracy opens a space for alternative understandings of it, as well as of the history of African American rhetoric more generally.

If one drives down Ashley Avenue in Charleston, South Carolina, today, heading north out of the pristine historical district and into a predominantly African American neighborhood on the other side of Meeting Street, one will eventually come to an enormous tree growing in the middle of the street. The "Ashley Avenue Oak" or "Vesey's tree," as some locals call it, forces motorists to slow down as the road splits and curves around its formidable circumference. There is no name or historical marker by the tree, but it was left by avenue residents—silent and standing—to signify Vesey's hanging. If, by interrupting the flow of traffic, the Ashley Avenue Oak prompts reflection and sustains memory, then historians of rhetoric might do well to linger over Vesey's silence, too. I argue that a current and ongoing effect of Vesey's silence is like that of "Vesey's tree": it gives pause. If we slow down enough to hear moments of silence in the archival documents, rather than attend exclusively to the effusiveness attributed to Vesey in myriad constructions and reconstructions of the event, we confront the stark possibility that even the most well-chosen words may not have ever saved Vesey or changed the course of history—a difficult reality that Vesey himself may have been more attuned to than those telling and retelling his story.

Notes

1. Since the 1980s, for example, there has been heated debate about whether and how to memorialize Vesey in Charleston (see, e.g., Denmark Vesey File; *Denmark Vesey Spirit of Freedom Monument*; Hampson; Waldo; Wiener).

2. This narrative of Vesey and the alleged conspiracy is taken from the main contemporary sources on the Vesey affair, including academic historians Her-

bert Aptheker, Douglas R. Egerton, Robert L. Paquette, Edward A. Pearson, and Robert Starobin, as well as novelist John Oliver Killens, journalist John Lofton, and playwright Julian Wiles (*Denmark Vesey: Insurrection*; see also Freehling; Robertson; Rucker; Stuckey)—all of whom agree that a slave conspiracy existed and that Vesey was its leader. Other historians, such as Richard C. Wade and more recently Michael P. Johnson, take issue with this dominant narrative, arguing instead that the primary historical sources do not point unequivocally to either Vesey or a slave conspiracy. Johnson even goes so far as to suggest that Vesey himself was the victim of a conspiracy on the part of Charleston authorities who framed him for a nonexistent slave revolt. See Gross for the current scholarly debate about the historical accuracy of the Vesey affair. See Paquette as well as Paquette and Egerton for the most recent interventions and interpretations.

The main historical sources pertaining to the Vesey affair include the following: (1) Charleston mayor James Hamilton's fifty-page pamphlet, *An Account of the Late Intended Insurrection among a Portion of the Blacks in the City of Charleston, South Carolina*, published in August 1822; (2) the court's account, *The Official Report of the Trials of Sundry Negroes*, written by the presiding magistrates, Lionel H. Kennedy and Thomas Parker, published in October 1822; and (3) South Carolina governor Thomas Bennett's gubernatorial papers, which hold three versions of the transcripts, one of which, "Evidence Document B," has been determined to be the earliest extant record of the court proceedings (see Johnson, "Denmark Vesey" 921–25). In addition, Bennett's personal letters and gubernatorial statements express his doubts about the conspiracy.3. This letter (June 16, 1822) is addressed to William Lowndes, who served as South Carolina's influential member of Congress from 1811 to 1822. When Lowndes resigned midterm, Hamilton was elected to fill his position in October 1822 and served until 1829.

4. See Egerton, Lofton, Pearson, and Robertson for various contemporary retoolings of Vesey's courtroom panache.

5. Noted legal scholar Paul Finkelman describes Kennedy and Parker's *Official Report* as, at the very least, "incomplete" and "confusing" (207–8). By legal standards alone, the court's documentation of the secret trials is severely wanting. See Johnson for more on Kennedy and Parker's rearrangement of testimony and dates.

6. The council's charge is reprinted on the inset page of Hamilton's pamphlet.

7. It should be noted that researchers disagree about the use of torture in the conspiracy investigation and trials, especially as it pertains to the credibility of resulting testimony (e.g., Johnson, "Reading" 194; Starobin, *Blacks* 125; Egerton, "Forgetting" 146, and *He Shall Go Free* 237; Freehling 46).

Works Cited

Aptheker, Herbert. *American Negro Slave Revolts*. 5th ed. New York: International, 1983. Print.

Aristotle. *The Nicomachean Ethics*. Trans. David Ross. Rev. ed. New York: Oxford UP, 1987. Print.

———. *On Rhetoric: A Theory of Civic Discourse.* Trans. George A. Kennedy. New York: Oxford UP, 1991. Print.

Bacon, Jacqueline. *Freedom's Journal: The First African-American Newspaper.* Lanham, MD: Rowman and Littlefield, 2007. Print.

———. *The Humblest May Stand Forth: Rhetoric, Empowerment, and Abolition.* Columbia: U of South Carolina P, 2002. Print.

Bacon, Jacqueline, and Glen McClish. "Descendants of Africa, Sons of '76: Exploring Early African-American Rhetoric." *Rhetoric Society Quarterly* 36.1 (2006): 1–29. Print.

Beach, Mary Lamboll Thomas. Papers, 1822–1890 (43/225). South Carolina Historical Society, Charleston. Print.

Bennett, Thomas. "The Late Conspiracy; A Letter from the Governor of the State of South Carolina, Charleston." Aug. 10, 1822. Records of the General Assembly, 1822, Governors' Messages #1328. South Carolina Department of Archives and History. Columbia. Print.

———. "Message No. 2." Nov. 28, 1822. Records of the General Assembly, 1822, Governors' Messages #1328. South Carolina Department of Archives and History. Columbia. Print.

Bontemps, Alex. *The Punished Self: Surviving Slavery in the Colonial South.* Ithaca: Cornell UP, 2001. Print.

Brown, William Wells. "Denmark Vesey." *The Black Man, His Antecedents, His Genius, and His Achievements.* New York: Thomas Hamilton, 1863. 142–48. Print.

Denmark Vesey: Insurrection. By Julian Wiles. Dir. Julian Wiles. American Theater, Charleston, SC. June 9, 2007. Performance.

Denmark Vesey Spirit of Freedom Monument. The Denmark Vesey Spirit of Freedom Monument Committee, 2007. Web. Dec. 15, 2009.

Egerton, Douglas R. "Forgetting Denmark Vesey; or, Oliver Stone Meets Richard Wade." *William and Mary Quarterly* 59.1 (2002): 143–52. Print.

———. *He Shall Go Free: The Lives of Denmark Vesey.* Madison: U of Wisconsin P, 1999. Print.

———. *Rebels, Reformers, and Revolutionaries: Collected Essays and Second Thoughts.* New York: Routledge, 2002. Print.

"Evidence Document B." Records of the General Assembly, 1822, Governors' Messages #1328. South Carolina Department of Archives and History. Columbia. Print.

Finkelman, Paul. *Slavery in the Courtroom: An Annotated Bibliography of American Cases.* Washington, DC: Library of Congress, 1985. Print.

Foucault, Michel. *Discipline and Punish: The Birth of the Prison.* Trans. Alan Sheridan. 1977. New York: Vintage, 1995. Print.

———. *The History of Sexuality.* Vol. 1. Trans. Robert Hurley. 1977. New York: Vintage, 1990. Print.

Freehling, William W. "Denmark Vesey's Antipaternalistic Reality." *The Reintegration of American History: Slavery and the Civil War.* New York: Oxford UP, 1994. 34–58. Print.

Gilyard, Keith. "African American Contributions to Composition Studies." *CCC* 50.4 (1999): 626–44. Print.

Gross, Robert A., ed. "The Making of a Slave Conspiracy." Pts. 1 and 2. *William and Mary Quarterly* 58.4 (2001): 913–76; 59.1 (2002): 136–202. Print.

Hamilton, James, Jr. *An Account of the Late Intended Insurrection Among a Portion of the Blacks of the City of Charleston, South Carolina.* 2nd ed. Boston: Joseph W. Ingram, 1822. Print.

———. Letter to William Lowndes. June 16, 1822. James Hamilton Jr. Papers, Southern Historical Collection. The University of North Carolina at Chapel Hill. Print.

Hampson, Rick. "Ex-slave's Legacy Disputed." *USA Today*, Nov. 20, 2007. Web. Dec. 15, 2009.

Higginson, Thomas Wentworth. "Denmark Vesey." 1865. Rpt. in *Black Rebellion: A Selection from "Travellers and Outlaws,"* by Thomas Wentworth Higginson. New York: Arno, 1969. 215–75. Print.

Jamieson, Kathleen Hall. *Beyond the Double Bind: Women and Leadership.* New York: Oxford UP, 1995. Print.

Johnson, Michael P. "Denmark Vesey and His Co-conspirators." *William and Mary Quarterly* 58.4 (2001): 915–76. Print.

———. "Reading Evidence." *William and Mary Quarterly* 59.1 (2002): 193–202. Print.

Kennedy, Lionel H., and Thomas Parker. *An Official Report of the Trials of Sundry Negroes.* Charleston: James R. Schenk, 1822. Print.

Killens, John Oliver, ed. *The Trial Record of Denmark Vesey.* Boston: Beacon, 1970. Print.

Lerner, Gerda. *The Grimké Sisters from South Carolina: Pioneers for Women's Rights and Abolition.* New York: Schocken, 1971. Print.

Lofton, John. *Denmark Vesey's Revolt: The Slave Plot That Lit the Fuse to Fort Sumter.* Kent, OH: Kent State UP, 1983. Print.

Logan, Shirley Wilson. *"We Are Coming": The Persuasive Discourse of Nineteenth-Century Black Women.* Carbondale: Southern Illinois UP, 1999. Print.

———, ed. *With Pen and Voice: A Critical Anthology of Nineteenth-Century African-American Women.* Carbondale: Southern Illinois UP, 1995. Print.

Morgan, Donald G. *Justice William Johnson: The First Dissenter.* Columbia: U of South Carolina P, 1954. Print.

Olwell, Robert. *Masters, Slaves, and Subjects: The Culture of Power in the South Carolina Low Country, 1740–1790.* Ithaca: Cornell UP, 1998. Print.

Paquette, Robert L. "From Rebellion to Revisionism: The Continuing Debate about the Denmark Vesey Affair." *Journal of the Historical Society* 4.3 (2004): 291–334. Print.

Paquette, Robert L., and Douglas R. Egerton. "Of Facts and Fables: New Light on the Denmark Vesey Affair." *South Carolina Historical Magazine* 105.1 (2004): 8–48. Print.

Pearson, Edward A. *Designs against Charleston: The Trial Record of the Denmark Vesey Slave Conspiracy of 1822*. Chapel Hill: U of North Carolina P, 1999. Print.

Plato. *Gorgias*. Trans. W. C. Hembold. New York: Macmillan, 1952. Print.

Richardson, Elaine B., and Ronald L. Jackson, ed. *African American Rhetoric(s): Interdisciplinary Perspectives*. Carbondale: Southern Illinois UP, 2004. Print.

Robertson, David. *Denmark Vesey*. New York: Knopf, 1999. Print.

Royster, Jacqueline Jones. *Traces of a Stream: Literacy and Social Change among African American Women*. Pittsburgh: U of Pittsburgh P, 2000. Print.

Rucker, Walter C. "'I Will Gather All Nations': Resistance, Culture, and Pan-African Collaboration in Denmark Vesey's South Carolina." *Journal of Negro History* 86.2 (2001): 132–47. Print.

Schilb, John. *Rhetorical Refusals: Defying Audiences' Expectations*. Carbondale: Southern Illinois UP, 2007. Print.

Simpkins, Ann Marie Mann. "Rhetorical Tradition(s) and the Reform Writing of Mary Ann Shadd Cary." *Calling Cards: Theory and Practice in the Study of Race, Gender, and Culture*. Ed. Jacqueline Jones Royster and Ann Marie Mann Simpkins. Albany: State U of New York P, 2005. 229–42. Print.

Starobin, Robert S., ed. *Blacks in Bondage: Letters of American Slaves*. New York: New Viewpoints, 1974. Print.

———. *Denmark Vesey: The Slave Conspiracy of 1822*. Englewood Cliffs, NJ: Prentice-Hall, 1970. Print.

Stuckey, Sterling. "Agitator or Insurrectionist? Remembering Denmark Vesey." *Negro Digest* 15 (1966): 28–41. Print.

Denmark Vesey File. South Carolina Historical Society, Charleston. Print.

Wade, Richard C. "The Vesey Plot: A Reconsideration." *Journal of Southern History* 30.2 (1964): 143–61. Print.

Waldo, Tenisha. "Denmark Vesey Memorial Plans Move Forward." *Charleston Post and Courier*, Sept. 5, 2007. Web. Dec. 15, 2009.

Wiener, Jon. "Denmark Vesey: A New Verdict." *Nation*, Feb. 21, 2002. Web. Dec. 15, 2009.

Williams, Juan, and Quinton Dixie. *This Far by Faith: Stories from the African American Religious Experience*. New York: HarperCollins, 2003. Print.

Living Pictures, Living Memory: Women's Rhetorical Silence within the American Delsarte Movement

Lisa Suter

I n the late nineteenth century, discouraged from using their voices in public forums, thousands of American women—most of them white, most middle- or upper-class—began exploring new methods of silent rhetorical delivery.[1] These women, the American Delsartists,[2] theorized the expressive potential of the body and the rhetorical usefulness of silence to communicate more effectively within the constraints of an oppressive gender ideology. So called because they employed a system of oratory called "Delsarte," the American Delsartists have all but been forgotten by rhetorical historians, but in their day they were a recognizable cultural force for many progressive reforms. In time, many became professors of college-level elocution in the United States. Their story begins, however, with the struggle to turn silence from a cultural imperative into a rhetorical tactic.

Who were the American Delsartists? No one answer seems sufficient to describe them, for they stretched across much of the United States at the height of the movement's popularity in the 1880s and 1890s (Ruyter, *Cultivation* xvii). They were also interested in many causes: women's education, women's health, dress reform, suffrage, and other social and political issues. What bound them together as a group was the desire to express themselves on such topics at a time when women were not encouraged to speak in public. They endeavored to study elocution, oratory, and rhetoric, formally and informally, but with a difference from their late-nineteenth-century male counterparts learning the same disciplines. As many of them noted, the Delsartists were aware that they would not soon be granted the same latitude to speak in public that men had. Regardless of whatever oratorical training they might obtain, the rhetorical situations they would face—their audiences, the topics they were expected to address, the rhetorical strategies they were expected to adopt or avoid—would in most cases be different from the situations of their masculine peers. As the women trained, then, they adapted received theories of elocution to suit these discursive proscriptions and their own purposes.

The Delsarteans devised new training techniques they called physical culture exercises to prepare women's minds and bodies for the stress of oratorical delivery. Often shedding their ladylike corsets, they wore loose-fitting neoclassical togas to improve their vocal power, to extend the range of their physical delivery, and to signify their classical rhetorical training. They revised received performance genres such as statue-posing and *tableaux mouvants*. Embodying these "living statues" or "living pictures,"[3] the American Delsartists performed publicly in the final decades of the nineteenth century: in professional theater and lecture halls, on public platforms at women's colleges, or at women's temperance meetings and church fund-raising events (see fig. 5.1). In this period, women in white togas were to be found almost everywhere.

5.1   A typical Delsartean tableau, showing women in their white toga-like gowns, in a pose intended to portray a carnival-like atmosphere. From Henry M. Soper's *Soper's Select Speaker* (490).

Fortunately, much of women's rhetorical history has been reclaimed in recent decades. Feminist historians have unearthed texts and recovered rhetors. Other scholars have worked to redefine rhetoric or regender the canon. Great tracts of rhetorical terrain have been rediscovered, and taken as a whole, these combined efforts have effectively remapped the field. Still, no scholar has yet undertaken a detailed explanation of the American Delsarte movement's unique significance to the field of rhetoric.

The pedagogy and praxes of the followers of the American Delsarte movement offer many rich sites of research, but their theories concerning the rhetoricity of silence will someday be counted among the most valuable of their lessons. Contemporary theorists in the field of rhetoric have begun to study the suasive power of silence (Glenn) and the importance of cross-cultural listening (Ratcliffe); the American Delsartists were there long before, however, and can offer us insights on both. In this chapter, I argue two things. First, I propose that the American Delsartists have been largely misrepresented by rhetoricians; they need to be reexamined in their own historical and cultural contexts so that we may appreciate their many contributions to the field. Second, I argue that their silent performances, far from being passive capitulations to cultural imperatives to be quiet, were often highly rhetorical in nature.

In this chapter, I attempt to read the Delsartists' purpose as they themselves described it. Beginning with a look at the origin of Delsarte theory in France, I track its arrival in the United States at the ostensible end of the American elocutionary movement—a time I suggest is better understood as the beginning of a second wave: a brief but frenzied era of interest in women's elocution. I analyze one Delsarte performance, showing its silent, embodied, and multimodal performance genres, and I offer pieces of archival evidence that demonstrate that Delsartean theory was being studied in women's colleges of oratory at the turn of the century.

At the end of this chapter, I forward the argument that Delsartists in the late nineteenth century were acutely aware of the absence of women in the rhetorical canon. The silencing of women's historical voices must have echoed loudly in the ears of women trying to establish themselves in the field of elocution, a professional field still dominated by their male colleagues. As the Delsartists established schools of expression, wrote elocutionary curricula, and authored books on delivery and more, I propose that they tried to reclaim earlier women's voices, too. Women practitioners of Delsarte had access to writings concerning a few historical women rhetors, but as I demonstrate, they were not afraid to imagine the existence of others, writing original dramas like *The Ladies of Athens*, a play highlighting women's rhetorical savvy in classical Greece. They then performed these dramas on public stages, giving new life to women's life experiences and oratorical triumphs.

More than a century later, all that remains of these performances are scattered textual references and blurry, grainy photographs. Naturally, we cannot hope to fully understand the American Delsartists from these scant traces. However, some of these artifacts do hint at a few of their hopes: the hope that the history of women's rhetorical achievements would not be forgotten (again) and the hope (paradoxical perhaps) that their silent performances might inspire more women in the late nineteenth century to take up the study of oratory.

Origin(s) of the Delsarte System of Oratory

Theorizing the rhetorical nature of silence might seem an incongruous subject for a system of oratory to take up. From their inceptions, however, each of the two branches of Delsartism, French and American, would codify its own relationship to silence. Within the French school, this interest focused on the use of silent gestures to accompany an oration's vocal delivery and silence as a way of timing the oration—both foci were used to augment a vocal performance, in other words. Within the American school, silent delivery would be studied as a way to replace vocal performance altogether.

The originator of the initial movement in France, François Delsarte, possessed a keen interest in physical expression. His curiosity regarding the body's ability to communicate may have arisen from the fact that he was a promising singer as a boy, but his voice was damaged, possibly due to poor training at the Paris Conservatory (Werner 290). He continued to perform throughout his life (1811–71); however, with his singing career thus limited, Delsarte devoted himself to a lifelong search for what he named the "universal" laws that govern gesture—how bodies "naturally" speak versus how they might be trained to communicate with rhetorical acumen. Eventually he developed a theorem that he termed "The Science of Expression," which he taught in his Course of Applied Aesthetics, opening a formal school in Paris in 1839 (Shaver 204).

Delsarte's theories were well received. Many famous singers and actors studied with him, and members of the nobility attended his lectures.

Of his many students, only one is known to have come from the United States, however (Shaver 206)—the American actor who became his protégé, Steele MacKaye. MacKaye studied under Delsarte for a number of years. After Delsarte's death in 1871, MacKaye returned to America, importing his teacher's theories with him. Soon he began a lecture circuit, touring the country. Then in 1877, MacKaye opened his own school of expression in New York City (208). By this time, already, as one historian put it, "the so-called 'Delsarte System of Expression' was probably the most popular method of speech training in the United States" (202)—but it was still expanding rapidly. The popularity of MacKaye's work led editor Edgar Werner to compile a volume of this popular new "science" in English: *Delsarte System of Oratory*. This anthology, published in the United States in 1882, was a compendium of translated notes by several of Delsarte's students.[4]

One of these students was a French clergyman, Abbé Delaumosne. In his notes on Delsarte's class, which he termed a "rational grammar of oratory" (Werner 163), Delaumosne attempted to locate the scientific principles underlying the art of vocal and bodily delivery. He argued (or recorded) that "the science of the Art of Oratory has not yet been taught. . . . Horace, Quintilian and Cicero among the ancients, and numerous modern writers have treated of oratory as an art. We admire their writings, but this is not science; here we seek in vain the fundamental laws whence their teachings proceed" (qtd. in Werner 3). Throughout his 170-page record of Delsarte's teachings, over 100 pages treat either the strategic use of silence or the rhetorical power of gesture. He noted that the two were related (27), but in this exposition they remain separate elements of a speech's delivery. Listed as "a powerful agent in oratorical effects," silence is recommended to would-be public speakers as a means of pacing themselves during their elocutionary efforts. A list of times to pause during an oration is offered, and speakers are reminded to remain silent until they are certain they are ready to speak and have their thoughts well in hand. The reader is also reminded that, often, silence can deliver more pathos than speech, as when an orator is too overwhelmed by emotion to continue speaking. Delaumosne observes that when this happens, the audience may be moved to tears: not by the speech itself but by the orator's inability to speak (27).

After the publication of *Delsarte System of Oratory* in the United States, a new wave of interest in elocution began to swell. Delsarte's "Science of Expression" was soon being studied by thousands of Americans who wanted to cash in on the promise of this "new elocution," as they were calling it—and most of them were women.

The Feminization of American Delsartism

For roughly twenty years, from approximately 1885 to 1905, American women of all ages studied Delsartean oratorical theory and applied its teachings to their personal and professional lives.[5] In *Reformers and Visionaries*, dance historian Nancy Lee Chalfa Ruyter divides American Delsartism into several stages. In the 1870s, she writes, the movement comprised mostly male actors and dancers looking to improve their crafts, but by the 1880s and 1890s, women constituted the ranks of the Delsartean faithful, almost exclusively (18). In another work, Ruyter estimates that 85 percent of the Delsartists in America during its entire time span were women (*Cultivation* 58).

What did this elocutionary movement look like? For starters, schools for women of all ages offered classes in this "new elocution"—from elementary school to college and beyond. Women's clubs put on Delsarte entertainments (often referred to as recitals) to raise money for various philanthropies. Anne Ruggles Gere remarks that among American women involved in literary societies, "the Delsarte science of attitude and gesture [became] enormously popular during the last decades of the nineteenth century" (35). Itinerant Delsarte scholars wandered the country, offering private tutoring to those women who could afford lessons in articulation, grace, posture, balance, breathing, and more; some scholars set up private schools in large cities and let the students come to them. Yet despite (or perhaps because of) the widespread scope of the movement, and despite its intimate connection to the field of rhetoric, American women's use of Delsarte theory has been curiously misrepresented by rhetoric scholars.

Rhetorical historian Robert Connors has written about the movement, noting that "the decline of oral discourse teaching in America" occurred as women began to enter colleges in larger numbers (57). He goes on to describe American Delsartism as "histrionics," "harmless thespianism," and "mummery" (58): a strangely tepid dismissal of women's first major foray into college-level rhetorical education. But Connors's depiction of the movement is skewed by his focus on traditional colleges, ones designed for men, and on what changed as they began to admit a few female students. He states, "After the Civil War . . . elocution—especially the old agonistic sort—fell on hard times. It was demoted from a requirement to an elective in most colleges and lost prestige rather sharply" (58).

Roxanne Mountford challenged Connors's claim concerning the "mutation" of rhetoric in this period. While Connors's overall research project is important, I agree with Mountford regarding the "dangerous stereotypes" that prevail in portions of his history (490). His focus on men's colleges prevented him from noticing the enormous upsurge in the popularity of elocution in women's colleges at this time—and, in fact, to the *creation* of new colleges of women's oratory to accommodate young women's demand for this new science. In these institutions, as course catalogs make evident, elocution remained a regular course offering (and often a substantial requirement) until the turn of the century. Both of these phenomena are directly connected to the influence of American Delsartism.

Only a few other rhetoricians have examined American Delsartism, and for the most part, those who have treated the subject have touched on it only briefly.[6] For example, in the otherwise exhaustive *Encyclopedia of Rhetoric and Composition*, only one paragraph concerns Delsartean theory and its connection to elocution. Citing Claude L. Shaver's observation that this was "the most popular method of speech training in America" at the turn of the century, Brenda Gabioud Brown's entry nonetheless sums up in four sentences the massive movement's size and complexity, asserting that it "reduced the study of rhetoric to the stilted expression of emotion through learned (and practiced) bodily gestures and positions" (214).

The "bodily gestures and positions" that Brown alludes to here refer to training in oratorical action. Like other American elocutionists, the American Delsartists studied and performed both halves of oratorical delivery: *pronuntiatio* and *actio*, the vocal and physical modes of delivering a speech. Action, the embodied half of delivery, was further divided into two performative elements: the attitude and the gesture. "Attitudes" were still poses or stances that the orator assumed, remaining frozen for a moment, mid-oration. These were stylized signifiers of emotions (fear, anger, and the like) that correlated to something happening in the text. "Gestures" were movements of an orator's hands or body to portray some action in the text through mimesis: miming the act of picking flowers, beckoning to a friend, or gesturing for silence (see fig. 5.2). Today, as we observe in Brown's analysis, rhetoricians often examine extant catalogs of Delsartean attitude and gesture and come to the conclusion that these emotional signifiers must have been employed by women performers in a nonreflective or "stilted" way.

FIG. 15: SILENCE

The index finger of the left hand seeks the lips—the portal of speech—and signifies thereby that they must be kept closed.

The right hand represents repression, the arm extending somewhat back, as if to silence a person standing behind or at the side of you.

5.2 An example of the rhetorical gesture of silence. In this compendium, Edward B. Warman offers 154 plates of various Delsartean attitudes and gestures that may be employed while delivering a speech. It should be noted that, in the particular example of indicating silence, there is only one option offered to an orator. Many attitudes offer more, however. For example, an orator can demonstrate that she is listening in four separate ways.

But the American Delsartists responded to this charge in their own day and defended their theory's worth. One Delsartean elocutionist, for example, parried a similar argument from a contemporary critic who worried that too much emphasis was being placed on learning artificial expressions. She responded, "The reader or the actor who is educated on Delsartean principles is necessarily no more self-conscious than a writer in the process of composition is handicapped by knowing the rules of syntax" (Morgan 599). Her argument (echoing many of her fellow Delsartists) was that these attitudes and gestures were not meant to be a straitjacket for the orator—they were mainly intended for study by beginners. The positions were meant to be studied with a trained instructor, expanded upon, influenced by the learner's individual style, then abandoned when no longer necessary. They were not intended to be repeated mechanically but rather were to inform a speaker's choices during delivery, just as rhetorical action had been used since classical times.

Yet another, larger dilemma exists if we are to understand this oratorical movement: namely, we cannot see or hear the Delsarte performance as it was enacted onstage in front of a listening audience. All we can see are frozen photographs of actors and orators striking a single pose for the camera. We cannot hear the music that accompanied the productions. We cannot see the full range of performance genres the Delsartists would typically enact—usually six to eight genres, at least—including but not limited to the aforementioned *tableaux vivants*, single statues, lectures on elocution, dramatic readings (voiced), and dialogues (also voiced). Without this full range of performance, we also cannot deduce any implied narrative emerging from the juxtaposition of these various genres, as one followed another.

Contemporary descriptions provide a glimpse into some of what scholars have been missing. One Delsarte recital put on by the students at a women's college in Oxford, Ohio, on May 2, 1892, was reviewed in a student newspaper this way:

> The entertainment was prepared under the entire management of Miss Anna B. Chew, our teacher of elocution. . . . After a brilliant piano selection . . . the second part of the programme, the Delsarte tableaux, began. The room was darkened, a bright calcium light was thrown upon the stage and to the soft strains of "Schubert's Serenade" the living statues—if we may speak so—slowly came forward on the stage, dressed in artistic robes of pure white. Then

with indescribable grace and ease they formed before us one group of statues after another. To a casual observer, who had never had any Delsarte training whatever, it seemed quite wonderful. ("Delsarte Evening")

One real problem, then, with analyzing the expressive potential of a live performance such as this one is that, obviously, the Delsarte performers had no recording devices capable of capturing the multimodality of their enactments. The "indescribable grace" of the performers' bodies, the music's affective power, the lighting and artistic nature of the scene: all these factors within productions of this type have been lost. Also of fundamental importance, I suggest, is the implied narrative emerging from the juxtaposition of so many representations of powerful female figures from history, literature, or mythology. In this performance, the "living statues" in the program included "Diana the Huntress, The Fates, The Graces, and a Scene from the Battle of the Amazons," among a host of others. What Victorian audiences felt, seeing these college-educated, uncorseted young women performing onstage, we can only surmise. Might they not have felt a growing realization of women's as-yet untapped potential?

Other crucial contexts also have yet to be properly recognized by rhetorical scholars. Joseph Francis Fahey's recent dissertation on Delsartism's impact on American theater points out another issue repeatedly overlooked—real, financial opportunities afforded women by this movement, such as teaching, writing, tutoring, and lecture and performance circuits. Delsarteans created careers as performers and elocutionists: here were professional activities and publishing opportunities that in other realms of the late Victorian world were routinely denied to women.

Fahey's observation is similarly cogent when applied to the current discipline of rhetoric. Perhaps the most surprising lacuna in the scholarship on the American Delsarte movement is that no historian has recorded the fact that the Delsartists broke new ground by becoming professors of oratory and by setting up new colleges of oratory for women in many major cities across the nation at this time—a fact made evident in advertisements in the Delsarteans' trade journal, *The Voice*. This chapter cannot do justice to the groundbreaking achievements of these nineteenth-century professional scholars; all it can do is gesture in the direction of all that was transpiring by examining one such school and its transformation in this period.

Colleges of Oratory for Women

Strikingly, to find sustained attention to Delsarte training in the colleges of oratory that were operating at this time, one must turn to James H. McTeague's book on the birth of professional acting in the United States. In *Before Stanislavsky: American Professional Acting Schools and Acting Theory, 1875–1925*, McTeague analyzes late-nineteenth-century curricular trends at schools such as the Emerson College of Oratory in Boston, the School of Expression in Milton, and the School of the Spoken Word in Brookline, all in Massachusetts. Anticipating critique concerning his choice of research sites, he explains that "the schools of expression . . . contributed substantially to the development of acting theory in America" (95). McTeague follows the acting innovations set in motion in the United States by Steele MacKaye, who developed Delsarte's science of expression into a codified theory (taught at these schools) for American actors. But while such institutions did teach acting theory to actors, they also taught expressive theory to orators. What's more, they represent only a fraction of the schools of expression or elocution accepting students in the late nineteenth century. Many of these were teeming with female students.

For example, Oxford, Ohio, claimed two postsecondary schools for women in the late nineteenth century: Western Female Seminary and Oxford College. Both had offered an elective course in elocution in their curricula since the 1870s. However, it was not until the first year that Delsarte courses were listed by name in the Oxford College catalog, in 1892–93, that the school's board of directors established the Oxford College of Oratory. Among the faculty listed in the catalog that year were four new professors: Estelle G. Clark and Annette Gault McClure, both from the Boston School of Oratory; Wilda Wilson Church, M.O., professor of expression and physical culture from the Emerson College of Oratory; and Mable Hester Coddington, instructor of expression and physical culture from the Northwestern University School of Oratory (Flower 215–16).

A local historian, Olive Flower, reported the many changes that were taking place in Oxford College at this time. Previously the college had had a school of expression, she explained, but it had been "unorganized." In the 1892–93 school year, however, in the year the College of Oratory was formed, "a systematic course of study was offered. For the first time diplomas for completing the two-year course were granted" (276–77). This two-year course swiftly became a four-year course, culminating in the award of the "Bachelor of Oratory degree."

Both Oxford schools at this time were providing the town's community with Delsarte recitals for entertainment and charity fund-raising. Newspaper articles and recital reviews in various student literary journals point to performances staged for the town every few months over the course of the following years. These public performances provided students and instructors of both schools with a platform for their progressive causes. And as a showcase for their learning, they surely acted as a form of advertisement for the schools, as well.

The obvious paradox inherent in the Delsarte performance is this: these young women were studying elocution and expressive delivery in colleges of oratory, yet their recitals often featured several performance genres that were partially or wholly silent (the statues, the tableaux). These wholly silent genres were almost never present in American men's Delsarte performances (Ruyter, *Cultivation* 59), nor had they been imported from the French school of Delsartism. The American women Delsartists' statues and living pictures can be seen as derived from older, mimetic traditions such as pantomime and crèches (Holmström 210–20)—but why would these young college women get so excited about reviving this type of performance?

Lindal Buchanan's recent book on delivery offers the insight that cultural constructions of gender and the ways they affect rhetors' strategies have not yet been fully taken into account in our analyses of many women rhetors. Buchanan might ask us to remember that the American Delsartists were taking the public stage in an era particularly hostile to women speaking in public, as a number of other feminist historians of rhetoric have already documented. At the end of the century, as women continued to fight for the franchise, women's education, labor reform, and temperance (among other causes), it became common to refer to female activists speaking their minds in public as "freedom shriekers" (Johnson 64), "shrieking sisters," or "screaming viragos" (Jorgensen-Earp 96). In this climate, the voice that male rhetors could take for granted was for women a dangerous means of expression: a rhetorical medium likely to backfire. Small wonder then, in this historical context, that many American Delsartists began to study the rhetoricity of silence. As we see in the last section, even when they were enacting voiced performance genres, these elocutionists were still attentive to silence's suasive power. They were also paying attention to other voices that were being muted and thinking about how to give those unfairly silenced their voices back.

The Ladies of Athens: A Performance of Women's Rhetorical Historiography

So far I have attempted to show that American Delsartism was a substantial social, cultural, and educational movement in the latter part of the nineteenth century—one that had a major role to play in how elocution and oratory were studied and enacted in women's colleges—but that this movement has gone either undocumented or misrepresented in the field of rhetoric. This, we know, is a common fate for much of women's history: to be lost, misread, or even erased. The act of canonical erasure is especially ironic when considered in light of the following Delsartean drama, however, because this play deals with exactly that subject: the absence of half of the narrative of classical rhetorical history—the women's half.

Unlike their silent performance genres, what the Delsarteans called a "dialogue" was a voiced theatrical production involving female actors who brought characters to life on stage—what we would call a play. Of the many dialogues in their textbooks, one theme recurs repeatedly: not surprisingly, the Delsartists loved stories about women's rhetorical savoir faire. For women who studied silence and occasionally enacted silent performances in public, they were at the same time elocutionists, and, as such, they were enamored of heroic tales of women rhetors. Many of these tales were respun from classical times, featuring historical figures such as Aspasia, Hypatia, Sappho, or Diotima; biblical figures such as Jephthah's daughter or Deborah the judge; even, as we saw from their *tableaux vivants*, mythological figures including the Fates or the Muses. When they ran low on known tales of classical women and their rhetorical cunning, the Delsartists wrote new tales that challenged the received rhetorical canon in comical yet telling ways.

The short drama *The Ladies of Athens* is a superb example of this iconoclastic genre. Mrs. M. A. Lipscomb, a professional elocutionist and instructor of women's finance, wrote this fictional scenario in which the wives and sisters of rhetorical icons (Socrates, Aristotle, and Demosthenes) come together to discuss various male shortcomings. Published in 1905 in Elsie M. Wilbor's *Delsarte Recitation Book*, the action is set at the home of Socrates, yet an audience viewing this play will never glimpse that familiar scholar. Instead, the narrative unfolds as seen through the eyes of his intelligent and long-suffering wife, Xanthippe, and her many friends.

Xanthippe addresses the audience first, delivering a heartfelt diatribe about how she is "shut up" within the four walls of her home. Her husband "wanders about the streets of Athens prating of justice and injustice," she says, yet he does not concern himself with her well-being or with their crushing state of poverty. "For months I haven't had a single drachma of his earnings," she informs the audience, but "if I perchance utter a single word of complaint, I am called a scold, a termagant" (Wilbor 78–79). Aspasia enters next. Listed in the bill of characters as the wife, not mistress, of Pericles, Aspasia praises her friend Xanthippe for having a husband whom everyone in Athens is "wild about." As for her own "husband," she says, "I but rarely see him now. *Once I could interest him on the subject of oratory* and we often read and studied together; but now he thinks there is no wisdom except what proceeds from the mind of Socrates" (79, emphasis added). Much ought to be pointed out here, from the way Xanthippe's legendary reputation as a scold is easily overturned to how Aspasia's character—much maligned, as Cheryl Glenn notes in her award-winning essay "sex, lies, and manuscript"—is calmly reestablished as a serious woman who wants to study with her partner as an equal. Of course, we notice what she most wants to study.

Other figures enter the scene: Philesia (wife of Xenophon), Pythias (wife of Aristotle), Cleobula (sister of Demosthenes), and Nicostrata (wife of Sophocles). Waiting for their men to return from the agora, the eponymous ladies of Athens argue whether philosophy is the right pursuit for a husband whose role in life is to provide for his family, or whether he ought to take up a practical career and get paid occasionally. The historical-fictional characters all display formal rhetorical training, ironically employing syllogism to lament that they are not permitted a formal education. Xanthippe complains: "[Socrates] says that husbands should instruct their wives in all they wish to know; he gives me no instruction, and, therefore, he wishes me to know nothing" (83). They also demonstrate knowledge of classical writings, quoting texts such as Xenophon's *Symposium*, Plato's *Apology* and *Symposium*, and Sappho's poetry. In fact, Wilbor represents the assembled ladies' erudition as superior to the men's, as they casually solve the riddle of the Sphinx that they note is "puzzling the minds of all wise Athenians" (85).

Throughout the work, the author of this canon-inverting dialogue is at pains to show that classical women not only wanted full and fair access to rhetorical education but also had already found the means of educating themselves in the field and, if given the chance, would love to work side by side with the men. At the end of the story, having been gone for two days and overnight, Socrates comes home. From offstage, he calls for Xanthippe to come to him and bring him his dinner. Seven times he calls, and seven times Xanthippe remains silent. Her friends scold her for neglecting her wifely duty, but she remains firm, telling them that it is Socrates who is neglecting his duty, not she hers. Her silence is assertive: she wants to be treated as a partner, not a domestic servant. After Socrates calls her for the eighth time, she gives in, but not happily. "Yes, I'll come," she says. "I'll feed you until you are well satisfied and ready to go again to the market-place to spend the night in thinking, thinking, thinking" (Wilbor 91).

Delsartean dialogues such as *The Ladies of Athens* delivered a number of messages to audiences: tales of women's abilities, desires, fears, and ambitions. In conjuring classical women's concern for oratorical training, Delsarte performers sought to attract more women to the study of elocution in their schools. These performances also spoke to other contemporary women's issues prevalent in public discourses circulating at the end of the century—agonistic questions of access to education, women's rightful sphere, and women's financial independence, as we see here—but in a comical way, allowing laughter to soften the blows of their demands. Finally, these dialogues attempted to reconfigure the rhetorical canon.

As women clamored in the nineteenth century for more rhetorical space, then, I contend that the Delsartists argued (sometimes silently, sometimes not) for a women's history of rhetoric. With living pictures and creative dramas, they enacted a collective, living memory to preserve their rhetorical past and to secure their material futures. Modern-day rhetorical scholars would do well to listen to the American Delsartists' silence now as audiences listened to it then . . . attentively.

Notes

1. I wish to thank Cindy Lewiecki-Wilson, Kate Ronald, and Katie Johnson of Miami University for their assistance. Thanks are also due to Nan Johnson of the Ohio State University for the loan of rare, nineteenth-century rhetorical

handbooks from her personal library as well as for her time spent discussing this project.

2. Substantial differences exist between the original French branch of Delsartism and its American counterpart (Georgen; Bishop). Therefore, I refer to my field of study as "American Delsartism" to differentiate between the two movements.

3. "Living statues" and "living pictures" were performance genres in which artists recreated famous artworks or memorable scenes from literary works with their bodies. Taking the stage in white togas—to resemble marble—the performer(s) would assume poses for the audience to read. Statues were recreated by individual performers; pictures were usually done as a group.

4. Other than a few notes obtained from his widow after his death, Delsarte left no writings. What is known of his theories, therefore, we have from his students' transcriptions of his classes.

5. Archival evidence indicates this was primarily a white women's middle- and upper-class movement. See also the next note.

6. One notable exception is Jane Donawerth, who included the Delsarteans in her 2002 book, *Rhetorical Theory by Women before 1900: An Anthology.* Her book offers sections of two rare, rhetorical chapbooks by an African American elocutionist named Hallie Quinn Brown (Donawerth 173–94). Explicitly and implicitly, both texts offer evidence of Delsarte training.

Works Cited

Bishop, Emily. *Americanized Delsarte Culture.* Meadville, PA: Chautauqua-Century, 1892. Print.

Brown, Brenda Gabioud. "Elocution." *Encyclopedia of Rhetoric and Composition: Communication from Ancient Times to the Information Age.* Ed. Theresa Enos. 1996. 211–14. Print.

Buchanan, Lindal. *Regendering Delivery: The Fifth Canon and Antebellum Women Rhetors.* Carbondale: Southern Illinois UP, 2005. Print.

Connors, Robert J. *Composition-Rhetoric: Backgrounds, Theory and Pedagogy.* Pittsburgh: U of Pittsburgh P, 1997. Print.

"A Delsarte Evening." *Oxford Ladies Collegian,* May 1892. Print.

Donawerth, Jane. *Rhetorical Theory by Women before 1900: An Anthology.* Lanham, MD: Rowman and Littlefield, 2002. Print.

Fahey, Joseph Francis. "Americanized Delsarte Culture as Physical and Political Expression: How American Women Shaped François Delsarte's System of Applied Aesthetics into a Progressive Force for Social Reform, Performance, and Professionalism." Diss. Ohio State U, 2000. Print.

Flower, Olive. *The History of Oxford College for Women: 1830–1928.* Oxford, OH: Miami University Alumni Association, 1949. Print.

Georgen, Eleanor. *The Delsarte System of Physical Culture.* New York: Butterick, 1893. Print.

Glenn, Cheryl. "sex, lies, and manuscript: Refiguring Aspasia in the History of Rhetoric." *CCC* 45.2 (1994): 180–99. Print.

———. *Unspoken: A Rhetoric of Silence.* Carbondale: Southern Illinois UP, 2004. Print.

Hochmuth, Marie, and Richard Murphy. "Rhetorical and Elocutionary Training in Nineteenth-Century Colleges." *History of Speech Education in America.* Ed. Karl R. Wallace. New York: Appleton-Century-Crofts, 1954. 153–77. Print.

Holmström, Kirsten Gram. *Monodrama, Attitudes, Tableaux Vivants: Studies on Some Trends of Theatrical Fashion 1770–1815.* Stockholm: Almqvist and Wiksell, 1967. Print.

Johnson, Nan. *Gender and Rhetorical Space in American Life, 1866–1910.* Carbondale: Southern Illinois UP, 2002. Print.

Jorgensen-Earp, Cheryl R. *"The Transfiguring Sword": The Just War of the Women's Social and Political Union.* Tuscaloosa: U of Alabama P, 1997. Print.

McTeague, James H. *Before Stanislavsky: American Professional Acting Schools and Acting Theory, 1875–1925.* Metuchen, NJ: Scarecrow, 1993. Print.

Morgan, Anna. "The Art of Elocution." *The Congress of Women: Held in the Women's Building, World's Columbian Exposition, Chicago, U.S.A., 1893.* Ed. Mary Kavanaugh Oldham Eagle. Chicago: Monarch, 1894. 597–99. Web. Jan. 10, 2010.

Mountford, Roxanne. "Feminization of Rhetoric?" Rev. of *Composition-Rhetoric: Backgrounds, Theory, and Pedagogy,* by Robert J. Connors. *JAC* 19.3 (1999): 485–92. Print.

Ratcliffe, Krista. *Rhetorical Listening: Gender, Identification, Whiteness.* Carbondale: Southern Illinois UP, 2006. Print.

Ruggles Gere, Anne. *Intimate Practices: Literacy and Cultural Work in U.S. Women's Clubs, 1880–1920.* Urbana: U of Illinois P, 1997. Print.

Ruyter, Nancy Lee Chalfa. *The Cultivation of Body and Mind in Nineteenth-Century American Delsartism.* Westport, CT: Greenwood, 1999. Print.

———. *Reformers and Visionaries: The Americanization of the Art of Dance.* New York: Dance Horizons, 1979. Print.

Shaver, Claude L. "Steele MacKaye and the Delsartian Tradition." *History of Speech Education in America.* Ed. Karl R. Wallace. New York: Appleton-Century-Crofts, 1954. 202–18. Print.

Soper, Henry M., ed. *Soper's Select Speaker.* 1901. Print.

Stebbins, Genevieve. *Society Gymnastics and Voice-Culture.* New York: Werner, 1889. Print.

Warman, Edward B. *Gestures and Attitudes: An Exposition of the Delsarte Philosophy of Expression, Practical and Theoretical.* Boston: Lee and Shepard, 1892. Print.

Werner, Edgar S., ed. *Delsarte System of Oratory.* 4th ed. New York: 1893. Print.

Wilbor, Elsie M. *The Delsarte Recitation Book.* 1905. Freeport, NY: Books for Libraries, 1971. Print.

Part Two

THEORY AND CRITICISM

6

Silence: A Politics

Kennan Ferguson

Political conflicts, identities, and ideologies are negotiated linguistically, language being both the instrument by which humans interact and the means of constructing what it means to be human.[1] That voice and speech are central to the construction of community and political action is practically a truism within political theory. The assumption that language is deployed unproblematically and ubiquitously—that is, that language "just is" and that all people use language identically and constantly—is, unfortunately, just as much a truism in political discourse.

For example, take what has served as the archetypal community for political theorists from Aristotle to Locke to present-day philosophers: the family. A family is made up of disparate individuals, with often conflicting values, commitments, interests, even affections, who yet still (generally) consider themselves a close-knit community. But of course, close relatives do not necessitate unanimity; indeed, some of the most brutal and unforgiving conflicts emerge within family structures. Families, instead, use a variety of mechanisms to persevere. Of interest here is one particular strategy, often used in situations of profound disagreement (religion, politics, sexuality): that of silence. One important (though not exclusive) way to negotiate such differences is not to speak of them but to allow other, more uncomplicated topics of discussion to form the linguistic medium in which the family exists (Tannen, "Silence as Conflict Management"). These silences need not be total or universal, but they are often a useful strategy to enable domestic continuity in the face of radical discontinuity. This tactic is exemplary, too, for larger communities. Thus, commonalities, both real and imagined, are already based on lack of speech: political, ethical, and epistemological silences that are necessarily backgrounded to establish other, overlapping connections.

Yet those who wish to build and reinforce community mention silence only as a threat to community, as failure and malfunction. Silence is that which is imposed upon marginalized groups, for example, so it is easily assumed that silence must be overcome. Silence is indicative of miscommunication, so a model of community based on an image of language as transparent communication must eliminate silence.

Even if silence is recognized as an appropriate response, it may still be represented as absence. When Wittgenstein famously concluded his *Tractatus Logico-Philosophicus* with the aphorism "Whereof one cannot speak, thereof one must be silent," he supposed that since we cannot achieve truth in nonlogical matters—for example, ethics or aesthetics— they therefore have no place in philosophy (Wittgenstein §7; Ferguson 17–23). Wittgenstein recognized a place for silence (he certainly did not think such issues unimportant merely because they cannot be reduced to syllogistic demonstration), but this silence remains that of lack. Issues that cannot be adequately addressed should not be addressed at all; they are outside the realm of the proper and therefore rightfully languish.

But in fact silence, as Cheryl Glenn has convincingly argued, operates at different times on profoundly dissimilar affective registers (Glenn 15–16). Following Glenn, I am interested here in drawing out the implications of these dissimilarities by showing how silence operates in multiple ways toward (sometimes) divergent ends. If silence, as such, cannot be reduced to determinate purpose, it must be rethought as not only a site of repression but also a nexus of resistance or even as a potentiality for creation. This chapter begins by examining the common conceptions of silence's role through the lenses of communication theory, feminist criticism, and political theory, showing how disempowerment and oppression are the assumed political purposes of silence. Silence, though, can also serve as a refuge from power; this chapter thus turns to those fields that recognize the power inherent in silence, whether as a form of subjugation, resistance, or motivation. Finally, I point to the ways in which silence itself establishes private and public commonality, where it is not merely an impediment to connections between people. If silence can be used to create the self, or to create communities, then it is not always something to be feared, eliminated, or overcome. That silence resists any reductionistic political role, in other words, denotes a sweeping truth about both language and its lack: similarity in form is not equivalent to similarity in function.

Denigrated Silence

"Silence is weird," read the tagline for a 2001 advertising campaign in the United States for Cingular cellular phone service. It is perhaps less surprising that such an approach to silence prevails in contemporary society than that the aphorism declaring silence golden still has wide enough provenance to be thus transposed. There exist, it seems, few states less desirable than silence. Silence is linked to the horror of absence, of aporia; Pascal held that the silence of space "strikes terror" (qtd. in Steiner 32). Insofar as communication between people is popularly considered the acme of human endeavors and silence is seen as the failure of communication, to be silent means to betray the goals and hopes of humanity, to renounce ties with fellow citizens.

If in popular discourse the idea of silence is denigrated, its fate is hardly better in academe. As the concepts of identity and activity have become increasingly connected to a lingual politics, the existence of silence has in turn been increasingly seen as the subjugation of these identities and activities. If language, in other words, is identity, then lack of language can only be the demise of identity. Communication is presumed to reside within, or be constituted by, language; words might be demarcated by the lacuna between them, but the words remain the elementary objects of analysis.

Those few who do recognize silence as a constitutive aspect of language often regard it as merely the lack of sound—perhaps between utterances or as an individual response to certain behaviors. For example, silence may be defined as referring to pauses between words (Crown and Feldstein) or "to the failure of one addressee to produce a response to a request" (Dendrinos and Pedro 216) or as an initial reluctance and delay in reaction (Rochester). In its most extreme form, the total disappearance of a particular language is metonymically the disappearance of a people, the extinction of a culture (Crystal).

A second analysis of silence has emerged in recent decades from feminist theorists who embarked on the project of discovering how, when, and why women's voices have been silenced by a patriarchal culture. In some important ways, this approach has overlapped with that of the linguists, who criticize silence as a failure or denial of communication and examine the social and political causes of this aphonia. But a critical difference in the feminist analyses remains: silence is politicized. That some people (women) are encouraged or forced to remain silent can be traced to cultural norms that use silence to deny them agency.

This approach has caused a central ambivalence in recent feminist theory: how both to explicate the abusive power relationships that have historically kept women's voices from being heard and also celebrate the work that women have done within the spheres allowed to them. Tillie Olsen's work epitomizes this. In *Silences*, she describes and critiques myriad silencings that have occurred in contemporary American society and the history of literature and the ways and times that the voices of women have been defamed, ignored, stilled, or precluded. Olsen calls for a rediscovery of women's work that has been purged from literary history while also advancing a cultural critique of those who attacked (and continue, she argues, to attack) women's voices. If the most talented and original voices among us are stifled, then such systems must affect the less resistant even more severely. What, she asks, do such destructions "explain to the rest of us of possible causes—outside ourselves—of our founderings, failings, unnatural silencings?" (141). Similarly, Adrienne Rich, perhaps the best-known feminist critic to connect women's experience to silence, argues that women as women have been repeatedly and forcefully obstructed from entering the public realm of speech. "The entire history of women's struggle for self-determination," she states, "has been muffled in silence over and over" (11).

Nor is this reading limited to feminist theory. Silence qua absence/powerlessness appears in a variety of political contexts. See it used as absence within history: the lacunae in official archives are termed "silences" in the historical record.[2] See it used as vulnerability in political science: Elisabeth Noelle-Neumann describes the inability to express one's political preferences in the face of contrary public opinion (however slight) as the "spiral of silence." See it used legally as implied consent (Tiersma). See it used as the opposite of organized political contention:

ACT UP's famed anti-AIDS slogan "Silence = Death" intrinsically calls for political speech as action.

Underlying each of these critical conceptions of silence is a model that conflates community, communication, and speech. Silence, whether that of a subaltern group or as perpetuated by institutional mechanisms, represents a threat to that nexus and, by extension, a threat to politics. If silence is that which means the lack of articulation, and such an articulation is the primary—even sole—means of creating and continuing community, then silence is incompatible with community and society.

This implicit and explicit denigration infects not just those who decry silence but also theoretical perspectives that presume the mutuality of community/communication/speech. Theorists using this model generally either condemn a disempowered group's lack of authority within a society or suggest new strategies to promote equality and democracy by encouraging speech.

Jürgen Habermas's conceptual approach to social power and equality exemplifies this latter approach. Having developed and deployed over the years an ambitious and meticulous critique of the privileging of enlightenment subjectivity, Habermas later began to champion speech as the formulation for democratic practice. Beginning with a rather simplified "ideal speech situation" and moving to more complex conceptions of discursive social space, Habermas's solution to the dilemmas of difference and inequality is resolutely verbal. For example, in his thorough treatment of law and equality, *Between Facts and Norms*, he champions, in turn, "discourse theory," "communicative reason," "communicative action," "communicative power," "communicative freedom," "discourse principles," and his previous stepping-off point, "speech act theory."

Habermas's ideal, a nomologically neutral realm of power, is certainly a valid and laudable ambition. Nor is he wrong in his understanding that speech comprises a constitutive part of law and fair access to law remains partially dependent on discourse equality. He is certainly not the only political or social theorist to reduce freedom and the very possibility of justice to the availability of speech; the vast majority share this approach. But in reinforcing a normative communicative theory as the ideal formulation of political democracy, he positions silence exclusively on the side of partiality, inequality, and oppression. If linguism is the sole site of community and connection, then fragmentation is inevitable.

In other words, Habermas's theoretical approach not only ignores the ways silence figures within people's lives but also makes the grounds of community (which he ostensibly defends) insupportable and implausible.

These various assumptions of words as axiomatic for communication, identity, and politics are popular, widespread, and deeply ingrained. Each serves to make speech/noise normative and silence deviant; as sociolinguist Ron Scallon puts it, "hesitation or silences" are thought to indicate "trouble, difficulty, missing cogs" (26). But positioning silence exclusively as absence and speech as the substantive aspect of these powerful concepts makes possible a striking set of possibilities. As Michel Foucault has argued, "Silence and secrecy are a shelter for power, anchoring its prohibitions, but they also loosen its hold and provide for relatively obscure areas of tolerance" (101). The very existence of silence thereby becomes a form of resistance, of nonparticipation in these practices of community building, identity formation, and norm setting. Silence, in other words, betokens a rejection of these practices of power.

Resistant Silence

In its most moderate understanding, silence is seen as basic withdrawal, whether from a conversation or from the business of modern life. Silence is a ceasing of participation, a discovery of self by cutting off external stimuli, whether the creation of "a time for quiet," a spatial or temporal retreat, or particular venue in which to read, think, or relax. Silence, in this conception, is as much metaphorical as literal. The "silence" of the wilderness, for example, is not really a literal quiet, as anyone who has spent a night camping there well knows. Instead, it is a figurative slowing-down, an escape from the quotidian pressures of its imagined opposite, city or suburban life. Yet this metaphorical quality prevails precisely because silence is seen as a rejection, however temporary, of those metaphorically noisy practices that are being escaped.

If silence is not privileged as imperative for personal growth, then, why does it have this reputation? One answer may lie in this metaphorical position it holds: if silence is a form of withdrawal, then those aspects of life that require a degree of withdrawal from the assumptions and involvements of that life are metonymically linked to silence. Silence, in other words, functions as a representation of withdrawal; the assumed tranquillity of silence bars the nontranquil involvements of the outside world.

This does not, however, constitute a particularly overt power of resistance, even if it implies a form of disavowal. Linked to the withdrawal conception of silence is a more overt refusal to participate in the normative linguistic practices of a state or society. Silence can prove to be powerful not only as isolation but for the social function of self- or group withdrawal as a resistance.

Sociolinguist Perry Gilmore gives one familiar example: that of the student whose silence in the classroom serves to resist the authority of the teacher, whose power in turn cannot force an answer. The studied silence, or "sulk," can be used against a teacher's attempt to settle, understand, or appropriately punish a student; in refusing to speak, the student resists participating in the linguistic management of a classroom. Gilmore notes that while teachers may refer to persistent silence in a variety of ways, such as "'pouting,' 'fretting,' 'acting spoiled,' 'being rebellious,' 'acting nasty,' 'having a temper tantrum,' and so on," in each case it is seen as a threat to the normative standards of a classroom and usually causes a teacher to respond and pay attention to the silent student (154).

Silence can serve as resistance to any institution that requires verbal participation (which is virtually all). In the face of forced speech, as Thomas L. Dumm says, to "speak may be to justify what is unjustifiable" (30). On a macroscopic political scale, states often require such participation and subsequently employ a variety of means to compel it. The state-sponsored requirement to take an oath is a particularly overt form of obligatory speech. Loyalty oaths, public recantations of heresy, self-incrimination, enforced pledges of allegiance, and required judicial affirmations all oblige certain well-circumscribed speech acts. Haig Bosmajian has illuminated a profound trajectory of the ways that coerced speech has been used to control, imprison, and even kill those who dissent, from Thomas More and Galileo to the victims of the U.S. House Un-American Activities Committee and employees forced to sign oaths as a condition of employment. Most notably, these institutional forces consider silent dissent threatening; declining to support a king's or legislative body's activities is judged tantamount to opposing the nation.

This role of silence is meticulously captured and illustrated by Jane Campion's film *The Piano*. The protagonist, Ada, played by Holly Hunter, is mute. Early in life, she says, she decided to stop speaking: "My father says it is a dark talent and the day I take it into my head to stop breathing will be my last." Her silence weighs heavily on her husband, Stewart (who selected her by mail order), but his inability to listen carefully to the silence in which she lives distinguishes him from his blunt, illiterate, but ultimately more responsive neighbor Baines, who learns to treat her as a fierce, independent, full person. Ada's silence adds to her humanity in that she demands more from her noninterlocutors, yet her silence clearly demonstrates a constant defiance rather than any sort of passivity.

The silence of a nineteenth-century woman is not an uncommon affair, especially as represented by the strain of feminist criticism epitomized by Rich. Ada, unlike the archetypal silenced woman, uses her silence to discomfit those who regulate social behavior with speech. Her primary communication through the eponymous piano is available only to those with the ability or will to listen; that she does not speak seems both the literalization of the norms of her society and her rebellion against those norms. One way of viewing the relationship of silencing and being silenced is as a "self-contained opposite," where silence can be reclaimed from the mechanisms of power to be used as a practice of self-creation (Clair 147–64).

Silence can be used against others, but not just in resistant ways. To see such usage as merely wresting a tool from an oppressive system, as a self-contained opposite, is to miss that silence's power extends beyond resistance. Silence, both as withdrawal and as pointed avoidance, can be used to manipulate, control, and harm others just as easily as to protect the self.

Again, to turn to children to understand its uses, their deployment of silence against one another shows a silence that itself does violence. The "silent treatment," the calculated withdrawal of communicative words from an unfavored member of that societal group, can be devastating. Importantly, this does not literally silence the individual in the sense of negating that person's attempts at speech but attacks by revoking accepted social forms of recognition. Similarly, so-called passive-aggressive behavior, using silence to punish someone who relies on verbal interaction within a relationship, also wields silence to castigate and discipline (Sattel). In each case, silence operates on an exoteric register.

In each of these cases, silence is not something that is done to one but a practice that one aggressively performs. Active and reactive silence does not fit well into the predominant model of silence as powerlessness. However, this is not to say that silence as power is better, or more often true, than silence as denigration. Indeed, insofar as normative speech structures both, discourse equally constitutes both models, since each works with and against the norms of speech. Wendy Brown points out that these conceptions, far from being oppositional, are in fact mutually structured: that it is possible for silence, she argues, "both to shelter power and to serve as a barrier against power" (316).

Yet before moving beyond this dialectical relationship, one more model of silence as power exists, one that is not reducible to either a passive, resistant, or aggressive posture: that used on the analysand. Professional psychotherapeutic relations are premised on an evocative silence, yet one that is certainly far from neutral as structured by organizational power. The therapist's silence, at least relative to the client, intends to promote, or even provoke, disclosure. Similar situations include a professor's use of silence used to draw out a class, a journalist's to encourage elucidation, a priest's hearing a confession, or indeed any interlocutor to induce conversation. If silence can function to provoke a discursive subjectivity, then, its power is neither defensive nor aggressive. It may operate on both registers at once, as in Jean-François Lyotard's description of the "differend" as speech that is simultaneously demanded and impossible, as in those who insist upon eyewitness accounts by victims of genocide (3–31). Or, it may operate on neither, as the evocative silence does. It may be that *silence has no predetermined structure of power at all*. If this is the case (and it is my contention here that it is), silence can play an infinite variety of roles in social, political, and linguistic networks. If it can be destructive, defensive, and evocative of selves and social relations, then it can also contribute to the constitution of these identities. The remainder of this essay therefore examines some ways silence operates at this formational level, with particular emphasis on its use as a strategy to negotiate the competing realities of incommensurability and community.

Constitutive Silence

Silence can operate in multiplicitous, fragmentary, even paradoxical ways. The politics of silence, in other words, are not reducible to any particular political functionality; even more than its putative opposite, language, silence resists absolution. Insofar as silence cannot be literalized or universalized, it is not reducible to one singular function. If silence was strictly resistant, or oppressive, it could be neatly categorized as salutary, or sinister; instead, it both embodies and transcends these neat categorizations.

Condemnations of silence, especially in institutionalized contexts, arise from this very indeterminacy. Gail Griffin describes classroom silences for the college professor thus:

> A stretch of silence may mean any number of things. It may mean "We have no idea, as we have not yet even glimpsed the frontispiece of this text." Or "You appear to be operating under the naive delusion that we care." Or "I will never drink orange vodka again." Or "If she doesn't call me tonight I will throw myself off the chapel tower." Or "If you'd just break down and tell us the answer, we could all go home and sleep." Very often it means "I am a cretin in a classroom of geniuses." But teachers, often bad translators, usually interpret it as follows: "We despise and loathe you." (219)

Griffin clearly means to remind teachers that silence is not necessarily to be feared, but her multitude of meanings is not quite so reducible to the moral lesson she intends. For the classroom, silence may well mean loathing; its very irreducibility to any of these territorializations makes the lack of speech threatening to those organizational structures and their representatives: teachers are often justified in distrusting silence.

This particular capability significantly differs from the customary political roles of silence, even among those discussed above who recognize some of its potential kinds of power. If silence is comprised solely as lack, communication becomes impossible; if it is limited to force, either as resistance or as aggression, it separates and partitions relationships. If it can function within, say, families in various ways, both to create divisions and to resist power, then the nature of silence is in fact no intrinsic nature at all.

That it has no necessary form, however, leads to an unexplored and unacknowledged capability: it can also enable and produce. Silence, in other words, can be constitutive. It can create identities and enable communities. It can, in the words of Glenn, "engender," "witness," "attest," "command," even "open" us to the world. Once understood as freed from interpretive structures that necessarily condemn (or celebrate) it, the unlimited aspects of its multiplicitous functionality are freed for their creative and productive capacity.

Friedrich Nietzsche, as Zarathustra, conceives of silence as the method for the most profound individual changes. An anthropomorphized Solitude welcomes him from the world of men, the "world below," where "everything among them speaks, everything is betrayed" (Nietzsche 202–4). To the "fire-dog," the creature of the underworld, he argues against the cacophony of the so-called world-changing events. "The greatest events— they are not our noisiest but our stillest hours. The world revolves, not around the inventors of new noises, but around the inventors of new values; it revolves *inaudibly*" (Nietzsche 131). Zarathustra, in a parable he calls "The Stillest Hour," explains how he changed from his comparisons with other men to his creation of himself. Repeatedly, "something" spoke to him "voicelessly," helping him realize how to escape his childhood, his pride, his shame, and his limitations imposed upon him by society.[3]

Yet if silence can be constitutive of individual subjectivity, it can also serve to constitute commonality. The very existence of social silence depends upon its acceptance. Silence must always be a collusion, as Deborah Tannen points out; social silence cannot be limited to one side. Silences between two or more people must be actively maintained as such ("Silence: Anything But").

That any communal silence must be socially preserved is obvious, especially when cases of those who disturb it are taken into account—for example, the response of an audience watching a theatrical production or listening to symphonic music. Noise, be it speaking or mere rustling, is seen as disruptive to the experience of the performance; an audience member who cannot learn silence is commonly seen as failing in his or her place. Nor is this limited to those moments when dialogue emanates from the stage or sounds issue from instruments. An audience member who speaks loudly during a tense emotional standoff in a Harold Pinter play or applauds between movements in a Mozart concerto implicitly breaks an alliance of silence, an alliance to which other audience members (and occasionally venue staff) are deeply invested.

This is of course a partial silence (one on the part of the audience, not the performers), but instructive nonetheless. The audience members recognize the necessity of silence on their part for the experience they desire and go to great lengths to protect it. In doing so, they create a particular kind of audience, one with its own norms and mores: a community. Yet this is a limited example. To better explore this aspect of silence, I turn to two cases that actively and overtly use silence to constitute a community, instances where silence plays a far more active and recognized role than in the familial example with which this essay began. These two illustrations, traditional Quaker meetings and the prominent John

Cage piano piece *4'33"*, show silence bringing together disparate people in common experience.

Quaker worship is famed for being conducted, in the most part, in silence. Friends, as Quakers often call themselves, were not the only Christian group to promote silent worship; even within the Catholic church, the apophasis tradition gained strength in the late seventeenth century in the quietist movement led by Miguel de Molinos.[4] But Quakers are the best-known historical and contemporary sect to worship in this way, and the centrality of silence in their worship and daily life is overtly justified as conducive to theological truth and community creation by Quakers themselves.

From the denomination's beginning, this form of worship drew considerable attention and criticism. In his *Apology*, the 1678 explication of Quakerism, Robert Barclay spends considerable time defending silent worship, especially once he has declared that "there can be nothing more opposite to the natural will and wisdom of man than this silent waiting upon God . . ." (qtd. in Bauman 22). Barclay saw silence as a method of diminishing the automatic demands of the self, allowing the word of God to emanate instead. Speaking, thereby, became representative of all activities of the body, which could through practice become secondary to listening to God's voice (Bauman 22). For Quakers, silence has long been the foremost way to allow the overcoming of the egocentric mind. In the words of an 1805 pamphlet written by Thomas Colley, "there is no exercise whatever where self is more shut out" (qtd. in Hodgkin 97).

This is not the silence of constantive individualism; like most religious ceremonies, it is practiced as a community. This silence must take place communally, Barclay argued: it is the "duty of all to be Diligent in assembling of themselves together, and when assembled, the great work of one and all ought to be to wait upon God" (qtd. in Brook 27). The Quakers considered congregation vital, even in the absence, as was their convention, of a central speaker/priest/minister. When "these who came together, to meet after this manner in Silence, so that they would set together many hours in a deep Silence and Quietness," they practiced silence together, as a community (Keith 17).

Those who attempt to theorize silence often remark on Quaker practice, but its communal aspect remains consistently overlooked. Even Richard Bauman, in his admirable treatment of the interplay between speech and silence in seventeenth-century Quakerism, treats silence as something ultimately individualistic (22–31). But the literature of the period, though primarily concerned with the overcoming of self in the service of "the Light," continually refers to the necessity of assembly. Even in the twentieth century, Quaker theologians take pains to differentiate the experience of individualized silence from the authentic communal worship: silence, argued L. Violet Hodgkin in 1919, must arise not from "each soul alone, but united as a community" (97).

Silence, in this social role, creates the community. It provides emotional, theological, and political sustenance in many of the same ways any denominational organization does. Silence functions as shared experience, but one whose meaning is not necessarily (or even likely) shared. Silence's "primary object is group unity"; the unarticulated yet contiguous experience of silence itself forms the community (Zielinski 23).

Cage's famous piece *4′33″* invokes similar experiences. A performer sits at a piano for four minutes and thirty-three seconds without touching the keys; an audience hears what would usually be considered incidental noises instead of notes from the piano. While not silence in the sense of absence of sound (Cage held there is no such thing as absolute silence), Cage's piece throws all sound into stark relief (Cage 8). In doing so, it encourages the audience to consider the nature of music (the most common interpretation of *4′33″*) but also, more importantly, to become aware of itself as an audience.

Cage's study of the role of silence within Zen Buddhism convinced him that music's ideal role was not to unilaterally communicate emotion or ideas to listeners but rather to create awareness of surroundings: in this case, the surroundings of the performance hall (Kostelanetz). Cage's interest in the creation and reception of music is testament to this focus: his dislike of recordings as "the end of music"; his insistence on a score, page turnings, and note durations for the performance of *4′33″*; and his fundamental interest in the art of everyday experience.[5] As Susan Sontag has pointed out, the dialectical nature of the silence that Cage created necessitates a surrounding fullness of response in the audience (10–11). It is as though the silence constitutes the awareness of the audience *as such*, both within its self-awareness and in the arrangement of its relation to the "music."

The audience, then, transcends its assumed identity as passive recipient and actively partakes in the piece. Cage's is not a form of performance art that primarily relies on shock, or even that of transgression. Instead, the surprise of 4′33″ emerges from its use of silence to enable the recognition of the audience as integral to performance, as making up the piece as much as the composer or performer. Silence, in this role, does not distance, resist, nor overpower; it forms the artistic and intellectual basis for the recognition and constitution of communal identity. For Cage's musical composition, as for the Quaker theological tradition, silence creates community.

These creative productions, from Zarathustra's self-creation to Barclay's theological assembly to Cage's communal experience, make singular interpretations of silence's functions problematically simplistic. If silence cannot be fixed to the singular interpretation of powerlessness, or of resistance, then neither can it be easily and clearly constitutive. No sure way exists of determining if all members of a community are affected by silence in ways that actually create community; no silence is indisputably formative or reactive.

A search for *the* politics of silence, for the determinative classification of the power dynamics inherent within silence, is consequently doomed to fail. The multiple, fragmentary, and overlapping dynamics of silence can be iterated, investigated, and explored, but they cannot be fixed nor predetermined. Indeed, the implications of this impossibility may well have more to do with how politics gets conceptualized in contemporary theory than with the particularities of silence. Perhaps power itself, like silence, is radically indeterminate, open to processes of domination, emancipation, and resistance that can never be fully contained, represented, or comprehended.

Both the creation of community and the disruption of organization compose silence's constitutive aspects. Each of these forms is linked to silence as oppressive or resistant power, but silence does not ultimately, necessarily perform any one of these functions. Or, more properly, silence does not perform only one of these tasks in only one way. Silence functions as a negotiation of the disparate and the common, but like any true negotiation it takes more than one path and more than one meaning. In silence, as in few other mechanisms, individuality, incommensurability, and community coexist.

Notes

1. My thanks to Jane Bennett, Melissa Orlie, Kathy Ferguson, Carolyn Eichner, Carolyn DiPalma, William Connolly, Verity Smith, Cheryl Hall, Matthew

Moore, and Raia Prokhovnik, whose discussions (and occasional silences) have been particularly helpful in constructing this essay. My thanks also to Pendle Hill and Swarthmore College, whose collections of Quaker literature proved invaluable.

2. See, e.g., Allen. Allen's overt use of "silence" means the lack of a self-created historical record by those whose sole historical documentation resides as objects of police surveillance and custody, such as prostitutes in Victorian-era England.

3. At least eight times, Zarathustra says something along the lines of, "Then something said to me voicelessly . . ." (Nietzsche 166–69).

4. Both likely inherited the tradition from the Seekers, though their theological underpinnings cause both to be loath to admit historical influence or precedent. See Zielinski and Fraser, especially chapter 1.

5. Pianist Larry J. Solomon is particularly interested in these structural aspects of the piece.

Works Cited

Allen, Judith. "Evidence and Silence: Feminism and the Limits of History." *Feminist Challenges: Social and Political History*. Ed. Carole Pateman and Elizabeth Gross. Boston: Northeastern UP, 1986. 173–89. Print.

Barclay, Robert. *Truth Triumphant, Through the Spiritual Warfare, Christian Labors, and Writings, of that Able and Faithful Servant of Jesus Christ, Robert Barclay: To Which is Prefixed an Account of his Life*. 1692. 3 vols. Philadelphia: B. C. Stanton, 1831. Print.

Bauman, Richard. *Let Your Words Be Few: Symbolism of Speaking and Silence among Seventeenth Century Quakers*. Cambridge: Cambridge UP, 1983. Print.

Bosmajian, Haig. *The Freedom Not to Speak*. New York: New York UP, 1999. Print.

Brook, Mary. *Reasons for the Necessity of Silent Waiting, in Order to the Solemn Worship of God; to Which are Added Several Quotations from Robert Barclay's Apology*. 1795. Philadelphia: Friends Bookstore, 1977. Print.

Brown, Wendy. "Freedom's Silences." *Censorship and Silencing: Practices of Cultural Regulation*. Ed. Robert C. Post. Los Angeles: Getty Research Institute for the History of Art and the Humanities, 1998. 313–27. Print.

Cage, John. *Silence*. Middletown: Wesleyan UP, 1961. Print.

Cingular. Billboard advertisement. 2001.

Clair, Robin Patric. *Organizing Silence: A World of Possibilities*. Albany: State U of New York P, 1998. Print.

Colley, Thomas. *An Apology for Silent Waiting Upon God in Religious Assemblies; With Some Observations On the Nature and Ground of True Faith, and the Application Thereof in the Important Concern of Worship*. Philadelphia: Joseph Crukshank, 1805. Print.

Crown, Cynthia L., and Stanley Feldstein. "Psychological Correlates of Silence and Sound in Conversational Interaction." Tannen and Saville-Troike 31–54. Print.

Crystal, David. *Language Death*. Cambridge: Cambridge UP, 2000. Print.

Dendrinos, Bessie, and Emilia Ribeiro Pedro. "Giving Street Directions: The Silent Role of Women." *Silence: Interdisciplinary Perspectives.* Ed. Adam Jaworkski. Berlin: Mouton de Gruyer, 1997. 215–38. Print.

Dumm, Thomas L. *A Politics of the Ordinary.* New York: New York UP, 1999. Print.

Ferguson, Kennan. *The Politics of Judgment: Aesthetics, Identity, and Political Theory.* Lanham, MD: Lexington, 1999. Print.

Foucault, Michel. *The History of Sexuality.* Vol. 1. Trans. Robert Hurley. New York: Vintage, 1980. Print.

Fraser, Russel. *The Language of Adam.* New York: Columbia UP, 1979. Print.

Gilmore, Perry. "Silence and Sulking: Emotional Displays in the Classroom." Tannen and Saville-Troike 139–62. Print.

Glenn, Cheryl. *Unspoken: A Rhetoric of Silence.* Carbondale: Southern Illinois UP, 2004. Print.

Griffin, Gail. *Calling: Essays on Teaching in the Mother Tongue.* New York: Trilogy, 1992. Print.

Habermas, Jürgen. *Between Facts and Norms: Contributions to a Discourse Theory of Law and Democracy.* Trans. William Rehg. Cambridge: MIT P, 1998. Print.

Hodgkin, L. Violet. *Silent Worship: The Way of Wonder; Swarthmore Lecture 1919.* London: Swarthmore P, 1919. Print.

Keith, George. *The Benefit, Advantage, and Glory of Silent Meetings, both as it was Found at the Beginning, or first Breaking Forth of this Clear Manifestation of Truth, and continued o to be Found by all the Faithful and Upright in Heart at this Day.* London: Andrew Sowle, 1687. Print.

Kostelanetz, Richard. *Conversing with Cage.* New York: Limelight, 1988. Print.

Lang, Beryl. *Heidegger's Silence.* Cornell: Cornell UP, 1996. Print.

Lyotard, Jean-François. *The Differend: Phrases in Dispute.* Trans. Georges Van Den Abbeele. Minneapolis: U of Minnesota P, 1988. Print.

Nietzsche, Friedrich. *Thus Spoke Zarathustra.* Trans. R. J. Hollingdale. London: Penguin, 1969. Print.

Noelle-Neumann, Elisabeth. *The Spiral of Silence: Public Opinion—Our Social Skin.* Chicago: U of Chicago P, 1984. Print.

Olsen, Tillie. *Silences.* New York: Delacorte Press/Seymour Lawrence, 1978. Print.

The Piano. Dir. Jane Campion. Perf. Holly Hunter, Harvey Keitel, and Sam Neill. Artisan Entertainment, 1993. Film.

Rich, Adrienne. *On Lies, Secrets, and Silence: Selected Prose, 1966–1978.* New York: Norton, 1979. Print.

Rochester, S. R. "The Significance of Pauses in Spontaneous Speech." *Journal of Psycholinguistic Research* 2.1 (1973): 51–81. Print.

Sattel, Jack W. "Men, Inexpressiveness, and Power." *Language, Gender, and Society.* Ed. Barrie Thorne, Cheris Kramarae, and Nancy Henley. Rowley, MA: Newbury, 1983. 119–24. Print.

Scallon, Ron. "The Machine Stops: Silence in the Metaphor of Malfunction." Tannen and Saville-Troike 21–30. Print.

Solomon, Larry J. "The Sounds of Silence: John Cage and 4'33"." 2000. Web. Dec. 1, 2002.

Sontag, Susan. "The Aesthetics of Silence." *Styles of Radical Will.* New York: Farrar, Straus and Giroux, 1969. 1–34. Print.

Steiner, George. *Language and Silence: Essays on Language, Literature, and the Inhuman.* New York: Atheneum, 1976. Print.

Tannen, Deborah. "Silence: Anything But." Tannen and Saville-Troike 93–111. Print.

———. "Silence as Conflict Management in Fiction and Drama: Pinter's *Betrayal* and a Short Story, 'Great Wits.'" *Conflict Talk: Sociolinguistic Investigations of Arguments in Conversations.* Ed. Allen D. Grimshaw. Cambridge: Cambridge UP, 1990. 260–79. Print.

Tannen, Deborah, and Muriel Saville-Troike, eds. *Perspectives on Silence.* Norwood, NJ: Ablex, 1985. Print.

Texas v. Johnson. 491 U.S. 397. 1989. Print.

Tiersma, Peter. "The Language of Silence." *Rutgers Law Review* 48 (1995): 1–99. Print.

Wang, Youru. "Liberating Oneself from the Absolutized Boundary of Language: A Liminological Approach to the Interplay of Speech and Silence in Chan Buddhism." *Philosophy East and West* 51.1 (2001): 83. Print.

Wittgenstein, Ludwig. *Tractatus Logico-Philosophicus.* 1922. Trans. C. K. Ogden. Mineola, NY: Dover, 1999. Print.

Wright, Dale S. "Rethinking Transcendence: The Role of Language in Experience." *Philosophy East and West* 42.1 (1992): 113–38. Print.

Zielinski, Stanislaw. *Psychology and Silence.* Wallingford, PA: Pendle Hill, 1975. Print.

7

"Down a Road and into an Awful Silence": Graphic
Listening in Joe Sacco's Comics Journalism

Andrea A. Lunsford and Adam Rosenblatt

With his graphic novels about life in Palestine and the former Yu-goslavia under conditions of war and occupation, Joe Sacco has almost single-handedly invented a genre, comics journalism. While influenced by sources as diverse as Flemish painter Pieter Brueghel, Hunter S. Thompson, and Art Spiegelman, Sacco's comics journalism is unique for the ways in which it combines methodologies of war corre-spondence with the art of comics. Sacco travels to war zones and refugee camps with notebook, camera, and press pass, creating works that are not quite editorial cartooning, not quite memoir, and certainly not quite the straightforward war reporting of newspaper correspondents and the photojournalists who travel with them. Sacco uses caricature and self-critique to question traditional journalistic "objectivity" and highlight the agency of his subjects, with all of their human strengths and weak-nesses. Always self-critical, Sacco documents both his triumphs and his failures at escaping from the dominant paradigm of war reporting, a paradigm in which people's stories of suffering often become com-modities, pre-packaged and even given new narrative trajectories by the journalists who collect them and by the newspapers, television channels, radio stations, and Web sites that market them.

Journalism often involves intense listening, followed by a journalistic "report" of that experience of listening. The interview, key to a journalist's work, is in some ways a paradigmatic example of listening, as the reporter attempts to get a story "just right" by drawing on eyewitness sources, often representing multiple perspectives of the same event. But other journalistic methods call for listening as well: Sacco often gathers information by "listening" not only with his ears but with his eyes and other senses. The use of synesthesia enables Sacco to inch closer to the truth of a situation than would otherwise be possible.[1] His methodology is of course intimately bound up with the fact that the "report" of his listening will take the form of comics, with their unique language of text and image. This chapter asks how Sacco uses his acute self-awareness, as well as the unique properties of the comics medium, to fashion a model of listening that suits his ethos as a reporter, storyteller, and humanist. In doing so, we will look to work on empathic and rhetorical listening, especially as articulated by Krista Ratcliffe, and will introduce two other forms of listening, which we call "instrumental listening" and "voyeuristic listening," that we find in Sacco's comics journalism. Together, these four forms of listening capture a wide range of motives practiced by listeners whose job is often to tell a story that represents, invokes, or shapes what comes to be taken for the "truth."

In interviews, Sacco describes himself as working very hard to capture the voices of those he talks with, to catch the nuances of speech and sound that lie on the hyphen or just below the surface of what they say. For an English speaker working in Palestine and the former Yugoslavia, of course, this work faces the limitation of language difference. The work of translators is usually rendered invisible in the columns of newspapers, with translators themselves almost never sharing a byline. In Sacco's work, by contrast, translators and guides like Edin, Sacco's closest friend in Bosnia (*Safe Area Goražde*), and Neven, his "fixer" in Sarajevo (*Fixer*), become major characters in Sacco's books. Readers are, in other words, always aware of translation and of the human beings—themselves both victims of and participants in violence—who mediate between Sacco and the worlds he enters. In fact, while in most journalism, the translator or guide often appears (if at all) as a reporter's underling, Sacco frequently portrays himself as inadequate to the generosity and traumatic experiences of guides like Edin and Neven the fixer, though also subject to their tolerance and caprice. Knowing that his dependence on mediators, as well as the complexity of the situations he is faced with, makes it impossible to tell even a single absolute or positivistic "truth" about war or occupation, Sacco is content to try for the truth as he apprehends it. That truth, significantly, turns out to hinge on a series of human relationships involving everything from friendship to codependence and commerce. More often than not, the relationships Sacco builds in search of his "story" wind up *becoming* the story.

Sacco also distinguishes his work from mainstream journalism with his choices about *what* to listen to and *how* to listen. Upon arriving in Sarajevo in 1995, during the final stages of the war in Bosnia, Sacco writes, "Put yourself in my shoes. You've just arrived at the Great Siege . . . your teeth are still rattling from the APC ride over Mt. Igman . . . and someone has just pointed you down a road and into an awful silence . . ." (*Fixer* 11). This remark is followed by a stunning wordless drawing, spread across the next two pages, of a very small Sacco, hunched over, walking past burned-out buildings toward a desolate, shell-marked Holiday Inn (see fig. 7.1). The lonely quietude of the image, like Sacco's remark about silence, comes as a surprise, given that we are following a war reporter to the scene of the "Great Siege" of Sarajevo, a siege marked by exploding shells, gunfire, and a very noisy media circus.

7.1 In Sarajevo, Sacco heads into "an awful silence." From Joe Sacco's *The Fixer*.

These few pages establish Sacco's quest, not only in this book but also in the entire body of his work, to document both the noises and the silences of war, the speech of his subjects, and the experiences they find unspeakable. Sacco arrives in the town of Goražde, for example, with a flotilla of other foreign journalists, just in time for its moment of fame. As the journalists descend upon the town, microphones at the ready, he narrates: "Goražde! Which had just wrested the spotlight from that media darling Sarajevo! Goražde! Which was getting CNNed! NPRed! BBCed! But its proverbial 15 minutes were ticking away! Pretty soon no one was gonna remember Goražde! . . . We didn't have a moment to lose" (*Safe Area Goražde* 6). Long after the other journalists have moved on, however, Sacco keeps returning to Goražde. He documents the story of its stunning outbreak of violence among neighbors, but he also wanders into living rooms, pubs, even an abandoned cultural center, recording the quiet process by which the town emerges from war into peace, as well as the hunger that accompanies its silence. Describing his interactions with the town's young people, Sacco writes: "After an hour's chat about this and that, Alma told me she'd recall aspects of our conversation for a long time, that it'd keep her going for another month. . . . And I'd throw out every scrap I knew . . . Stuff off the top of my head. They gathered in my crumbs" (75). Here, as in other places, Sacco discovers that in order to get the story he is looking for, he will be called upon to speak as well as to listen.

Instrumental Listening, or Listening as Consumption

As in Sacco's phrase about "crumbs," hunger and listening are frequently twinned in Sacco's work, raising questions about the relationship between listening and consumption. In *The Fixer*, just after the wordless spread depicting Sarajevo's "awful silence," Sacco passes a man in the nearly empty Holiday Inn lobby. The first words to break the silence come from the figure, who says, "I want to talk to you." This man, Neven, will become Sacco's "fixer," finding him interview subjects, translating for him, and narrating, perhaps unreliably, his own experiences of the war. This meeting, however, perfectly captures the mutual need that will come to characterize Sacco and Neven's relationship: Neven says "*I* want to talk to you," when really it is Sacco, the reporter in Sarajevo collecting stories, who should "want" to talk to Neven, not the reverse.

What Neven wants (or so it seems at first) is not so much to talk as to earn the money that comes from talking. Sacco spends much of *The Fixer* documenting how stories become commodities in a war zone. He and Neven feed off one another's different and occasionally intersecting hungers, and Sacco's journalistic search for "truth" becomes increasingly compromised as talking and listening become a shared compulsion for him and Neven, driven by Sacco's hunger for a story and Neven's own hunger, ultimately not just to gain cash but to create a narrative of meaning for his war experience. In a magazine story in which Sacco interviews two Iraqi men captured and tortured by U.S. forces, he similarly describes his interactions with his subjects in the language of transaction, starting with the piece's title, "Trauma on Loan." "They are nervous, exhausted, filling their hotel room on Times Square with cigarette smoke," he writes. "But I have been lurking for three days—good-naturedly, patiently—and they feel they *owe* me" (1, emphasis added). The commodification of war stories, Sacco reminds us, exists not only between himself and his subjects but also between him and us, his readers: "Let's face it, my comics blockbuster depends on conflict; peace won't pay the rent" (*Palestine, Book 1*, 76).

What seems to bother Sacco most about this form of listening, even (or especially) when he is implicated in it, is how it blurs the agency of his subjects, making them objects of study rather than actors in their own history. It is, ultimately, a purely *instrumental* form of listening, where the reporter listens not to know a person or to form a relational connection through listening but to obtain that person's objectified experience, which in some ways then no longer belongs to him or her. On one hand, we see the process by which subjects and their war experiences turn into objects to be consumed by the listening "reporter." On the other hand, we also see a larger political process in which a conflict zone like Goražde becomes, rather than a place humming with resilient life (as pictured in fig. 7.2), an object that can be "traded" to "facilitate" a peace settlement (*Safe Area Goražde* 3). Sacco seems to suggest that the objectification of experiences by journalists and the trading of territories by distant politicians are connected, perhaps even co-constitutive. For the reporter, instrumental listening turns the person and the experience into a commodity to be sold to the news; for politicians, this form of listening renders whole territories and their people into property that can be used to barter, trade, or coerce.

7.2 Sacco highlights resilience and agency, as much as or more than violence or trauma, in his stories from Bosnia. From Joe Sacco's *Safe Area Goražde*.

Instrumentalism is opposed, in Sacco's work, to agency. Foreign photographers come to Goražde, "throwing candy at kids to capture the predictable mad scramble" that feeds their craving for "top of the hour" stories to tell (*Safe Area Goražde* 131). Almost as bad to Sacco, other journalists develop complicated "policies" of candy distribution, which, in their high-handedness, their intention of setting "a good example," seem to replicate the superiority and distance in the political relationship between the United Nations and the people left unprotected in its so-called safe areas. When giving out "candy" of his own (whether bonbons for the kids in Goražde or money to Neven), Sacco does not to try to rise above instrumental listening to some pure and noncommodified ideal. Rather, he insists on the agency of his subjects even within a commodified relationship. He explains, "*My* bon-bon policy was to give them out to every kid asking so long as they all got one. As to how they ought to eat their bon-bons, I couldn't care less. I figured the children in Goražde could make their own bon-bon decisions" (*Safe Area Goražde* 131). This last sentence appears in a panel depicting a child against a backdrop of bombed-out buildings, reminding us of the gap in lived experience between the inhabitants of Goražde and the foreign journalists, so eager to "set an example." When we listen instrumentally, we listen through preformed schema we impose on those we "listen" to.

In a perfect example of instrumental listening, one of Sacco's acquaintances calls Neven "a tower of information" (*Fixer* 62), thus turning him from a person into a thing, a walking archive. Sacco, in turn, despite the compromises he makes in hiring Neven, begins his chapters with the repeated call for the reader to "put yourself in Neven's boots" or shoes (*Fixer* 63, 50). In doing so, he not only models his own form of what we will be calling "empathic listening" but also asks his reader to do the same.

The Voyeuristic Listening of a "War Junkie"

To Sacco, even more troubling than the instrumental model of listening are the ways in which wartime reporting winds up replicating the aggressive and even parasitic relationships of war itself. Sacco finds himself on both sides of these relationships, besieged by Neven's manipulations and ploys for money but also preying on his own subjects. In *Palestine*, he calls himself "a vulture" and confesses his hunger for violent and disturbing images that even other journalists turn down (*Palestine, Book 1*, 71, 77). In "Trauma on Loan," Sacco uses both drawings and language to imply a comparison between the interrogation the Iraqi men faced during their detainment and their "interrogation" by Sacco the reporter. As his interview with them ends, Sacco sits in shadow, only partly visible, facing away from us, with the two men in front of him facing the light (and us) (see fig. 7.3). They are exposed, and he—his implements of pen and notebook in hand—is in the position of the listener/interrogator. As the session ends, he writes, "And, once again, they are released," drawing a direct link between the end of their detention and the end of his interview (8).

Sacco has been concerned about the voyeuristic quality of his work since he began crafting his method of comics journalism. In an early strip called "War Junkie," he chronicles how he simultaneously vocally opposed the first Gulf War and became addicted to watching it on television: "Yep, each explosion was proving me right, here it was all in the open, I had a tangible bloodbath to dangle in people's faces, who could deny it?" (*Notes* 178). We see the "war junkie" instinct accompanying him on his first major comics journalism project in Palestine. In one sequence from Sacco's comic series *Palestine*, a Japanese photojournalist, Saburo, describes seeing a picture of a Palestinian baby's swollen head, which the baby's family believed was caused by Israeli tear gas inhaled by the pregnant mother. Whereas Sacco's later work, such as *Safe Area*

7.3 Sacco portrays himself as an interrogator as he interviews Iraqi torture survivors. From Joe Sacco's "Trauma on Loan."

Goražde, will often show his disgust with the exploitative and voyeuristic practices of other journalists (as in the bonbon episode), here he admits to the opposite instinct. Telling his reader, "It's good to get your finger in the wound. Your whole head would be better," Sacco asks Saburo if he was able to take a picture of the swollen-headed baby. "I don't want take picture," Saburo replies, "but they want me take picture [. . .] I take picture . . . very hard." Sacco then confides to us, "Man, I wish I'd seen the soldiers firing tear gas . . . wish I'd seen that baby" (*Palestine, Book 1*, 77).

In *Palestine*, more than in later works like *Safe Area Goražde*, Sacco's drawings also seem like documents of intrusion. The angles are off-kilter, as if Sacco's "camera" were everywhere from right above the heads of his subjects to underfoot. Sometimes he zooms in so close that we feel as if we have invaded the personal space of his interviewee, can see his broken fingernails and maybe even smell his breath (see *Palestine, Book 1*, 40; compare, for example, to the final page of "Trauma on Loan"). If *Safe Area*

Goražde, *The Fixer*, and other recent works seem less voyeuristic, it is not only because Sacco spends less time critiquing his journalistic fervor. It is also because of the way he builds these later books around a central subject or two (Neven, Edin, and Riki). As character begins to play a larger role in Sacco's work, he includes more scenes of the mundane along with wartime experiences, rather than roving from person to person in search of a condensed picture of violence, as he often did in *Palestine* (though his most recent book, *Footnotes in Gaza*, again focuses on two particular, violent episodes—this time in the more distant past—and chronicles them through the eyes of an almost overwhelming number of interview subjects.). Sacco's art style has, for the most part, adapted to this shift in his journalistic instincts, pulling back to less intrusive (though often less visually arresting) angles.[2] Whereas the images in *Palestine* are often most notable for ways in which bodies crowd the page (a style that may in part reflect the cramped reality of Palestinian cities and refugee camps; see *Palestine, Book* 2, 114, 126), his work afterward makes more room for the landscape as a character, graphically obsessing over the relationship between people and the places they inhabit (*Safe Area Goražde* 15, 128) (see figs. 7.4 and 7.5).

7.4 Sacco depicts the manic energy of a crowded, conflictive occupation. From Joe Sacco's *Palestine: In the Gaza Strip*.

Empathic Listening

Against instrumental and voyeuristic models of listening, Sacco also searches for a way forward. He is, for instance, not *only* a voyeur or

7.5 Yet he can also capture the desolation of a traumatized, abandoned Bosnian town. From Joe Sacco's *Safe Area Goražde*.

instrumental listener (though he certainly implicates himself in those practices) but an empathic listener as well.[3] Sacco expresses the empathy of his listening, the driving ethos of his work, through drawings as much as through words. His lines, compositions, and lights and darks respond directly to the stories of his subjects. In *Safe Area Goražde*, Sacco again listens to stories in which hunger (this time literal) plays a central role, as the United Nations fails to get food relief through Serb blockades and into the Muslim village of Goražde. "Nobody had enough food. Children were coming very often, old people, poor people, on the main road, they knocked, looking for food" (135). Accompanying these words are Sacco's haunting drawings of starving children, their eyes glazed over, shuffling through the snow, which villagers called the "white death." The ensuing pages of *Safe Area Goražde* record the dangerous and deadly trek made by the villagers as they march through Serb-controlled territory to reach food supplies: the drawings grow darker, dense with cross-hatching that etches the suffering on the faces of the marchers (see fig. 7.6). Many fall by the wayside, left to die. When they finally reach supplies, the amount of food seems paltry in comparison to the suffering and death the group has suffered on their trek: "I'd brought food for my family, for four people

7.6 Sacco's heavy cross-hatching emphasizes the muted depth of this man's suffering. From Joe Sacco's *Safe Area Goražde*.

for 20–25 days," Edin tells Sacco. "But that's only if we ate a little" (143).

In this example and others, Sacco practices the kind of empathic listening aimed at getting as close to the characters' experience as possible. In empathic listening, an idea often associated with the work of Carl Rogers,[4] listeners seek to understand another's experiences, thoughts, and feelings from that other person's point of view. This is the way Sacco listens to Ghassan, a Palestinian man arrested for "security reasons" and subjected to two weeks of torture by Israeli police. In this chapter of *Palestine*, as in so much of his work, Sacco lets Ghassan speak for himself, quoting him extensively from panel to panel: "They tied me tighter than before. I was in a different sort of chair. I had a lot of pain in my back, my shoulders, my knees, my wrists . . . I couldn't lean against the wall" (*Palestine, Book 1*, 108). Accompanying this reported speech are Sacco's minutely detailed drawings of Ghassan, his head covered by a urine-soaked bag, his hands tied behind the chair he slumps in (see fig. 7.7). Sacco listens, it seems to us, empathically, inviting readers to hear

7.7 Sacco's cramped panels echo the process by which torture shrinks a man's world down to the space of his body. From Joe Sacco's *Palestine: A Nation Occupied*.

Ghassan and to inhabit, at least in these panels, his unique point of view.

No matter how empathically we listen, however, the reality is that most of us will never know how Ghassan really felt, and Sacco must both accept and work against this limitation: this is the most Sisyphean, but also most humane, aspect of Sacco's work. The sequence about Ghassan shows Sacco using the comics medium in sophisticated ways to communicate as much as he can of experiences that frequently elude description. In *The Body in Pain*, Elaine Scarry argues that pain actively destroys language, making it an experience of which the person in pain is always "vibrantly certain" but the person hearing about it is always in doubt (4). Pain, in other words, is one of the greatest challenges to the model of empathic listening described above, the place where what Scarry has elsewhere called "the difficulty of imagining other people" becomes nearly insurmountable. And torture, Scarry claims, seizes on this language-destroying, imagination-defying aspect of pain to "unmake" the world before the eyes of those tortured, leaving them sealed into the terrifyingly private experience of pain that is caused by another person but seems to emanate from their own bodies. From the beginning, Sacco's chapter about Ghassan is concerned with this very same phenomenon of how torture imprisons the victim within his or her own body, what Scarry calls "the prisoner's steadily shrinking ground" (36). Sacco traces the shrinking ground of the torture victim, who is both strangely close to and completely removed from the world he or she once inhabited: "On the surface streets: traffic, couples in love, falafel-to-go, tourists in jogging suits licking stamps for postcards. . . . And over the wall behind closed doors: other things, people strapped to chairs, sleep deprivation, the smell of piss . . ." (*Palestine, Book 1*, 102). On the page, the images echo this movement, this coming to the body's ground zero. As Ghassan recounts his long confinement, interrupted by violent interrogation sessions, the panels on the page shrink: at the beginning of his story, when he is arrested, they are large enough that only three panels fit on one page (103), while by the end of his confinement, there are twenty panels to a page, laid out in a tight grid (107–12). The panels are so small that frequently the only piece of the world they can depict is Ghassan's body on a stool or a cot. Sacco's drawings thus come to illustrate the aspect of torture that Scarry calls "a destruction experienced spatially as either the contraction of the universe down to the immediate vicinity of the body or as the body swelling to fill the entire universe" (35). The tortured person becomes "a colossal body with no voice" while the torturer (who in Sacco's tiny panels often appears in fragments only: a hand, or a head and part of a shoulder; *Palestine, Book 1*, 110) becomes "a colossal voice . . . with no body" (Scarry 57). Working this experience out visually on the physicality of the drawn and printed page and listening empathically to the voice of the tortured Ghassan, Sacco works to restore voice where there was none as well as to provide a material record of torture that exists outside the privacy of the body.

Toward Listening Rhetorically

Listening and drawing empathically, Sacco also traces, sometimes self-consciously and sometimes not, the limits of his listening. He often falls short of what Ratcliffe identifies as "rhetorical listening,"[5] which calls for pairing empathetic listening with radical self-critique to achieve what Ratcliffe, echoing Jacqueline Jones Royster, terms "codes for cross-cultural conduct" (17). In short, rhetorical listening asks the listener not only to understand another person's perspective but to understand the belief system, the "terministic screen," to use Kenneth Burke's phrase, that guides the listener's understanding—and to work just as hard at understanding and interrogating his or her own terministic screens. As we've shown earlier in this chapter, one of Sacco's signature moves is self-scrutiny. Though he would not use Ratcliffe's or Burke's terms, it is clear that he seeks to create and use "codes for cross-cultural conduct" (with culture defined here not only as American, Muslim, or Serb but as the "cultures" formed among journalists, refugees, people living under occupation, and others) even as he realizes his failures in this regard.

In *Palestine*, Sacco attempts to practice what Sonja K. Foss and Cindy L. Griffin dub "invitational rhetoric," expending great effort to inhabit the perspective of the Palestinians, listening to their stories, and trying to take on the terministic screens that shape their lived experience, constant fear, and simmering anger. Toward the end of the series, however, in a chapter called "Through Other Eyes," Sacco finds himself serving as an impromptu guide to two "young Tel Aviv ladies" on a trip through Jerusalem's Old City. "I know my Jerusalem!" says Sacco. Later, as Sacco guides the women toward the Western Wall, he drops his listening stance and tells them he is collecting stories about the Palestinians and their trials. "Shouldn't you be seeing OUR side of the story, too?" one of the women asks, and Sacco immediately sees the biases that have become part of his listening, understanding that his invitation has been both limited and limiting: "It occurs to me that I have seen the Israelis, but through Palestinian eyes—that Israelis were mainly soldiers and settlers to me now, too . . ." (256). Perhaps to reverse this trend—and in spite of the Israeli women's fears—Sacco talks one of them into walking through the historic Arab market. Nothing will happen to them, he says: "This'll take 15 minutes." The panels that follow take Sacco and his companion through the Arab market's crowded streets, full of vendors hawking their wares. Then, in a stunning full-page panel, Sacco creates a collage of thumbnail portraits of himself as he begins to experience the market through other—Israeli—eyes (see fig. 7.8). Increasingly panicked, Sacco hurries through the market in a full sweat, worrying over passing glances and his own appearance. As he emerges with his companion from the market, thoroughly chagrined, he can only say, "See, we made it: that wasn't THAT bad, was it?" (259). In other words, Sacco has lost control over his terministic screen, lost the careful balance of his characteristic self-criticism and sensitivity to others' perspectives: he has traveled all the way from dismissing the Israeli women's perspective to becoming, over the course of "15 minutes," captive to what he clearly thinks are the most irrational elements of their viewpoint, the very fears he had hoped to dispel. What we see here is Sacco caught between two seemingly incommensurable terministic screens, trying and failing—just as so many of the region's political compromises have failed—to find a critical stance between or outside of them.[6]

7.8 Sacco loses his own perspective in one of Jerusalem's Arab markets. From Joe Sacco's *Palestine: In the Gaza Strip.*

In the end, however, we judge Sacco not against some ideal model of the listener, especially since he would be the first to point out the ways in which he falls short. Rather, we have tried to unpack the complexities of the four types of listening we see in his work and to provide a rhetorical reading of how listening functions in Sacco's comics journalism. The comic we ultimately read is a record not only of listening but also of a series of translations: from one human being to another, from other languages into English, from oral testimony and reference photographs into the language of comics. In focusing on the ethical, political, and journalistic concerns that shape and haunt Sacco's method, we have only begun to touch on the choices he makes in translating the record of his listening into the text, lines, and spaces of the page. And while we are aware of the gaps and fissures that accompany such choices and the constant tension accompanying every attempt to listen well, we admire Sacco's tenacity and his decision to go on looking for and listening to— and reporting—not an absolutist truth-with-a-capital-T but the truth as *he* can best apprehend it. As he says in "Some Reflections on Palestine," "My idea was not to present an objective book, but an honest one" (*Palestine: The Special Edition* ix). As we have shown, any attempt at honest reporting will necessarily draw on a panoply of ways of listening.

Notes

1. Examples of Sacco's synesthesia abound in his work. See, for example, the chapter "Moderate Pressure, Part 2" in *Palestine*, in Sacco's report on the experience of Ghassan, discussed below. In this section, the drawings show Sacco "listening" with his eyes while using other senses, particularly smell, to allow him to hear Ghassan's full story (*Palestine, Book 1*, 102–13). Ghassan himself, in fact, experiences a similar synesthesia in his cell, with a hood thrown over his head: "I *felt* I was in a yard with a corrugated zinc roof," he remembers; "I could *feel* other people there" (106, emphasis added).

2. As Sacco has become a more experienced and controlled comics journalist, his drawing style has become steadily more conservative. We are frequently torn between respect for his more nuanced reporting and regret for the loss of vibrancy, even an appropriate sort of manic energy, in his art.

3. Many thanks to our colleague Laurie Stapleton for sharing her insightful and provocative dissertation work on empathic, rhetorical, and present listening.

4. In *A Way of Being*, Rogers describes the kind of therapeutic listening in which the listener sets aside personal perspectives and views so as "to enter another's world without prejudice" (143).

5. Ratcliffe's rhetorical listening is related to what Wayne Booth, in *The Rhetoric of Rhetoric*, calls "Listening-Rhetoric," which he defines as the kind of listening in which "I am not just seeking a truce; I want to pursue the truth behind our differences" (46). In this kind of listening, Booth says, "both sides

join in a trusting dispute, determined to listen to the opponent's arguments, while persuading the opponent to listen in exchange. Each side attempts to think about the arguments presented by the other side. . . . Both sides are pursuing not just a victory but a new reality, a new agreement about what is real" (46–47). While Sacco certainly desires "to pursue the truth behind . . . differences," his kind of reporterly listening doesn't fit easily into Booth's argumentative model.

6. In these Tel Aviv interactions, Sacco is painfully aware of his own failures at listening rhetorically. Perhaps this encounter with the Israeli women is so memorable, so pronounced, because it is one of the very few occasions during which Sacco achieves some measure of what Burke would call "consubstantiality" with women. Indeed, in our study of his work, we have found that his rhetorical listening is often strongly gendered: men, such as Edin, Riki and Neven, emerge from the scenes of Sacco's listening as complex, highly-nuanced individuals, whereas women are often grouped together, as in the ironically designated "Silly Girls" who appear in a series of chapters in *Safe Area Goražde*. In this and other cases, Sacco seems limited in his capacity to inhabit the experiences and spaces of women, as he is so able to do with his male subjects.

Works Cited

Booth, Wayne. *The Rhetoric of Rhetoric: The Quest for Effective Communication*. Oxford: Blackwell, 2004. Print.

Burke, Kenneth. "Terministic Screens." *Language as Symbolic Action*. Berkeley: U of California P, 1966. 44–62. Print.

Foss, Sonja K., and Cindy L. Griffin. "Beyond Persuasion: A Proposal for an Invitational Rhetoric." *Communication Monographs* 62 (Mar. 1995): 2–18. Print.

Ratcliffe, Krista. *Rhetorical Listening: Identification, Gender, Whiteness*. Carbondale: Southern Illinois UP, 2005. Print.

Rogers, Carl. *A Way of Being*. New York: Houghton Mifflin, 1980. Print.

Royster, Jacqueline Jones. "When the First Voice You Hear Is Not Your Own." *CCC* 47 (1994): 29–40. Print.

Sacco, Joe. *The Fixer: A Story from Sarajevo*. London: Jonathan Cape, 2004. Print.

———. *Footnotes in Gaza*. New York: Metropolitan/Henry Holt, 2009. Print.

———. *Notes from a Defeatist*. Seattle: Fantagraphics, 2003. Print.

———. *Palestine: A Nation Occupied (Book 1)*. Seattle: Fantagraphics, 1993. Print.

———. *Palestine: In the Gaza Strip (Book 2)*. Seattle: Fantagraphics, 1996. Print.

———. *Palestine: The Special Edition*. Seattle: Fantagraphics, 2007. Print.

———. *Safe Area Goražde: The War in Eastern Bosnia, 1992–95*. Seattle: Fantagraphics, 2000. Print.

———. "Trauma on Loan." Guardian (weekend mag. supp.), Jan. 21, 2006. Print.

Scarry, Elaine. *The Body in Pain: The Making and Unmaking of the World*. Oxford: Oxford UP, 1987. Print.

The Ideology of African Philosophy: The Silences and Possibilities of African Rhetorical Knowledge

Omedi Ochieng

> Salt comes from the north, gold from the south, and silver from the country of the white men, but the word of God and the treasures of wisdom are only to be found in Timbuctoo.
>
> —Sudanese proverb, quoted in Felix
> Dubois, *Timbuctoo the Mysterious*

Odera Oruka's sage philosophy project arguably signaled the boldest intervention in the debate over the existence and boundaries of African philosophy. In research that spanned over two decades, Oruka set out to "search for and expose traditional African sages (men and women) who have the capacity for critical, philosophical thinking" (Oruka, *Trends* 27). The main purpose of the project, he argued, was to "disprove the well-known claim that real philosophical thought had no place in traditional Africa," a claim Oruka took to imply that "any existence of philosophy in modern Africa is due wholly to the introduction of Western thought and culture" (52). Contrary to the notion that African philosophy was "basically intuitive, mystical and counter- or extra-rationalistic," in contrast to European philosophy that was alleged to be marked by "critical and rigorous analysis, . . . logical explanation and synthesis" (13), Oruka argued that his finding of sages whose "outlook and cultural well-being remain[ed] basically that of traditional rural Africa" was proof that philosophy was practiced in Africa prior to the European colonization of the continent (51). The upshot, Oruka concluded, was that philosophy "in the strict sense" (14)—which he argued is "critical," "reflective," "individualistic," and "dialectical"— exists in Africa.

In this critical study of Oruka's project, I argue that the sage philosophy project is articulated and emerges from two intimately related forms of knowledge whose condition of possibility emerge from two types of "silences." The first form of knowledge is *forensic knowledge*. This knowledge, I contend, emerges from the attempts of African philosophers in the academy to legitimate their own knowledge by contrasting it with the beliefs of Africans outside the academy. I argue that these attempts at legitimation are parasitic on the colonial and neocolonial silencing of African knowledge by the "Western" academy. Such silencing is by no means restricted to African knowledges. LuMing Mao has documented similar strategies of silencing in relation to Chinese rhetoric (216). The second form of knowledge I discuss is *sapiential knowledge*. This form of knowledge is a reference to the silenced, fugitive, secret, and/or conspiratorial knowledges of oppressed and exploited Africans who have been ruled out of consideration and delegitimized by dominant institutions of knowledge production. Vorris Nunley has revealed that such knowledges are emergent in public spheres that are dismissed as marginal or unimportant, such as beauty shops, barber shops, and women's clubs (221).

The articulation of these two forms of knowledge, I argue, indicates that epistemology is rhetorical. This claim is true insofar as a consideration of forensic and sapiential knowledge draws attention to articulations of what counts as knowledge and who counts as legitimate knowledge makers. Such a view of knowledge as embedded in power relations may offer an outline for a praxis oriented to engaging the embodied, institutional, and global structures that determine the division of knowledge and labor. This study thus seeks to extend the work of Cheryl Glenn in excavating the institutional dynamics that determine "who speaks, who remains silent, who listens, and what those listeners can do" (23).

Literacy and the African Public

A mapping of the contours of the terms of debate is in order here. Belgian anthropologist Placide Tempels posited that the distinction between

African philosophy and Western philosophy was based on "race." African philosophers based in the newly independent African countries vigorously contested this claim. Led by the Beninois philosopher Paulin Hountondji, arguably the most implacable critic of Tempels and his "ethnophilosophy" followers, they derisively described as *ethnophilosophy* the notion that African philosophy consisted of communal beliefs, little more than a grab bag of stories, proverbs, poems, and maxims packaged as philosophy. According to Hountondji (whose proffered conception of true philosophy draws heavily from the arguments of his teacher and mentor, French Marxist Louis Althusser), insofar as there is a distinction between "European" and "African" philosophy, that distinction pivots on "literacy": the ability to read and write endowed Europeans with a "theoretical philosophy" against African "popular ideology" or "spontaneous philosophy" (Hountondji 47–48). Other African philosophers such as Kwasi Wiredu, V. Y. Mudimbe, and Kwame Anthony Appiah would follow Hountondji in arguing that African philosophy had been so far unable to develop because of the lack of literacy among Africans. Odera Oruka was the one African philosopher in the academy whose philosophy was arguably furthest from the other professional philosophers. Like other African philosophers in the university, he opposed the ethnophilosophers, but unlike them he made a case for the existence of a ratiocinative thought in traditional Africa.

The claim that writing leads to superior cognitive abilities is now a well-established myth in the European American academy. As Ruth Finnegan has demonstrated, there are widespread claims that "literacy" is "responsible for just about all the 'goods' of modern Western civilization" (5). Harvey Graff draws attention to the breathtakingly "daunting number of cognitive, affective, behavioral, and attitudinal effects" made on behalf of literacy (13–14). Finnegan draws attention to other miracles said to have been birthed by literacy, including "'rationality,' abstract thought, sophisticated literary expression, individual self-consciousness, or the growth of science" (5). Roy Harris, a literacy enthusiast, argues confidently that "the writing revolution was not merely of political and economic significance. The autonomous text was naturally suited to become the basis not only of law but of education and literature" (qtd. in Finnegan 6). Walter J. Ong goes further, arguing that writing fundamentally restructured the mental architecture of the brain (78).

Literacy as Cultural Capital

I would argue that the claims to "literacy" name a symptomatic relationship of the institution of the African university to other forms of knowledge. The African university, as it were, wants to claim itself as the only site of official knowledge, which it is concerned to contrast with other knowledges, specifically the wisdom or sapiential knowledges that exist in the margins of officialdom. It is this claim to officialdom that renders African philosophical knowledge forensic. This relationship is named symptomatically by African scholars in the "literacy" versus "illiteracy" debate, which they posit transcendentally, following the writings of scholars such as Jack Goody. But, as John Guillory has aptly noted, literacy is "not simply the capacity to read but . . . the *systematic regulation of reading and writing*, a complex social phenomenon corresponding to the following set of questions: Who reads? What do they read? How do they read? In what social and institutional circumstances? Who writes? In what social and institutional contexts? For whom?" (18).

Conceived in this manner, the definition and assessment of literacy is grounded in particular institutional sites—in this context, in the institution of the school. African philosophers such as Hountondji and Appiah who fetishize "literacy," deeming it the ladder to "modernity," insulate themselves from coming to terms with the institutional processes of credentialing and legitimizing that authorize them as literate vis-à-vis those they deem illiterate. In other words, their attempts to legitimize African philosophy is also an attempt to legitimize their own practices as teachers of African philosophy, a claim to what Pierre Bourdieu has described as cultural capital (247).

Hountondji's definition of African philosophy as much as points to the self-referential, solipsistic process that structures the appropriation and accumulation of cultural capital—in this case, to African philosophy as cultural capital. According to Hountondji, African philosophy is "the set of texts written by Africans themselves and described as philosophical by their authors and themselves" (33). This statement aptly describes the power to name and claim a form of cultural capital—philosophy—allowed an author with the credentials Hountondji possesses. But in much the same way that his mentor Althusser brackets science from ideology, Hountondji refuses to recognize that insofar as he can name and claim his work as "philosophy," a claim to cultural capital, this emerges from a context of power relations endowed him by the institutional apparatus of credentialing that is the university.

The upshot is his Althusserian distinction between "theoretical" philosophy and "spontaneous" philosophy, which symptomatically—in an age distinguished by its fetishization of the natural sciences and mathematics—falls back on the technical expertise claimed by the chemist, the physicist, and the mathematician to legitimize philosophy:

> African philosophical literature . . . rests on a confusion: the confusion between the popular (ideological) use and the strict (theoretical) use of the word "philosophy." According to the first meaning, philosophy is any kind of wisdom, individual or collective, any set of these principles presenting some degree of coherence and intended to govern the daily practice of a man or a people. In this vulgar sense of the word, everyone is naturally a philosopher, and so is every society. But in the stricter sense of the word, one is no more spontaneously a philosopher than one is spontaneously a chemist, a physicist or a mathematician. (Hountondji 47)

The Althusserian fetishization of "science" forgets its own *contextual* conditions of possibility.

But if the transcendental conceptualization of "literacy" as special knowledge sanctions a self-legitimation of African philosophers such as Hountondji, Oruka's own sage philosophy, which rejects claims that "literacy" is a prerequisite for the existence of philosophy, is not completely unproblematic either. Oruka thinks it sufficient therefore to interview sages whose statements he then exhibits as proof of the existence of African philosophy. But in not examining the question of "literacy" as an institutional ideology—that is, not just consisting of reading and writing but a whole gamut of verbal and nonverbal performances of legitimation, credentialing, and authority—Oruka fails to break in any significant way with the presuppositions of "philosophy," instead reifying it on another register.

His debate with Nigerian philosopher Peter O. Bodunrin is especially telling. Bodunrin questioned Oruka's claim that his interviews represented the thoughts of the sages. According to Bodunrin, "The product of the joint inquiry of the traditional sage and the trained philosopher is a new phenomenon. Both inevitably enter the dialogue with certain presuppositions. What they come out with is a new creation out of their reflections on the beliefs previously held by them" (168). Bodunrin rejects Oruka's claim that "sage philosophy" represents a return to how philosophy was conducted in ancient Greece: "Socrates' interlocutors, if Plato's dialogues have any verisimilitude, are his intellectual peers. Among them were etymologists like Euthyphro . . . after whom Plato named the *Euthyphro*, renowned orators like Gorgias . . . and mathematicians like Theactetus" (168).

Bodunrin's objection to "sage philosophy," which he believes is a straightforward question of qualification, is actually one of "literacy": in what way can Oruka's sages be said to be qualified? After all, Bodunrin appears to say, they are not as intellectually gifted as the "classical" Greek philosophers. But rather than challenge the enthymeme that gives force to Bodunrin's objection, which invokes the fetish of ancient Greece as cultural capital, Oruka's response is telling: "They [the sages] do not need to be the equal of Plato, for even in ancient Greece, there was only one Plato and one Socrates while there were a host of many other much less profound thinkers who deserve to be called philosophers." And he adds: "Plato as a philosopher was a genius of the first rank" (Oruka, "Sage" 65). History shows, Oruka argues, that most philosophers "come to create new ideas or style of philosophy only as a result of responding to the ideas or works of some other philosophers or persons" (Oruka, *Sage* 51). Moreover, he continues,

> The trained philosopher, interviewing the sage, plays the role of philosophical provocation. The outcome no less belongs to the sage than the thoughts of professional philosophers, reacting to others, belongs to them. It is a fact that without philosophical debates, conferences, and rivals, many philosophers including even the most prolific of them would remain reproductive. (51–52)

It is significant that Oruka does not confront the question of "literacy" or qualification, opting here for outright denial, defensively stating that the sages did not have to be Plato's equal. Instead he claims that philosophers create new ideas by responding to the work of others (an odd admission for Oruka to make, given that it contradicts his insistence that "true philosophy" is strictly individualistic), and he insists that the thought of the sages "belongs" to the sages (the word "belonging" revealing the prized item of cultural capital, *ownership*). But the eventual effect is only to reify, not question, the legitimacy of this seemingly acontextual, ahistorical cultural capital.

But Oruka has to work hard to prove that his sages are "literate." For example, aware that "school philosophy" demands a performance, even a language, of "logic," conceived narrowly as propositional statements, he invokes narration as a means of reasoning, once again tellingly reaching to the ancient Greeks for legitimation:

> There is a tendency to treat a Greek sage such as Heraclitus as a philosopher but to deny the label to an African sage such as Mbuya Akoko. The African sage is seen as a mere peasant storyteller. Philosophy may indeed employ stories, poetry or oracles. Indeed, Heraclitus, the dialectician, and Parmenides, the founder of abstract logic in the West, expressed their philosophies using oracular epigram, epic poem and storytelling. (Oruka, *Sage* 8)

F. Ochieng-Odhiambo has argued that Oruka's thought underwent an evolution from an uncompromising hostility to ethnophilosophy, where his favored term for describing his project was "philosophic sagacity," to a much more accommodating stance, where he preferred using the term "sage philosophy" to describe his project. Ochieng-Odhiambo suggests that Oruka evolved in the face of criticism that the sages whom he proffered as exemplars of philosophic sages "proved only that there were sages, but not necessarily philosophical ones" (29). I am inclined to go further than Ochieng-Odhiambo in arguing that this was more than an evolution in Oruka's thought: it was, rather, symptomatic of his attempts to assimilate sage philosophers into the "literacy" of the school without having to confront the institutional mechanisms that established this literacy in the first place.

There arise the antinomies that bedevil Oruka's thought. Oruka's refusal to engage with the power of his institutional location only condemns him to invoke it without accounting for it. Thus he states, concerning the process that goes into the selection of the sages: "The best judge [of who qualifies as a sage] must be the community from which the person hails. The researcher[, however,] must follow up the guidance of the community and be capable of assessing those alleged to be sages and dismissing others" (qtd. in Masolo 237). Dismas A. Masolo is therefore correct when he notes, "So, after all, it is the professional practitioner who produces the sage according to her/his institutionalized definitions of the categories of knowledge" (237)—in other words, Oruka himself.

It is therefore not surprising, given his failure to critique it at the institution of the university, that the forensic versus sapiential divide is reinstated by Oruka in another register. Echoing Hountondji's distinction of "spontaneous philosophy" versus "*theoria*," Oruka is anxious to separate what he calls "popular wisdom" from "didactic wisdom" (Oruka, *Sage* 57). Based on this distinction between popular and didactic wisdom, he argues that there are two types of sages:

> Findings in Kenya show that there are two main divisions of sage philosophy. One is that of the sage whose thought, though well informed and educative, fails to go beyond the celebrated folk-wisdom. Such a sage may not have the ability or inclination to apply his own independent critical objection to folk beliefs. He is, therefore, a folk sage in contrast to the second type of sage, the philosophic sage. The former is a master of popular wisdom while the latter is an expert in didactic wisdom. (34)

Thus, what would have seemed to be a break with the institutional ideology of the university—its absolutistic insistence on transcendence—is now reaffirmed by Oruka.

Universities as Institutional Spaces for the Production of Cultural Capital

The reasons for this reification have been spelled out by Guillory in a different context—one, however, that holds a cautionary lesson in *this* context. According to Guillory, the abstraction of "oral literatures" from their contexts for the purposes of exhibition as "non-Western" works without accounting for the school as an institution of mediation in the distribution of cultural capital only serves to absorb these works to the interests of a coterie, notwithstanding these oral literatures' claim to be "inherently subversive":

> When the condition of oral production is on the other hand ignored in the context of interpreting or evaluating these works (by treating oral works as though they were other written works), the real difference between school culture and the culture of a culture which gives rise to works disappears from view. By suppressing the context of a cultural work's production and consumption, the school produces the illusion that "our" culture (or the culture of the "other") is transmitted simply by contact with the works themselves. (43)

The upshot of this erasure is the absorption of the works of the sages toward the end of constituting the cultural capital of the university.

I would argue, therefore, pace Masolo, that the four trends outlined in African philosophy by Odera Oruka—ethnophilosophy, nationalist-ideological philosophy, the professional philosopher, and sage philosophy—are not so much useful as analytical constructs, as Oruka believes, but rather ought to be seen as symptomatic of the contestation within which the "sage philosophy" project was articulated and performed. Masolo has argued, citing the Foucauldian Mudimbe, that "in the wake of the emphasis of plurality of *epistemes* as separate fields of forms of reflection, the idea of sage philosophy becomes an interesting and important channel for identifying, understanding and articulating the philosophical task through a reconciliation of different epistemic fields" (237).

When, however, conceived *institutionally* rather than as forms of reflection—for as has been shown, "sage philosophy" can be attributed to Oruka's "sages" only by ignoring Oruka's institution altogether—the "four trends" name the conflict *within* the institution of Oruka's university between a dominant "Western" philosophy striving to silence "African" philosophy and Oruka's own attempts to gain recognition of his philosophy by silencing sapiential forms of knowledge. For example, questions of legitimation were clearly at stake when he commenced on his "sage philosophy" project. Oruka had joined the Department of Philosophy and Religious Studies at the University of Nairobi in 1970 as a "special lecturer." The odds stacked against him—as a knower—and against his research program in philosophy were immediately apparent.

First, the head of the department, British Anglican bishop and theologian Stephen Neill, believed that Africans were incapable of philosophizing, ostensibly because they were congenitally illogical (Masolo 233). This must have posed a formidable challenge to Oruka, who not only was prevented from teaching logic but also believed that philosophy was distinct from religion and wanted a separate department of philosophy.

Second, the intellectual zeitgeist at the University of Nairobi was overwhelmingly in favor of "ethnophilosophy," that is, the notion that African forms of thinking were grounded in collective myths (Masolo 233). This idea not only was flattering to nationalists interested in portraying "blacks" as the polar opposite of the hated "white colonialists" but also was congenial to "white" racialists at the University of Nairobi such as Neill who had always believed in this notion anyway.

Third, there were questions of personal-professional legitimation at stake. Oruka joined the department as a special lecturer and thus was not in a regular faculty position. He was also only twenty-six years old. These factors underscore the struggle for legitimation that Oruka did not articulate and account for as part of his "sage philosophy" project. The point here is not that Oruka's need to legitimate "sage philosophy" in any way vitiates his project. His rejection of Neill's racialist position is, for example, unimpeachable. The point is, rather, that an engagement with the contested field from which "sage philosophy" emerged would have allowed for a historical perspective on its significance and, ultimately, opened up space for a more informed definition of its *telos*.

African philosophers have generally occluded a critical engagement with the university institution that is the locus of their intellectual work as it has been constituted *in relation to* other more powerful university institutions (for example, those located in imperial formations of capital), other institutions in their own nationalities (for example, the state), and other cultural and economic institutions (for example, popular culture and the market). Because these relationships are not conceived historically, an exploration of their nature is foreclosed; instead, they emerge only symptomatically in the debates that have defined African philosophy: in the hypostatization of "the West" and "Africa" (in the form of debates over what African philosophy is) and in the debates over "literacy" versus "illiteracy" (that is, whether philosophy can exist in cultures labeled "oral"). By taking as their premise and thematic a metaphysically conceived "West" and an "Africa" seen through romantic lenses, the question of institutional locus is elided in favor of monolithic entities. Yet is clear that the fact that African philosophers feel compelled to locate themselves in relation to what they call "the West" is an indication of their occupation of *some* institutional locus that has to take into account its subordination to a more powerful center. Whether in the form of rejection, therefore, as in John Mbiti's notion of an ontologically Different Africa, or in the form of adulation, as in Bodunrin's celebration of "the West," both positions symptomatically indicate a positioning for *recognition* vis-à-vis the powerful institutional university of imperial capital.

It is, however, telling that the overwhelming anxiety of African philosophers has focused on recognition. Oruka's sage philosophy project, premised on proving the existence of "indigenous" African philosophers, is indicative of this anxiety. But it is captured as well in Appiah's pithy comment: "The Western emperor has ordered the natives to exchange their robes for trousers: their act of defiance is to insist on tailoring them from homespun material" (60).

The failure of African philosophers to critique their institutional locus is thus revelatory of not only their silenced position vis-à-vis "Western" philosophy but also of their silencing of other forms of knowledge. Because their failure to engage the privileged institution of the university stems primarily from a debilitating ahistoricity, it ensures that many of the claims that African philosophers have made to legitimate African philosophy reiterate the same racialist motifs that marked European dismissals of African philosophy. Another limitation of the failure to engage their institutional locus is that it leads to a failure to examine the overwhelmingly economic determinants that may account for much of the devastation and precariousness of the African university (and thus the weakness of African philosophy as an intellectual, cultural, and social force).

Listening as Critique, Engagement, Solidarity, and Practice

The analysis above invites thought on its implications for conceptualizations of silence and listening in particular and of "African philosophy" in general. The first implication is that African philosophy ought to articulate a *critical program*. I would hold with Guillory, speaking here in a different context about the American literary canon but nevertheless striking a note, that African scholars ought to heed, that "a rather different pedagogy, one that emphasizes historical contextualization, would at the very least inhibit the assimilation of cultural works to the agenda of constituting a national culture, or the Western culture which is its ideological support" (43). Thus, there is need for a critique of the metaphysical and idealist presuppositions—the *topos* of an essential "West" versus transcendent "Africa"; the fetishization of "literacy"—that have frozen African philosophical debate in ideological torpor. Such a critique would lead to an accounting for the political, economic, and cultural structures that are the condition of possibility for "African philosophy." It would articulate the symbolic and material violence that has gone into the construction of "Western" and "African" philosophy, specifically the violent exploitation and oppression of African polities by ruling classes of imperial capital.

Specific areas of investigation can be ventured but not elaborated here. A specific task of African philosophy, should such a critical contextual critique be carried out, is that of engaging and remapping the educational philosophies of African institutions. Such philosophies would identify the contextual needs in Africa and the particular ways of radically confronting contextual solutions to these needs, including of course the obstacles that stand in the way of solutions and the "unintended aftershocks" that may ripple from suggested solutions. Certainly some areas of consideration would be poverty, health pandemics, violence, and the destruction of educational and socialization institutions; the ideologies that go into the constitution of these scourges (capitalism, racism, ethnic prejudices, sexism); and the alternatives to them (participatory and egalitarian economics, pacifism, critical cultural pluralisms, and feminism).

The articulated troika of capitalism, racism, and sexism is illustrated grotesquely in the area of health, to take an example, where the gutting of rudimentary services such as hospitals and rural dispensaries by the African ruling classes and the G8 economic oligarchy has led to the horrific deaths of millions of the poor, while other barely surviving millions are unable to afford medicines because of the extortionist prices set by multinational pharmaceutical industries. And even as imperial formations—such as the U.S. ruling class—work tirelessly to cultivate the false consciousness of their populace by making facile "promises" of "aid" (Reynolds), they ruthlessly crush attempts to manufacture generic drugs in the stricken countries, all in the name of intellectual property rights (Bwomezi).

These blatant injustices should be articulated with more subtle inquiries into the military-medical connections that drive much research in viral infections, such as Ebola (Starr), and the use of the poor in Africa as guinea pigs (Solomon). This horrific callousness toward Africans finds ideological legitimation as well, for example in the claim advanced by the then U.S. AIDS coordination administrator to the effect that because Africans have no sense of time, they were unlikely to follow the regimen required for the taking of anti-retroviral medicines. The pernicious falsehood of this statement (research subsequently revealed that Africans put on the regimen were more faithful to the regimen than patients in the United States [McNeil]) is not easily dismissed in the context of African philosophy as more of the same scapegoating of African victims, though such indeed it was. What ought to give African philosophers pause, however, is how this statement reprises ethnophilosopher Mbiti's claim that Africans have neither a sense of the past nor of the future (Oruka,

Trends 8). Be that as it may, such are the ideologies that legitimate the continued withholding of drugs from poor patients. Instead, what gets yelps of indignation, also critiqued here as atrocious, are the claims of South African president Thabo Mbeki that HIV may not be the cause of AIDS, which was thus a reason for the withholding of anti-retrovirals from patients. Mbeki's stance is despicable, for it lacks not only pragmatism (by the time his point was made, millions had already perished) but also any indication of solidarity with AIDS patients. It should therefore be concertedly critiqued as part of the power play that makes pawns of poor patients in Africa. Nevertheless, avowals that Mbeki's stance represents the "African suspicion of Western medicine" are simplistic and vulgarly ethnocentric. A critical stance toward the ideological positions here, even such "basic" measures as the number of AIDS victims in Africa—which, contrary to the popular adage, do not speak for themselves—should be invitations to investigation, not calls for the reassertion of "Western supremacy" or "African particularism."

The second implication for the above analysis is that it calls African philosophy to an openness to *pluralism*. African professional philosophers ought to engage in a self-reflexive critique of their practice vis-à-vis knowledges that they have too easily dismissed as "spontaneous," "popular," or "illiterate," stances that have also underwritten class, gender, racial, and ethnic violence. Such critique would then allow for considered articulations of different knowledges and the "literacies" that they demand—forensic versus sapiential. Some concrete contemporary issues come to mind.

Take, for example, the "informal" sector, which provides much of the utilities, services, employment, and subsistence desperately needed by many of Africa's poor. By and large, African governments pay lip service to this sector, such as the Kenyan government's sessional paper on this area. These informal industries, such as Kenya's Jua Kali industries, have barely managed to survive in the face of Washington's free market fundamentalism that demanded unrestricted access to African markets and, when it got its way, launched a massive campaign of dumping its semifunctioning, used, and tattered exports onto these markets. Meanwhile, the almost complete collapse of "polytechnics"—that is, schools (even though they were, in the main, elitist) that provided a modicum of training in technology, arts, and crafts—also went some way in damaging "informal" industries. Eventually, however, there would be need to critique how "polytechnic" training was grounded on the colonial notion that Africans are capable only of psychomotor skills.

I envision such a task as also actively engendering a critical pedagogy of the knowledges of the poor and the literacies that they perform. For example, Colin Tudge has drawn attention to the racist contempt for "traditional farming" methods that has been used to legitimize the notion of Genetically Modified Food as a panacea to the famines ravaging Africa. Tudge points out how effective, and environmentally friendly, particular "traditional" farming methods have been and reveals the vested capitalist profits that have driven the aggressive marketing of Genetically Modified Food. Other pertinent issues would nevertheless also have to be taken into consideration, such as land tenure issues. Similarly, Sue Mayer has critiqued the British establishment's scientism that contemptuously rides roughshod over thoughtful objections to Genetically Modified Food. Such critiques need not imply a fetishization of forms of "knowledge" considered "traditional." Indeed, a critical contextual epistemology involves precisely a critique of this valorization. It is cognizant and critical, for example, of the invocation of "indigenous knowledges" by powerful elites under various monikers, from the "African socialism" advanced in the high noon of nationalist fervor by the African bourgeoisie to consolidate their hold on power to more contemporary versions of "Hindu Civilization" propounded by the right-wing Hindutva in India or the "Asian values" flag-waving.

Third, African philosophy must be oriented toward praxis. A critical stance means articulating engagements and solidarity with the exploited and involves critical dialogues that would seek nonviolent resistances to the expropriation and conquest of these knowledges, whether by imperial formations through multinational patenting or by local elites in the name of "indigenous knowledges" (a critique of intellectual property rights must be articulated with stopping the legitimation of the continuing confiscation of rights under the World Trade Organization and Trade-Related Aspects of Intellectual Property Rights regimes).

The upshot of these critical-contextual inquiries would be aimed toward the cultivation of more robust, ethical forms of agency. Such agency must begin with an active listening to forms of knowledge that lack official sanction. It would articulate struggles for recognition with those of distribution (Fraser and Honneth).

Works Cited

Appiah, Kwame Anthony. *In My Father's House: Africa in the Philosophy of Culture*. New York: Oxford UP, 1993. Print.

Bodunrin, Peter O. "The Question of African Philosophy." Oruka, *Sage Philosophy* 163–77. Print.

Bourdieu, Pierre. "The Forms of Capital." *Handbook for Theory and Research for the Sociology of Education*. Ed. John G. Richardson. Westport, CT: Greenwood P, 1986. 241–58. Print.

Bwomezi, Anne Mugisha. "How US Is Turning AIDS into Big Business." *Monitor*, July 20, 2004. Web. Jan. 4, 2010.

Caffentzis, George. "The World Bank and Education in Africa." Federici, Caffentzis, and Alidou 3–18. Print.

Cooper, Frederick. "Conflict and Connection: Rethinking Colonial African History." *American Historical Review* 99 (1994): 1516–45. Print.

Dubois, Felix. *Timbuctoo the Mysterious*. Ed. and trans. Diana White. New York: Negro Universities, 1969. Print.

Federici, Silvia. "The Recolonization of African Education." Federici, Caffentzis, and Alidou 19–24. Print.

Federici, Silvia, George Caffentzis, and Ousseina Alidou, eds. *A Thousand Flowers: Social Struggles against Structural Adjustment in African Universities*. Trenton, NJ: Africa World, 2000. Print.

Finnegan, Ruth. *Literacy and Orality: Studies in the Technology of Communication*. New York: Basic Blackwell, 1988. Print.

Fraser, Nancy, and Axel Honneth. *Redistribution or Recognition? A Political-Philosophical Exchange*. Trans. Joel Golb, James Ingram, and Christiane Wilke. London: Verso, 2003. Print.

Glenn, Cheryl. *Unspoken: A Rhetoric of Silence*. Carbondale: Southern Illinois UP, 2004. Print.

Goody, Jack, *The Domestication of the Savage Mind*. New York: Cambridge UP, 1977. Print.

Graff, Harvey. "The Legacies of Literacy." *Journal of Communication* 32 (1982): 12–26. Print.

Guillory, John. *Cultural Capital: The Problem of Literary Canon Formation*. Chicago: U of Chicago P, 1993. Print.

Hountondji, Paulin, *African Philosophy: Myth and Reality*. Bloomington: Indiana UP, 1983. Print.

Mao, LuMing. "Studying the Chinese Rhetorical Tradition in the Present: Re-presenting the Native's Point of View." *College English* 69.3 (2007): 216–37. Print.

Masolo, Dismas A. "Decentering the Academy: In Memory of a Friend." *Sagacious Reasoning: Henry Odera Oruka in Memoriam*. Ed. Anke Graness and Kai Kresse. Frankfurt: Peter Lang, 1997. 233–40. Print.

Mayer, Sue, "Blinded by the Light of Technology." *Guardian*, Feb. 20, 2004. Web. Jan. 4, 2010.

Mbiti, John. *African Religions and Philosophy*. South Africa: Heinemann, 1969. Print.

McNeil, Donald, Jr. "Africans Outdo Americans in Following AIDS Therapy." *New York Times*, Sept. 3, 2003. Print.

Nunley, Vorris. "From the Harbor to Da Academic Hood: Hush Harbors and an African American Rhetorical Tradition." *African American Rhetorics: Interdisciplinary Perspectives*. Ed. Ronald Jackson and Elaine Richardson. Carbondale: Southern Illinois UP, 2004. 221–41. Print.

Ochieng-Odhiambo, F. "The Evolution of Sagacity: The Three Stages of Oruka's Philosophy." *Philosophia Africana* 5.1 (2002): 19–32. Print.

Ong, Walter J. *Orality and Literacy: The Technologizing of the Word*. New York: Methuen, 1982. Print.

Oruka, H. Odera. "Sagacity in Development." Oruka, *Sage Philosophy* 57–65.

———, ed. *Sage Philosophy: Indigenous Thinkers and Modern Debate on African Philosophy*. Nairobi, Kenya: African Center for Technology Studies, 1991. Print.

———. "Sage Philosophy: The Basic Questions and Methodology." *Sagacious Reasoning: Henry Odera Oruka in Memoriam*. Ed. Anke Graness and Kai Kresse. Frankfurt: Peter Lang, 1997. 61–67. Print.

———. *Trends in Contemporary African Philosophy*. Nairobi, Kenya: Shirikon, 1990. Print.

Reynolds, Michael, "The Abstinence Gluttons." *Nation*, June 18, 2007. Web. Jan. 4, 2010.

Simpson, Christopher. *Science of Coercion*. New York: Oxford UP, 1994. Print.

Solomon, John. "AIDS Research Chief Altered Safety Report." *Newsday*, Dec. 15, 2004. Web. Jan. 3, 2010.

Starr, Barbara. "Researcher Isolated after Possible Ebola Exposure." *CNN.Com*, Feb. 19, 2004. Web. June 19, 2010.

Tudge, Colin. "Bad for the Poor and Bad for Science." *Guardian*, Feb. 20, 2004. Print.

Finding Democracy in Our Argument Culture:
Listening to Spike Lee's Jazz Funeral on the Levees

Joyce Irene Middleton

> At the end of the film, [Spike] Lee returns to the procession, but, . . .
> in adherence to New Orleans custom, the men are playing the hymn
> up-tempo, with a defiant swing; the Katrina casket has been rudely
> placed on the street, and the men shimmy around it.
>
> —David Denby, "Disasters"

In 1998, Deborah Tannen's book *The Argument Culture: Stopping America's War of Words* found its way into both academic and popular culture. At the time, many of her academic readers found her book neither compelling nor provocative. But in the aftermath of September 11, 2001, a new politically conservative leadership would exploit the dualistic thinking and adversarial language of the culture that she described ("you're either with us or against us"). In today's argument culture, America's multiracial and pluralistic citizens live in a society—a culture of critique—that has been rendered fearful, cynical, tragically misinformed, and politically polarized. In an American discourse that is saturated with so many military metaphors, Tannen cautions us to remember that "words matter" and that "when we think we are using language, language is using us" (14).

Listening has become a major casualty of this war and, perhaps, so has American democracy. This casualty was politically and rhetorically strategic, of course, but new research and further understanding of the actions made by the Federal Communications Commission during the 1990s can help more of today's rhetoric students, teachers, and scholars to align themselves with Tannen's observations on America's growing civil war in the media. Since 1998, two remarkable books on the role of listening and one on the role of silence have appeared, almost simultaneously, in rhetorical studies—Krista Ratcliffe's *Rhetorical Listening: Identification, Gender, Whiteness*, Wayne Booth's *The Rhetoric of Rhetoric: The Quest for Effective Communication*, and Cheryl Glenn's *Unspoken: A Rhetoric of Silence*. These authors help us to affirm that a healthy vision for the future of our pluralistic democracy is present, as always, but we, as a diverse body of citizens, have to collectively choose it.

Building on this research, I argue three interrelated claims in this chapter. First, I contend that Tannen's warning about America's argument culture in the 1990s demonstrates the need for listening as a rhetorical tactic. Second, I maintain that Tannen's description of an argument culture, a culture of critique, helps to explain the American tragedy that followed Hurricane Katrina in 2005. Spike Lee's film on the breaking of the levees in New Orleans will help to illustrate the rhetorical connections between listening and silence. Third, I argue that the aftermath of Hurricane Katrina offers American citizens a renewed, progressive vision for a reconstituted democracy, if we practice strategic and intentional uses of rhetorical listening and silence. These rhetorical acts help to promote critical transformation, intervention, and honest conversations (rather than pointless agonistic debates) about democracy and rhetorical identity in our time.

The Argument Culture One Decade Later

The war metaphors that Tannen observed in the late 1990s are even more commonplace today and magnify their power through rhetorical repetition in the electronic media. Tannen wrote that Americans "talk about almost everything as if it were a war" (13), and since 1998, Americans have been engaged, literally, in four wars and numerous shocking high school and college shootings. What happened to the rhetorical training that might help us to avoid physical violence? After all, rhetoricians like Booth remind us that rhetoric "is our primary resource for *avoiding* violence and building community" (xii). *The Argument Culture* implicitly described the emerging clashes of political identities in the two-party structure of American politics, which is inherently adversarial, and Tannen noted that Americans "seem to be *unlearning*" how democracy can work (103).

The new and varied media outlets that have appeared since the 1990s have bolstered the effects of spurious arguments and have effectively become great sources of misinformation for American citizens, such as the belief that Saddam Hussein was linked to 9/11, or that Barack Obama is a Muslim, or that intelligent design should be taught in public high school science classes, or that abstinence-only sex education programs prevent pregnancies, or that global warming is still debatable, or that college teachers should not be trusted because they are too liberal (Kristol; Mosk).

The uncivil practices in the media illustrate "an increasing meanness of spirit and practice in our public discourse" (Tannen 125). Booth describes this kind of win-rhetoric as rhetrickery, aimed to create "noncommunities in which winner-takes-all" (40). He contrasts this with a listening rhetoric that aims to build trust and communities. But he also admits that both kinds of rhetoric can be effective and persuasive (40). How might the essential acts of rhetorical listening and silence influence this political and educational problem? If misinformation is one of the effects of the argument culture, then perhaps we should ask ourselves what kind of rhetorical listening is going on.

The Importance of Rhetorical Listening in a Pluralistic Democracy

Tannen's primary interests are in linguistics, and so she does not provide detail about the crucial role of historical and classical rhetoric regarding practices of democracy in her book. For this background, I will focus on Ratcliffe's concept of rhetorical listening and the historical thinking about rhetoric and democracy that her rhetorical art suggests. In 2005, when Ratcliffe published her research on the role of listening in rhetorical theory, *Rhetorical Listening* helped to generate waves of new thinking about rhetorical theory and practice, consistent with the way that new scholarship in the re-gendering and re-racing of rhetorical history have broadened our scholarship and teaching in the field (see, for example, Donawerth; Glenn; Logan; Lunsford; Middleton; Morrison; Royster; and Welch).

Importantly, her book gives readers a context for thinking about how to reconceive the role of rhetoric in a pluralistic democratic polis. Ratcliffe's research explores the unacknowledged role of listening in relation to rhetorical theory and offers an intimate description of why that role matters to rhetorical studies. She defines listening as an essential part of rhetoric, especially for "identifications across *commonalities* and *differences*" (33). Listening is central "to conceptualize tactics for negotiating ... troubled identifications" in our rhetorical practices (8), Ratcliffe writes, and these kinds of observations in her definition help to identify some specific rhetorical strategies that are missing in Tannen's research. For example, the concept of listening should give us new, important, and progressive ways to think about a rhetor's audiences. The importance of this concept cannot be understated, since a rhetorical focus helps researchers to create new pluralistic civil discourses and to build unity in a democracy that was originally imagined on the "logic" of reifying differences between people (both in classical Greece as well as in America). Ratcliffe's contribution helps to highlight the central role of rhetoric in any new democracy since the classical period: to forge citizen allegiances, a collective understanding of itself, and a harmony of identity within a society of cultural differences.

The very title of Tannen's book on the "argument culture" found its way, quite easily, into popular culture, the media, rhetoric, and other academic studies. But a title on "listening" would not have been "heard" in the media, according to Ratcliffe's definition of it. Our Western culture, and its disciplinary studies, has inherent disciplinary biases against listening, and Ratcliffe outlines three of them—gender, race, and ocularcentrism—noting that "U.S. culture privileges sight" (22). These biases implicitly inhibit our ability to bring "blurred intersections [of identity] together" (22). Gender or race in rhetorical studies, the first two biases against rhetorical listening that Ratcliffe describes, are probably familiar to most readers, with decades of research to help in rereading rhetorical studies from feminist and racial disciplinary points of view. But Ratcliffe's third bias of "ocularcentrism," grounded in Martin Heidegger's divided *logos*, links her work in rhetoric to a variety of disciplinary debates on Western and non-Western cultural conflicts (22–23; also see McKee). Ratcliffe observes that even in Aristotle's ancient theory of rhetoric, he "never delves into *how* to listen" (20). Perhaps this part of his rhetoric, designed for male elites, was left unnoticed in a less pluralistic view of rhetorical studies. Ratcliffe's inclusion of the ocularcentric bias against listening, implicit in Heidegger's divided logos, points her readers to an important Western bias in studies of rhetorical identity. She writes: "We inhabit a culture where 'saying' has assumed dominance and 'laying' (and, thus, listening) has been displaced" (24).

The implications of Ratcliffe's third Western cultural bias against listening are easily seen—and heard—in Michael Moore's 2002 documentary film, *Bowling for Columbine*. Moore famously asked Marilyn Manson a question about his views on the gun violence at Columbine High School. Manson's ethos and music had been heavily blamed in the media for the tragedy because the murderers had listened to his music just prior to the shootings. For illustration, Moore's scene includes, first, a visual litany of video clips of media citations from a variety of politicians and individuals in the media who all blamed Manson for the tragedy. But then Moore asked Manson what he would *say* to the kids and the Columbine community if he could answer these accusations and speak to them. Manson replied, "I wouldn't *say* a word to them. I would *listen* to what they had to say, and that's what no one did." His words reflect those of a good rhetorician who understands the awful power of a war-rhetoric in an adversarial climate and recalls Booth's words about the importance of rhetoric to avoid war. Connecting the lack of rhetorical listening with physical acts of violence and militancy, both Moore and Manson point out that the Columbine tragedy occurred on the same day of the heaviest bombing in the war in Kosovo. Thus, Moore connects domestic physical violence with international military violence, not as direct cause and effect but as resonances of the same kind of rhetoric. Booth also observed that, "whatever the historical causes, the United States now practices more violence per day, domestically, than most other nations" (124). Unfortunately, Moore's question in his film about why there are extremely high episodes of domestic gun violence in the United States remains unanswered.

Ratcliffe cites noted Italian and feminist scholar Gemma Corradi Fiumara's philosophical writing on listening to analyze the Western bias against listening—a logos that speaks but does not listen. Ratcliffe suggests that restoring the role of listening "would offer us other codes for conducting ourselves in the world" (24). With a reinterpretation of listening, Ratcliffe argues passionately for a better Western rhetoric and an "undivided *logos*": "through listening, people can engage more possibilities for inventing arguments that bring differences together, for hearing differences as harmony or even as discordant notes" (25). After all, the difference between listening *for* intent and listening *with* intent reflects a rhetor's choice to truly understand a speaker's (or writer's) intent (28). This "difference" in our understanding of listening shifts the aims of rhetoric from one of simple "mastery" to a rhetoric that promises to move an audience "beyond original beliefs to some new version of the truth" (Booth 46). With rhetorical listening, there is at least the possibility of truly changing one's mind and finding the common ground of American democratic citizenry.

Rhetorical Listening and Mutual Trust in a Pluralistic Democracy

Danielle Allen, a classical studies and political science scholar and MacArthur Award fellow, analyzes in her book *Talking to Strangers: Anxieties of Citizenship since Brown v. the Board of Education* how the effect of the *Brown* decision in 1954 reconstituted the grounds for American citizenship and democracy. In doing so, she provides a vivid assessment of the cross-cultural implications for Ratcliffe's arguments on the intersections of democracy, rhetoric, and listening. *Talking to Strangers* opens with a visual rhetorical analysis of an iconic photograph of the scene at Little Rock High School, prominently featuring Elizabeth Eckford, a black high school student, and Hazel Bryan, a white high school student. By analyzing this photograph (and others in the book), Allen makes persuasive inferences about the state of democracy and the ordinary habits of citizens in a racially segregated public sphere in the United States in 1957. Allen's claims highlight an important feature of Ratcliffe's definition of rhetorical listening as "a trope for interpretive invention" that can facilitate a "cross-cultural conduct" (18). There are failures in an argument culture, leading to what Allen describes as "interracial distrust" (xiii). In fact, like Tannen's work in the 1990s, Allen's book effectively describes an earlier American, politically polarized argument culture in the early 1950s. Helpful to those who teach rhetoric, Allen's book features a signature chapter on Aristotle's well-known text on rhetoric. Her analysis focuses on that work as a manual that offers citizens in a democracy a way to locate, maintain, and affirm a political friendship. She writes that "a democracy's legitimate strength and stability derives from the allegiance of citizens [and] . . . endures only so long as citizens trust that their polity does generally further their interests" (xviii). I add to her description that rhetorical listening as a strategic practice encourages political friendship among citizens.

Music and H(ear)ing Metaphors in Rhetorical Listening

Readers will note that throughout Ratcliffe's book, she plays with the visual root of the word "ear" in "h(ear)" as she thinks through her work on defining rhetorical listening as a trope of interpretive invention. Rhetorical listening will necessarily align itself, even modestly, with the subject of music, and Allen, Booth, and Ratcliffe all provide some discussion of music and listening as a rhetorical strategy for building trust in a democracy. In a 1995 interview with Cornel West, multi-award-winning jazz musician Wynton Marsalis linked the subject of rhetorical listening to the success of the American democratic experiment. America's path toward a pluralistic democracy began in New Orleans with the music of jazz as "the only original American music" (136). Marsalis emphasizes the link between music and the rhetorical interests of listening in a democracy, telling West that "jazz is an art form that was created to codify democratic experience and give us a model for it. Jazz music was invented to let us know how to listen to each other, how to negotiate" (136). Marsalis's description of jazz as the only original American music acknowledges a central role of this music and America's global influences through this music.

Ratcliffe uses the metaphors of music, but she also asks her readers to think about how rhetorical listening enhances a speaker's persuasive power by linking her definition to Kenneth Burke's theory on persuasion. "Burke argues," she writes, "that identification must precede persuasion . . . [but this] chapter argues that rhetorical listening may precede *conscious* identifications" (19). Music teacher W. A. Mathieu writes provocatively about listening to classical music in *The Listening Book: Discovering Your Own Music*, but in doing so he underscores rhetoric's interdisciplinary interests with music and gives readers some insight about how Ratcliffe's unconscious identification occurs: "There are many types of thinking, and listening is not any of them," he states (35). Mathieu tells us that "as a culture we have forgotten how to listen to music;" one interesting effect of this is that we have become "undiscriminating consumers" (37). His keen observations on listening and music raise a good interdisciplinary question about rhetoric: without acts of rhetorical listening and silence, are we simply undiscriminating consumers of ideas in an argument culture?

The metaphors of music provide a good context for Ratcliffe's theory on listening, and it is little wonder that her musical references give us the means "to cultivate the *unconscious* identifications" that she argues for as one of its goals. Her allusions to music—listening for discordant notes, dissonance, contradictory sounds, rhythms, aural echoes, tone— are linked to another part of her definition of rhetorical listening: its ability to help facilitate a "code of cross-cultural invention" (17), both domestic and global. One additional requirement for Ratcliffe's definition for rhetorical listening is to encourage a good deal of reflection. A rhetor must practice rhetorical listening from "a stance of openness" and must listen "with intent" (25). A stance of openness is difficult but crucial in our pluralistic democracy, where the act of identification is central to developing trust among all U.S. citizens. But, again, what Mathieu observes on music and listening has strong implications for rhetoric: "Noncritical listening is the way to learn the sound of your own speaking voice" (25).

A film clip from Julie Taymor's *Across the Universe* helps to illustrate Ratcliffe's definition of rhetorical listening across commonalities and differences. Using a gospel-inflected version of the Beatles' song "Let It Be" as the musical score to this scene in her film, Taymor racially integrates the moment when a white mother learns of her son's death in the Vietnam War with a collage of images from black race riots in the 1960s. Then, she integrates two narrative scenes even more with images from two distinct burial scenes—one of a white family who lost their eighteen-year-old, upper-middle-class son in Vietnam and one of a young black male who was killed in the riots.

The characters quietly express deep feelings of remorse, helplessness, and contemplation as they search for meaning in the deaths of their loved ones and as they share, unknowingly, their sense of personal and human loss. The film reminds the audience of a hard-won, collective identity and of the human loss during the Vietnam War and the civil rights movement. In fact, Allen calls this historical period a second Civil War, not only a civil rights movement. The scene also serves as a trope of interpretative invention for Taymor's film audience and for Ratcliffe's idea of unconscious persuasion made available through music for audiences who intentionally practice listening for rhetorical identification.

Listening and Music in Spike Lee's *When the Levees Broke*

In a panel discussion at the 2007 Feminism(s) and Rhetoric(s) Conference in Little Rock, I asked the audience a question related to the political dominance of the Reagan-Bush years: "What might have happened to American citizens who marched and protested during the 1960s for civil rights if a Republican government similar to the recent, second Bush administration's had been running the country instead of the Democratic Kennedy-Johnson administration at the time?" All session participants shared thoughtful memories and responses as we reflected on the status of our government and the future of American democracy. That session helped to shape my rhetorical response to Spike Lee's documentary film *When the Levees Broke: A Requiem in Four Acts*, "an examination of the U.S. government's role and its response to Hurricane Katrina." The film gives viewers a huge text for sustained thinking about the role of rhetorical listening, silence, music, and perceptions of American citizenship (for a total of 245 minutes, plus two additional DVD chapters). In addition to the narrative insight and listening that Lee encourages, he also uses "silence as a strategic choice" in his film editing, which effectively heightens the "empathic exchange" between the visual text of the film and its rhetorical audience (Glenn 13, 16). In *Unspoken*, Glenn describes a range of ways to think about silence as a rhetorical practice. Although Glenn does not address the topic of film in her book, her broad rhetorical theory clearly provides great tools for thinking about strategic practices of silence in fiction and nonfiction film (especially on the rhetorical canon of delivery in the silent film era or in today's global foreign language films).

First, the momentary and intentional use of verbal silence throughout the film (with music) gives Lee's viewers the rhetorical space to contemplate the meanings and magnitude of the horrific images of death, destruction, the flood, the heat, and the political abandonment in New Orleans and Mississippi in 2005. Effectively, Lee's film exposes a great inequality in American democracy that today's viewers rarely see in reported films or in news video reports on commercial television. In fact, I argue that this film serves as a counter-hegemonic film narrative. It tells the unabashedly emotional story of the aftermath of Katrina in a way to allow for the kind of rhetorical listening that Ratcliffe has urged us to engage and to address the adversarial argument culture that both Tannen and Allen describe. After examining a few broad issues from the entire film project, I will analyze some of Lee's persuasive detail about the breach of the levees. But I will also analyze two specific film excerpts with a focus on Lee's uses of rhetorical silence and his illustrations of *kairos*.

As a "requiem," Lee's film mourns the loss but also celebrates the life of the culture in New Orleans, as David Denby keenly observes in his review of the film. Using the cultural frame of a "jazz funeral," unique to New Orleans, Lee opens the film with a slow, mournful trumpet, piano solos, and string music to serve as the score to these images. The haunting tones of this musical introduction reflect Lee's lamentation on the death of a beloved American city. But then the film ends with an upbeat score that celebrates the life of a great city. Framed in this way, the film offers a broad range of voices from American citizens who survived the tragedy and who tell their stories about what happened, about the lessons they learned, and about the lingering questions that remain for them.

In an early scene, Lee presents a bit of oral history about U.S presidential responses to two prior hurricanes in New Orleans of a similar magnitude, one in 1927 and one, Hurricane Betsy, in 1965. John Barry, author of *Rising Tide: The Great Mississippi Flood of 1927 and How It Changed America*, told Lee that the flood of 1927 (before hurricanes were named) was the worst natural disaster in American history, before Katrina. In addition, David Brinkley, Clark Professor of History at Tulane University, told Lee about such forty-year floods. But as a resident of New Orleans, Brinkley also described the stark contrasts in U.S. governmental responses to his city in 1965 and in 2005. When Hurricane Betsy occurred in 1965, there was an intentional breach of the levees (with dynamite) that flooded much of the lower Ninth Ward. Brinkley, who wrote *The Great Deluge: Hurricane Katrina, New Orleans, and the Mississippi Gulf Coast*, spoke eloquently about President Lyndon Johnson's response to the citizens of New Orleans who lost their homes during this crisis; then he compared Johnson's engagement with President Bush's response and Bush's "flyover" stance in 2005. In the interview, Brinkley helped Lee to hear the clear contrasts in the earlier and later governmental styles: the former, one of openness, intimacy, and care for his citizens who faced a tragedy; the latter, one that reflected a lack of openness and a distance from his citizens in the face of a tragedy. Brinkley continued, telling Lee that

> [Bush] needed to have put his boot heels on the ground, to have touched the floodwaters, to have smelled the death. Lyndon Johnson in 1965 came down to the Ninth Ward and in the pitch-black-

ness of night, in his awkward Texas way, had a big ol' flashlight with him and went out there and put a flashlight on and said, "This is your president. I am here." In some ways that's a funny LBJ story, but what Johnson was saying is, "We care. I represent the American people and you may have lost your home . . . you may have lost all of your heirlooms . . . but we care . . . you mean something to us."

With such a clear and contrastive point of view about the different governments, Brinkley helped to answer my lingering question about possible differing political responses to the civil rights movement in the 1960s.

Two visual narratives in this documentary remind viewers of both the tragedy and the humanity that they are witnessing. The film encourages rhetorical listening, enabling identification, persuasion, and cross-cultural codes of invention. In the first narrative, Lee shows images similar to those from scenes in a war zone, complete with helicopter rescues, bloated dead bodies, and people lingering for days without food, water, or medicine in the 100-degree heat and humidity of a Louisiana and Mississippi summer; we see grown men and women crying (and then apologizing for their tears) and the infamous Superdome. Effectively, we witness the magnitude of the problem and the need for a government to respond to its impoverished citizens. This narrative influenced the media to refer to these American citizens as "refugees" (with its "third world" implications). But in a second equally important narrative, Lee offers the stories of people who demonstrated love, faith, humanity, heroism, compassion, and a great religiosity; their controlled anger in the face of such total devastation and the interruption of their personal lives is remarkable and inspiring. Lee contrasts these two narratives with a third bureaucratic and impersonal narrative: an exceedingly slow government administration whose members were on vacation, fishing, playing tennis, shopping, attending a Broadway play, and fund-raising; this narrative included the iconic "flyover" photograph of the president's viewing the scene of the aftermath of Hurricane Katrina below.

Lee includes an additional "act 5" on the DVD collection that offers a seven-minute silent film tribute (a slide show of photographs with accompanying music) to all of the people who were interviewed for the film. Many of the photos include Lee, his small crew, and a selection of the interviewees in the film. Rhetorically, this segment is completely nonverbal, accompanied only by the celebratory, upbeat music to emphasize the end of a jazz funeral, and the silence invites viewers to reflect on and identify with these citizens' narratives. The pace of the photographs in the slide show matches the pace of the upbeat jazz. We are reminded of a pluralistic America—people of many races, social classes, disabilities, and gender differences. Each interviewee appears with a literal frame around his or her face, which gives these moments a sense of "portraiture" and themes of dignity and citizenry as the audience "listens" to these silent pictures. Lee shares an unspoken faith in seeing New Orleans return to health. In fact, he ends his lengthy film with a beautiful still photograph of a blue coastal sky over the serene water below on the Gulf Coast.

One of Spike Lee's strongest illustrations of rhetorical listening in the film was in his inquiry about two notable moments of *kairos* in the media in response to the tragedy after Katrina: when rap singer/producer Kanye West exclaimed on unedited, live television that "George Bush doesn't like black people," and when Dr. Ben Marble, an ER physician in Gulfport, Mississippi (driving with his friend Jay Scully), said to Vice President Dick Cheney, very emphatically, "Go fuck yourself." In the film, West and Marble talk to Lee about the government's failure of rhetorical listening.

West was invited to speak during a national telethon event for Katrina victims. His exclamation that "George Bush doesn't like black people," repeated several times during this brief film clip, polarized his audience, lost commercial endorsements, and was edited out of the programming for the later timing of the show on the West Coast. West told Lee that his comments were unplanned but that his previous rehearsals were not as "heartfelt," not as empathetic, as he wanted them to be. He wanted to express something on television that would share his genuine feelings: "I was more concerned about [what I could say] . . . if I was in these people's shoes." Commenting on this point in his book, *Rhetorical Refusals,* John Schilb suggests that West's moment of a "rhetorical refusal" actually resembles "[Frederick] Douglass in criticizing injustice toward black Americans instead of engaging in the discourse of national unity expected of him" (157).

Immediately following West's interview, Lee cuts abruptly to new scenes with footage of the disaster in Gulfport, where Marble and his friend are driving a rental truck to Marble's home. Their driving path has been interrupted not only by the demolished trees, completely destroyed homes, and general chaos from the effects of the hurricane but also by

Vice President Cheney's visit to this hard-hit area, which was almost directly across from Marble's home. Marble told Lee: "I remembered what [Cheney] had said to Senator Leahy from Vermont on the floor of the Senate, when he had told him to go fuck himself, so I thought it would be poetic justice to quote the Dick to the dick." Thus, in another *kairic* moment in front of the camera, Marble shouts out, in an almost lyrical but pained voice, "Go fuck yourself, Mr. Cheney." As Marble drives away from the area, his anger is palpable, and viewers see the absolute and complete destruction of the entire community where he lived.

Acts of genuine listening that Ratcliffe, Booth, and Allen want us to practice is very different from what we hear within the competitive walls of our classrooms. Tannen addresses the problem of agonistic behavior in our classrooms, a problem exacerbated by television, radio, and other forms of electronic and commercialized media. Students bring reported "sound bites" directly into class discussions and simply repeat them instead of engaging in genuine exercises on civic discourse on serious provocative issues. I asked a graduate class on cultural rhetoric to talk about what they heard in the selected film clips highlighting Kanye West and Ben Marble from Lee's film (the scenes play for under six minutes). The responses that I got from the first two of three nontraditional white female graduate students in a southern university show the difficulty of practicing listening from "a stance of openness" or listening "with intent" or seeking "identifications across commonalities and differences." Instead, the agonistic form of win-rhetoric is much easier, or at least it's more familiar and generally rewarding:

Student #1

I wonder . . . what Danielle Allen would comment on after seeing this film. Would she describe this one-sided documentary as politically friendly? Was the intent of the film to actually document the horrific event of the hurricane . . . or to lay blame of the entire event on a political party? . . . I wonder what such a documentary would be comprised of had employees of FEMA [Federal Emergency Management Agency] created one.

Student #2

I hadn't really thought about the rhetorical implications on a broader scale of Kanye [West]'s statement. It really assumed that the poor black residents were the only people injured. There were plenty of poor white, Hispanic, and other members of other cultural groups injured I'm sure. I have to wonder also about the responsibility of the mayor. He was black and Kanye didn't comment on his response to the hurricane. [Lee comments on the mayor in his DVD commentary.]

These samples of student writing reflect the kind of performances that professors have consistently rewarded—prove why the "opposition" is wrong and why "your position" is right. But these responses also show, implicitly, how the adversarial nature of today's media that Tannen describes intrudes in our classrooms. The simplified media arguments fit in neatly with the expected agonistic behavior of graduate and undergraduate students, where the "sheer fun of asking and answering questions" and an engagement of rhetorical listening or listening sympathetically are relatively absent (Booth 103). In most cases, these students believe that they are asserting their own points of view (instead of the views of cable news or other media) rather than demonstrate any sense that they have listened for a "cultural logic" that may have informed the lessons, experiences, and stories of the people in Lee's film. I would not conclude that these students would not be able to change their minds about their initial rhetoric. But it would seem that a training in rhetorical listening and silence would enable them to see how their traditional form of academic listening undermines their ability to hear *all* of the sounds, speech, and meaning in the film and to genuinely listen to that beyond the frame of their own rhetorical lens—not at all an easy task. In fact, it impedes them from being able "to hear their own voices," as Mathieu might suggest.

The third graduate student, also a nontraditional white female student, responded to what she "heard" in a way that reflected both her own rhetorical identification with Lee's interviewees and her responsibility as an American citizen, to be a "political friend":

Intentionally raw emotion, an unapologetic appeal to pathos, the voice of the people—this is what I saw in Spike Lee's *When the Levees Broke*. . . . Spike Lee lets the audience feel some of the chaos while leading us to examine tough questions this disaster exposed. He also creates audience identification and investment through his choice of people to feature. Any audience member can see herself or himself reflected in this documentary and can understand Spike Lee's message—Post Katrina New Orleans is EVERYONE's business.

This student's arguments reflect the important connection between rhetoric and democracy, including intentional acts of listening and silence. This moment was every American citizen's business—the government is "we," the people. Spike Lee wanted to make this film because he believed it would have an impact on the future of American democracy. In an interview on the HBO Web page for the film, Lee says: "I think when we look back on this many years from now, I'm confident that people are gonna see what happened in New Orleans as a defining moment in American history. Whether that's pro or con is yet to be determined. And that's one of the reasons why I wanted to do this film" (Nauffts). For now, this film has become an eye-opener, revealing how the federal government (as well as local or state governments) responds to the needs of its citizens in American national disasters.

Rhetorical Listening: Strengthening American Pluralism

We may agree that American identity has always been shaped by an argument culture and that the democratic idealism that America represents is always growing to accommodate the true history of this country's pluralistic identity (against its beginnings of illusory yet reified human differences—race, whiteness, ethnicity, gender, sexuality, religion, and so on). Historian Richard Cullen Rath suggests that perhaps *e pluribus pluribum* would make more sense for the image of American identity and citizenship today rather than "the myth of *e pluribus unum*" (176).

The agonistic discourses in the media that Tannen observed in the late 1990s or the discourses of race, whiteness, and citizenship that Allen recognized in the 1950s should persuade more rhetoric scholars to reject the history of American identity as linear, static, color-blind, post-racial, or even progressive. American identity is cyclical, always a work in progress, and reflective of many hard-won battles to expand laws for civil rights for all of America's citizens. The film samples in this essay help to illustrate some of these American identity battles, and indeed, so do the reflections on listening to music. Rhetorical listening—a genuine listening, with an accountability logic and the intent to change one's own rhetoric—gives American citizens a huge responsibility for practicing the kind of discourse, dialogue, and rhetorical silence that can help us to find a common ground in our public sphere. Spike Lee's jazz film on the levees in New Orleans, a trope for American democracy, shows how acts of listening and silence offer the promise to move us beyond the "win-rhetoric" of the adversarial, argument culture that limits what rhetoric can be. But, as always, for American citizens to truly achieve this promise, we have to collectively choose it.

Works Cited

Across the Universe. Dir. Julie Taymor. Sony, 2007. DVD, 2008. Film.

Allen, Danielle. *Talking to Strangers: Anxieties of Citizenship since Brown v. Board of Education*. Chicago: U of Chicago P, 2004. Print.

Barry, John. *Rising Tide: The Great Mississippi Flood of 1927 and How It Changed America*. New York: Simon and Schuster, 2007. Print.

Booth, Wayne C. *The Rhetoric of Rhetoric: The Quest for Effective Communication*. Malden, MA: Blackwell, 2004. Print.

Bowling for Columbine. Dir. Michael Moore. Perf. Michael Moore. MGM, 2002. Film. DVD, 2003.

Denby, David. "Disasters." *New Yorker*, Sept. 4, 2006. Web. Jan. 4, 2010.

Donawerth, Jane, ed. *Rhetorical Theory by Women before 1900*. New York: Rowman and Littlefield, 2002. Print.

Glenn, Cheryl. *Unspoken: A Rhetoric of Silence*. Carbondale: Southern Illinois UP, 2005. Print.

Kennedy, Tammie, Joyce Irene Middleton, and Krista Ratcliffe, eds. "The Matter of Whiteness; Or, Why Whiteness Studies Is Important to Rhetoric and Composition Studies." *Symposium on Whiteness Studies*. Spec. issue of *Rhetoric Review* 24 (2005): 359–402. Print.

Kristol, Bill. "Both Sides Now." *New York Times*, Sept. 15, 2008: A-25. Print.

Logan, Shirley. *Liberating Language: Sites of Rhetorical Education in Nineteenth-Century Black America*. Carbondale: Southern Illinois UP, 2008. Print.

Lunsford, Andrea. *Reclaiming Rhetorica: Women in the Rhetorical Tradition*. Pittsburgh: U of Pittsburgh P, 1995. Print.

Mathieu, W. A. *The Listening Book: Discovering Your Own Music*. Boston: Shambala, 1991. Print.

McKee, Patricia. *Producing American Races*. Durham: Duke UP, 1999. Print.

Middleton, Joyce Irene. "'Both Print and Oral' and 'Talking about Race': Transforming Toni Morrison's Language Issues into Teaching Issues." *African American Rhetoric(s): Interdisciplinary Perspectives*. Ed. E. Richardson and R. Jackson. Carbondale: Southern Illinois UP, 2004. 242–58. Print.

———. "Race Matters Rhetoric: Reading Race and Whiteness in Visual Culture." Royster and Simpkins 243–54. Print.

Morrison, Toni. *Playing in the Dark: Whiteness and the Literary Imagination*. New York: Vintage, 1992. Print.

Mosk, Matthew. "An Attack That Came Out of the Ether." *Washington Post*, June 28, 2008: C01. Print.

Nauffts, Mitch. "Teaching 'The Levees.'" Web log entry. *Philantopic*. Philanthropy News Digest. Sept. 14, 2007. Web. Feb. 19, 2010.

Ratcliffe, Krista. *Rhetorical Listening: Identification, Gender, Whiteness*. Carbondale: Southern Illinois UP, 2005. Print.

Rath, Richard Cullen. *How Early America Sounded*. Ithaca: Cornell UP, 2003. Print.

Royster, Jacqueline Jones. *Traces of a Stream: Literacy and Social Change among African American Women*. Pittsburgh: U of Pittsburgh P, 2000. Print.

Royster, Jacqueline Jones, and Anne Marie Simpkins, eds. *Calling Cards: Theory and Practice in Studies of Race, Gender and Culture*. New York: State U of New York P, 2005. Print.

Schilb, John. *Rhetorical Refusals: Defying Audiences' Expectations*. Carbondale: Southern Illinois UP, 2007. Print.

Tannen, Deborah. *The Argument Culture: Stopping America's War of Words*. New York: Random, 1998. Print.

Welch, Kathleen E. "Who Made Aristotle White?" Kennedy, Middleton, and Ratcliffe 373–77. Print.

West, Cornel. "Wynton Marsalis." *Restoring Hope: Conversations on the Future of Black America*. New York: Beacon, 1995. 113–40. Print.

When the Levees Broke: A Requiem in Four Acts. Dir. Spike Lee. HBO, 2006. Film.

Gesturing toward Peace: On Silence, the Society of the Spectacle, and the "Women in Black" Antiwar Protests

Ashley Elliott Pryor

ccording to contemporary Italian philosopher Giorgio Agamben, we live in an age of the "complete triumph of the spectacle" (82). Agamben argues that since the Industrial Revolution, human activity finds its value increasingly and perhaps irrevocably against the matrices of efficiency, productivity, and other predetermined ends that serve to perpetuate Western-style capitalist states. Whatever we might have in common and whatever relations might constitute a social realm are "inverted" and given back to us as the common good. As a consequence, Agamben believes that authentic and free human political action—that is, human action not directed entirely toward predetermined ends or goals—is endangered. When we are no longer able to value human *being* apart from its potential to contribute to a future goal or activity and the question of human being is decided and becomes just another product, human freedom becomes inoperable and politics as such collapses.[1] In place of the political, we have the spectacular.

The Society of the Spectacle names the condition of modern, Western capitalist societies in which all human thought and activity—even the impulse to modes of political resistance and dissent—are co-opted to serve the society's insatiable desire for entertainment and consumption. In the Society of the Spectacle, acts of political resistance (such as the recent protests at the Copenhagen climate change conference) are more likely to occasion twenty-four-hour CNN and Fox "news vigils" in which the borders of news reporting, punditry, and pandering are hopelessly blurred than they are to inspire consumer boycotts of the transnational corporations that trivialize or overlook human rights abuses or to inspire people to educate themselves further about the political struggle in the Tibet Autonomous Region. In the Society of the Spectacle, Nelson Mandela's birthday becomes an occasion to buy M&Ms, as in the case of the South African advertisement featuring the antiapartheid activist's beaming face fashioned completely out of M&Ms and a birthday wish: "Thanks for encouraging us to embrace all our colours. Happy Birthday, Madiba." An image of Mahatma Gandhi once enticed us to "Think Different"—and especially while using a Macintosh computer—and more recently became the "G" in "Google."[2]

This chapter explores the meaning(s) of silence as a medium of antiwar protest in the context of the "Women in Black" (WIB) movement. By reading the WIB narratives on silence through the rhetorical category of the "gesture," which was developed by second century C.E. Roman rhetorician Mareus Terentius Varro and later theorized by contemporary Italian philosopher Giorgio Agamben, I argue that we can retrieve a strategy within the Western rhetorical tradition that potentially resists the tendency toward the "noisy" commodification or appropriation of political protest that is characteristic of the Society of the Spectacle. Both Agamben and Varro present gesturing (*gegere*) as a third modality of human activity, challenging Aristotle's simple binary categorization of human activity into *poesis/facere* (an activity that finds its value or end in the product that it fashions—that is, a means to an end) and *praxis/agere* (an activity that is undertaken and valued in and for itself—that is, an end in itself). While the value of acts of *poesis* and *praxis* are determined against measurable ends or outcomes (*teloi*), the gesture by contrast draws attention to the "pure mediality" of an activity; that is to say, it does not yield a singular definable "end" or value. Insofar as the gesture reveals "itself" as pure mediality or means without end for Agamben, the gesture functions more like an arch-transcendental, the condition that first makes any means-ends activity possible as such and that is not reducible to any particular content or message. In its relative "emptiness," Agamben likens the gesture to silence.

While the WIB narratives do not refer to Varro's or Agamben's theory of the gesture, this chapter argues that in their attention to the ways that silence defies easy appropriation or reduction to a singular meaning about what protest "means," the WIB participants often understand their silence more like a medium or mediality rather than as an end or means to an end. As we will discover, a common but by no means exclusive thread in the WIB narratives concerns the ways that silence opens a "space" that potentially transforms the passive spectator into a more active participant who helps determine the meaning of protests. While it could be argued that the desire to transform human consciousness is itself a predetermined end, it diverges from most other political agendas in that it does not seek to proscribe an exact course of action or strategy. Thus, I suggest that the WIB accounts attend to silence in terms of mediality, as a medium in and through which political resistance and dissent take place without necessarily reduplicating the economies of dogmatism, imperialism, neocolonialism, and patriarchy they critique. Not only is silence central for communicating the WIB antiwar/pro-peace message, but it also grounds the ethical legitimacy of the protest as it opens up a deeper dimension of political responsibility. Thus, I am interested in the potential of Agamben's thinking of the gesture in relation to the problem of the systematic co-optation of the political realm and to silent forms of protest. I also consider how the concrete practices of the WIB protests might advance the still very provisional reflections on how silence as mediality might move us from a Society of the Spectacle to something like a Society of the Gesture.

Gesture and Spectacle

Agamben's essay collection *Means without Ends: Notes on Politics* is concerned with reclaiming a dimension of authentic human activity that is not co-opted by or directed to a predetermined aim, outcome, or common good. In his essay "Marginal Notes on Commentaries on the Society of the Spectacle," Agamben defines the twentieth century as the culmination of modern capitalist production in which the value of human production shifts from its use and exchange values to its value as image or representation—as a commodity. For Agamben, the Society of the Spectacle extends well beyond the sum total of commodities to name an entire social relation whereby everything that was once directly lived or experienced has receded into a representational form, is distanced from its use value, and is replaced by "fetishistic" powers to stimulate awe, wonder, desire, fantasy, and deep identification. As such, the Society of the Spectacle is capitalism's "extreme figure" and represents "the commodity's final metamorphosis, in which exchange value has completely eclipsed use value and can now achieve the status of absolute irresponsible sovereignty over life in its entirety, after having falsified the entire social production" (76). The triumph of commodity fetishism over all other aspects of life is so familiar and omnipresent in contemporary Western capitalist societies that more often than not it is mistaken for the natural order of things. Commodity fetishism appears to be an all-but-permanent part of the human condition as its processes are rendered invisible to us and the fruits of our labor increasingly become removed from actual human needs as they are displaced, falsified, and co-opted by commodity-fetishes.

The second trait of the Society of the Spectacle is the way that processes of commoditization shape the political realm. Commodification co-opts the possibility of authentic political activity and effectively nullifies or neutralizes forms of resistance to the state by turning them into spectacles, into commodities for consumption. Examples of the co-optation and political protest abound, but among the most salient examples is Chrysler's recent ad campaign "Your Face of Freedom," which features Nobel Peace Prize winner and political dissident and prisoner Aung San Suu Kyi. The implicit message of the campaign is that our ability to buy a Chrysler is made possible by the great wealth and power that American democracy affords us. By buying the Chrysler, they suggest, we best support Aung San Suu Kyi's quest to bring democracy and freedom to the people of Myanmar, linking democracy to wealth, power, and mobility. In the wake of such abject attempts to trivialize the nature of human freedom, Agamben rightly observes that it is hard not to conclude that the realm of politics offers anything but "a hasty and parodic *mise-en-scène*" (80). Hence, any attempt to challenge fascism or other forms of authoritarian tyranny requires that we first expose and disrupt the ideological ground that attempts to co-opt and appropriate all gestures of dissent in service of its own aims.

Agamben finds a potential resource for this task in Varro, who, in *On the Latin Language*, offers a critique of Aristotle's categories *poesis* (making) and *praxis* (acting) by proposing a third category of human activity, *gegere*, or "gesturing." As it is thought by Varro, gesturing contrasts with *facere* (making) and *agere* (acting), which are valued against a determinate outcome, product, or goal in that the value of the gesture consists in how well it manifests the conditions that make its enactment possible. Varro elucidates his meaning of gesturing by contrasting it with two other modalities of action: acting and making, modes of activity in which the agent either brings forth an object through her activity or transforms it in some way. "For a person can *facere* something and not *agere* it, as a poet *facit* 'makes' a play and does not act it" (Varro 245; qtd. in Agamben 57). By contrast, the actor "acts" (*agit*) the play but does not "make" (*facit*) it. Here, Varro draws a clear distinction between two kinds of concerns and relationships an agent might have to an object—in this case, a play. For the poet/playwright, the activity relates to bringing into existence (*facere*) something that had not existed before. By way of contrast, the actor is concerned with bringing the play to life through his or her interpretation of it. Varro then describes a third mode of action, one that results neither in the production nor in the interpretation or transformation of its object: "The general [*imperator*] in that he is said to *gegere* 'carry on' affairs, in this neither *facit* 'makes' nor *agit* 'acts,' but *gerit* 'carries on,' that is, supports, a meaning transferred from those who *gerunt* 'carry' burdens, because they support them" (Varro 245; qtd. in Agamben 57). As Varro describes it, what makes the general's activity different from that of the poet or the actor is that it does not significantly transform an object: it is neither the origin or cause of a state of affairs, nor does it interpret or otherwise transform the state of affairs. The general's job is only to support and carry on the state of affairs that is handed down to him. While we may disagree with Varro's description of the scope and nature of the general's work (especially within the context of modern-day warfare), Agamben's appropriation of the Varronian gesture here provides a resource for thinking about a form of human activity that exhibits the conditions (mediality) that make our activity possible in the first place. The gesture exhibits "the sphere of pure and endless mediality" (Agamben 59).

Unlike the categories of *poesis* and *praxis* that are conceived in relation to a final goal, end, or product, "the gesture is the exhibition of a mediality: it is the process of making a means visible as such" (Agamben 58). As mediality, the gesture is empty and devoid of any particular content and is intimately bound up with silence. "[T]he gesture is essentially always a gesture of not being able to figure something out in language; it is essentially always a *gag* in the proper meaning of the term, indicating first of all something that could be put in your mouth to hinder speech" (59). Gesture is not a "way of speaking" or a language unto itself, which would make it a *facere*—a bringing forth of something into language. Nor is it repressed speech, for if it were, gesture would ultimately or potentially give way to speech, and the specific mediality proper to gesture in Varro's classification would be compromised by what gesture really wants to say. The importance of Varro's analysis is that gesture is the exhibition of mediality without reference to what is said, to the goals, ends, or origins of speech. Gesture, then, as the medium and mediality of authentic human action is in fact nothing other than silence. It is the silence from which all human actions and words emerge, the space in which something is unsaid and unsayable and yet on its way to being "figured out" in language. Thus, words and actions are not silently waiting for expression but are essentially always entwined with silence.

Agamben believes that when thought functions by way of the gesture, what becomes significant in a given human activity is less how well it accords with a pre-given structure or schema (what we could call its sense of responsibility) but rather the character or quality of its enactment within its given environment or context (what we could call its sense of responsiveness). In contrast with the Society of the Spectacle in which lived relationships are obscured, distorted, and replaced with abstractions and predetermined ideas about what people should want and do, Agamben begins to imagine something like a Society of the Gesture.

This form of experience would attempt to render visible and apparent the multiform, dissenting, and often messy sphere of human relations and with it allow "the emergence of the being-in-a-medium of human beings," thus opening up "the ethical dimension for them" (Agamben 58). It is a form of experience or way of thinking that remains open to the gesture and that provides a space in which the gesture comes to sense without being superimposed on a means-ends schema or understood as a deficient form of communication. "The gesture [is the] communication of a communicability. It has precisely nothing to say because what it shows is the being-in-language of human being as pure mediality" (59).

Although his essay is ultimately concerned with the recovery of an authentic political domain, Agamben does not give an example of the way that silence might be used as a medium of political resistance or dissent.

This is a curious omission, though perhaps it reflects the fact that that so much of what passes as political protest and activism, such as antiwar and pro-peace rallies, is framed by limiting identities such as self/other or victim/victimizer and thus tends to repeat some of the very structures and hierarchies it seeks to repudiate. And most antiwar activists carry signs and shout out slogans—in short, they tend to be quite noisy. In any event, one would not want to look to overt political action and protest to give resources for the recovery of an authentic political domain. On the other hand, the "gesture" is unavoidable in multiple contexts: the gesture accompanies even the most banal political protest no less than it inhabits cinema or philosophy, though cinema and philosophy are where gesture is problematized as such. Protests and political actions too often compromise the mediality of the gesture and lend themselves to commodification and spectacle, but conversely, attention to gesture's mediality may shed light on the political possibilities of concerted, communal action.

Were Agamben interested in illustrating his theory of the gesture of silence with a concrete example, however, he might find in the WIB silent protests a perfect example of the way that silence functions as a medium of and means for political dissent. Indeed, more often than not the women speak about their silence in spatial rather than in instrumental terms. They experience silence as something that one occupies rather than as something one uses. As we will see in the WIB narratives that follow, the meaning or sense that each of the women draws from the practice of silence is multilayered and complex. Their silence functions to engage the spectator, relying on the gesture as opposed to the employment of silence as a tool to a definable end, as a determined practice with determined effects. I do not examine these gestures in order to establish the value of WIB's use of silence according to how closely it conforms to the Varronian/Agambenian conception of gesture as medium or mediality. Rather, I offer them as a help in finding potential commonalities and affinities (but so too differences and potential points of incompatibility) between the experiences of silence that share a commitment to the gesture in its resistance to commodification and spectacle.

Women in Black

"Women in Black" was inspired by earlier women's grassroots protest movements refusing violence, militarism, and war, such as Black Sash in

South Africa, the Madres de la Plaza de Mayo in Argentina, the Women's International League for Peace in the United States, and the Greenham Common Women's Peace Camp in the United Kingdom. The group began in Israel in 1988 at the outset of the Palestinian intifada when some Israeli Jewish women began to gather in public and stand to protest the Israeli occupation. To signify their grief and mourning, they dressed in black. Although the first vigils were not "silent," they were sober events: there was no chanting or recitation of slogans. Their more deliberate silence developed gradually out of a shared commitment not to repay violence with violence by shouting back at hecklers who would frequently hurl abuse at them.[3] Thus silence functioned less as an expression of any particular political view but rather as a strategy for resisting the continuation or proliferation of violence. Silence became a medium for peacemaking. From Israel, the movement gradually spread to Canada, the United States, Australia, and Europe. As tensions and violence between Israelis and Palestinians proliferated and began to have increasingly serious and immediate consequences for people around the world, the WIB continued to stage antiwar/pro-peace actions, holding silent vigils during the Gulf War, the U.S. invasion and occupation of Afghanistan, and more recently the U.S. invasion and occupation of Iraq. Since the time of the first silent protest vigils, when the women responded to the heckling crowds with silence, the purpose and meaning of WIB's silence has become a more complex medium. Indeed, we risk distorting the gesture of silence(s) if we settle on any one meaning or use. In this way, it is difficult to justify the use of silence as a worthwhile strategy on any simple, practical grounds. Part of what I take to be at stake in the group's frequent use of silence is the attempt to create an opening for others to actively participate in the protest by thinking through the apparent ambiguities inherent in members' refusal to speak or tell their spectators what to think.

Where the WIB's silence was in some ways an immediate and crafty response to abuse, it changed over time. It was never formally implemented or woven into a group charter. It remains a gesture. Silence functions as a medium to open exchange and dialogue rather than as a concrete political message or recommendation. In order to explore their practice and its sense, I highlight four distinctive gestures of silence that I find at play in the recorded narratives of one American WIB group: silence as the gesture of (1) resisting the trivialization or co-optation of

political discourse, (2) resisting dogmatism, (3) cultivating an awareness of women's oppression and historic silencing and the possibility of
occupying silence differently, and (4) effecting transformative practice
through self-cultivation.

In what follows, I will briefly examine these four gestures of silence,
connecting them with some of the WIB narratives (of Susan Pearson,
Eileen Kurtz, Craigen Healy, Jo Josephson, Judy Rawlings, Ellen Grunblatt, Rita Kimber, and Lee Sharkey) from the Farmington, Maine, group
that were collected by Lee Sharkey on the group's Web site.[4]

*Silence as the gesture of resisting the trivialization or co-optation of po-
litical discourse.* In reflecting on her own use of silence in the Farmington
WIB group, Susan Pearson notices how words, images, and even actions
of resistance and dissent are subject to co-optation and censorship and
are consumed as forms of entertainment. Silent protests dodge manipu-
lation and co-optation in a way that signs, banners, or protest "speech"
cannot. At the very least, silent protests do not produce readily usable
and co-optable slogans or sound bytes. Instead, Pearson observes that
silence provides her with an alternative discourse that disrupts the "idle
chatter" that seems characteristic of an age: "Words have lost reliability
in this age of advertising, public relations, speechwriters, and deception
by euphemism. Politically charged words, laden with cultural history,
lose their ability to label accurately or to invite critical thinking."[5] Where
"chatter" is as easily co-opted as it is ignored, silence "invites curiosity, leaves space for creative engagement of the observer's imagination."
Eileen Kurtz, another Farmington WIB protester, shares with Pearson
the experience of silence providing a space or refuge apart from banal or
trivializing accounts of the war: "To me the silence feel to be a true and
honest response to all the 'chatter of the times'—we have heard now for
months of yet another upcoming 'war'—almost like a new movie release.
Silence lets it all sink in—and offers a place from which to sort it all out."

By practicing silence, Pearson and Kurtz seem to understand silence
less as a tool or instrument that one uses and more as a space that one
can "occupy," if only temporarily. Silence is restorative: it grants them
a space for reflection, and in it they resist taking on prefabricated ideas
about the war and can examine their own feelings in a more spontaneous
and honest way. As Craigen Healy, another WIB Farmington member,
says, silence communicates the very incommunicability of the evils of

war and thus for her is a more authentic expression of what is in her heart: "I love the silence. It is a vital part of the experience for me because . . . no words can express the horrors of war, whereas silence speaks in a way everyone can understand"—an idea that echoes Agamben's own description of the gesture as a communication of something that is unsaid or unsayable, "a gag" (Agamben 59).

Silence as the gesture of resisting dogmatism. As many WIB women note, they are never exactly sure how passersby will interpret their silence. Because they do not tell people what they should think about their silence, it can be and is read in many ways. For some the silence is full of ambiguity or mystery. For others it constitutes a refusal to communicate or to cooperate. WIB protests provoke a variety of responses, some favorable, some not. According to Jo Josephson, usually people seem curious: "[WIB silent protest] is time when I observe the faces of the people walking and driving by. It tells me that there are people surprised and curious and, yes, even confused about our presence. . . . At times I even detect a sense of relief in their faces: 'I am not alone; there are others who think as I do.' And of course there are the faces and gesture that tell me how wrong I am." As a gesture, silence does not lend itself easily to the propagation of a specific ideology or political platform and thus potentially creates openings and questions for spectators. This is also the case for the women who engage in silence. Judy Rawlings writes, "What attracted me to the WIB vigils was—and still is—the silence. I really like not having to say anything or to respond to either positive or negative responses from those who observe our silent witness." For Rawlings, silence creates a space by and through which she can show her dissent without having to engage in potentially futile or pointless debate, testimonial, and argumentation. As Susan Pearson puts it, "To stand each week outside of labels (at least by my intent, if not always in others' perception) leaves room for others to think without having to defend themselves against whatever threat they may perceive us to represent. It defines a safe territory for us to meet." In each case, silence draws attention to its own mediality. Silence is not itself the message—it does not aim at a particular ideological stand or dogma—rather, silence opens a communal space in which the gesture can occasion reflection and deflect violence.

Silence as the gesture of cultivating an awareness of women's oppression and historic silencing and the possibility of occupying silence differently.

In their accounts of the Farmington protests, Ellen Grunblatt and Susan Pearson thematize ways that silence produces a historic memory in them of women's oppression and the manifold ways that women's voices have been suppressed or silenced. While the women do not offer sophisticated theories of the categories of sex and gender in their work, several do thematize their own silence in relation to the historical silencing of women and minorities who have been dispossessed of the power to speak out in public (Glenn 23). For Grunblatt, the memory of women's systematic disenfranchisement from public speaking makes her relationship to her own silence difficult: "I dislike silence. Communication, engagement, dialogue is what I want. I accept silence as part of street theater, but it makes me uncomfortable. When I stand there I am aware of women's silence serving as a blank slate on which others, usually men, have written their fear and sometimes their hate. I am often afraid." While acknowledging that the knowledge of women's historic oppression and silencing is disquieting, Pearson suggests that in silence she finds resources for challenging oppression and sexist discrimination: "Silent vigil provides space for entry into the construction of reality that women's voice has been. And that voice has been for too many centuries ignored, degraded, or absent. To invite others into a new understanding, a safe entryway must be prepared." For both Pearson and Grunblatt, silence offers an important space of access and process and potentially transforms women's silence. Both recognize a performative aspect of silence—both grasp the mediality of silence. For Grunblatt, in silence she is able to attend to the feelings of discomfort and unease that arise as she reenacts the role of one who is momentarily silenced, while Pearson reports finding in silence a potential space through which the meaning of women's silence could open to new possibilities and understandings.

Silence as the gesture of effecting transformative practice through self-cultivation. Since its inception as a response to the Palestinian intifada, participants of the WIB movement have dedicated themselves to promoting interfaith dialogue and community among women of different religious and spiritual traditions. This is particularly apparent in the WIB Farmington chapter, where women self-identify as Christians, Quakers, and Jews and some as having no particular religious affiliation. Many of the women talk about silence as a medium of inner transformation and healing, and many of them relate this healing through silence back to their own religious or spiritual practice. Craigen Healy, for instance, describes how her silent protest takes the form of a silent prayer in which she prays for her enemies but also for "guidance to become a peacemaker." Rita Kimber identifies a "spiritual part" of her silence as well and describes an extension of her silent practice in Quaker meetings: "In the silence we try to feel our connection to God or the world soul or whatever you want to call it . . . trying to be an atom weighing in on the side of peace in the great universe." Lee Sharkey explains the way silence helps her mourn and work through her anger at the policies of the Israeli state: "As a Jew, I have been appalled by Israel's response to the second intifada. I take this personally. . . . I came to WIB in solidarity with Israeli WIB to make my resistance to war on all fronts visible, without hatred, to say 'Dai! Enough already! I mourn all dead.'"

While Healy, Kimber, and Sharkey all talk about the ways their experience with silence connects them to a particular religious identity or practice, Susan Pearson frames her experiences in terms of self-transformative practice:

> While I stand vigil with Women in Black, I treat each of my thoughts of judgment or anxiety as a mushroom cloud on the bright noonday sun. We humans will not change what has been assumed to be our natures easily, and scant resources from the culture are offered in its support. I believe I must use each conscious waking moment I am able to counter that tendency in myself that I am urging humanity to do as a whole. The stakes get higher and time speeds on more quickly, at the expense of self-reflection. Inner change does not preclude action, but I trust that the more I am able to hold peace within, the greater the likelihood that my actions will reflect my values. The Women in Black vigil is a time for me when new ways of relating to myself and those around me come most easily.

For Pearson, what is most significant in her practice of silence is its potential for helping her to transform negative emotions that keep her from connecting more deeply with others. Silence gives Pearson a kind of distance from herself, a space in which she is able to "move beyond [our] respective disagreements and fears."

Silence potentially provides a medium that allows for the pluralistic and peaceful coexistence of different religious and spiritual traditions at the same time that it provides a mediality through which the women can meet in and through their differences to resist forces that threaten the possibility of peace and interfaith community. As such, it provides a model of the potential use of silence as means for healing, peacemaking, and self-transformation.

Conclusion

Giorgio Agamben's presentation of the gesture of silence is intimately connected with the project of restoring to human being an experience of freedom rooted not in any predetermined essence or goal (political or otherwise) but in the open-ended question of its possibilities. If this space of freedom is to have any meaning whatsoever, the question of human being must be raised as a question that concerns not only humanity in general but also individual, concrete, singular lives. The question of human being also involves the question of the meaning(s) of *my* life and is answered in the ways that I live this life. Agamben concludes his essay with the promise that philosophy (at least a certain form of philosophizing) may hold for deconstructing or de-centering limited views of human being's end or of the "autistic" form of subjectivity that keeps so many of us locked in a perpetual battle against a nameless, faceless "they." Yet he never offers suggestions as to the concrete, practical ways the gesture or "gesturing" might be of use in our own political or social struggles. This omission no doubt is tied to Agamben's commitment to create the conditions in and through which silence finds expression in our own lives. As such, Agamben's own silence on the gesture of silence might be read as gesture in light of Varro's provocation to think of human being in its mediality without recourse to a final end or product.

WIB members do advocate for specific ends and use silence as a means of achieving an end. Despite the different social and political contexts in which their protests are embedded, the WIB protesters all seek the end of war and the establishment of peace. But as I have tried to suggest, their use of silence is complex and variable. While the women share in common the medium of silence, the way that each woman occupies and experiences this silence reflects the particularities of her own situation. At the heart of the WIB accounts is a commitment to values that resist the trivialization or co-optation of political discourse and that address and account for women's oppression and historic silencing while occupying silence in new and potentially transformative ways. The four gestures of silence, in exposing the ways silence functions more as a medium and less as an instrument or tool, constitute a pragmatic gesture, organizing key themes that emerge in the WIB accounts. The WIB, in "giving voice" to our singular experience of silence, helps us find a medium in which we might stand together in silence with others to begin the process of transforming the "Society of the Spectacle" into a "Society of the Gesture."

Notes

1. Emphasizing human being as a process rather than as a state, fixed essence, or even condition, Agamben offers a very different definition from those substantialist versions of classical Western philosophy. "Because humans beings," Agamben writes, "neither are nor have to be any essence, any nature, or any specific destiny, their condition is the most insubstantial of all: it is the truth" (95). Accordingly, the authentic task of politics is to restore human beings to the essential question of their being—a question that turns not on the determination of an end but rather on the very means, mediality, or gesture, of living.

2. The slogan "Thanks for encouraging us to embrace all our colours" finds its concrete instantiation in an advertisement created by BBDO Advertising Agency in Capetown, South Africa, for the Mars Candy Corporation. The ad features the smiling face of Nelson constructed out of M&M candies; see http://adsoftheworld.com/media/print/m_ms_nelson_mandela. For the Google ad, see http://www.p2pnet.net/story/29287.

3. According to the Women in Black Web site's history page, the WIB protesters were frequently "heckled and abused" and were sexualized and called "whores," as well as labeled as "traitors." See http://www.womeninblack.org/en/history.

4. All quotations from representatives of the WIB movement are drawn from the Web site of the Farmington, Maine, chapter, http://wibfarmington.org/. There, in the Writings section, one can find the narratives in their entirety, as well as essays, poems, and press releases related to their protests.

5. I find Cheryl Glenn's comments on the limitations of relying on gender as a central category of analysis in the study of silence helpful in the context of reading the WIB narratives. Glenn writes, "Whether people are male or female, masculine or feminine, is not so important to their purposeful use of speech as their willingness to use silence or speech to fulfill their rhetorical purpose, whether it is to maintain their position of power or resist the domination of others" (23). Even as they evoke their identity as women in these narratives, Grunblatt and Pearson both seem to do so within the framework of the silencing, that is, within the differential relationship of those who have historically enjoyed more freedom to speak (men) and those whose freedom to speak has been more restricted (women).

Works Cited

Agamben, Giorgio. *Means without End: Notes on Politics (Theory Out of Bounds)*. Trans. Vincenzo Binetti and Cesare Casarino. Minneapolis: U of Minnesota P, 2000. Print.

Glenn, Cheryl. *Unspoken: A Rhetoric of Silence*. New York: Southern Illinois UP, 2004. Print.

Sharkey, Lee. "Women in Black: The Transformation of Silence into Language and Action." *Women in Black, Farmington, Maine, USA*. Web. Jan. 11, 2010.

Varro, Mareus Terentius. *On the Latin Language*. Trans. Roland G. Kent. Cambridge: Harvard UP, 1977. Print.

Women in Black, Farmington, Maine, USA. Web. Jan. 11, 2010.

Hearing Women's Silence in Transitional South Africa: Achmat Dangor's *Bitter Fruit*

Katherine Mack

Isocrates, one of rhetoric's founding figures, famously asserted: "Of all human capabilities [speech] is responsible for the greatest goods. . . . If one must summarize the powers of discourse, we will discover that nothing done prudently occurs without speech (*logos*), that speech is the leader of all thoughts and actions, and that the most intelligent people use it most of all" (sections 251–52). Growing interest in embodied, visual, and silent rhetorics as both complementary to and counterparts of verbal rhetoric now complicates the field's traditional privileging of speech, particularly public speech. Rather than determining whether or how the rhetorical tradition has downplayed silence as a rhetorical art (Glenn 2), this essay considers the assumptions that exist about silence in a specific historical moment—transitional South Africa—and the gendered effects of those assumptions. It analyzes the silences that led to the South African Truth and Reconciliation Commission's (TRC) "special hearings on women" and a novelistic response to those hearings: Achmat Dangor's *Bitter Fruit*.

The TRC's belief in the causal relationship between public speech and the construction of self and society echoes the Western rhetorical tradition's deeply held assumptions about the transformative power of speech. In 1996 and 1997, the commission held "special hearings on women" (hereafter referred to as the "women's hearings") to encourage women victims of apartheid to "break the silence" surrounding their experience of gross human rights violations. Indeed, "silence" was the subheading of one of the sections of the commission's report on these hearings (*Truth* 4:293). The commission's attempt to elicit women's stories formed part of its broader effort to generate "as complete a picture as possible of the causes, nature and extent of the gross violations of human rights that were committed during the period from 1 March 1960 to the cut-off date [April 1994]" and to "validat[e] the individual subjective experiences of people who had previously been silenced or voiceless" (1:112). The first goal is historical, concerning what happened, to whom, and, to a lesser extent, why. The commission understood that these facts alone, and the historical record that they would jointly create, would not restore victims' dignity; such restoration would instead result from victims' ability to speak their experiences of abuse. Hence, the commission's second goal is to "restor[e] the human and civil dignity of such victims by granting them an opportunity to relate their own accounts of the violations of which they are the victims" (1:55). In spite of the commission's efforts to elicit their participation, some female victims remained silent, opting not to participate in its process.

Achmat Dangor's novel *Bitter Fruit* constitutes a literary response to these female victims' silence and to the women's hearings that their silences generated. Through the voice of the main character, Lydia, a woman who opts not to testify about her experience of an apartheid-era rape, the novel responds critically to the guiding assumptions of the TRC, specifically its central maxim: speaking is healing. *Bitter Fruit* depicts a way of dealing with the past that disrupts the commission's implied binary of speech as liberation versus silence as repression. Its characters' journey into an uncertain future is neither exclusively verbal nor oriented toward the goal of nation-building but rather, for the most part, unspoken and personally motivated. *Bitter Fruit* thus invites readers to move beyond the commission's opposition of speech and silence by demonstrating the fluid relationship between imposed and chosen silences, by revealing silence to be both a capacious and consequential rhetoric, and by exploring silence as a condition wherein transformation can occur. In the novel, silences are imposed, chosen, and co-created. At times, they stifle action, but at other times, they generate the grounds for action. What unites *Bitter Fruit*'s diverse silences is their rhetorical power—their ability to generate effects through the withholding of language—and the fact that these silences, contra the commission's logic, do not signify a lack of voice or dignity. To the contrary, they at times constitute and at other times create the grounds for action and agency.

Taking seriously, then, Cheryl Glenn's claim that "silence is an absence with a function" (4), this chapter examines the myriad effects of some women's rejection of the commission's appeal to speak. "Bearing witness" to their silence, to borrow Fiona C. Ross's apt term, poses both methodological and ethical challenges to feminist rhetorical historiographers. Most obviously, their silences do not materialize into an object that can be easily analyzed, though they certainly have material effects that rhetoricians can trace. Studies of rhetoric on the margins provide different models for examining rhetorics that, like silence, complicate traditional methods of analysis due to the absence of a textual record or the presence of only secondhand accounts (Bizzell and Jarratt; Romano). By tracing the institutional and literary effects of these women's silence, this chapter models another way to study silence as "a specific rhetorical art" (Glenn 2). It conceives of the various institutions, such as the TRC's women's hearings, and texts, such as Dangor's *Bitter Fruit*, that respond to their silence as participants in a "cultural conversation," one that occurs over time and in a variety of forms (Mailloux 54). This chapter thus offers rhetorical historiographers a method with which to account for the rhetoric of silence in a specific cultural context. It also shows silence to be a generative rhetoric, the effects of which reveal competing assumptions about its meaning, significance, and power in a particular time and place.

Limitations of the TRC's Mandate and Process

The TRC sought to create a more inclusive history of South Africa's recent past by incorporating the voices of those who were "silenced" by apartheid. Apartheid was a system of legal separation of the races created and enforced by the Nationalist party from 1948 until the democratic elections in 1994. Apartheid categorized South Africans into four main "racial" groups: black, coloured, Indian, and white. The system controlled every aspect of life: it denied the right to vote to non-white South Africans, dictated where different groups were allowed to live, controlled the movement of non-white South Africans through "pass laws," and managed private life through regulations that prohibited interracial relationships.

Despite the TRC's intentions to generate "as complete a picture as possible," its timeline, definitions, and process ironically reproduced some of the silences it sought to address (*Truth* 1:112). To an extent, both its institutional form and pragmatic concerns—the TRC was only one component of a costly and complicated transition—made it impossible for the commission to do otherwise. Though it had a bigger staff and budget than prior truth commissions (Hayner 41), the commission's seven-volume *Truth and Reconciliation Commission of South Africa Report* reminds readers that the commission had "neither the lifespan nor the resources to implement a broadly constituted interpretation" of the key terms and requirements of its mandate (1:60). Indeed, the report acknowledges that the commission's timeline, which extended from the Sharpeville Massacre of 1960—a peaceful demonstration against the "pass laws" that culminated in a police shoot-out and the death of sixty-nine protesters—to the democratic elections of 1994, covered "only a small part of a much larger story of human rights abuses in South and southern Africa" (1:24, 63). The report claims, however, that the thirty-four years the commission addressed were "possibly the worst and certainly, in regard to the wider region, the bloodiest in the long and violent history of human rights abuses in this subcontinent" (1:24–25). As Madeline Fullard, a historian and senior national researcher for the TRC, points out, the time frame thus consciously "propose[d] a certain circumscription of focus to physical violence" (10). In its definition of human rights violations, "the Commission [likewise] had to walk a tightrope between too wide and too narrow an interpretation" (*Truth* 1:60). The commission defined "gross violations of human rights" as "bodily integrity rights" (1:64), including "killing, torture, abduction and severe ill treatment" (1:60, 63, 64), a narrow definition that worked in tandem with its constricted time frame to sideline the other kinds of abuses—socioeconomic, legal, and cultural—that South Africans suffered under apartheid.

Given the limited scope set by the Promotion of National Unity and Reconciliation Act No. 34 of 1995 (the parliamentary act that established the TRC), the commission was unable to analyze the racism and structural violence of the apartheid system and the colonial system that had preceded it. In an oft-cited critique of the TRC, scholar Mahmood Mamdani calls the product of the TRC's work "an institutionally produced truth [that] was established through narrow lenses, crafted to reflect the experience of a tiny minority. . . . [It] defined over 20,000 South Africans as the 'victims' of apartheid, leaving the vast majority in the proverbial cold" (177–78). A different mandate, Mamdani observes, might have "illuminated apartheid as a reality lived by the majority" (180). While the report claims the commission's awareness "of this systemic discrimination and dehumanisation" (*Truth* 1:63), it explains repeatedly that the terms of its establishing act limited the scope of its inquiry (1:48–102). The commission's exclusive focus on victims of human rights violations also precluded inquiries into the varied and complex subjectivities that apartheid, and the struggle against it, engendered. "Victims" who sought to address the everyday violations and violence of the apartheid era, or their resistance to that oppression, had to work against the commission's unintended silencing of these more complex accounts of the past.

From January 1996, the TRC's official starting date, through December 1997, when the work of the Human Rights Violations Committee (HRVC) concluded, the commission gathered and processed about 21,000 victims' statements. Some who gave statements also desired to speak at the public hearings, but not all had the opportunity to do so. The commission selected deponents who represented the demography of the region where the hearing was taking place and whose stories conveyed varied perspectives on the violence and the types of human rights violations that had occurred there (*Truth* 1:146). While the commission claimed that it sought to give everyone "a chance to say his or her truth as he or she sees it" (1:112), it is more accurate to state that it elicited stories that conformed to the traditional discourse of human rights. Victims' stories had to undergo a series of translations to become legible to the commission's information management system. Lars Buur, anthropologist and member of the regional investigation unit of the TRC based in Johannesburg, describes this system as a "bureaucratic machinery of truth production," with its attendant categories, codes for violations, controlling vocabularies, and demand for "in mandate" statements (67). Indeed, statement takers' questions shaped victims' narratives even before they were recorded on the commission's official protocol, which itself, due to time constraints, became shorter and more formulaic over the course of the commission's process. Through the many stages of the commission's work, this process of translation served to transform victims' narratives into "*signs* of gross human rights violations under apartheid, inscribed in statement protocols, the database, investigative reports, the Commission's archives, the final report, and, ultimately, the national archives" (Buur 80). Participants in the commission's process thus constantly negotiated between the narratives they wanted to share and the primarily forensic report the commission could hear, quantify, and incorporate into its final report. Deponents contended with these constraints by offering layered testimonies that conformed to, but also exceeded, the narrow boundaries established by the commission's mandate (Fullard; Ross).[1]

Several months into the hearings held by the HRVC, a gendered pattern of testimony became apparent. The commission expressed concern that while more women were testifying than men, they were doing so as so-called secondary witnesses, speaking as relatives or dependents of victims rather than "as direct victims" (*Truth* 4:283–84). On June 14, 1996, at a meeting with representatives of nongovernmental organizations and academics about the commission's work, Commissioner Mapule Ramashala spoke of the TRC's concern regarding the absence of women's stories about their direct experience of human rights violations: "If women do not talk then the story we produce will not be complete" (qtd. in Ross 22). The commission sought to address this gender imbalance in victims' testimony by acting on the recommendations in "Gender and the Truth and Reconciliation Commission," a paper that Beth Goldblatt, research fellow in political studies at the University of Witwatersrand, and Sheila Meintjies, lecturer in political studies at the same school, delivered at a workshop on the TRC and gender that was held in anticipation of the public hearings phase of the commission's process. Committed to the TRC's goal of eliciting all victims' stories and concerned that women would be reluctant to speak about their own experiences of gross human rights violations, Goldblatt and Meintjies made several recommendations. They urged the commission to reconsider the questionnaires used by statement takers to elicit more details about women's experiences; not to probe too deeply for graphic details, and yet not to avoid "embarrassing" or "private" subjects like sexual abuse; and to offer closed hearings, staffed only by female commissioners, to make it easier for women to speak of experiences not commonly discussed around men, such as rape and/or other forms of sexual abuse. They also proposed holding special hearings in which community leaders could testify on behalf of those women who were not comfortable speaking before the commission themselves.

In response to these recommendations, the commission amended the form used to record statements; held workshops in which participants explored ways to bring more women into the process; and conducted three "special hearings on women" in Cape Town, Durban, and Johannesburg (*Truth* 4:283). Fiona Ross shows how the commission's interventions created "woman" as a particular kind of harmed subject, one who experienced sexual violations that could be investigated and quantified. She argues that "sexual violence was represented in the hearings and in public discourse as a defining feature of women's experiences of gross violations of human rights . . . about which women *could* and *should* testify, and about which they *would* testify under certain conditions" (24). Despite the commission's efforts to elicit their stories, however, some women remained absolutely silent, refusing to participate in the TRC's process, and it is on their silence—its motivations, meanings, and effects—that this chapter focuses.

The Commission's Theoretical Assumptions about Voice and Agency

The architects of the TRC believed that giving victims the opportunity to recount their experiences of abuse before a public audience would both contribute to its goal of truth-recovery and promote the restoration of their dignity. Indeed, the commission claimed the interrelatedness of these two processes in its report: "Establishing the truth could not be divorced from the affirmation of the dignity of human beings" (*Truth* 1:114). The report cites the act that established the TRC to explain the commission's understanding of the relationship between victims' verbal account of their experiences and the recovery of their dignity: "The Act required that the Commission help restore the human and civil dignity of victims 'by granting them the opportunity to relate their own accounts of violations of which they are the victim'" (1:128). The commission here refers not only to the content of victims' accounts—"[their] individual subjective experiences"—but also to the form in which those accounts were relayed. Victims contributed "their own stories in their own languages" to what the commission called "the South African story" (1:112). Implicit in the commission's approach, and stated explicitly in the report's summary of the human rights violations hearings, is its understanding of victims as "people who had previously been silenced or voiceless" (1:113–14). To be silenced is not necessarily to be without voice, nor is to be silent indicative of voicelessness, subtle distinctions that the commission's rhetoric tends to obscure and that *Bitter Fruit* helps to illuminate.

The TRC's heady rhetoric about the transformative potential of victims' stories weaves together diverse discourses that nevertheless all hinge on the assumed relationship between speech and selfhood. By linking memory, voice, narrative, and healing, the commission drew on what anthropologist Rosalind Shaw describes as "a dominant memory discourse of therapy and remembering that has developed since the late nineteenth century" (7). This discourse merges psychiatric and psycho-analytic claims about the pernicious effects of repressed memories, the difficulty of articulating traumatic experiences, and the benefits afforded to victims of trauma who successfully narrate their experiences of abuse. According to this theory, the creation of narrative order transforms what was once formless, unspeakable, and unmanageable into a coherent story. The process of creating and then narrating this story to oneself and to others ostensibly restores the agency that the trauma had threatened or destroyed. The work of psychiatrist Judith Hermann and legal theorist Teresa Godwin Phelps conveys this chain of assumptions: that personal and political trauma affects victims in similar ways—by inhibiting their ability to speak—and that "recovery" quite literally entails the "recovery" of speech. These theorists thus posit "coming to speech" as an essential component in the reconstruction of traumatized persons and societies.

The assumed relations between speech and subjectivity coalesce in much of the literature on rape and its aftermath. Louise Du Toit writes about the rape epidemic in post-apartheid South Africa and its disen-franchisement of women citizens. Her assertion that "the loss of self and world is thus in both rape and torture accompanied by a loss of voice, by a loss of agency and self-extension which is carried or embodied by the ability to speak" could appear in feminist literature about rape victims anywhere in the world (277). Du Toit collapses the distinction between voice, agency, and self-extension; the loss of one necessarily entails the loss of the others. Thenjiwe Mtintso's opening statements at the women's hearings in Johannesburg express this *doxa* of feminist scholarship and convey its centrality to the work of the TRC: "[This hearing] is the beginning of giving the voiceless a chance to speak, giving the excluded a chance to be centred and giving the powerless an opportunity to empower themselves" (*Truth* 1:110). For Mtintso, as for Du Toit, speech, selfhood, and empowerment are inextricably linked.

For victims' dignity to be restored, according to the logic of the TRC, they not only had to speak about their violations—to move from silence to speech—but had to do so in the public realm of the hearings of the HRVC. The report claims that the "*public* unburdening of [victims'] grief" and subsequent "*public* recognition" (*Truth* 1:128, emphasis added) enacted the transformation of knowledge into acknowledgment, a process that it explains as follows: "Acknowledgment refers to placing information that is (or becomes) known on public, national record. . . . What is critical is that these facts be fully and publicly acknowledged. Acknowledgment is an affirmation that a person's pain is real and worthy of attention. It is thus central to the restoration of the dignity of victims" (1:114). Hannah Arendt's insights into the ontological effects of public speech illuminate the underlying premises of the commission's logic of acknowledgment. In *The Human Condition*, her response to dramatic events in the mid-twentieth century, Arendt asserts: "The presence of others who see what we see and hear what we hear assures us of the reality of the world and ourselves" (46). By authorizing those who were ostensibly invisible and voiceless under apartheid to speak in the official realm of its hearings, the commission believed that testifying publicly would also cultivate victims' identity as citizens. The report claims that public truth-telling "help[ed] citizens to become more visible and more valuable citizens through the public recognition and official acknowledgment of their experiences" (1:110). Through the public hearings, the commission sought to instill in victims a newfound trust of the state and the inclination to participate in civic affairs in a manner befitting the new democracy. The hearings thus functioned as a "technology of citizenship" (Cruikshank 2), educating and regulating citizens in the capacities and consciousness of liberal democratic governance. In them, victims learned how to perform in their capacity as fully enfranchised citizens in South Africa's new democracy. Through their voluntary participation in this forum of liberal democracy, they implicitly endorsed this state-sponsored exercise and legitimized the new government, which offered them not revolution but rather sympathy, (limited) monetary compensation, and the "rule of law."

While victims' public storytelling ostensibly promoted their healing, the restoration of their dignity, and their ability to perform as citizens in the new South Africa, it also served the nation-building goals of the commission. Phelps explains how individuals' public storytelling fosters what she describes as "wider healing": "If the stories are told publicly, they have the potential to construct meaning for individuals and also for nations" (60). The presence of victims' narratives in the broader "story" of South Africa made that "story" more meaningful and emotionally resonant, most importantly to those who might otherwise deny the abuses of the apartheid era. The report recalls their didactic and emotional effect: "[Victims' stories] provided unique insights into the pain of South Africa's past, often touching the hearts of all that heard them" (*Truth* 1:113–14). The broader historical narrative subsumed individuals' stories, making them the "pain of South Africa's past," a shared legacy of the entire nation. Like the public speech that forms the "common world" in Arendt's metaphor of "the table," victims' stories formed a historical narrative that the commission hoped would gather South Africans of all backgrounds around the "table" of the new nation (Arendt 48). In short, the commission's transitional logic required speaking subjects whose public speech would simultaneously promote their healing as individuals and that of the nation as a whole. Women's silence about their experiences of abuse hindered the commission's construction of a unifying historical narrative and threatened the national community the commission hoped that narrative would cultivate.

Bitter Fruit Responds to the TRC

Achmat Dangor's *Bitter Fruit* counters the commission's logic of transition, challenging in particular its emphasis on the relationship between public verbal truth-telling, the restoration of self, and the construction of the new nation. The main character Lydia's decision not to speak at the TRC's women's hearings—to maintain a public silence—responds to its claims about the dynamics of speech and silence in the "new" South Africa. Lydia's transition entails speech, silence, and written communications about the past, communications that circulate primarily in the private sphere and that lead to actions that complicate, if not subtly undermine, the commission's citizen- and nation-building project.

Bitter Fruit traces the dissolution of a coloured family literally born of—and ultimately undone by—the violence of apartheid. The novel is set in 1998, as the TRC's women's hearings are taking place, a year described by the narrator as "a twilight period, an interregnum between the old century and the new, between the first period of political hope and the new period of 'managing the miracle'" (255). The event that drives the action of the novel, however, occurred twenty years earlier, in December 1978. Two of the main characters, newlyweds Silas and Lydia, both coloured according to apartheid-era racial designations, are caught in a police roundup. During the roundup, Du Boise, an Afrikaans policeman, rapes Lydia in a police van while the police-battered Silas listens and bangs helplessly on its sides.[2] The rape leaves Lydia pregnant with Michael, a fact she never shares with Silas, who believes Michael to be his biological son. Lydia recalls the reasons behind her silence about Michael's paternity in the journal entry she wrote after the rape: "Silas and I walked down the quiet, peaceful street, both of us silent. He had stopped moaning, but did not know how to reach out and touch me. . . . His fear, that icy, unspoken revulsion, hung in the air like a mist. It would enable me to give life to Mikey, my son. At that moment, in Smith Street, Noordgesig, I crossed over into a *zone of silence*" (129, emphasis added). Eighteen years later, Silas interrupts that "zone of silence" when he tells Lydia about his chance encounter with Du Boise in a supermarket in a scene that opens the novel (3). Their discussion-cum-argument sets the action of the novel in motion and initiates another series of rhetorical silences.[3]

Through its depiction of the aftermath of the rape, *Bitter Fruit* explores the complicated origins and evolution of the silences that the commission sought to address through its women's hearings. Lydia's journal entry suggests that she was able and willing to speak the night of the rape but that Silas's "fear, that icy, unspoken revulsion," prevented that conversation from taking place (129). Silas's silence continues and begets further silences. Indeed, the rape and the resulting silence become what Lydia wants to address. Silas knows this but finds himself incapable of undergoing the frank exploration that she seeks. He explains his preference for silence—or, if not silence, then words that muffle and mitigate:

> Lydia really wanted to explore some hidden pain, perhaps not of her rape, but to journey through the darkness of the silent years that had ensued between them. He was not capable of such an ordeal, he acknowledged. It would require an immersion in words he was not familiar with, words that did not seek to blur memory, to lessen the pain, but to sharpen all of those things. (63)

Lydia imagines a similar silencing would occur if she were to speak about the rape with her parents, who, like Silas, prefer to deny difficult or painful experiences by not speaking about them: "They will also demand of me a forgetful silence. Speaking about something heightens its reality, makes it unavoidable" (127). In both these reflections, we hear echoes of the commission's logic—that verbalizing an experience compels acknowledgment of the reality of that experience. Unlike the "voiceless" victims that the TRC imagines in its report, however, Lydia has a "voice" and seeks to verbalize her experience but finds herself stymied—trapped in a "zone of silence"—by the discomfort of those who are closest to her. She is both silent and silenced but certainly not voiceless.

Though Lydia wants to speak about the rape, and is frustrated and disappointed by Silas's and her parents' inability to do so, she nevertheless rejects the commission's offer to speak at the women's hearings. She recalls the words of "the young lawyer from the TRC" in whose eyes she detects "an evangelist's fervour": "This is an opportunity to bring the issue out into the open, to lance the last festering wound, to say something profoundly personal" (156). In addition to exaggerating to the point of mockery the commission's rhetoric in her recollection, Lydia points to the permanence and immutability of the rape to challenge its promise of closure as the result of public testimony. She confronts its hyperbolic goals for the women's hearings with her own assertion that testifying will change "nothing": "Nothing in her life would have changed, nothing in any of their lives would change because of a public confession of pain suffered. Because nothing could be undone" (156).[4] Here Lydia calls into question the allegedly therapeutic and ontological effects of public speech that motivate the commission's effort. That she refers to the experience as "a public confession" suggests that she perceives the women's hearings as a trial in which she (ironically) is the defendant (for only the guilty "confess"), not as a space of healing for victims. Lydia seeks dialogue with interlocutors of her choosing, not the opportunity to display herself before an audience of strangers who represent the state and need her story to construct a "complete" history for the new nation (*Truth* 1:112). Tellingly, in these reflections, Lydia does not refer to the personal shame that the bulk of the literature on women and rape and, more specifically, the CALS submission to the TRC suggest might disincline women victims from speaking about their experiences. Nor does she refer to the shame her public account might cause her parents or Silas. It is rather the futility of the public confession—the fact that "nothing could be undone"—that she cites to explain her decision to maintain a public silence.

Bitter Fruit further implies that sexist attitudes within the anti-apartheid struggle might have encouraged Lydia to maintain a silence that was initially imposed by Silas and her parents, to choose silence rather than the public speech now elicited by the commission. As a former operative in the underground African National Congress and the current liaison between the TRC and the Department of Justice in the transitional government, Silas is simultaneously associated with the sexism of the struggle and the commission's efforts to address its legacy on women victims in the present. In the course of the heated conversation following his encounter with Du Boise, Silas rehearses several contradictory arguments, all of which subordinate Lydia's needs and desires to Silas's or to "the struggle" against apartheid. At first he insists that there "was no need to [talk about the rape]" (13), a position he quickly modifies by insisting that the initial silence was called for by the political exigencies of that time: "It was a time when, well, we had to learn to put up with those things [that is, in Lydia's case, to put up with rape]" (13). Silas does not elaborate on this point, leaving the reader to infer that the anti-apartheid struggle required equal amounts of sacrifice from everyone and that complaints would not be countenanced then or now. His comment hearkens back to an earlier episode in their marriage in which he similarly justified an extramarital affair that he had with "a comrade in the 'movement'" (12). Lydia recalls that he told her then that "people in the underground were in constant danger . . . and this created a sense of intimacy, it was difficult to avoid such things" (13). Silas explained that Lydia "had to be told [this] so that she would understand the 'context,' so that her rage would not be 'misdirected'" (12–13). In other words, Silas suggested that the psychological demands placed on active agents in "the movement" eclipsed Lydia's personal needs and expectation of fidelity to their marriage. Though Silas subsequently acknowledges that he did not have the right to determine whether she "needed" to discuss the rape, he maintains the notion that Lydia's personal experience was rightly subsumed, at least at that time, to the ostensibly distinct, and more important, movement to end apartheid.

Silas, so resistant to discussing the rape and its consequences within the privacy of their home, nevertheless encourages Lydia to speak at the women's hearings. At the conclusion of their argument, he tells Lydia,

"*We* have to deal with this" (15, emphasis added), by which he means that *she*, Lydia, should speak at the women's hearings and thereby deal with her anger. Lydia, however, doubts his motivations and, moreover, resists having her voice and experience become stepping stones in his ascendancy in the new government. She recognizes that Silas is disappointed when she refuses the commission's offer, as "her appearance would have given him the opportunity to play the brave, stoical husband. He would have been able to demonstrate his objectivity, remaining calm and dignified, in spite of being so close to the victim" (156). Lydia suggests that her public testimony would not shame Silas but would rather strengthen his reputation; having a wife who was the victim of a political rape that he could not prevent and maintaining his composure during her public testimony before the TRC might indeed be a source of pride. In light of Silas's insistence that she participate in the commission's process, and given their contentious history concerning the hierarchy of personal and political needs, Lydia's decision to maintain a public silence about the rape—not "to deal" with her anger as Silas demands (and desires)—constitutes a subtle form of rebellion against being told what, why, when, and how much to feel. For so often when "women's issues" are taken up, as in the TRC's women's hearings, the attention given to them serves a broader agenda, such as nation-building, in which such issues have been deemed topical or convenient. In other words, attention to "women's issues" does not necessarily demonstrate a foundational shift in priorities or thinking about gender. As Helene Strauss observes in her review of *Bitter Fruit*, "Lydia's refusal to let [Silas and the commission] determine the moment of release serves as an attempt at reclaiming female agency amidst the overdetermining constraints of patriarchal benevolence" (para. 4).

While the commission's logic implies that to be silenced or voiceless entails a lack of agency, Lydia's evolution over the course of the novel suggests otherwise. Within the "zone of silence," one imposed initially by Silas but then maintained by her own choice, she grows. This "zone of silence" creates a safe space for her. The narrator refers to Lydia's emergence from her "cocoon" and to her "transformation," one with which neither she nor her family feels entirely at ease: "[Lydia] is also rapidly being transformed, terms and thought processes that astonish everyone. . . . All look at her as if she is a strange insect emerging from a cocoon" (169). Lydia is "a strange insect" not only to them but also to herself: "Wondrous, [but] fearful of her own new wings, Lydia is hesitant at times, speaks as if seeking approval and permission" (169). In spite of that hesitance, Lydia develops a professional life that makes her increasingly independent from her family. She works longer hours for an HIV-AIDS research team; becomes fluent in a new professional discourse, one "slick and coded" (169); and buys a car so that she can commute to a hospital far from where they live. Indeed Silas comments on Lydia's new mobility: "That car had become the real instrument of her freedom. Gave her the ability to cover great distances without his help" (272). His reflection foreshadows the "journey" away from Johannesburg—away from Silas and Michael, away from the demands of the TRC—that Lydia will soon commence (279). In this "transformation," Lydia does not remain a wholly silent subject; she speaks the "new language" of her profession (169). But she is the agent behind these moments of speech, moments that take place neither in the home nor in the state-sanctioned space of the TRC hearings.

Silas's fiftieth birthday party provides the occasion for Lydia's final acts of separation from her biological and national families and the burdens that they place upon her. She decides to give Silas his father's diary, which Silas's mother had entrusted to her "for safekeeping" in the early days of their marriage (251). As she wraps the diary, Lydia reflects: "Only women, wombed beings, can carry the dumb tragedy of history around with them. History is a donkey's arse. . . . Hand Silas his heritage, say something short but profound, kiss him on the cheek, then walk away, free of him and his burdensome past" (251). Here Lydia chooses to speak, but again it is speech that she initiates and that will further separate, rather than implicate her in, weighty familial and national legacies. For Lydia, the diary is the repository of these complicated and intertwined legacies, ones that she no longer feels compelled to address or confront. Her decision to return the diary, and the national history of the "old" South Africa that it contains, echoes her rejection of the commission's appeal to collaborate in its creation of an official history for the "new" South Africa. In the first instance she resists maintaining, while in the latter she resists adopting, the gendered historical subject position of "woman-as-nation"—that "wombed being [who carries] the dumb tragedy of history."

In the closing scenes of the novel, Lydia's final moves to liberate herself from the dual and, as figured in *Bitter Fruit*, imbricated bonds of family and nation are embodied more than spoken. At Silas's birthday party, she dances and has sex with João, a young, very dark-skinned Mozambican. Seeing them together, first on the dance floor and then in a passionate embrace in a deserted room of the house, Silas reflects: "His wife had found relief at last from both her captive demons: from Du Boise and from himself. Now not every man would be a rapist to her" (267). Lydia dances rather than speaks her way to this final release, experiencing it in her embodied interactions with a young man who carries none of the historical baggage, particularly around race, of South Africa.[5] When Lydia calls Silas after the birthday party from a hotel outside of Johannesburg, he tells her: "We can sort it out" (279). Lydia refuses his offer and "remains quiet, hopes that her silence will signal her determination to end their relationship" (279). Her silence speaks here as well, simultaneously marking the end of her marriage and the start of her less historically and personally encumbered existence as a professional woman in the "new" South Africa.

Contra the commission's ontological claims of becoming via public speech, then, Lydia's "journey" to selfhood entails speech *and* silence, and it directs her away from the TRC's nation-building exercise and the demands of domestic life. While falling asleep the evening of Silas's party and upon waking in the morning, Lydia entertains thoughts of returning home, finding herself fighting "the temptation to slow down, turn back" (280). She resists, though, and continues her literal and metaphorical "journey" away from home and family (279). The narrator observes: "Time and distance, even this paltry distance, will help to free her. Burden of the mother. Mother, wife, lover, lover-mother, lover-wife, unloved mother. . . . Even Du Boise does not matter any more" (281). The "transformed" Lydia sheds these gendered roles in her pursuit of a different, as-of-yet unknown future. Listening to a Leonard Cohen song, Lydia laughs at her ability to paraphrase its lyrics—"Carry your own burdens" (281)—a decisive rejection of her role as the "donkey's arse" of history (251). Her directive seems intended as much at the "new" South Africa as at Silas, her husband and representative of that new state. This final image of the novel—of Lydia driving into the veldt to an unknown destination—underscores that her freedom and agency lie not in her becoming a speaking subject of the "new" South Africa, as the TRC suggests, but rather in her ability to disentangle herself both from family and the new nation.

Conclusion

Through its imaginative exploration of the motivations and consequences of one woman's decision not to testify about her experience of an apartheid-era rape, *Bitter Fruit* contributes to the commission's goal of furthering understanding of the violence of the past while respecting the decision of real women not to speak before the TRC. *Bitter Fruit*'s Lydia does not seek a "voice" with which to articulate her experience of a sexual violation nor an official audience to hear her story. While she does not disavow the influence of the rape, she does reject the suggestion that the commission's orchestrated verbal encounter with the past is the preferred way of dealing with its influence in the present. The trajectory she desires and enacts is the inverse of the commission's public verbal encounter with complicated personal, social, and political histories. Lydia employs silence and her body to create distance between her new existence, one not enmeshed in national politics or politicized familial relations, and that complicated past. This representation of Lydia helps readers to conceive of some contemporary South African women's silence not as a monolithic absence or lack of voice but rather as a way of opting out of oppressive familial and state structures, however well-intended such domestic and political ligatures may be. The novel thus addresses different iterations of gendered power structures that have persisted despite the change in South Africa's government. A drama of intimacy, *Bitter Fruit* offers a compelling version of this political critique.

Beyond extending the geographical scope of rhetorical studies through an analysis of silence in transitional South Africa, this chapter's methodology might serve scholars who seek to account for the rhetorical power of silence but find themselves stymied by its immateriality. For, by its very nature, silence eludes analysis. One way to gauge the rhetorical power of silence is by attending to its effects. As this chapter demonstrates, these effects may take a variety of forms, including the institutional and the literary. A cultural rhetoric approach, which understands all texts to be rhetorical participants in a "cultural conversation" (Mailloux 54), broadens the range of materials that scholars can access to understand the workings of silence in a given context. Given that silence, like all rhetorical acts, is culturally inflected and embedded, future studies might contextualize and situate their analyses of silence through consideration of literary and other artistic texts that harness the powers of the imaginary to make silence speak.

Notes

1. In *Bearing Witness*, Fiona Ross argues that the commission misconstrued women's testimony about violations experienced by others as constituting "silence" about the abuses they suffered themselves. She suggests that the so-called secondary witnesses embedded personal narratives into their testimony about family members—that women were in fact speaking "their" stories but that the commission was unable to hear them (28).

2. Afrikaners are white, Afrikaans-speaking people of northwestern European descent. During apartheid, they were classified as "white."

3. The novel has other significant subplots that do not appear in this summary. Michael embarks on a quest to learn more both about his putative biological father, Du Boise, and about Silas's Muslim heritage. Ultimately, Michael murders Du Boise before the TRC has the opportunity to hear Du Boise's application for amnesty, and he plans to exile himself to India to escape prosecution. Michael and Lydia also verge on an incestuous relationship about which Silas represses his awareness: a different "code of silence" develops around this family secret (151).

4. Ross points to the "paucity of currently existing grammars . . . [and] the need for a new language of social suffering that . . . recognizes the fragmented and unfinished nature of social recovery, and does not presume closure" (165).

5. Both Lydia and Silas comment on the darkness of João's skin, reveling in his seeming lack of internalized racism, a *topos* of *Bitter Fruit* and its engagement with the conditions of South African "coloureds." Silas, for example, recalls Lydia's knees "against his skin so black it was almost blue. . . . There was something so ineluctably beautiful about Lydia pulling the young man to her, embracing his black body in her lovely olive-skinned arms" (266–67). Lydia similarly calls attention to João's color in her recollection of him as "black João, beautiful as jet" (281).

Works Cited

Arendt, Hannah. *The Human Condition: A Study of the Central Dilemmas Facing Modern Man*. Chicago: U of Chicago P, 1958. Print.

Bizzell, Patricia, and Susan Jarratt. "Rhetorical Traditions, Pluralized Canons, Relevant History, and Other Disputed Terms: A Report from the History of Rhetoric Discussion Groups at the ARS Conference." *Rhetoric Society Quarterly* 34 (Summer 2004): 19–25. Print.

Buur, Lars. "Monumental Historical Memory: Managing Truth in the Everyday Work of the South African Truth and Reconciliation Commission." *Commissioning the Past: Understanding South Africa's Truth and Reconciliation Commission*. Ed. Deborah Posel and Graeme Simpson. Johannesburg: Witwatersrand UP, 2002. 66–93. Print.

Cruikshank, Barbara. *The Will to Empower: Democratic Citizens and Other Subjects*. Ithaca: Cornell UP, 1999. Print.

Dangor, Achmat. *Bitter Fruit*. New York: Grove/Atlantic, 2001. Print.

Du Toit, Louise. "A Phenomenology of Rape: Forging a New Vocabulary for Action." *(Un)thinking Citizenship: Feminist Debates in Contemporary South Africa.* Ed. Amanda Gouws. Burlington: Ashgate, 2005. Print.

Fullard, Madeline. "Dis-placing Race: The South African Truth and Reconciliation Commission (TRC) and Interpretations of Violence." Race and Citizenship in Transition Series. *Centre for the Study of Violence and Reconciliation.* 2004. Web. Aug. 5, 2004.

Glenn, Cheryl. *Unspoken: A Rhetoric of Silence.* Carbondale: Southern Illinois UP, 2004. Print.

Goldblatt, Beth, and Sheila Meintjies. "Gender and the Truth and Reconciliation Commission: A Submission to the Truth and Reconciliation Commission." Department of Justice and Constitutional Development Web site. May 1996. Web. July 12, 2004.

Hayner, Priscilla. *Unspeakable Truths: Facing the Challenge of Truth Commissions.* New York: Routledge, 2002. Print.

Hermann, Judith. *Trauma and Recovery: The Aftermath of Violence—from Domestic Abuse to Political Terror.* New York: Basic Books, 1992. Print.

Isocrates. *Antidosis.* In *Isocrates 1.* Trans. David Mirhady and Yun Lee Too. Austin: U of Texas P, 2000. 201–64. Print.

Mailloux, Steven. *Reception Histories: Rhetoric, Pragmatism, and American Cultural Politics.* Ithaca: Cornell UP, 1998. Print.

Mamdani, Mahmood. "The Truth According to the TRC." *The Politics of Memory: Truth, Healing, and Social Justice.* Ed. Ifi Amadiume and Abdullahi An-Na'im. London: Zed Books, 2000. 176–83. Print.

Phelps, Teresa Godwin. *Shattered Voices: Language, Violence, and the Work of Truth Commissions.* Philadelphia: U of Pennsylvania P, 2004. Print.

Romano, Susan. "The Historical Catalina Hernández: Inhabiting the Topoi of Feminist Historiography." *Rhetoric Society Quarterly* 37 (Fall 2007): 453–80. Print.

Ross, Fiona C. *Bearing Witness: Women and the Truth and Reconciliation Commission.* London: Pluto, 2003. Print.

Shaw, Rosalind. "Rethinking Truth and Reconciliation Commissions: Lessons from Sierra Leone." *United States Institute of Peace.* Feb. 2005. Web. Apr. 20, 2005.

Strauss, Helene. "Intrusive Pasts, Intrusive Bodies: Achmat Dangor's *Bitter Fruit.*" *Post Colonial Text* 1.2. (2005): n. pag. Web. Mar. 14, 2008.

Truth and Reconciliation Commission of South Africa Report. Ed. Department of Justice. Vols. 1–5. Cape Town: Juta, 1998. Print.

Part Three

PRAXES

With Our Ears to the Ground: Compassionate Listening in Israel/Palestine

Joy Arbor

> How do we listen? How do we demonstrate that we honor and respect the person talking and what that person is saying . . . ? How do we translate listening into language and action, into the creation of an appropriate response?
>
> —Jacqueline Jones Royster, "When the First Voice You Hear Is Not Your Own"

> From different listening comes different speaking.
> —Yosseph Naim, Israeli planner and communication teacher

In response to Jacqueline Jones Royster's call to ensure that speakers, especially those with marginalized voices, are "well-heard" (38), rhetoricians' interest in listening and engaging across difference has been growing: Linda Flower and her colleagues at the Community Literacy Center focus on intercultural inquiry and rhetoric, communicating across difference in order to make change in the community (Flower, Long, and Higgins; Flower); Donna Qualley focuses on self-other relations, developing "self-reflexive inquiry" as an ethical practice for questioning one's own assumptions while encountering the difference of the other; Krista Ratcliffe has developed "rhetorical listening" as interpretive invention and a "code for cross-cultural conduct" (17). Listening across difference is fundamental to the "different speaking" and "exchang[ing] perspectives, negotiat[ing] meaning and creat[ing] understanding" necessary to cooperation and intercultural engagement (Royster 38). But rhetoric's historical devaluation and naturalization of listening in favor of speaking has meant that rhetoric's concepts of listening, especially listening across difference, are still nascent (Ratcliffe 20). Yet groups outside of the academy sharing rhetoric's commitment to intercultural engagement and social justice, such as conflict resolution and reconciliation groups, have developed theories and practices for listening across difference worthy of rhetorical study.[1]

In conflict resolution and reconciliation work, people listen across difference in order to learn more about each other, solve problems, and develop possibilities for peace. Moreover, conflict resolution and reconciliation groups focus specifically on dialogue and cooperation between peoples in conflict, often with a history of oppression and/or bloodshed. One activist group for conflict resolution and reconciliation of particular interest for rhetorical conceptions of listening across difference is the Compassionate Listening Project (CLP), which leads annual citizen delegations to Israel/Palestine where delegates learn Compassionate Listening and listen to people on all sides of the Israeli-Palestinian conflict.

Compassionate Listening, a model of listening across difference that highlights the humanity rather than the political positions of the other in order to effect long-term social change, provides theories and practices for listening across difference that complement and complicate rhetorical studies' inquiry into listening. What follows draws on my Institutional Review Board–approved research of and participation in the CLP's November 2005 citizen delegation to Israel-Palestine. In order to introduce and argue for Compassionate Listening in this small space, I first narrate a transformative encounter from the CLP's citizen delegation, attempting to show the possibilities of Compassionate Listening for engaging across difference, then describe the citizen delegation training in Compassionate Listening's theories and practices. Finally, I argue for two important offerings from Compassionate Listening for rhetorical concepts of listening: (1) a concrete and active method for attending to emotions and resistance in listening across difference and (2) a multilayered theory of listening as an intervention for social change.

"Different Speaking" at the Bat Ein Settlement:
Compassionate Listening in Action

At the Bat Ein settlement, our group of about twenty Compassionate Listening citizen delegates listened to an orthodox Jewish settler advocate his beliefs that Jews should take all of the "land of Israel" for a Jewish state, leaving no land for a Palestinian state. A settlement of Jews located in the disputed lands called, variously, the West Bank, the Occupied Territories, and Judea-Samaria, the Bat Ein settlement is infamous for its residents' violent encounters with Palestinians in neighboring villages. (Frontline documentary *Israel's Next War* recounts two longtime residents' plan to bomb a school for Palestinian girls in Jerusalem.) Not only did this ultraorthodox Jew narrate his transformation from American secular Jew to ultraorthodox rabbi living in the West Bank, he also spent the day with us, showing our group all around the grounds of the settlement, including a historical *mikvah*, or traditional Jewish purification waters; it seemed he was trying to invoke the common argument that because Jews had lived there over a thousand years ago, Jews had a historical right to the land, though the Bat Ein settlement is among those that many promoting a two-state solution to the conflict argue should be evacuated. When we were finally seated in the yeshiva where he taught, he told us that he believed in a strategy of claiming all of the land of Israel because then, according to Talmudic juridical practice, Jews would likely be awarded half to three-quarters of the country. He said he believed Jews should be sovereign in the land of Israel: other peoples could live there with cultural and personal rights but not sovereign or political voting rights. He also encouraged us to ask him "the hard questions," inviting us to engage him in oppositional debate.

By the time our group sat listening to this settler, we had been practicing Compassionate Listening for nearly two weeks, listening to Israelis and Palestinians on all sides of the conflict, determined to be open-minded and to create a non-oppositional and safe space for people to speak. Even so, listening to the settler's advocacy of "tit-for-tat" when it came to violence with Palestinian villagers and his denial of their political rights was difficult. A member of our group, Jacob,[2] had been reluctant to visit the settlement at all, seeing in settlement ideology all he abhorred as a professional human rights activist and a Jew. Furthermore, Jacob had been skeptical initially about Compassionate Listening's long-term approach to social change and reconciliation; instead, he was in favor of the oppositional strategy of direct advocacy and law-making, a practice that Compassionate Listening asserts further entrenches people in their positions. Once the settler was done speaking, we began the usual Compassionate Listening practice of "giving back," reflecting back what we admired in what he told us. When Jacob began to speak to the settler, he engaged him in strategic questioning, another Compassionate Listening strategy. He told the settler that he was a Jew but also a human rights activist. He explained that in the last couple of weeks, we had spoken to many Palestinians and visited a refugee camp, talking with people who also share a deep connection to this land. Then he asked what the settler would do if the State of Israel ordered an evacuation of these lands in order to allow for a Palestinian state.

The settler grew quiet and seemed to be considering the question, then said: "If the Jewish people in their short-sightedness decided to abandon and give this land to a Palestinian state, I'd cry, but I'd move. The Jewish people are my people—and I should be with my people." Then the settler began to weep.

Later, in the "processing" session that often followed our listening sessions, we discussed how Compassionate Listening—and Jacob's careful questioning in particular—encouraged a transformation in the tone with which the settler addressed us, moving from oppositional advocacy to engagement and emotional introspection. Coming on the heels of our non-oppositional "giving back," Jacob's question seemed to allow the settler some space to reconsider his commitments without becoming defensive. Clarifying that his commitment is to the people rather than to the land may encourage him to make (perhaps only slightly) different decisions.

For me, this encounter with the settler demonstrates the transformative possibilities of Compassionate Listening for listening across difference. First, the Compassionate Listening training allowed us to listen to the settler in an open-minded and empathetic way without our feelings of difference stifling engagement. While I, for example, certainly did not identify with his ideas or agree with his denial of Palestinian people's political autonomy, I came to understand the connections between his life experiences and his political positions, seeing him as a person rather than as a representative of settlement ideology. Initially resistant, Jacob, too, was able to listen to the settler without getting angry or too uncomfortable to continue, seeking the settler's humanity at least long enough to ask him a respectful question.[3] Second, we listeners created a safe space for the settler to tell his story without feeling threatened and defensive by our different opinions. The settler appeared committed to thinking through Jacob's question because of, I believe, the base of trust and respect that we had created as a group as well as the thoughtful and compassionate way in which the question was posed. We listeners were able to create the space for this transformative experience for both Jacob and the settler because we had trained in and practiced Compassionate Listening for over a week.

Compassionate Listening Training in Israel-Palestine

A U.S.-based nongovernmental organization that teaches peacemaking skills, the CLP provides training and certification in Compassionate Listening throughout the United States and leads annual citizen delegations to Israel-Palestine. The CLP emerged in 1997 when its founder and director, Leah Green, who had been leading citizen delegations to Israel/Palestine since 1990, met and collaborated with Gene Knudsen Hoffman, founder of the U.S./U.S.S.R. reconciliation program for the Fellowship of Reconciliation and developer of Compassionate Listening as a reconciliation and peacemaking tool, to use Compassionate Listening as a framework for citizen delegations (Green).

Hoffman's Compassionate Listening advocates a new way of engaging the peace process: "We peace people have always listened to the oppressed and disenfranchised. . . . One of the new steps I think we should take is to listen to those we consider 'the enemy' with the same openness, non-judgment, and compassion we bring to those with whom our sympathies lie" (*Compassionate Listening* 311). Compassionate Listening's commitment to listening across difference to "the enemy" makes this activist approach different from "telling truth to power." In fact, far from foregrounding oppositional protests to promote change, Compassionate Listening "call[s] for peacemakers to initiate humanizing contact and cultivate compassion for those on all sides of a conflict" (Green). Compassionate Listening's advocates believe that listening is the foundation of reconciliation. Carol Hwoschinsky, a trainer of Compassionate Listening, explains: "[Listening] is the basis of what may become sustained dialogue. Successful dialogue can only take place when people are ready to really listen to each other and themselves. Dialogue then becomes the basis for problem solving and, ultimately, for advocacy" (3). The CLP's commitment to listening to the other with nonjudgment and compassion forms the basis of future cooperation.

From the training with Leah Green and Compassionate Listening advocate Maha El-Taji, we learned about Compassionate Listening's goals, the progression of a standard listening session, the importance of listening to one's self, exercises to help us listen beyond our triggers and defenses, and the possibilities of strategic questioning. The goal of Compassionate Listening is "to anchor us [listeners] in our core [rather than our defenses], inviting others" to do the same.[4] Ideal Compassionate Listening is completely nonjudgmental and nonreactive; the listener is not persuaded by the speaker's words but maintains his or her own ideas without feeling threatened by the presence of the other's. In this way, listeners model for the speakers how to move beyond their defenses and advocacy in order to speak from the heart. If people can speak and listen in non-oppositional ways with the goal of understanding one another, Green and El-Taji assert, change becomes possible.

A Compassionate Listening session begins with a person speaking. The people we listened to were often advocates promoting a particular position. Because Compassionate Listening teaches that positions are defensive and make others defensive, we listeners asked each speaker to move beyond speaking about positions to the speaker's personal story; Compassionate Listening asserts that an individual's personal story helps listeners connect with the speaker's humanity (through identification, though the trainers did not use that word). Recounting one's personal story, Compassionate Listeners assert, also allows the speaker to hear the connections between his or her experiences and positions. The listeners then engage in "reflective listening," mirroring what they have heard from the speaker, in order to make the speaker feel "well-heard." In experiencing being listened to and understood, the speaker also encounters a non-oppositional method of engaging with people across difference. The listeners, on the other hand, learn to hold themselves open to, and make sense of, stories very different from their own. Generally after listening for an hour, we "gave back," thanking speakers for what they had shared with us. Even if we completely disagreed with their positions, we found ourselves responding to their values or personal qualities, such as bravery, perseverance, or commitment to their ideals.

Listening compassionately to others depends on listening compassionately to one's self, attending to what Green and El-Taji called "triggers." Triggers are those emotional and physical responses "in your body, stomach, heart" that make a person want to jump in and respond to another's words and stories, ending listening. Triggers show us which ideas, positions, and stories provoke our defenses. When listening across difference, the goal is not to ignore one's triggers but to recognize the moments where one has reacted or experienced changes in one's body that impeded listening, note them, and gently refocus attention on the speaker.

In order to help us listen to those whose stories may seem threatening to our own, Green and El-Taji taught us a number of practices to help us listen beyond our triggers and defenses, such as reflective listening and the facts, feelings, and values exercise. Reflective listening is similar to Rogerian rhetoric; the listener engages in "say back" until both people come to an agreement about what has been intended and said. The facts, feelings, and values exercise, which Green calls "the life raft of Compassionate Listening," helps listeners to learn to listen beyond positions that divide to values and needs, which transcend facts and feelings. For this exercise, we got into groups of four—one speaker and three listeners. Each listener listened for a different facet—facts, feelings, or values/needs transgressed—during a story that the speaker told. Then the listeners reflected back what they heard until the speaker felt "well-heard."

Green and El-Taji then taught us inquiry or strategic questioning, based on the ideas of activist Fran Peavey. A strong strategic question might include, "What action might you take to address this problem?," building the assumption of action into the question in order to urge the speaker to begin to contemplate possible actions or solutions. Green explained that strategic questions "open up options" and "allow people to rethink their ideas" but warned that because we "want people to feel connected, trusting, open, cared about" in Israel/Palestine, there might be few opportunities for strategic questioning on our trip.

Compassionate Listening and Listening as a Rhetorical Art

Compassionate Listening and the citizen delegation to Israel/Palestine offer a number of points that merit further consideration within rhetorical studies. Two aspects include Compassionate Listening's concrete methods and practices for listening across difference and the various layers of Compassionate Listening's theory of listening as an intervention or rhetorical art.

Compassionate Listening focuses on actively learning and practicing a kind of listening across difference that makes speakers feel safe to speak. Hwoschinsky describes it this way: "Compassionate Listening is a quality of listening which creates a safe container for people to be free to express themselves and to go to the level of their deep concerns. It simply and profoundly means empathizing with the feelings and condition of people who have been affected by effects and circumstances, sometimes of their own doing, and sometimes out of their control" (3). If listeners want to create a "safe container" and to empathize with others' feelings, they have to intend to do so. Listening across difference is not a passive process. As Hoffman asserts: "[Compassionate Listening] requires a particular attitude. It is non-judgmental, non-adversarial, and seeks the truth of the person questioned" (Preface xiii). Here, listening to the other, no matter what one's personal beliefs are, necessitates a certain attitude, an openness. Similarly, both Flower and her colleagues and Ratcliffe affirm that assuming an open stance is necessary to engagement across difference (Flower, Higgins, and Long 5; Ratcliffe 26).

But maintaining a nonjudgmental, nonadversarial attitude in the face of the other is difficult work. Speaking of philosopher Emmanuel Levinas's ethics, performance and testimony scholar Julie Salverson explains: "The call by the other, by what he calls 'the face,' is the encounter through which, in allowing myself *to open*, I *am opened* and taken beyond myself" (61). Listening and trying to understand beyond one's experiences and abilities requires a commitment to listening through pain. Ratcliffe too describes how difficult and painful listening across difference can be: "It may be . . . another's truth . . . that hurts us; however, this challenge, this conviction, this hurt exposes a space of dissonance. When responding to this dissonance, we should not accuse the person foregrounding it, deny its existence, or bristle defensively. Rather, we should question ourselves. . . . If such questioning makes us more uncomfortable, so be it. In fact, good" (34). Here, Ratcliffe states that the pain of listening to another's truth should turn listeners inward to do the difficult work of questioning the self. Similarly, Qualley's notions of self-reflexivity depend on the encounter with the other in order to question and examine one's assumptions (11).

While I champion and agree with Ratcliffe's and Qualley's claims that such work should be undertaken no matter the discomfort, I am concerned that without concrete practices and strategies for addressing the difficulty of listening, listeners are left without resources and will too often allow their discomfort to paralyze efforts to listen across difference. We must have a method to attend to the emotional threat and discomfort of those who engage this work, such as already defensive members of groups in conflict, undergraduate students under our tutelage, and ourselves, or we risk underestimating the difficulty of listening across difference. In her chapter that most focuses on resistance, Ratcliffe champions "moves" to address resistance, such as studying the tropological nature of language and historicizing and localizing seemingly universal tropes under contention—particularly intellectual approaches to resistance that work well within the intellectual environment of the classroom (146–58). But resistance may not be merely intellectual but also emotional, as Ratcliffe notes but does not fully explore in her discussion of resistance in the classroom (138). Certainly empathizing or identifying with another person has an intellectual component, but it also has an important affective dimension. Countering the powerful forces of us-them thinking that underpin identity-based discrimination, such as racism, and that often have their basis in one's self-definition takes more than intellect.[5] To consider others in the sphere of human obligation, which implicates one's self, one must feel *moved* by the other.[6] Yet, intellectualizing moves do little to address these emotional factors and are thus more limited in emotionally charged encounters, outside of the classroom, and away from teachers/mentors who take responsibility for moving emotional content to a more intellectual register. Certainly, providing emotional support is sometimes viewed as an additional burden in the academy and the public sphere. But, as Laura Micciche argues, emotion is "crucial to how people form judgments about what constitutes appropriate action or inaction in a given situation" and therefore is "central to rhetoric" (169). Practices that attend to the emotional threat of listening across difference should be considered to complement the intellectual and theoretical concepts in order to form a more comprehensive rhetorical theory of listening.

In answer to emotional threat, Compassionate Listening claims that listening must begin with the self. Compassionate Listening's emphasis on practical exercises to recognize resistance and triggers in one's self lays this groundwork. Not only does attending to one's bodily responses help with resistance, but the facts, feelings, and values exercise provides a structure to use when struggling. Fellow group members and I found the facts, feelings, and values exercise incredibly useful for transforming moments of difficulty and resistance into moments of learning about ourselves and our values, similar to Qualley's self-reflexive inquiry. Moreover, the group leaders constantly supported the practice of our listening to ourselves through "processing" the overwhelming experience of listening to the stories and pain of many others with the group throughout our journey. Green and El-Taji emphasized throughout the citizen delegation that "holding ourselves open" was emotionally taxing, encouraging listeners to take time off when needed. Compassionate Listening is an active process that gives us tools for addressing the emotional difficulties of listening to others and ourselves across difference.

Listening as Intervention

Compassionate Listening emphasizes that listeners give "the gift of listening" to the speaker, which is, in itself, an intervention in the conflict. This intervention is made up of three facets: the speaker feeling heard, the listeners modeling engagement across difference, and the speaker hearing himself or herself in a new way.

One important aspect to social change is making the speaker feel heard. Reflective listening is particularly suited to helping people feel as if they have been heard. Hwoschinsky explains how listeners provide support for the speaker, making listening an intervention: "[Listening] becomes a gift through recognizing the possibilities embedded in each event. Through the words, we often witness great strength and courage in the midst of suffering which, through that recognition, is reflected back to its source. Often people feel empowered by listening to themselves" (3). Because Compassionate Listeners are committed to reflecting back aspects of the speakers' stories, speakers may feel empowered. Engaging in such "say back," however, does not include making speakers feel that listeners are condoning their behavior. Reflective listening is the learned practice of being able to state what the listener heard while still presenting it as difference (as Jacob did when speaking to the settler). Also, it is common to express appreciation for the speaker at the end of each listening session, often for what listeners have learned. For Compassionate Listening, appreciating difference is not just an idea but enacted in conscious practices during every listening session.

Because these conscious practices focus on making a person feel understood, Compassionate Listening may provide one possible answer to rhetorician Jacqueline Jones Royster's important question about how to make others feel "well-heard." Reflective listening and engaging in the necessary work on the self in order to listen intently to others demonstrates to speakers that listeners value their speaking, actively going against the idea that there is, in Ratcliffe's words, "an absence of listening ears" (85). If a person feels heard, then, at least in Compassionate Listening's model of change, a person is less likely to feel wounded and defensive—defensiveness being one of the functions of Ratcliffe's "rhetoric of dysfunctional silence" that compounds conflict and encourages people to construct barriers rather than engage with one another (90). While it is impossible to determine or premeditate exactly how this "feeling heard" might manifest in a speaker's future behavior, listening in order to make a speaker or other feel heard is itself a rhetorical intervention.

Another "gift of listening" includes Compassionate Listeners' modeling a way of engaging with the other without conflict or bloodshed. Leah Green believes this act of listening attentively and compassionately can lead to conflict resolution and reconciliation, effecting a slow revolution of change. Helping resistant people to see the possibilities of listening and inquiry, rather than thinking that conflict resolution lies in oppositional advocacy or bloodshed, is a challenge. We listeners modeled for the speakers what an inquiring and attentive listener might look like, rather than the one who knows (or the one who is victimized). If speakers feel listened to and heard by listeners, especially across difference, they might engage in attentive listening with others; this could lead to speakers' eventually listening to their own others. Again, this listening as a new model for engagement is itself an intervention.

Modeling listening across difference is a practice we might consider more in rhetorical studies. If modeling peaceful engagement with the other is an intervention in itself, then one way of encouraging listening across difference to resistant people may be to listen deeply to them. After being listened to and "well-heard" by committed listeners, those people might be more motivated to listen to others. If being listened to makes a person more open to others, this has important ramifications for engagement across difference and anti-racist education.

Finally, Compassionate Listening offers speakers the possibilities of hearing themselves in new ways. As Hwoschinsky states, "When we tell our story, we hear ourselves and what is important to us" (11). When listeners create a safe space for speakers to tell their stories, speakers hear them as well, perhaps discovering new connections and possibilities for meaning. Hwoschinsky also sees in reflective listening the possibility of deeper learning and getting to the roots of conflict: "Reflecting back or restating the essence of what you heard the other person say clarifies that person's position and can also bring forth the underlying issues. . . . The reason conflict recycles is that the underlying interests, needs and concerns have not been addressed" (7). During reflective listening, listeners offer the speakers' discourses back to them. That reflective listening can help a speaker see his or her story in a new way mirrors Ratcliffe's claim that the encounter with the other "return[s] our discourses to ourselves somehow unchanged but changed" (28). Such reflection lends the speakers the possibility of seeing themselves differently, as does being asked to "translate" one's stories and positions to outsiders.

Compassionate Listening's emphasis on externalizing this internal rhetoric (Jean Nienkamp's term) helps people engage in praxis, or the thinking through the interrelations of their ideas and experiences, an act highly valued in rhetorical studies. This attempt to make meaning is aided by the presence of listeners who can help attend to the gaps, contradictions, and excess; if nothing else, speakers are asked new questions by the listeners. Strategic questioning—that is, listeners asking questions to open up new possibilities in someone's thinking—can greatly aid in helping speakers move to praxis. Encouraging people to investigate the relationship between their experiences, ideas, and actions and open up new possibilities in their thinking is fundamentally an intervention, moving people to change, albeit slowly.

The various "gifts of listening"—helping people feel heard, modeling a peaceful engagement with the other, and providing a way for speakers to investigate themselves—demonstrate that Compassionate Listening is not only active but activist and rhetorical. Compassionate Listening demonstrates that listening across difference can itself *be* an intervention, with important rhetorical effects, helping people feel "well-heard" and aiming at long-term social change, one speaker at a time.

Of course, no theory or practice is without its limitations; practitioners and scholars must also be aware of certain hazards with Compassionate Listening. The desire to have empathy, to identify with the speaker/other, can lead to confusion about people's positions and differences, causing theoretical and practical problems. The (Quaker) spiritual base upon which Compassionate Listening was founded assumes that people across difference are similar and can identify across difference, a contested idea in rhetorical circles.[7] Furthermore, language that communicates can also obscure.[8] For these reasons and others, I believe further research is vital. If Compassionate Listening were studied in other contexts besides Israel/Palestine (such as other citizen delegations or dialogue groups in the United States), different insights may be gleaned. Also, the connections between rhetorics of listening, Compassionate Listening, and witnessing/testimony need to be investigated more thoroughly. Finally, other conflict resolution and reconciliation groups and theories should be studied and worked with. Perhaps by listening across difference to these organizations, community-academy partnerships can be developed that will enrich conflict resolution groups, rhetorical studies, and the communities we all hope to serve.

Notes

1. I would like to thank the Human Rights Human Diversity Initiative and the Norman and Bernice Harris Center of Judaic Studies at the University of Nebraska-Lincoln for funding this research. Thanks also to Cheryl Glenn and Krista Ratcliffe for help in focusing this article.

2. Names have been changed. This event is discussed with "Jacob's" permission.

3. In an e-mail describing this experience to friends and Compassionate Listeners, Jacob wrote that this encounter with the settler—his "enemy"—was transformative for him.

4. All quotes from Green come from my field notes, unless otherwise stated.

5. For fascinating discussions of us-them dynamics that lead to genocidal violence from a social-psychological perspective, see James Waller's *Becoming Evil* and Ervin Staub's "The Psychology of Bystanders, Perpetrators, and Heroic Helpers."

6. In *States of Denial*, Stanley Cohen discusses the passive bystander effect's finding that an individual's intervention in the sufferings of a visible other is less likely "when people *are unable to identify with the victim*" (16, emphasis in original). My work "Never Again: Interventionist Rhetoric and Social Justice for the Other" explores Cohen's premises and their ramifications for rhetoric, social justice, and engagement across difference.

7. Ratcliffe's *Rhetorical Listening* provides a useful synopsis of scholarship pertinent to rhetorical studies in which identification is suspect (60–67).

8. For example, the leader of a Palestinian women's organization wanted to "stop the occupation," which I took to mean ending the settlements and

Israeli Defense Force's presence in the West Bank. Later, I learned she meant that having Jews in the Middle East was an occupation, and she wanted Jews to "go back where they came from." With language that obscures as much as it reveals, true engagement and reconciliation become difficult.

Works Cited

Arbor, Joy. "Never Again: Interventionist Rhetoric and Social Justice for the Other." Diss. U of Nebraska, 2007. Print.

Cohen, Stanley. *States of Denial: Knowing about Atrocities and Suffering.* Cambridge, UK: Polity, 2001. Print.

Flower, Linda. "Talking across Difference: Intercultural Rhetoric and the Search for Situated Knowledge." *CCC* 55.1 (2003): 38–68. Print.

Flower, Linda, Elenore Long, and Lorraine Higgins. *Learning to Rival: A Literate Practice for Intercultural Inquiry.* Mahwah, NJ: Lawrence Erlbaum, 2000. Print.

Green, Leah. "A Short History of the Compassionate Listening Project." *The Compassionate Listening Project.* 2009. Web. Jan. 8, 2010.

Hoffman, Gene Knudsen. *Compassionate Listening and Other Writings.* Ed. Anthony Manousos. Torrance, CA: Friends Bulletin, 2003. Print.

———. Preface. Hwoschinsky xii–xiii. Print.

Hwoschinsky, Carol. *Listening with the Heart: A Guide for Compassionate Listening.* 3rd ed. Indianola, WA: Compassionate Listening Project, 2002. Print.

Micciche, Laura. "Emotion, Ethics, and Rhetorical Action." *JAC* 25.1 (2005): 161–84. Print.

Nienkamp, Jean. *Internal Rhetorics: Toward a History and Theory of Self-Persuasion.* Carbondale: Southern Illinois UP, 2001. Print.

Qualley, Donna. *Turns of Thought: Teaching Composition as Reflexive Inquiry.* Portsmouth, NH: Boynton/Cook, 1997. Print.

Ratcliffe, Krista. *Rhetorical Listening: Identification, Gender, Whiteness.* Carbondale: Southern Illinois UP, 2005. Print.

Royster, Jacqueline Jones. "When the First Voice You Hear Is Not Your Own." *CCC* 47.1 (1996): 29–40. Print.

Salverson, Julie. "Anxiety and Contact in Attending to a Play about Land Mines." *Between Hope and Despair: Pedagogy and the Remembrance of Historical Trauma.* Ed. Roger I. Simon, Sharon Rosenberg, and Claudia Eppert. Lanham, MD: Rowman and Littlefield, 2000. 59–74. Print.

Staub, Ervin. "The Psychology of Bystanders, Perpetrators, and Heroic Helpers." *Understanding Genocide: The Social Psychology of the Holocaust.* Ed. Leonard S. Newman and Ralph Erber. New York: Oxford UP, 2002. 11–42. Print.

Waller, James. *Becoming Evil: How Ordinary People Commit Genocide and Mass Killing.* New York: Oxford UP, 2002. Print.

13

A Repertoire of Discernments: Hearing the Unsaid in Oral History Narratives

Frank Farmer and Margaret M. Strain

I n a volume dedicated to silence and listening as rhetorical arts, a chapter that discusses oral history narratives may seem odd, if not out of place. After all, what do oral historians, ethnographers, and researchers who rely on oral testimony set out to capture with their tape recorders and carefully composed questions if not the voices of interview subjects? Is not the value of the interview or videotape as a research tool to be found in the communicative power of sound? And consider the degree to which transcribers employ punctuation, auditory cues, and other speech markers to replicate the individual rhythms of the subject's speech, the cumulative effect of which permits listeners/readers/viewers to appreciate not only the content of the other's conversation but his or her personality as well.

As you may have surmised from our title, we believe much resides at the site of the oral interview, much that holds value for the researcher beyond what is merely heard. Take, for instance, the following passage excerpted from an interview Margaret M. Strain conducted with Edward P. J. Corbett in 1994 and later published in a print version in 2000:

> I took this [book] down and it opened to one of Blair's four lectures on the "Critical Examination of the Style" [of] a *Spectator* essay. And I said, "Oh my God, I'm going to be teaching this [in the survey course]. This is some way I can talk maybe about the form

of the thing instead of just talking about the contents." So I stood there and I read that essay: It's a sentence by sentence analysis . . . (I think it was 411 in the *Spectator*). Well, I turned the pages. . . . I must have been there for an hour. I said, "My God, where has this book been?" (4)

What does the first set of ellipses indicate? Did Corbett's stream of speech momentarily go off topic, so the interviewer chose to excise what follows for greater cohesion? Did Corbett pause and insert conversation holders (for example, "Um," "Hmmm," "Let me see") as he recollected the exact issue of the *Spectator*? Did ambient noise captured on the audio recording prevent the transcriptionist from deciphering what Corbett said? Of both sets of ellipses, we might ask, "Is there silence here?" If this is the case, is it possible that the silence resounds differently in each example? Listening to the actual audio recording might reveal that the first set of ellipses marks a moment of Corbett's silent mental recall. Yes, he was reading no. 411 of the *Spectator*. The second set poses another—and for our purposes, more rhetorically nuanced—understanding. If in listening to the recording, we detect an extended silence between Corbett's two statements, we may realize that we are witness to an important moment in our field's disciplinary history. Perhaps between the framing of "turn[ing] the pages" and "I must have been there for an hour" lies a moment of dawning awareness for a young professor who recognized that classical rhetoric might provide a theoretical framework for teaching writing.

Our chapter examines those moments when (seemingly) nothing—or perhaps, *nothing important*—is said, moments that are often excised from sonic transcriptions or, as the saying goes, left on the cutting room floor. We direct your attention to the oral interview event itself, urging you to consider not only how silences get represented in oral history narratives but also how silence shapes the meanings that emerge between interlocutors in the interview event. We wish to demonstrate how paying attention to what is *not* said might help scholars develop what we call a repertoire of discernments to inform the use and interpretation of oral histories. At a time when our pedagogies and research methods keep pace with developing technologies, visual media, and expanding global discourses, recognition for the ways silence accompanies these forms has never been more salient.[1]

An appreciation for what has been termed a rhetoric of silence is not new. In Plato's *Phaedrus*, Socrates advises his eager companion to "listen to [him] in silence" so that Phaedrus might learn from his mentor's instruction (145).[2] Classical rhetoricians such as Aristotle, Cicero, and the author of *Rhetorica ad Herennium* take note of how silence, carefully deployed, might prove a useful vehicle for addressing audiences. In fact, Roman teachers developed a host of terms—*obtincentia, praecisio, reticentia, interpellatio*—all of which correlate roughly to the Greek term *aposiopesis*, "a becoming silent" (Lanham 20). Feminists, too, have reanimated the voices of women who have historically been silenced and demonstrated how women have strategically used nondiscursive communication to achieve agency. Most famously, perhaps, in her fiction and essays, Tillie Olsen illuminates the effects of silencing in the lives of women writers. Julie E. Bokser has examined the letters of Sor Juana Inés de la Cruz, a seventeenth-century nun and poet, who first ignored a bishop's command to abstain from writing by composing her *La Respuesta (The Answer)*, then used the same document to explain that she would refrain from writing but not before assuring her readers that the silence to come was her conscious choice (15). Cheryl Glenn has helped to reclaim the contributions of women to classical rhetoric and has, more recently, surveyed the importance of silence in gendered, cultural, and communal spaces.[3] These uses of silence illustrate its power as a purposeful response to sound (that is, a deliberate non-sound) and an equally suasive effort to privilege certain sanctioned sounds at the expense of others. Yet in a Western culture that valorizes sound as the preeminent signifier of life, productivity, and meaning, where can oral historians look for help in the project of rehabilitating silence?

The first section of this chapter examines instances of silences that routinely occur as a part of the oral interview and the transcription/editing process that follows. We turn to the oral interview because these records—aural, oral, and visual—provide an ideal point of departure for understanding how a revaluation of silence might advance our methodological practices and legitimate its place in our public work and private lives. In the next section, we extend the conversation on silence using the ideas of Mikhail Bakhtin and V. N. Vološinov, a prominent member of Bakhtin's circle.[4] In brief, we explore how each theorist's understanding of the utterance provides a way to acknowledge and recuperate the importance of silence in understanding speech. That is, we highlight how

Bakhtin's notion of *logosphere* provides a means to investigate the temporal and spatial qualities of silence that exist as a part of (yet simultaneously distinct from) the spoken utterance. Our final section suggests how developing a repertoire for discerning silences might enhance our appreciation for those moments in human experience when silence speaks.

Representing Silence in Oral Interviews

Oral and written interviews underpin many of our discipline's research agendas and forms of scholarly inquiry. Scholars conducting case and longitudinal studies, ethnographies, and focus groups rely on the data collected via oral or videotaped interviews with their research participants. Edited interviews populate many of our print and online journals, and the Rhetoric and Composition Sound Archives serves as a repository for audio recordings that might otherwise be inaccessible to researchers.[5] If, to borrow a phrase from David Silverman, our discipline has become an "interview society," researchers would do well to investigate that more complex realm that sound and silence inhabit together (822).

Certainly, oral interviews are conducted for a variety of reasons, but there comes a point in any oral or audiotaped interview when the researcher must decide whether to transcribe the sonic record (whether it be a verbatim record or heavily edited manuscript) or leave the tape as a raw primary source. It is during the process of translating sound into print that a transcriber begins listening for what he or she deems representative of the interviewee's talk and meaning, and it is here where silences can go unattended. A trained transcriptionist may employ a coding system to capture phenomena that accompany an exchange between interlocutors (for example, overlaps in speech, turn transitions, changes in intonation or pitch) because the primary emphasis rests with what the interviewee says and how he or she says it. Typically, a transcribed interview will go through several permutations from the original, and any number of factors governs a transcriber's or editor's decisions about what and how much conversation is depicted.[6] In the interest of creating a seamless narrative, for example, an editor may move sections of text around so that topics are grouped together or strands of conversation cohere (Yow 237). As Studs Terkel observes, sometimes the space devoted to the interviewer is limited purposely to highlight the featured speaker in the exchange (Grele, *Envelopes* 36). Or, an interviewee may excise material during the editing process. Finally, a scholar intending to publish an interview as a stand-alone text may be subject to the space limitations of a print journal.

What, then, do manipulations of silence—deleting it, altering its presence to authorize one voice over another, changing its location—say about how researchers value it? In these instances, the potential fullness of silence is lost or, at the very least, diminished. This is not to say that silence goes completely unrecorded in transcriptions. Scholars who engage in conversation or discourse analysis do employ transcription symbols to account for frequencies and locations of silence during interviews. But here silence is reduced to a temporal measurement between sounds and between speakers. George Psathas suggests that in denoting time intervals between utterances, transcribers mark silences in seconds and tenths of a second (72–73). Following Psathas' directives, a transcription might appear thus:

> SAM: When will you (.4) be finished?
> (.6)
> MEG: Are you talking to me?

Anything less than a tenth of a second appears as a period enclosed by a single set of parentheses (.). Another option is to use dashes to signify a tenth of a second and a plus sign for a full second, enclosing both in parentheses:

> ANN: How's uh, (——+——) what's-her-name?

If the silences are not timed, the word "pause" in double parentheses is used for a silence within one speaker's turn. "Gap" refers to the silence between speakers:

> ANN: How's uh, ((pause)) what's-her-name?
> ((gap))
> SALLY: Jean? She's good.

The terms "gap" and "pause" are gestures toward silence, yet the terms themselves connote silence as lack, a space where no sound resides. Scholars' attempts to contain silence between the fragile ends of a typographical symbol suggest the limitations of transcription practice. Furthermore, we are reminded how transcription strips the interview scene of context.

There may be occasional asides to punctuate an exchange (for example, "Joe reaches for a book on the shelf"), but such references usually are inserted to explain an interruption in speech flow.

In the dialogues above, the transcriber *represents* the silences of others rather than *interprets* what the silences mean to the parties involved. The shift in emphasis from external audience to the participants themselves signals a change in the goals of interviewing. It is not uncommon for interviewing handbooks to advise researchers to remain as neutral as possible while collecting data, thereby defending oral interview practices against challenges to the objectivity, validity, and reliability of such practices (Hoffman; Cutter). While we understand the desire for rigor in our methodological practices, we are concerned that much may be lost if oral historians do not attend to the hermeneutics of the interview event. We thus support the view expressed by those who regard the interview as a mutual endeavor wherein speakers create knowledge together (Grele, "Private Memories" 257; Mishler 52).[7] That is, we understand the scene of the interview as an ecology in which silence, sound, and other sensate activity resides.

Understood this way, oral interviews constitute what Bakhtin calls an "open, (unfinalized) totality" (*Speech Genres* 134). If interviewers attend to silence as much as they do speech when participating in oral dialogues, how might these silent moments enrich our discipline's understanding of what is communicated? How would our knowledge of these silences moderate our use of written transcriptions? Or complicate how we respond to videotaped exchanges? To be sure, this approach to "reading" the site of the interview event precludes any final, authoritative interpretation of oral and audiotaped records. But unless researchers consider the spoken word to be readily transparent in its intended meaning—a view most reject as naive—and unless researchers consider the spoken word to be the sole source of meaning, they will be wise to interpret both words and silences *together* if they hope to acquire a larger, more nuanced understanding of the interview event. Before such is possible, we believe that silence must be rehabilitated so that researchers may become more attuned to silence as a world worth knowing. In the next section, we explore how Bakhtin and Vološinov illustrate the interpretative plurality that arises during a minimal exchange between speakers, a fictionalized example but one that has implications for oral interviewing that we explore later.

Bakhtin, Vološinov, and the Logosphere of the (Un)Said

Bakhtin offers a useful distinction between "quietude," in which "nothing makes a sound (or something does not make a sound)," and "silence," in which "nobody speaks" (*Speech Genres* 133). The former is a condition of nonspeaking phenomena; the latter, an inextricable part of the "human world (and only for a person)" (134). The tension between the two, Bakhtin adds, is "always relative," never absolute (134). And yet, for our purposes, the more interesting distinction is not between quietude and silence but rather between the spoken word and the silence that accompanies it. When taken together, these constitute, for Bakhtin, "a special logosphere, a unified and continuous structure" (134). Rejecting the notion that silence is mere absence or negation, Max Picard likewise describes silence as "a positive, a complete world in itself. . . . It is always wholly present in itself and it completely fills out the space in which it appears" (17). It is not visible, yet its presence is recognized; it is not tangible, yet it is felt palpably. And though they have distinct approaches to the question of silence, Bakhtin and Picard identify silence as a phenomenon coincident *to* and *with* all human experience. Of particular interest to us, both use spatial metaphors to locate silence within that matrix of sound, sensation, affect, and materiality in which oral history narratives typically unfold.

To illustrate how this is so, we borrow a scenario from Vološinov, a contemporary of Bakhtin's. In a now-famous discursus on a single, uttered adverb, "Well!," Vološinov asks us to imagine that "two people are sitting in a room. They are both silent. Then, suddenly, one of them says, 'Well!' The other does not respond" (99). Vološinov observes that this utterance is "utterly incomprehensible" to outsiders—unless, that is, we who are looking in on this scene have access to some privileged knowledge of the situation that shaped the utterance. Could we acquire such knowledge by defining the "phonetic, morphological, and semantic factors of the single word, *well*?" Vološinov asks. Hardly. But might some awareness of the personalities of speaker and listener—their values, intentions, feelings, and the like—enable us to better comprehend this situation and its utterance than we do on first reading? Perhaps, Vološinov might answer, but only to a limited degree, especially if readers focus solely on the isolated psychological states of the participants (99).

In fact, as Vološinov points out, the only way those looking in can understand "the sense and meaning of this colloquy" is for us *to know what they know but do not say.* That is, consider if, as outsiders, we somehow knew that

> at the time the colloquy took place, both interlocutors *looked up* at the window and *saw* that it had begun to snow; both *knew* that it was already May and that it was high time for spring to come; finally, *both* were *sick and tired* of the protracted winter—*they both were looking forward* to spring and *both were bitterly disappointed* by the late snowfall. On this "jointly seen" (snowflakes outside the window), "jointly known" (the time of year—May), and "unanimously evaluated" (winter wearied of, spring looked forward to)— on all this the utterance *directly depends*, all this is seized in its actual living import—is its very sustenance. (99)

If readers could unpack the accompanying silences inherent in the word "Well," it would become apparent that all of the information elaborated above would be assumed within the uttering of that single word. In fact, Vološinov maintains that any utterance, however poetic or prosaic, can be understood only with adequate knowledge of the extraverbal context. Such context, Vološinov adds, is constituted of "the *common spatial purview* of the interlocutors . . . the interlocutors' *common knowledge and understanding of the situation*, and . . . their *common evaluation* of that situation" (99). As readers learn a few more particulars of this situation, they can begin to see how the speaker is at once addressing the listener, whom he hopes to enlist as an ally, as well as the hero (theme) of his utterance, a seemingly eternal winter. No linguistic or psychological approach to our speaker's single-word utterance could possibly account for the complexities discovered in Vološinov's sociological analysis. These complexities could be revealed only in the relationship between the utterance and the extraverbal context in which it is uttered. And what makes possible a sense of this relationship at all, according to Vološinov, is the *intonation* of the utterance. It is tone that "establishes a firm link between verbal discourse and extraverbal context"; it is tone that "always lies on the border of the verbal and the nonverbal, the said and the unsaid" (102).

Vološinov insists, however, that the extraverbal context does not "cause" the utterance, for that would be to regard the extraverbal context as something external and mechanical to the utterance. Rather, it is more exact to say the situation itself becomes "an essential, constitutive part" of the utterance, which means that the utterance is not merely composed of "the part actualized in words," the said, but also "the assumed part," the unsaid (100). And it is here that Vološinov suggests that the utterance can be likened to the classical enthymeme, since the "missing premises" definition of the enthymeme would seem to account for "the assumed part" in a conversation.[8] Yet, for Vološinov to speak of "premises"—for example, in his analysis of the "Well!" scenario above—would seem to impoverish the rich complexity of that exchange. True, one might theoretically make explicit the "unsaid" in a series of interlocking syllogisms, but doing so would hardly capture the subtleties, the nuanced communication that actually occurs between the two interlocutors. What's more, serializing those assumptions would artificially (and inaccurately) represent that which occurs coincidently in the moment.

Vološinov's example is instructive in a number of ways, but for our purposes, we will draw attention to two. First, and as we noted above, his illustration rejects any conventional understanding of silence as the mere absence of speech, of silence as a phenomenon somehow *opposed* to the voiced word. Rather, from a dialogic perspective, the word and its accompanying silences are of a piece, inseparable. Silence, thus understood, is a constituent aspect of every utterance, and for Vološinov, we realize this is so because through intonation, the relationship between the word and its silences are revealed to be parts of something larger than both. And while oral historians typically give preeminence to the spoken word as the primary locus of meaning, Bakhtin reminds us that "to a certain degree, one can speak by means of intonation alone, making the verbally expressed part of speech relative and replaceable, almost indifferent. How often we use words whose meaning is unnecessary, or repeat the same word or phrase, just in order to have a material bearer for some necessary intonation" (*Speech Genres* 166). The word "Well" serves precisely this function. Having little (if any) semantic content, its tones carry the unsaid (but mutually shared) social evaluations of the two interlocutors. Without hearing that single word's intonations, however, most of us would be discursively adrift. For those who locate meaning exclusively in what is or has been said, Vološinov's illustration would amount to pure nonsense. The significance of any communicative event, when divorced from the evaluative tones that point us toward possible meanings, is diminished when listeners do not hear the intonations of the saying, as well as the content of the said. Think here of a friend, or student perhaps, who seems unable to hear irony in conversations or texts. Such persons serve as an unhappy reminder that our interpretations of other's words can be wildly mistaken or inappropriate without an ability to hear what tones (and the silences they represent) say to us.

Our second point is one regarding the vignette's narrator, the interpretive source of information. From what vantage does this person speak? Where, exactly, is he speaking from? And how is it that our narrator came to *know* all the details and particulars of this event? How, for example, does Vološinov (as narrator) know that "they both were looking forward to spring and [that] both were bitterly disappointed by the late snowfall"? Is this something the two men could actually know of one another, unless they told each other as much? It would seem, then, that our interlocutors are positioned squarely in the realm of the assumed (the enthymematic) that Vološinov so carefully describes. Yet while the participants in this imagined event are limited to what they assume about their situation and each other, Vološinov and his readers enjoy a measure of privileged knowledge of the two men that they do not have of each other. Vološinov's readers, in other words, know more about the characters in this scenario than do the characters themselves.

Of course, we understand that Vološinov conjures a fictional scene so that he may explicate its complexities for his readers. We realize that he does this for rhetorical purposes, to illustrate both the subtleties and complexities of what would otherwise be a fairly uninteresting scenario. To reveal the deeper significance of that word, "Well!," Vološinov has to draw upon knowledge that only an omniscient narrator could possess. He does so in the apparent belief that for a full understanding of this event, he cannot be limited strictly to what the two men know of each other or of the situation in which they found themselves. Vološinov surely could not have provided us with his insights had he not been able to stand above the situation he imagines, enjoying a surplus knowledge the rest of us do not have. And yet by virtue of elaborating the context of a fictional scene, he is able to reveal just how profoundly meaningful the silences are that occur in even the most ordinary of situations. The authorial privileges that Vološinov reserves for himself allow him to accomplish his purposes—purposes, needless to say, that are far different from those of the oral historian.[9] While the oral historian understandably might yearn for the kind of encompassing knowledge that Vološinov seems to possess, it is, in fact, this very difference between them that underscores the importance of attending to the tonal silences of oral interviews.

Unlike the fictional narrator, the oral historian and interviewee *strive for* an insider knowledge presumed to be always already incomplete.[10] The knowledge to be acquired must emerge from their active participation in the event and *only* from this participation. This means, among other things, that the work of the oral historian and interviewee is thoroughly and inescapably hermeneutic. Together, the two parties know their conversation is, and will remain, situational, partial, limited, and fallible—in a word, interpretive. The silences that Vološinov can explain from a privileged vantage are fully alive and realized in the world of the interview where tonal silences are *heard*, not narrated. This is a world rife with surprises, particularities, and random oddities, not to mention much that simply cannot be accounted for—all of which oral historians must, well, attempt to account for. It is they who must construct an insider's knowledge, and it is they who must do so from within an actually occurring conversation, rather than from outside a fictional one. It is they who may be uniquely poised to listen for, reclaim, and interpret silences that occur in our dialogues with others.

If oral historians do not have omniscience at their disposal, neither do they have the objectivity that many desire. Some accepted practices in oral history research endorse the view that the interviewer should be a *non*participant in the exchange that occurs between interviewer and interviewee.[11] Much methodological thinking holds that any attention devoted to the researcher as a full participant in the interview event tends to appropriate, subtract from, or interfere with what the interview subject has to say. From this point of view, some think it better that the researcher *not* be actively present (figuratively speaking) at the very interview he or she conducts. Failing that, and in the name of objective rigor, some may also think it prudent for the researcher's presence to be minimally acknowledged to other researchers. Such is the case when interviewers are designated by initials (for example, FF, MS) or when effaced entirely in question and answer formats.

But we think much is lost in this abdication of the participant role. While it may be true that the research interview is not the most dialogic of language events, we maintain that each interview has its own dynamics, its own peculiarities, its own uniqueness as an event, and that these qualities largely derive from the relationship between both speakers. One might argue that such qualities are negligible concerns, that what matters are the interviewee's responses to the questions addressed to him or her. But this reductive understanding does not take into account the fact that what the respondent tells us is, in some degree, always shaped by the interested participation of the researcher—or, perhaps more exactly, what Bakhtin might call the researcher's "active responsive attitude" (*Speech Genres* 68). And why might such an attitude be valuable for the researcher?

In an early philosophical essay that slightly predates Vološinov's example, Bakhtin is interested in the ethics of the act—that is to say, the act as a singular, unrepeatable event. In this essay, Bakhtin makes the rather large claim that "the world in which an act or deed proceeds . . . is a world that is seen, heard, touched, and thought, a world permeated with the emotional-volitional tones of the affirmed validity of values" (*Toward* 56). But what does it mean to say that the world is "permeated" with "emotional-volitional tones"? His basic point, we think, is that our experience of the world—our inescapable, induplicable experience of the world—is steeped in valuation. To act, to think, to feel, and, of course, to speak is to possess an attitude, is to assume an evaluative stance toward someone or something. In this way, Bakhtin reminds us that our experience of the world is never one of complete rationality, of object relations, of indifference, of, in a word, *non*participation. Actual lived experience cannot be neutral. Indeed, Bakhtin hints that it might be oxymoronic to talk of disinterested experience: "an object that is absolutely indifferent, totally finished," according to Bakhtin, "cannot be something one actually becomes conscious of" (32). The same may be said of those particular acts called utterances: when any of us speak about, of, or to the world, our acts of saying are hardly neutral or objective. Apart from what we say *about* the world, our words, our tones, and, yes, our silences position us *toward* the world, revealing our evaluative attitude regarding the things of which we speak. The oral historian could ill afford to dismiss those evaluations as insignificant.

Therefore, as an interested participant in the interview event, as one who embraces active responsive understanding, the oral history researcher is in a position to be especially attuned to the silences that accompany that event. Indeed, these are the silences one hears only when participating fully in the interview event itself. And while we cannot enumerate all the kinds of silences possible during an interview, we offer a preliminary map for imagining what some of these silences might be, and we invite readers to help us develop a repertoire for discerning and interpreting others.

Toward a Repertoire of Discernments

As rhetorical phenomena, silences differ according to a variety of situational contexts and purposes.[12] In what follows, we want to begin to identify certain specific genres of silence that accompany oral history narratives. While some may object that the use of the term "genre" here is too imprecise, we believe that if it is legitimate to speak of "speech genres" (as Bakhtin does), and if, as we have argued, silence is concomitant to speech, then we are merely shifting Bakhtin's emphasis from *speech* genres to genres of *silence*, convinced that one cannot exist without the other. We do not claim that the genres noted below are limited exclusively to oral history research, but we do think that some silences are more likely to emerge in the interview event than in others. Nor do we mean to suggest that our catalog exhausts the potential silences that might be recognized at the site of any given interview. Having made the case for the uniqueness of each interview event, we would hardly be inclined to foreclose on the possibility of surprise, to discredit the unforeseeable and spontaneous silences that might become apparent to the parties involved. Still, we offer the catalog below as a starting point for investigating the many silences that researchers would do well to listen for.

First, we observe that *ambient* silences are always present in conversations, dialogues, interviews, and in most discursive forms that occur throughout all verbal contexts. This silence is deeply, thoroughly contextualized (by location, time, space, and material exigencies). Ambient silence, for example, is the "open totality" of silence that precedes that uttered word, "Well!" It is the silence that comes with no apparent urgency to be broken. It is the all-encompassing silence against which words may be heard, yes, but against which other silences may be heard as well. For the oral historian, its importance cannot be overestimated because it is what makes our work possible; it is "what allows speech to take place. It endows speech with the capacity to bear meaning" (Pinchevski 71). For this reason, ambient silence is also the ground for the relationship between interviewer and interviewee.

Another genre of silence that accompanies the interview event is *enthymematic* silence. Our discussion of Vološinov's example above details how it is that meaningful silences reside in the shared but unspoken assumptions between interlocutors. As Vološinov demonstrates, what goes unstated may often be apprehended through intonation alone, distinct from what the voiced word actually says (as in irony, for example). For the oral history researcher, enthymematic silences would likely occur when the interviewer and interviewee have a shared history, a shared identity, or perhaps a meaningful shared experience. Moreover, it may be that in oral histories developed from multiple interviews over time, the likelihood of enthymematic silences gradually increases with each subsequent interview, as the two interlocutors become more familiar with each other's habits, values, patterns, responses, and so on. In fact, whenever the two parties involved establish the grounds for any familiarity whatsoever, the oral historian would be wise to listen for the enthymematic silences that may encompass the interview event.

Meditative silences are typically discovered in those moments when an interviewee reflects on his or her understanding of a question, or carefully considers how to phrase a response, or ponders alternate responses to the same question, or evaluates the possible consequences of a certain answer, or patiently tries to reconstruct a vague or fading memory of a past event. The interviewer, too, has occasion for meditative silences. When the interviewee offers a response that opens up a new line of questioning, the interviewer may take considerable pains (and time) in the formulation of those questions, since they are not the prepared ones with which he or she began the interview. It may sometimes even be the case that the interviewee bestows upon the interviewer a "moment or two" for the interviewer to gather his or her thoughts, a permitted space for the meditative silence needed to understand something that was said.

A closely related genre would be what we call *kairic* silences. These silences we regard to be largely spontaneous, and if *kairos*, in its traditional rhetorical sense, can be understood as timeliness—the right words at the right time—*kairic* silences, then, ought to be understood to be the right silences at the right time: the appropriately mute, rhetorically powerful, and well-placed silences that occur in dialogues with others. Whether silences occur by fortuitous chance or by the creative efforts of interlocutors is, of course, a matter of some importance to the oral history researcher. If the former is true, if the *kairic* opening is a happy accident of conversation, the researcher must be prepared to receive that moment and the potential meanings that its silences might reveal. If, on the other hand, a silent moment (or the conditions for that moment) can be created, then the researcher would do well to consider how meaningful silences might be fostered in the interview event itself.

Finally, as many oral history researchers know, *strategic* silences (from either speaker) can be especially powerful. A purposely delivered or performed silence can be read in any number of ways. In deploying this particular genre of silence, for example, speakers can convey resistance, lack of interest, comfort, anger, weariness, embarrassment, and a host of other sensibilities. One intent of these calculated silences, for example, might be to hasten the end of the interview. Or to leave the interviewer with doubts about the veracity of the interviewee's statements. Or to protect the interviewee from the discomforts of answering truthfully to an especially sensitive question. It is the determined and savvy interviewer who is able to navigate potentially disruptive moments in ways that preserve the purposes of the interview and thereby sustain the interview dynamic. Of course, it is not the interviewee alone who deploys strategic silences. Interviewers, too, withhold spoken words, typically to provoke the interviewee into elaborating more than he or she was originally inclined to do. Far more worrisome, though, would be scenarios when the interviewer deploys strategic silence in order to provoke the interviewee into an anxious search for a response that the interviewer desires.

All of the silences identified here require something more than ellipses marks, something beyond editorial or typographic representations. They require the full presence, the active responsive understanding of the oral history researcher as a participant in the interview event itself. They demand of that researcher (and of his or her texts) a sophisticated interpretive awareness—what we call a repertoire of discernments—that will enable the researcher to hear the meaningful silences that inevitably emerge in any given interview.

We freely admit that interpreting other people's silences is, at best, a problematic enterprise, one riddled with uncertainties and potential misunderstandings. And while we do not want to posit an equivalence, we recognize that the same could be said of all efforts to interpret spoken (and written) words as well, whether those words appear in ordinary conversation, literary texts, or oral history interviews. As researchers, we can hardly refuse the obligation to interpret the words spoken to us—and to report our understanding of those words to others. But our challenge is that we have very little practice attending to and interpreting the kinds of silences that routinely occur in our interviews. For this reason, we should be eager to ask: How might the dialogic nature of the oral interview be enriched if both participants attended to silences and attempted to explain their importance? Who better to make sense of the exchange than those involved? What would it mean to rethink how *meaningful* silence gets represented in discourse analysis transcripts?

We do not yet know how such silences might be faithfully expressed in our work. But we do know that if, as we have argued, there is much meaning to be found in silences, then we must at least be favorably disposed to hearing silences as utterances. We must be actively receptive to listening for what the unsaid says to us. In doing so, our inquiries will be richer, our knowledge more complete, our appreciation for the unspoken more deeply understood.

Notes

1. On the relationship of silence to teaching writing, see Pat Belanoff's "Silence." Michelle Grijalva focuses on silence as a cultural value in "Teaching American Indian Students."

2. This admonition must, of course, be read as somewhat ironic, for what Socrates ultimately desires from Phaedrus is not his silence but his companion's voiced participation in a dialogue about the true nature of rhetoric. One of Socrates' objections to rhetoric is the compulsory silence that continuous (uninterrupted) discourse seems to require from listeners, a silence that preempts the give and take of dialectic.

3. See Cheryl Glenn's *Rhetoric Retold* and *Unspoken*. In the latter, Glenn identifies silence as a form of delivery. In a similar vein, Bernard P. Dauenhauer argues that silence is performative in *Silence*.

4. See also Frank Farmer's *Saying and Silence*.

5. *Writing on the Edge, Composition Forum, JAC* (formerly *Journal of Advanced Composition*), *Issues in Writing*, and *Kairos: A Journal of Rhetoric, Technology, and Pedagogy* are among a few scholarly journals that include interviews in their issues. Oral narratives can also be found as part of the special collections of several university libraries, collections of textbooks (University of New Hampshire), personal papers (University of Rhode Island), writing centers (University of Louisville).

6. In an ideal setting, the oral historian would record, transcribe, and edit an interview; however, it is not uncommon for another person to complete the transcription process or for an editor to assist in the preparation of a print interview.

In such cases, researchers are advised to listen to the original recording while reading the edited version(s) to detect mistakes in transcription and, for the purposes of this paper, moments of silence. (See Baum; Dunaway and Baum.)

7. Ronald Grele eschews the term "interview" altogether when referring to oral history work, preferring the phrase "conversational narratives" ("Private" 257–60).

8. In a footnote, Vološinov alludes to the enthymeme as a form of the syllogism, "one of whose premises is not expressed but assumed" (100 n). This is, of course, a standard definition and one that has been questioned in some recent literature on the enthymeme. One unfortunate result of Vološinov's use of such a comparison, we think, might reside in its implicit approval of the formalities of Aristotelian logic when, more precisely, his analysis moves us from the strictly logical to the dialogical.

9. We are reminded here of Ivor A. Richards's famous definition of rhetoric as "the study of misunderstanding and its remedies" (3). We are also reminded of Bakhtin's examination of narrative privilege in "Author and Hero." Here, Bakhtin observes the artistic challenge faced by the literary artist and what he chooses to do with that "surplus" or excess of seeing that authors may possess but that some (notably Dostoyevsky) refuse.

10. As Alessandro Portelli writes, "The interviewees are always, though perhaps unobtrusively, studying the interviewers who 'study' them" (70). Researchers studying interview dynamics have observed how participants "read" one another, enacting a version of themselves in response to particular interview topics (see Barrick, Patton, and Haugland; Paunonen, Jackson, and Oberman; and Rapley).

11. Certainly, the aims and uses of the oral interview affect the interviewer's degree of representation in a transcribed interview. Oral historians such as Grele adopt a more social epistemic view toward oral interviews, as does behavioral scientist Elliott Mishler.

12. In her *Unspoken: A Rhetoric of Silence*, Glenn, citing Richard L. Johannesen, provides readers with an impressive but "inexhaustive" list of the many meanings that silence can fulfill in various rhetorical contexts (16). While neither author links those meanings to specific contexts, we wish to attempt to do something along those lines here. More recently, Thomas Huckin has also explored genres of silence, though not genres related to a specific research methodology.

Works Cited

Bakhtin, Mikhail M. "Author and Hero in Aesthetic Activity." *Art and Answerability: Early Philosophical Essays*. Trans. Vadim Liapunov. Austin: U of Texas P, 1990. 4–256. Print.

———. *Speech Genres and Other Late Essays*. Trans. Vern W. McGee. Ed. Caryl Emerson and Michael Holquist. Austin: U of Texas P, 2002. Print.

——. *Toward a Philosophy of the Act.* Trans. and notes Vadim Liapunov. Ed. Michael Holquist and Vadim Liapunov. U of Texas P Slavic Series, 10. Austin: U of Texas P, 1993. Print.

Barrick, Murray R., Gregory K. Patton, and Shanna N. Haugland. "Accuracy of Interviewer Judgments of Job Applicant Personality Traits." *Personnel Psychology* 53 (2000): 925–51. Print.

Baum, Willa K. *Transcribing and Editing Oral History.* Nashville: American Association for State and Local History, 1991. Print.

Belanoff, Pat. "Silence: Reflection, Literacy, Learning, and Teaching." *CCC* 52 (2001): 399–428. Print.

Bokser, Julie E. "Sor Juana's Rhetoric of Silence." *Rhetoric Review* 25 (2006): 5–21. Print.

Cutter, William, III. "Accuracy in Oral History Interviewing." Dunaway and Baum 99–106. Print.

Dauenhauer, Bernard P. *Silence: The Phenomenon and Its Ontological Significance.* Bloomington: Indiana UP, 1980. Print.

Dunaway, David K., and Willa K. Baum, eds. *Oral History: A Disciplinary Anthology.* 2nd ed. Walnut Creek, CA: AltaMira, 1996. Print.

Farmer, Frank. *Saying and Silence: Listening to Composition with Bakhtin.* Logan: Utah State UP, 2001. Print.

Glenn, Cheryl. *Rhetoric Retold: Regendering the Traditions from Antiquity through the Renaissance.* Carbondale: Southern Illinois UP, 1997. Print.

——. *Unspoken: A Rhetoric of Silence.* Carbondale: Southern Illinois UP, 2004. Print.

Grele, Ronald. *Envelopes of Sound: The Art of Oral History.* 1975. 2nd ed. Chicago: Precedent, 1985. Print.

——. "Private Memories and Public Presentation: The Art of Oral History." Grele 243–83. Print.

Grijalva, Michelle. "Teaching American Indian Students: Interpreting the Rhetorics of Silence." *Writing in Multicultural Settings.* Ed. Carol Severino, Juan C. Guerra, and Johnnella E. Butler. New York: MLA, 1997. 40–50. Print.

Hoffman, Alice. "Reliability and Validity in Oral History Interviewing." Dunaway and Baum 87–93. Print.

Huckin, Thomas. "On Textual Silences, Large and Small." *Traditions of Writing Research.* Ed. Charles Bazerman et al. New York: Routledge, 2010. 419–31. Print.

Johannesen, Richard L. "The Function of Silence: A Plea for Communication Research." *Western Speech* 38 (1974): 25–35. Print.

Lanham, Richard A. *A Handlist of Rhetorical Terms.* 2nd ed. Berkeley: U of California P, 1991. Print.

Mishler, Elliot. *Research Interviewing: Context and Narrative.* Cambridge: Harvard UP, 1986. Print.

Olsen, Tillie. *Silences.* New York: Feminist P of City U of New York, 2003. Print.

Paunonen, Sampo V., Douglas N. Jackson, and Steven M. Oberman. "Personnel Selection Decisions: Effects of Applicant Personality and the Letter of Reference." *Organizational Behavior and Human Decision Processes* 40 (1987): 96–114. Print.

Picard, Max. *The World of Silence.* Chicago: Henry Regnery, 1952. Print.

Pinchevski, Amit. "Freedom from Speech (or the Silent Demand)." *Diacritics* 31 (2001): 71–84. Print.

Plato. *Phaedrus. The Rhetorical Tradition: Readings from Classical Times to the Present.* Ed. Patricia Bizzell and Bruce Herzberg. 2nd ed. Boston: Bedford/St. Martin's, 2001. 138–68. Print.

Portelli, Alessandro. "What Makes Oral History Different?" *The Oral History Reader.* Ed. Robert Perks and Alistair Thomson. New York: Routledge, 1998. 63–74. Print.

Psathas, George. *Conversation Analysis: The Study of Talk-in-Interaction.* Thousand Oaks, CA: Sage, 1995. Print.

Rapley, Timothy John. "The Art(fulness) of Open-Ended Interviewing: Some Considerations on Analyzing Interviews." *Qualitative Research* 1 (2001): 303–23. Print.

The Rhetoric and Composition Sound Archives. Texas Christian U. Web. Feb. 15, 2008.

Richards, Ivor A. *The Philosophy of Rhetoric.* New York: Oxford UP, 1950. Print.

Silverman, David. "Analyzing Talk and Text." *Handbook of Qualitative Research.* Ed. Norman K. Denizen and Yvonna S. Lincoln. 2nd ed. Thousand Oaks, CA: Sage, 2000. 821–34. Print.

Strain, Margaret M. "'A Serendipitous Moment': An Interview with Edward P. J. Corbett." *Composition Forum* 11 (2000): 1–19. Print.

Vološinov. V. N. "Discourse in Life and Discourse in Art." *Freudianism: A Critical Sketch.* Ed. I. R. Titunik and Neal H. Bruss. Bloomington: Indiana UP, 1976. 93–116. Print.

Yow, Valerie Raleigh. *Recording Oral History: A Practical Guide for Social Scientists.* Thousand Oaks, CA: Sage, 1994. Print.

14

Cultivating Listening: Teaching from a Restored Logos

Shari Stenberg

> We must remember that one of the most insidious ways of keeping
> women and minorities powerless is to . . . let them speak freely and
> not listen to them with serious intent.
> > —Mitsuye Yamada, "Invisibility Is an Unnatural Disaster:
> > Reflections of an Asian American Woman"

Within both composition and critical education discourse, few concepts are as highly valorized as voice. Consequently, as a teacher who aims to help students assert authoritative and engaging voices and to create spaces for those voices that have been historically marginalized and silenced, I often conflate loud, rousing debate with a successful class. Lately, however, I am concerned that the sound of voices is not enough. As women's studies teacher-scholar Margaret Stetz points out, the 1990s brought an abundance of texts that offer students models of young women "speaking up"; as a result, she finds that her students feel increasingly able to voice their ideas in class. While this is a positive shift, I am aware, like Stetz, that the addition of voices makes little difference if there isn't equal attention devoted to careful listening. As Carmen Luke reminds us, it is insufficient to invite new voices to speak without altering the structures that excluded them in the first place. And one means of exclusion is cultural inability—or refusal—to listen.

In this chapter, I examine how the exclusion of listening has been normalized in the academy by considering what Krista Ratcliffe calls "the organizing principle" of both disciplinary and cultural biases: a diminished notion of *logos*. According to Martin Heidegger, the West inherited "logos" as the Greek noun, understood as a system of reasoning and forming logic, but lost its verb form, *legein*, which means not only to speak but also "to lay down, to lay before"—that is, to listen (Heidegger qtd. in Fiumara 3).

The result is an impoverished notion of language that relies on an "arrogant" logos, ignoring knowledge deemed "irrational" or "illogical" (Fiumara 6). In addition to excluding particular kinds of voices, logos without listening also perpetuates a homogenized mode of speech based on competition rather than dialogue—or, as Wayne Booth puts it, a rhetoric that overvalues the question of "How can I change your mind?" and undervalues that of "When should I change my mind?" (Booth and Elbow 379). Consequently, opportunities for genuine listening—and thus for dialogue and self-reflection—are diminished.

In what follows, I build on Ratcliffe's theory of rhetorical listening by extending its implications into the classroom to show what a pedagogy of listening makes possible. With Joy Ritchie and Kate Ronald, I agree that the best way to deepen the impact of crucial new visions offered by feminist rhetoric, including rhetorical listening, is to document and theorize their enactment in local contexts (2).

To do so, I first examine the consequences of academic exchange—in the classroom and in scholarship—informed by a divided logos. I contend that a logos that places listening and speaking in opposition prevents us from the kind of receptivity necessary to overcome other dualisms that limit genuine dialogue: assent and critique, logos and pathos, and rationalism and excess. Drawing from specific moments in a course called Rhetoric of Women Writers, wherein listening proved essential to the pedagogy, I consider the possibilities opened by cultivating listening as a vital component of critical-feminist teaching.

Assent and Critique

From the Greeks, the West inherited a notion of logos that conflates rational thought with forceful speech acts such as probing, scrutinizing, critiquing, examining, and exploring (Fiumara 16). This notion of logos, however, represents only one side of a two-sided coin: speech without listening. When listening is considered at all, it is deemed speech's passive subordinate, its unequal partner.

A restored definition of logos, however, disrupts this speech/listening binary to encompass both saying and *laying* as reciprocal, active modes of invention. Here, listening enables what Heidegger calls "laying-to-let-lie-before," reminiscent of harvesting or gathering a crop. Within this conception, we listen, or let something lie before us, not to accumulate another's ideas but to safely keep them, to provide shelter for what has been gathered (Fiumara 4). There is no production of wine without a gathering and safekeeping of the vintage, just as there is no genuine dialogue without dwelling in another's ideas.

This gathering is not how academics typically conceive of knowledge formation, however. As Fiumara contends, a divided notion of logos shapes the intellectual heritage of the West and makes Western logic the (seemingly) "most reliable cognitive standpoint" (9). Consequently, academic culture is built upon a notion of logos that is more "involved in hunting than in cultivation" (10). Others' ideas are seized, appropriated, and discarded according to a predetermined agenda. In contrast, laying-to-let-lie-before—listening—requires us to nurture, tend to, and safely keep that which we engage.

To cultivate rather than hunt—that is, to capture and destroy—another's words or ideas is to rethink entrenched academic practices that value critique at the expense of assent (Booth and Elbow) and that position disciplinary members in agonistic relation to one another. Listening, Fiumara writes, is "characterized by the requirement that we dwell with, abide by, whatever we try to know; that we aim at coexistence with, rather than knowledge-of" (16).

Indeed, normative academic practices do require that close attention be paid to the words of others before one offers a contribution. We see an example of this expectation in Chris Thaiss and Terry Myers Zawacki's 2006 cross-disciplinary study wherein faculty across disciplines emphasized the importance of a writer attending to and reflecting on the conversation he or she seeks to enter (5). In fact, they point out that faculty are "invariably harsh toward any student or scholar who hasn't done the background reading" (5). While we may teach students to do the "background reading," however, this is not necessarily the same as fostering in them an ability to *listen* to the scholarly dialogue in which they engage. In fact, within the divided logos, attending to the words of others before contributing one's own idea tends to function not so much as an act of safekeeping and dwelling within as an *accumulation* of knowledge or demonstration of mastery. Evoking one's knowledge of a particular area of inquiry, then, often becomes a way to pave the road for one's own contribution, not to work in relation to other scholars.

Of course, as Peter Elbow points out, many educators are likely to argue that students do not have trouble with assent or belief; rather, they lack the ability to question, to achieve critical distance (Booth and Elbow 394). He contends, however, that while it is crucial to teach students to read against the grain, it is equally important to help them read *with* it. "Lack of critical distance is *not* the same as full, rich involvement—the ability to *dwell in* a text or an idea" (394). Ratcliffe names this distinction "understanding" or "standing under" another's ideas. Rather than reading or listening to accumulate another's ideas so as to impose one's own agenda, standing under requires us to let "discourses wash over, through, and around us" and then let them "lie there to inform our politics and ethics" (*Rhetorical Listening* 205).

This distinction becomes particularly pertinent when I teach texts that feature historically silenced voices—most recently, in a course called Rhetoric of Women Writers that examines rhetorical contributions by women from antiquity to the late twentieth century. While many of these students entered the class with associations of rhetoric as a canon of ancient texts or as the practice of persuasion, the feminist texts we engaged asked them to think differently about what constitutes rhetoric. These texts therefore have potential to foster new ways to think about what "counts" as rhetoric, how we discern "legitimate" knowledge and speech acts, and what form methods of persuasion can assume. The fulfillment of their potential depends, though, on their being heard.

Listening to them, however, was not easy for many students, largely because they responded to them as they had been trained to approach texts in English studies. That is, they demonstrated that they could articulate the piece's argument—they had completed the reading—and then they moved on to point to the piece's flaws, often with language like, "It is [the author's] methods of persuasion, however, I find a bit questionable," or, "In many cases throughout the work, I found myself doubting whether her message was legitimate." That is to say, they read *for* their own intent of critique (the textual "outcome" we privilege in English) rather than "*with* the intent to understand the claims made by the text, the cultural logics that shape those claims, and the rhetorical negotiations involved for both writer and reader" (Ratcliffe, *Rhetorical Listening* 205).

My concern with the kinds of responses that emerged is that critique (or dismissal) seems to be the end goal of the engagement, leading the reader to evaluate the texts for how they deviate from academic norms rather than for the possibilities they offer. Often, I noted that listening seemed to cease when the reader became offended by ideas that provoked discomfort. Critique then functioned as a mechanism to fend off these new ideas, offering justification for the reader to remain squarely in his or her current position. This mode of critique tends also to assume the writer's position as monolithic and thus immediately knowable. If one disagrees with or is put off by one rhetorical feature of the piece, the entire position is dismissed. As a result, the reader loses the opportunity to locate or build upon elements of the text with which he or she *does* connect or could engage to foster his or her own thinking.

While we have plenty of examples of the critique-and-dismiss model I describe, it is more difficult to find examples of standing under another's words. Standing under involves an examination of the intent and the cultural logics, the belief systems or modes of reasoning, that shape our own positions; it thus requires both self-reflexivity and a willingness to move beyond one's current position (Ratcliffe, *Rhetorical Listening* 205). I began to read my students' papers for examples of "standing under" so that I could consider what enabled this process and how to make it visible to my students. I found a good example in Lesley's response to Nomy Lamm's 1995 "It's a Big Fat Revolution," an essay that describes Lamm's experience as a woman who identifies as gay, disabled, and fat and her negotiation of the oppression that results.

In class, Lesley described feeling at first put-off by Lamm's seeming anger and arrogance. Rather than use her discomfort as a reason to disengage from the piece, however, Lesley dwelled within the argument, allowing herself to cultivate its layers of nuance and even contradictions. Ultimately, this enabled her to consider the rationale that may have shaped Lamm's rhetorical choices and to examine "fat oppression" from a new perspective:

> I was struck by Nomy Lamm's use of both anger and arrogance as rhetorical devices. The more I think about it, the better I think it

functions for what seem to be her rhetorical purposes. In a society where "Fatkikecripplecuntqueer" people are often openly, sometimes literally, frowned upon and shamed, Lamm's confident, frank rhetoric is jarring—and I think it's supposed to be. If a reader is prone to judging her [body], then he or she is in for a challenge: Lamm astutely argues against society's prejudices about fat. Said reader will find his or her usually unquestioned assumptions about fat met head-on, and not a little angrily. If a reader is prone to pity her [body], then he or she is jarred away from that response by Lamm's expressed pride in and openness about her body. While she critiques society's commonly held assumptions and attitudes about fat, she doesn't seem to want or need anyone's pity. Statements like "I know how fucking brilliant my girlfriends and I are" and "My body is fucking beautiful" show that pity is uninvited. Her confidence highlights the absence of shame and self-deprecation that society expects of fat people.

What's most important about Lesley's response is not, ultimately, her agreement with Lamm's points or strategies; rather, it is with what can be gained by dwelling within, rather than immediately critiquing, a text. To listen to Lamm's text is to hear it as multivocal, as a nuanced position cultivated over time and still under revision. To listen to Lamm is to assume responsibility for both asking difficult questions about a kind of oppression society often deems justified and thinking in deeper ways about what women are and are not allowed to say and feel about their bodies. Lesley's decision to cultivate rather than hunt Lamm's ideas led to a rich and changing rhetorical analysis.

If we begin with a conception of logos that requires a reciprocal relationship between speech and listening, we might likewise understand "critique" and "assent" to function dialectically. That is, while critique is often understood as a speech act that disrupts or rejects another's words, a restored logos may help us to imagine critique as incomplete without listening. As Ratcliffe notes, critique that encompasses rhetorical listening requires one to ask: "What's at stake? For whom? And why?" (*Rhetorical Listening* 97).

Standing under another's words further prompts us to consider the way our own intentions may limit our interpretation and capacity to listen to another. It asks listeners to move beyond a position whereby one holds a new idea or unfamiliar voice always at a safe distance, which can leave the listener unchanged and more firmly entrenched in his or her own thinking, and instead to leave open the possibility of being changed by the safekeeping of another's ideas.

Listening to Anger

During the week the Rhetoric of Women Writers class focused on silence, we discussed Gloria Anzaldúa's piece "How to Tame a Wild Tongue." Annie, a senior who had studied the author in another class, led us to engage a passage from Anzaldúa's *Borderlands* that wasn't part of our assignment reading but that she had read in another class. Since she readily embraced most of Anzaldúa's ideas, her resistance to the piece disturbed and preoccupied her.

She read this passage to the group: "[Chicano/as] need to say to white society: We need you to accept the fact that Chicanos are different, to acknowledge your rejection and negation of us. We need you to own the fact that you looked upon us as less than human, that you stole our lands, our personhood, our self-respect. We need you to make public restitution" (85–86). Several students spoke up to suggest that Annie was not wrong to feel offended by Anzaldúa's prose in this passage. "It's too angry to be useful," one student said. Another remarked that Anzaldúa simply "puts readers off" with these kinds of accusations, further dividing racial groups. One student labeled the passage a "rant."

Certainly prose that sounds angry defies institutional and cultural privileging of discourse deemed "rational"—meaning, devoid of emotion. A divided logos—which Fiumara contends is "ready even to ignore anything that does not properly fit in with a logocentric system of knowledge"—positions logos in opposition, rather than in dialogue with, pathos (6). Indeed, Thaiss and Zawacki found this notion echoed in their study, wherein faculty agreed that "in the academic universe the senses and emotions must always be subject to *control by reason*" (6). Logos is understood to discipline, control, or neutralize the wild and unrefined pathos, such that pathos is not considered, itself, a legitimate mode of reasoning—a rhetorical choice that one might craft and harness. It isn't surprising, then, that we often find it difficult to know how to listen to—or facilitate our students' listening to—pathos.

In our discussion of Anzaldúa's list of demands, several of us pointed to them as a rhetorical strategy rather than a spontaneous "rant." "Why might Anzaldúa have chosen to rely on such evocative language?" I asked. "Can one not be logical and angry at the same time?" Some other students joined in with their own questions. "Who is her audience?" and "Can't it be useful to evoke discomfort and anger in her readers?" I mentioned that in prior pages, Anzaldúa makes similarly charged demands to Chicano men, which presumably didn't evoke this kind of response in Annie. "Why not?" I asked.

Annie explained that she responded defensively to the charge against white people, and not to the equally impassioned directives toward Chicano men, because she felt blamed for a historical situation of which she had no part. Consequently, she met Anzaldúa's anger with anger of her own and didn't know how—despite her good intentions—to listen.

Within this divided logos that places reason in opposition to, or as a check on, pathos, affect is approached as something to contain or avoid rather than as something to engage and dwell within. Rather than listening to stand under or dwell within, readers are likely to approach pathos with what Ratcliffe terms "dysfunctional silence," resulting in three dysfunctional rhetorical stances: denial, defensiveness, and guilt/ blame (*Rhetorical Listening* 91).

In response to Annie, Marc, a student who had never before spoken in class—though certainly practiced rhetorical listening—raised his hand to describe his life in a small Nebraska town, where he was raised by his white father and Puerto Rican mother. In this town, where white people significantly outnumbered people of color, he said there existed a great deal of both "brown pride" and "brown anger." "But the anger isn't directed at any one individual," he insisted. "You shouldn't feel offended by anger of minority people. We're mad at the system; we're not mad at any one white person. And we need that anger. It can feel really good and empowering."

Marc's connection of anger to his own life, as well as the attention he called to the defensive response Anzaldúa's words raised, helped to make visible the dysfunctional logic of guilt/blame informing our dialogue. His comment nudged us to move out of a dysfunctional place of guilt and defensiveness in response to Anzaldúa's words and toward a deeper consideration of the contexts informing anger and the reasons she may have chosen to depict it. In other words, he helped us to listen to the piece.

Enacting the process of listening proved helpful in subsequent classes, particularly when we discussed Audre Lorde's "The Uses of Anger:

Women Responding to Racism." As she writes, "My anger is a response to racist attitudes and to the actions and presumptions that arise out of those attitudes. If your dealings with other women reflect those attitudes, then my anger and your attendant fears are spotlights that can be used for growth" (124). We began to ask what it means to use guilt, fear, or anger as a starting point for dialogue rather than as "bricks in a wall against which we all flounder" (124). What does it mean to live, at least momentarily, with painful or uncomfortable feelings that emerge when we understand that systems that have violated others have benefited us? Indeed, part of rhetorical listening, of gathering and dwelling in, requires lingering on one's own emotive response—often discomfort—long enough to allow oneself to be changed by one's hearing.

Ratcliffe argues that rhetorical listening—dwelling in rather than defending—can help us move away from dysfunctional positions of denial, defensiveness, and guilt/blame and instead offers three functional stances: recognition, critique, and accountability. Recognition involves an effort to understand the contexts that shape the speaker's words and choices. Critique is redefined by Ratcliffe as an evaluation that "moves beyond easy common-sensical interpretations (or the sense that a dominant culture holds is common): it is an evaluation that makes audible the echoes of that which is commonly rendered 'excess'" (*Rhetorical Listening* 97). This is a generative critique, then, that in some way moves the listener from a place he or she previously occupied. Finally, accountability requires us to recognize how our lives interlock with others' as well as how the past influences the present. Accountability also involves "forward-looking ways" to address social and individual wrongdoings. As Ratcliffe writes, "My purpose is to hold myself accountable for how I listen to [a] debate and what I choose to offer (or not offer) in return" (98).

As we discussed how to move from guilt/blame and make use of our discomfort, Melanie, a self-identified biracial student, offered a useful example. The story began when one of Melanie's coworkers picked up a cake whose message had omitted a "g" from "-ing." She told Melanie the decorator must have been black, since "black people drop off letters from words." Melanie said that while she fumed inside, she tried to remember her colleague's geographical background and lack of experience interacting with people of color. She then went on to explain to her coworker why some people would find that comment insulting. Listening rhetorically—contextualizing the comment and making a deliberate decision about how to act—enabled her to recognize her colleague's social location and thus to move from anger to education. For Melanie, accountability involves acting as what Joy Ritchie and Christine Stewart-Nunez call a "practitioner of critical anger," mining this emotion for action in the form of education (2). Melanie explained that she was ultimately motivated to approach anger as a resource—and not a final position—so as to keep it from destroying her emotionally. Engaging her anger in this way, she said, helps her to depersonalize such comments and to facilitate dialogue.

In both of these classroom moments, it was students of color who helped push their classmates to imagine possibilities beyond dysfunctional responses of guilt/blame or defensiveness. This begs the question of who carries the burden of listening. Who is more often required to listen, and who is allowed to assume his or her position is "natural"? Who is typically asked to do the work of accounting for how the past influences the present? The more difficult task, then, may be to help students in dominant positions recognize the contexts, histories, and experiences that shape anger expressed by minority speakers and to use their guilt or defensiveness as an impetus for action and self-reflection.

To that end, as we engaged particularly challenging texts, we began to consider the following questions: What affective responses prevent me from listening to this text? What enables me to listen to this text? What aspects of my social location inform that response? How do I want to listen to and participate in this debate? What are the effects of my response?

Listening to "Illegitimate Knowledge"

Interestingly, the more attention we devoted to listening in the women's rhetoric class—articulating it as a valuable process and practice—the more the students' responses to readings shifted, both in overt and subtle ways. One such shift came from a doctoral student, Alison, who had used most of her responses to relate the readings to topics she was considering for her dissertation: writing across the curriculum, audience theory, race relations. All offered compelling threads to pursue, but the writing and the connections sometimes seemed pressurized or strained, representing a struggle to control these voices so as to offer a sanctioned contribution. In their study, Thaiss and Zawacki found that the final agreed-upon fixture of academic writing is "an imagined reader who is coolly rational, reading for information, and intending to formulate a reasoned response" (7). For Alison, this presumably meant reading in a way that would create room for her contribution as a legitimate disciplinary member. Indeed, in our conversations in the hallway after class, Alison shared the urgency she felt to locate a dissertation project—and soon.

Something shifted, though, when Alison responded to Nancy Mairs's excerpt from "Carnal Acts," in which Mairs writes the connection between her disabled embodiment and her voice to demonstrate how shame of her body—her leg in a brace, her muscular control waning—translated into shame of her voice. She lets us see her husband lug her to the emergency room after a suicide attempt, "my hair matted, my face swollen and gray, my nightgown streaked with blood and urine. . . . I was a body, and one in a hell of a mess. I should have kept quiet about that experience. I know the rules of polite discourse" (398).

In class, Alison shared that her response to Mairs's piece was visceral—uneasy, a little embarrassed. Mairs broke the rules of polite discourse, which would have required her to hush the story of her suicide attempt. Or to narrate it without reminding us of the blood, the urine, the mess, the shame—to get on top of it, control it. In responding to the text, Alison had to make a decision, too. She could occupy the cool and rational role of the academic reader, which would require her to repress the visceral response that arose as she read Mairs, to hold the text at a safe distance as she critiqued it. Or she could listen to the piece, reflect on her own embodied response as a white, middle-class woman, and let her response be shaped by the hearing.

If, within a *divided* logos, listening serves as a mere waiting period while the hearer formulates his or her (reasoned) response to the speaker, within a *restored* logos, it provides an opportunity to dwell in another's experience, to reflect on—even shift—one's own position, and finally, to offer a revised response informed by cultivation. According to Fiumara, "listening serves to enhance the creation of language and the growth of the speaking person, thus freeing humans in the making from the forced role of users and imitators of whatever language happens to be most effectively propagated in the market" (167). As a result, we may hear speech acts typically deemed inappropriate, unreasoned (or unreasonable), or excessive, and those ideas may not only change the listener but also open the range of possibilities available for response.

Alison chose to write a piece quite different from her prior work but one that felt, at least to me, far more powerful. She wove theories of embodiment and language with stories of her own history as an embodied woman. When I shared with Alison that her voice sounded stronger, clearer, in this text, even as she felt less certain, she replied, "I just couldn't write in the same academic way in response to this piece. It called for a different kind of voice." It wasn't only Alison's voice that shifted, however; it was also her subject matter, which included stories of family history, of her relationship to her own body. Ratcliffe notes that while academic reading typically involves locating points of agreement or contention, rhetorical listening involves a *choice* to locate "exiled excess" and contemplation of "its relation to our culture and our selves" (*Rhetorical Listening* 203). And that contemplation just may result in a shift in how readers understand both their cultures and their identities.

This is not to say, however, that Alison did this easily or without the fear that accompanies risk-taking. When I wrote to her to ask if I could use her piece in this project, she responded: "I almost didn't turn this response in . . . because it felt risky in some way (even though I knew better). There were several times as I was writing it that I stopped and just decided I would write a more traditional response, but when I tried to do that . . . it just felt like writing in a way that didn't matter to me." Alison said she "knew better," because she and I have known each other for several years and from more than one class experience. She knows I value writing that challenges academic norms, and yet it doesn't remove the risk that comes with breaking with a larger, systemic academic practice, particularly as one strives to develop a sense of authority within this discourse.

Alison was not the only student who contemplated whether to exile the "excess" of Mairs's rhetoric or to dwell within it so as to create something else. Ella, a senior, was put off by Mairs's writing and suggested Mairs used her multiple sclerosis as a crutch, focusing too much of her energy on the "negative" aspects of her life rather than on the positives. Interestingly, at the end of our class discussion of Mairs, in which several students indicated a powerful response to her work and a deep frustration with the exclusion of so many crucial topics from academic and social discourse—sexuality, postpartum depression, and miscarriage all emerged in the dialogue—Ella stayed after class, writing on the bottom of her response paper.

"Maybe my frustration with Mairs is rooted in jealousy of how she can talk about her disability," she wrote. "Maybe deep down I'm a little ashamed of my CF [cystic fibrosis]. I need to process this through more personally and thoroughly." Though Ella had shared with me individually that she had CF, this was the first time she connected it to our course material, making it not just a personal issue but an intellectual one. The penciled response suggested a movement for Ella—a decision to shift from rejecting Mairs for that which made her uncomfortable to dwelling with her, to engage the complex contexts that shape her reading. Consequently, her listening opened a space for engagement of a subject she'd previously exiled—her relationship to her illness.

Learning to Listen

In *Noise from the Writing Center*, Elizabeth Boquet promotes a high-risk/ high-yield pedagogy that involves operating on the edge of our expertise, making mistakes, dwelling in the unfamiliar. To stand over a text, or another's voice, to assume that it is immediately knowable (and thus dismiss-able), is to remain squarely in the familiar. It is to remain safe. To listen, as the students above demonstrate, is to take a risk. Offering a response not typically sanctioned in the academy or dwelling in ideas that challenge one's privilege are certainly risks. So, too, is it a risk to teach listening, because it requires us to open our classrooms to different kinds of interactions, potentially allowing that which is typically deemed "excess" to enter in. It also means risking failure, because in attempting to teach rhetorical listening, I have found that, sometimes, genuine conversation—and thus rhetorical listening—is not possible. We cannot force rhetorical listening anymore than we can *make* students assume an open or reflexive stance. However, we can enact rhetorical listening, and we can call attention to examples of it, which is what I have tried to do in this chapter.

This piece is but one effort to explore what it means to engage a pedagogy of rhetorical listening. I hope that more such efforts will follow, particularly those that help us to consider strategies that might foster rhetorical listening as well as to negotiate the ever-present issue of how power differentials (both historically and presently) inform who is most willing or most required to listen.

As Fiumara suggests, a restored logos changes our relationship to discursive practices, inviting us to consider ourselves "apprentices of listening rather than masters of discourse" (57). While this is an apprenticeship that doesn't end—we must continually learn to listen as contexts and social locations shift—we can collaborate to help one another risk listening and thus to gain potential for richer yields of increased dialogue, previously exiled stories, and more complex thinking.

Works Cited

Anzaldúa, Gloria. *Borderlands: The New Mestiza = La Frontera*. San Francisco: Spinsters/Aunt Lute, 1987. Print.

Booth, Wayne C., and Peter Elbow. "The Limits and Alternatives to Skepticism: A Dialogue." *College English* 67.4 (2005): 378–99. Print.

Boquet, Elizabeth. *Noise from the Writing Center*. Logan: Utah State UP, 2002. Print.

Fiumara, Gemma Corradi. The *Other Side of Language: A Philosophy of Listening*. New York: Routledge, 1990. Print.

Lamm, Nomy. "It's a Big Fat Revolution." Ritchie and Ronald 454–61. Print.

Lorde, Audre. *Sister Outsider: Essays and Speeches*. Freedom, CA: Crossing, 1984. Print.

Luke, Carmen. "Feminist Politics in Radical Pedagogy." *Feminisms and Critical Pedagogy*. Ed. Carmen Luke and Jennifer Gore. New York: Routledge, 1992. 25–53. Print.

Mairs, Nancy. "Carnal Acts." Ritchie and Ronald 391–400. Print.

Ratcliffe, Krista. "Rhetorical Listening: A Trope for Interpretive Invention and a 'Code of Cross-Cultural Conduct.'" *CCC* 51.2 (1999): 195–224. Print.

———. *Rhetorical Listening: Identification, Gender, Whiteness*. Carbondale: Southern Illinois UP, 2005. Print.

Rayner, Alice. "The Audience: Subjectivity, Community and the Ethics of Listening." *Journal of Dramatic Theory and Criticism* 7 (1993): 3–24. Print.

Ritchie, Joy, and Kate Ronald, eds. *Available Means: An Anthology of Women's Rhetoric(s)*. Pittsburgh: U of Pittsburgh P, 2001. Print.

Ritchie, Joy, and Christine Stewart-Nunez. "Toward Critical Anger for Ethical Action." Unpublished article. 2008. Print.

Stetz, Margaret. "Listening 'With Serious Intent': Feminist Pedagogical Practice and Social Transformation." *Transformations: The Journal of Inclusive Scholarship and Pedagogy* 12.1 (2001): 7–27. Print.

Thaiss, Chris, and Terry Myers Zawacki. *Engaged Writers, Dynamic Disciplines: Research on the Academic Writing Life*. Portsmouth, NH: Boynton/Cook, 2006. Print.

Yamada, Mitsuye. "Invisibility Is an Unnatural Disaster: Reflections of an Asian American Woman." *The Bridge Called My Back: Writings by Radical Women of Color*. Ed. Cherríe Moraga and Gloria Anzaldúa. New York: Kitchen Table, 1983. 35–40. Print.

Making Ourselves Vulnerable: A Feminist Pedagogy of Listening

Wendy Wolters Hinshaw

> This is a women's studies course, and all assignments are expected
> to reflect an understanding of feminist scholarship. This does not
> mean that you are expected to be or become a feminist; it does
> mean that you will be expected to demonstrate the ability to apply
> feminist theories and critical methods in your work.

I included the above statement on the syllabus for a second-level writing course I taught in the Department of Women's Studies. Developed through initiatives in writing across the curriculum, this course is one of many options available to students to meet their second writing requirement, as well as an additional "diversity" requirement, at the large midwestern university where I teach. The majority of students who register for the course are not majors in, or even necessarily familiar with, women's studies and typically make their selection based on the time slot that best fits their schedules; because of this, I tried to anticipate students' resistance to the materials by insisting as part of my course policies that I did not expect them to become feminists but that I did expect them to take seriously the arguments that we read and apply them in their own writing—in other words, not to question feminism but to read, understand, and write about it. I reasoned, and they generally accepted, that they must first learn the fundamentals of any discipline before they could interrogate it. After all, it certainly wasn't appropriate for them to question the relevance or truthfulness of math in their algebra class; why would they question the relevance or truthfulness of feminism in my class? I feared such debates about feminism would likely become a platform for current "backlash" and antifeminist political rhetoric to infiltrate our class, undermine our discussions of our readings, and generally take time away from teaching my students how to improve their writing.

Asking students to withhold judgment in their initial encounters with feminist materials can be an effective way of temporarily disarming student resistance. Students enter our classroom discussions with various perceptions of feminism—both positive and negative—and withholding judgment is a key step in critical thinking. However, in my case, my course policy was as much about supporting critical thinking as it was about insulating me from student resistance. Rather than asking students to withhold judgment temporarily, eventually teaching them how to weave their own opinions and experiences into their interpretations of our texts, I asked them to accept our course materials, and my authority in the classroom, unconditionally. Although I professed critical thinking and feminist methods of analysis, I found myself demonstrating the opposite in my teaching practices.

I came to feminist pedagogy, and a pedagogy of listening more specifically, because I realized I'd created a structure that silenced debate, in part because I distrusted my ability to defend the feminist theories I read with my students. I felt, as I think many feminists do, that teaching the "F-word" meant arguing about and persuading our students of feminism and that if we are unsuccessful in this task, we not only are bad teachers but have reinforced dominant, patriarchal forces of oppression. This is a lot of pressure (especially for teachers who already have reputedly poor senses of humor) and also places a strong credence in student resistances that may be motivated by a number of issues beside political backlash against feminism.

In this chapter, I show how Krista Ratcliffe's theory of "listening pedagogically" can help us better recognize the power relations implicated in asking our students to withhold judgment of feminism and better negotiate the various types of resistance—resistance to dominant discourses of power as well as resistance to adopting new positions of thinking and learning—that are produced by students *and teachers* within classrooms attempting to communicate about and across cultural difference. By reinterpreting Kenneth Burke's theory of consubstantiality to account for communication through "non-identification" in addition to identification, Ratcliffe offers rhetorical listening as a means for acknowledging difference without "demand[ing] that differences be bridged" (53). Ratcliffe's pedagogical model reveals the multiple ways in which resistance can manifest in the classroom for both the teacher and the student and opens up possibilities for communication and learning across resistance. In doing so, she also represents a theoretical turn away from increasingly hostile characterizations of student resistance in recent composition scholarship, offering instead a model that preserves students' autonomy, and urges us to implicate ourselves in the risks and challenges that we ask our students to take.

Listening Pedagogically

In order to provide a foundation for feminist thinking in my writing class and to address my students' potential resistances to feminism, I started my course with readings designed to provide us with an initial feminist vocabulary. I hoped that essays such as Penny A. Weiss's "I'm Not a Feminist, But . . ." would provide us with an opportunity to communicate through identifications with popular myths and stereotypes. Similarly, I hoped that Peggy McIntosh's essay about white privilege would help provide a language for those of us in the class who occupied various kinds of privileged positions to talk about the "invisible knapsacks" we carried. My pedagogical approach followed models such as Dale M. Bauer's, who suggests that because our students often come to our classes with previously formed allegiances to politics that compete with or negate our own, we must "supply an authoritative word about potential sites of identification and of resistance to patriarchy" in order to get students to "identify with the political agenda of feminism" (392, 387). However, my attempts to galvanize students' identifications around the "political agenda of feminism" overlooked the fact that identification on such authoritative terms may prevent communication, and therefore learning, from taking place. Although the readings did provide opportunities for us to talk about resistance to feminism, this resistance was framed within a larger pedagogical strategy designed to eliminate resistance—to expose the flaws in these stereotypes and then put them aside—and consolidate students' identifications within a singular approach to feminism and feminist analysis.

Ratcliffe's theory of rhetorical listening premises a metonymic model of identification, disidentification, and non-identification that addresses the coercive power in such appeals for "common ground" and provides avenues for agency and dialogue that do not depend upon commonality. Whereas my pedagogy depended on my ability to accurately anticipate my students' reasons for resistance and then persuade them to identify with a new way of thinking about feminism, Ratcliffe's pedagogy reveals the coercion in this approach and provides alternative ways for communicating with students that are not premised on their identifications. For Ratcliffe, translating rhetorical listening into classroom practices or "listening pedagogically" involves, among other things, actively reflecting on the power dynamics that shape classroom relationships, and the experiences that we bring with us to these relationships, throughout the course of the class. She focuses specifically on how gender and whiteness function as tropes, both in relation to each other and in relation to other categories of difference, and how our language practices shape (and are shaped by) our experiences. By addressing difference through a rhetorical investigation of tropes, Ratcliffe is able to historicize and contextualize our cultural language and locate the terminology that students and teachers bring to their discussion of gender and race in larger cultural discourses. This strategy, like my attempt to build a feminist vocabulary, provides students who are uncomfortable (or simply unwilling to locate themselves in larger cultural discourses) a much-needed buffer zone. However, whereas my approach relied on identification, Ratcliffe insists that for her "the goal is not to discover some transcendent truth about gender and whiteness but rather to lay all gender and race 'cards' on the table in hopes of negotiating the existing (mis)perceptions about them and their intersections" (135).

Ratcliffe's pedagogy echoes commitments across contemporary feminist theory to raising students' awareness about issues of social inequality and locating our individual experiences within frameworks that identify sources of oppression as well as solutions for ending it. In her preface to *Emancipatory Movements in Composition*, Andrea Greenbaum makes a similar argument that "we, as citizens, scholars, and teachers, have an ethical imperative, a social responsibility and obligation to engage in actions that work toward transforming inequity and oppression" (xv). Susan Jarratt also proposes a vision for "composition courses whose instructors help their students to locate personal experience in historical and social contexts" (121). However, Ratcliffe's model is distinct from those proposed by Jarratt, Greenbaum, and others in its focus on both student and teacher resistances: Ratcliffe explores student moves of resistance to thinking about race and gender critically, as well as her own teacher moves of "pulling rank" in response to student resistance, by examining the underlying fears that may be at work in both acts of resistance.

Resituating Student Resistance

In order to foreground critical analyses of systems of social oppression and to address issues of inequality and difference in the classroom, many feminist theorists have proposed agonistic pedagogies as a means for modeling argumentative techniques and empowering students who might otherwise be silenced. Such pedagogical models take as their premises, one, that conflict and resistance are inevitable consequences of introducing new frameworks for thinking about relationships between identity and power and, two, that pedagogies that avoid conflict fail to acknowledge difference and risk reproducing oppressive power relations in the classroom (Jarratt 118). Jarratt argues that we should see such conflict as "the starting point for creating a consciousness in students and teachers through which the inequalities generating those conflicts can be acknowledged and transformed" and that such conflict is necessary in feminist composition pedagogies "fully engaged in issues of gender, race, and class" (119, 118). Similarly, Greenbaum draws from agonistic theories proposed by Jarratt, Bauer, and others to propose a "bitch pedagogy" that models female authority and argumentative discourse in order to empower all students "but particularly women students who . . . often lack the ability and confidence to assert positions" (*Emancipatory Movements* 53).

Agonistic pedagogies have provided frameworks for approaching student resistance and also draw important attention to differences in identity position and power relations that may be overlooked in efforts to preserve classroom harmony. Although such differences often represent points of discomfort in class discussions, they are also opportunities for putting theories of difference and critiques of power relations into practice. However, in building conflict into the premise for critical thinking, such models assume that because difference is inevitable, conflict over difference is also inevitable and that agonistic argument provides the best model for response. In contrast, Ratcliffe's model of rhetorical listening seeks to "supplement agonistic rhetorical strategies" by theorizing possibilities for communication across divisions and "non-identifications" (171). Although Ratcliffe also begins with the premise that students and teachers enter the classroom divided, with different beliefs and experiences framing their perspectives, rhetorical listening provides a means for communicating across divisions without requiring that identification be achieved. Conscious identifications and "non-identifications" are key components of rhetorical listening because they resist coercive identifications while still acknowledging the multiple contexts that help to form our identities and identifications. Although she holds up identification as one possible outcome of rhetorical listening, it is not the only goal and is not a requirement for communication or learning to take place: Ratcliffe suggests that "if disidentifications can be brought to the surface they may be negotiated and result in understanding" (63). Similarly, she argues that "rhetorical listening in a place of non-identification *may* precede conscious identifications; as such, rhetorical listening may help people consciously navigate troubled identifications and disidentifications. The operative term, of course, is *may*" (74). What this means is that while difference and division may be inevitable, conflict is not. Ratcliffe's model provides alternative ways for approaching difference while still acting within feminist goals of "fully engag[ing] . . . issues of gender, race, and class."

By opening up the possibility for learning within conditions of non-identification, Ratcliffe not only supplements agonistic rhetorical strategies but also initiates a theoretical turn away from increasingly hostile characterizations of student resistance in recent composition pedagogy. Composition scholars' approaches to student resistance have changed dramatically in the past few decades: once seen as evidence of students' rejecting oppressive and dominant discourses and power relationships, composition theorists have increasingly come to characterize student resistance as symptomatic of them. Earlier models, such as Robert Brooke's famous investigation of student "underlife," reflect commitments to fostering student resistance as a positive tool for institutional critique.

Brooke applies the sociological theory of "underlife" to the composition classroom in order to examine "behaviors which undercut the roles expected of participants in a situation" (141); he argues that what we might typically see as students' "misbehavior" is actually a sign of "constructive, individual stance-taking" and an indicator of critical thinking skills (144). Feminist theorists, however, responded to Brooke, and to similar uncritical embraces of student resistance and empowerment in critical pedagogy more generally, by pointing out the extent to which dominant power relations also structure relationships inside the classroom: while student "underlife" may demonstrate critical thinking and individual stance-taking, it may also reproduce privileged speaking positions for white and male students; while student resistance may be a tool for institutional critique, it may also further undermine already tenuous institutional authority held by female and nonwhite composition instructors.

Contemporary "post-process" critiques of expressivist pedagogies have further deepened the division between earlier pedagogical models open to and even embracing of student resistance and more recent models that are critical and even hostile to it. Jarratt's agonistic pedagogy is premised on a dichotomous positioning of "student-centered writing pedagogies" or "expressivist pedagogies" against a model in which conflict is central. Although she recognizes "transformative potential" in expressivist pedagogy's goal of decentering the teacher's authority, she argues that, despite its best efforts, expressivist pedagogy finds ways of "avoiding confrontations over social differences" (109). Greenbaum's edited collection *Insurrections* also provides an example of the current tendency to conflate student resistance and "process" pedagogies as uncritical and oppressive. In this collection of essays, the term "insurrections" refers not only to instances of student resistance in the classroom but also to the book's resistance to what Gary A. Olson describes in his foreword as an "increasing hegemonic struggle over how the field of composition studies should be defined" (xi). Here resistant students are firmly identified with larger "anti-feminist and anti-intellectual political backlashes," encouraging teachers not to listen pedagogically but to respond agonistically (xii). Resistance is no longer just enacted by students thinking critically about the institution but is now also a means for the teacher to distinguish between "critical" and "just functional" ways of teaching writing and to defend himself or herself against "a revitalized backlash against theoretical scholarship, especially that associated with critical literacy and with efforts to draw connections between the work we do in composition and the critical work done in other disciplines" (xii).

By emphasizing the larger social and political contexts for our teaching and by framing themselves in opposition to expressivist pedagogies characterized as avoiding conflict, agonistic approaches often end up foregrounding division and can result in increasingly hostile characterizations of student resistance and of student-teacher relationships more generally. Resistance, in *Insurrections*, is something that composition theorists and instructors do in response to dominant political ideologies—specifically ideologies of race, class, and gender oppression—that originate outside the classroom, as well as to the institutional hegemonies resulting from these ideologies. Because of this location, our students can resist critically, intellectually, and effectively, to the extent that they also express resistance to dominant political ideologies that propel race, class, and gender oppression. However, our students' resistance is complicated by the fact that although their resistance to larger dominant political ideologies, and even to the institution, is situated as critical, their resistance to us, because we are already located in resistance to the institution, is thereby situated as uncritical and reactive.

Pulling Rank

My own defensiveness about feminism and tendency to simplify my responses to perceived student resistance became clear to me when one particularly resistant student reinterpreted Gloria Anzaldúa's theory of borderlands in a close-reading assignment; he argued that borders are natural, geographic creations and drew evidence for support from academic and popular texts (all of them authored by men). Because the student had failed to engage and hardly even acknowledged Anzaldúa's intended use of this term, I demanded that he go back to the text, reread Anzaldúa's argument, and apply it in his paper. When he did not, I gave him a very low grade for failing to complete the requirements of the assignment. I interpreted what I saw as his blatant refusal to implement our assigned readings in his paper as deliberate resistance to my authority as both a teacher and as a woman. His refusal to even attempt to engage Anzaldúa was, I believed, evidence of the general backlash against feminism and other analyses of oppression in our culture and of students' resistances to thinking critically about the world around them. Although the student had, indeed, failed to meet basic assignment requirements by refusing to analyze the assigned readings in his paper, I had refused to see any explanation for his choices beyond a hostile resistance to me and to feminism more generally. I saw my authority as threatened and, in Ratcliffe's terms, "pulled rank."

Is it possible that the student didn't fully understand Anzaldúa's concept or was confused by her rearticulation of a term that previously seemed familiar and stable to him? Is it possible that he was trying to reconcile this new interpretation of borders as dynamic and political with the naturalized assumptions about borders that he saw Anzaldúa confronting? Is it possible that he was simply resistant to the limited assignment I had given and/or to other aspects of my teaching style and that his resistance had nothing to do with larger antifeminist backlashes? At the time, I was too busy, or perhaps too defensive, to find out.

Because we recognize that systems of domination in our culture shape dynamics within our classrooms as well, I believe we are quick to come to political conclusions about our students' resistance. In other words, because we are trying to teach our students to locate themselves within the forces and discourses that shape our society, we are prone to seeing their resistance or skepticism as always already a product of dominant, agonistic ideologies. But we are also encouraged to respond to student resistance as products of these larger "backlash" forces—and therefore as threatening. Jarratt argues that "when we recognize the need to confront the different truths our students bring to our classes—not only through self-discovery but in the heat of argument—feminism and rhetoric become allies in contention with the forces of opposition troubling us all," but aligning the "truths our students bring to our classes" with larger "forces of opposition" makes it more difficult to distinguish our students' voices, as they respond to the immediate context of our class, from the dominant public discourses that we anticipate when we engage in other contexts or in our scholarship (121). When we foreground concerns about the "political agenda of feminism," we can easily overlook the challenges and power dynamics at work in our individual classrooms. How, for instance, can we know whether a student's resistance to a feminist model of theory or teaching is a response to learned political objections to feminist ideologies or to the discovery of the pervasiveness of all kinds of ideologies in the classroom and the world around it? How can we tell whether a student is resisting feminist ideology, ideology in general, or just the particular feminist standing at the front of the room? A pedagogy of listening helps us avoid reactive responses to student resistance that may shut down communication.

Jarratt argues that "a female teacher who takes a position of uncritical openness toward the male student, especially if social-class differences also apply, invites the exercise of patriarchal domination to which every man in our society is acculturated" (111). But I suggest that openness to students, even to students acculturated in patriarchal domination, is not necessarily uncritical and may in fact be a strategy for teaching across such divisions. Like Jarratt, Greenbaum frames "bitch pedagogy" as an alternative to "ethics of care" models of feminist pedagogy and as a direct reply to perceived larger social trends resisting feminism specifically and women in authoritative positions more generally. She warns that ethics of care models, while they may seem to create positive and nurturing classroom environments, risk emotionally and materially exploiting the predominantly female body of composition teachers (*Emancipatory Movements* 56). I share Greenbaum's concerns about student perceptions of female authority in the classroom; as I stated earlier, my first response to a male student's resistance in my women's studies classroom was to interpret it as resistance to my authority. However, such models for argument and conflict, even when it's "productive conflict," lead us to create further divisions with our students, not just respond to them. When we begin by characterizing "the truths our students bring to our classes" in terms of the "forces of opposition troubling us all," then we impede some of our ability to communicate with our students, to *listen to them*, before we even enter the classroom.

A pedagogy of listening opens up wider possibilities for interpreting student resistance in order to consider the multiple contexts that shape our interactions with our students. This does not mean ignoring feminism's insights into how public discourses shape the discourses in our classrooms. However, it does require us to background the larger political stakes we bring to our scholarship and our classrooms long enough to listen for the potential identifications as well as disidentifications our students are making. For example, my quick assessment of my student's resistance to Anzaldúa may have prevented me from seeing the texts and concepts he *had* identified with, therefore causing me to miss opportunities to communicate with him (and other students) across these identifications and/or communicate about more "troubled identifications" or non-identifications through ones that were not as troubled.

Uneasy Listening

In encouraging us to listen for our students' identifications and non-identifications, "listening pedagogically" could easily evoke an image of a teacher/therapist and a pedagogy modeled after the "talking cure." The act of listening does not in itself require the listener to give up privileged positions or to reveal his or her own identifications, disidentifications, and non-identifications, let alone question them. That is why it is crucial that a pedagogy of listening implicates the teacher as well as the students and reminds us to anticipate and empathize with the difficulty that *anyone* experiences—ourselves included—when asked to realize and potentially change our current identifications.

Critical pedagogies have increasingly come to favor defamiliarizing moves designed to jar or otherwise awaken students to new insights about themselves and the culture around them and to use students' discomfort as a measure for the amount of critical development that has taken place. In *Talking Back*, bell hooks acknowledges that many students find her approach to an engaged, critical pedagogy "difficult, frightening, and very demanding. They do not usually come away from my class talking about how much they enjoyed this experience" (53). Similarly, David Bartholomae has suggested that "difficult and often violent accommodations . . . occur when students locate themselves in a discourse that is not 'naturally' or immediately theirs" (147). Students' defenses and fears were core concerns of "process" pedagogies. In "Emotional Scenarios in the Writing Process," Reed Larson draws from cognitive psychology to demonstrate the effect of fear and anxiety on writing: "Anxiety at best leads to impulsive and poorly controlled writing. At worst, it creates emotional and cognitive havoc that makes writing impossible" (27). Although "post-process" critiques have argued that process pedagogies were too individualistic and scientistic and that they detracted from our more pressing needs to emphasize "literate activities that challenge sociohistorical subjects" (Clifford and Ervin 179), recent contributions to composition theory mark a renewed interest in cognitive psychology, and theories of emotionality more generally. However, whereas earlier uses of cognitive psychology focused on the writing process, recent applications have been used more broadly to theorize students' emotional development, their processes of becoming aware of themselves as "sociohistorical subjects" (and the psychological basis of their resistances to these processes), and the consequences of these processes for classroom practices.

This recent cognitive and emotional (re)turn has helped compositionists complicate our understandings of psychic and social bases for our emotions, which thus positions us to be better listeners to the motivations of our students' resistances. Whereas Greenbaum constructs a binary opposition between "nurturance and empathy" and "modeling argumentative behavior" and argues that we must teach young women to "assert, insist, remove emotionality and position themselves as authoritatively as possible in order to become critical thinkers, speakers, and writers" (*Emancipatory Movements* 59), more recent "pedagogies of emotion," such as that offered by Marlia E. Banning, "address the affective component of experience, situate emotion historically, and account for emotions both as sites of social control and political resistance" (90). However, when applications of cognitive theory lead us to diagnose our students before we have met them, we have avoided the fundamental acts of listening necessary for communication in our classrooms. Mark Bracher proposes a method for reeducating students at the emotional and cognitive level, arguing that students often resist our attempts to promote social justice in our classrooms because our pedagogical strategies don't adequately address the psychological conditions that contribute to our students' "faulty" belief systems. However, although Bracher provides a model for correcting his students' "faulty cognitive schemas," he provides no models for addressing, let alone altering, our own psychic and social investments (485).

Especially in a feminist composition classroom, students will inevitably encounter new ideas that may contrast significantly with their previous ways of knowing. There is perhaps no way to make this encounter completely smooth, and smooth encounters (or "easy listening") are not Ratcliffe's goal; however, when we listen for our students' identifications, disidentifications, and non-identifications—as well as our own—we are better prepared to meet our students where they are, to address their own personal investments in their beliefs and the reasons and experiences that have affected their perceptions, and to provide a space for students to interact productively with our pedagogical agendas in order to create their own place in our classroom and in the world outside of it.

Conclusion

A pedagogy of listening does not promise that there will be no disagreement or conflict, and it does not even promise that there will be agreement in the end. However, it does better prepare us to communicate with our students and to help them communicate with us. By foregrounding listening as not just a considerate or conversational act but a rhetorical act, we are better able to position ourselves and our students as rhetorical audiences to each other and able to theorize how rhetorical processes of identification and division shape our communication and learning in our classrooms. Lisa Ede argues that "scholars in composition, like scholars in the humanities in general, have become accomplished at the kind of critique that exposes the working of ideology in both texts and lives. But we have generally aimed our critique at others, not ourselves" (49). By listening to my students' resistances to feminism, to critical race theory, or even to methods of critical thinking more broadly, I become more aware of the sources of my own identifications with these ways of thinking and better at recognizing my own defensiveness when it arises. I appreciate that my students are not always rational in their initial responses to the ideas we encounter because I am not always rational in defending my beliefs. Although teaching remains the goal in my classroom, the pressure to convince and win arguments is diminished because the stakes are diminished—my students' resistances don't have to symbolize a larger political backlash, and I don't have to defeat it.

It is no easy task to balance our commitments to social justice with the need to listen for and acknowledge students' potential resistances to them; issues of power and inequality are always already a part of our classrooms and our relationships with our students. However, I argue that we need to build identifications with students by addressing their suspicions and their personal experiences with and ideas about the issues that premise our pedagogy. Rather than lamenting, diagnosing, or explaining away the sources and motivations for their resistance to our theories, we must open them up to discussion and critique. It is our responsibility as teachers to fully recognize our students and address them relationally rather than confrontationally. It is the best way for feminists in the academy to keep all movements against social oppression, which exist both inside and outside the academy, vital.

Works Cited

Anzaldúa, Gloria. *Borderlands: The New Mestiza / La Frontera*. San Francisco: Spinsters/Aunt Lute, 1987. Print.

Banning, Marlia E. "The Politics of Resentment." *JAC* 26 (2006): 67–101. Print.

Bartholomae, David. "Inventing the University." *When a Writer Can't Write: Studies in Writer's Block and Other Composing-Process Problems*. Ed. Mike Rose. New York: Guilford, 1985. 134–65. Print.

Bauer, Dale M. "The Other 'F' Word: The Feminist in the Classroom." *College English* 52.4 (1990): 385–96. Print.

Bracher, Mark. "Teaching for Social Justice: Reeducating the Emotions through Literary Study." *JAC* 26 (2006): 463–512. Print.

Brooke, Robert. "Underlife and Writing Instruction." *CCC* 38.2 (1987): 141–53. Print.

Burke, Kenneth. *A Rhetoric of Motives*. Berkeley: U of California P, 1950. Print.

Clifford, John, and Elizabeth Ervin. "The Ethics of Process." *Post-process Theory: Beyond the Writing-Process Paradigm*. Ed. Thomas Kent. Carbondale: Southern Illinois UP, 1999. 179–97. Print.

Ede, Lisa. *Situating Composition: Composition Studies and the Politics of Location*. Carbondale: Southern Illinois UP, 2004. Print.

Greenbaum, Andrea. *Emancipatory Movements in Composition: The Rhetoric of Possibility*. Albany: State U of New York P, 2002. Print.

———, ed. *Insurrections: Approaches to Resistance in Composition Studies*. Albany: State U of New York P, 2001. Print.

hooks, bell. *Talking Back: Thinking Feminist, Thinking Black*. Boston: South End, 1989. Print.

Jarratt, Susan. "Feminism and Composition: The Case for Conflict." *Contending with Words: Composition and Rhetoric in a Postmodern Age*. Ed. Patricia Harkin and John Schilb. New York: MLA, 1991. 105–23. Print.

Larson, Reed. "Emotional Scenarios in the Writing Process: An Examination of Young Writers' Affective Experiences." *When a Writer Can't Write: Studies in Writer's Block and Other Composing-Process Problems*. Ed. Mike Rose. New York: Guilford, 1985. 19–42. Print.

McIntosh, Peggy. "White Privilege and Male Privilege: A Personal Account of Coming to See Correspondences through Work in Women's Studies." *Gender Basics: Feminist Perspectives on Women and Men*. Ed. Anne Minas. Belmont, CA: Wadsworth, 1993. 30–38. Print.

Olson, Gary A. Foreword. *Insurrections: Approaches to Resistance in Composition Studies*. Ed. Andrea Greenbaum. Albany: State U of New York P, 2001. xi–xii. Print.

Ratcliffe, Krista. *Rhetorical Listening: Identification, Gender, Whiteness*. Carbondale: Southern Illinois UP, 2005. Print.

Weiss, Penny A. *Conversations with Feminism: Political Theory and Practice*. Lanham, MD: Rowman and Littlefield, 1998. Print.

Revaluing Silence and Listening with Second-Language English Users

Jay Jordan

Perhaps the most compelling statistics about the growing numbers of nonnative users of English are the ones that cannot be reported. True, some statistics are fairly straightforward: the Institute of International Education estimates that over 620,000 international students were studying at U.S. colleges and universities during the 2007–08 academic year—a new all-time high. The plurality of international students come from China, India, South Korea, and other Asian countries, which have high levels of linguistic diversity, themselves. But, of course, not all international students are nonnative users, as the legacy of British colonial education in India would show. More to the point, not all residents and citizens of the United States are native English users. The Census Bureau projects that as many as 55 million U.S. residents speak languages other than English at home. However, unlike international visitors, such residents do not carry visas, and they are in no way obligated to report their language backgrounds and practices. Thus, they are hard to count.

While the numbers themselves are unclear, what is certain is that English—and the rhetorical practices that are often taught in English courses—is changing as it contacts thousands of other languages and countless English varieties locally and globally. As English spreads, it prompts linguists to consider the possibility of a new, emerging standard—one that would reflect the different traditions of diverse parts of the world in which English has had different trajectories but one that, nonetheless, also reflects a common desire to facilitate commerce and other interactions in a lingua franca. But English's spread also prompts linguists to think about the chasm between what David Crystal predicts as "World Standard Spoken English" and the present fact that most English speakers live in countries that have little English-language tradition. Indeed, Crystal's list of emerging examples of localized English usage is noteworthy for two reasons. First, it shows English's wide geographic dispersal. And second, it shows linguistic items that would immediately be marked as "errors" by most native English speakers. This response is, of course, understandable. Lacking a plausible way to unite such a massive proliferation of local varieties under anything like a "world standard," teachers of students who exhibit these varieties have little resort but to use the standardized categories they, themselves, inherited—categories that may not be equally relevant for all students and that may not be timely.

While the need to develop a more productive way to respond to increasing English language diversity is clear, the way to do it is not. And many colleges and universities do not make it easy to generate relevant ideas. More than ten years ago, Paul Kei Matsuda expressed frustration over the "disciplinary division of labor" between the fields of composition and second-language writing: while they frequently teach many of the same students (namely, second-language users of English), they are usually institutionally separated. Times—and the buildings that house separate departments—have not changed much. And the simultaneous specialization and growth of separate research agendas in rhetoric, in composition, and in second-language writing have made it increasingly difficult for scholars in those fields to communicate across the divide.

This chapter suggests a way forward based on a promising point of connection among the fields—specifically, work on silence and listening, which opens ways to reassess rhetorical productions that have too easily been overlooked or that have been misunderstood. Just as scholars of rhetoric, such as Lisa Ede, Cheryl Glenn, Shirley Wilson Logan, Andrea Lunsford, and Jacqueline Jones Royster have been trying to listen again—or for the first time—to women and to ethnic minorities in Western rhetorical traditions, applied linguists and second-language writing scholars, such as A. Suresh Canagarajah, Linda Harklau, Bruce Horner, Ilona Leki, and Min-Zhan Lu, have been trying to hear second-language users' speech, writing, and silences while suspending snap judgments. I believe theory-building about silence and listening in the field of rhetoric can inform studies of second-language users' emerging English use. And I believe that second-language users, as they challenge prevalent notions of silence and encourage careful rhetorical listening, can and will expand the range of rhetorical study.

Silence, Listening, and Language Learning Assumptions

A growing number of rhetoric scholars are reappraising silence as a productive communicative practice in historical and contemporary contexts. Western rhetorical traditions, following the Gospel of John's direct statement about the originary Word, have tended to value speech and writing as the best (if not the only) evidence of rhetorical production. As George Kalamaras notes, silence is widely and popularly perceived in Western societies as a lack or as evidence of annihilation. Unsurprisingly, then, many rhetors who remain even temporarily silent find it extremely difficult to get a fair hearing. Yet, to forget the role of silence and the rhetorical strategies behind both enacting it and listening to it is to overlook significant possibilities for meaning—even in the most canonical parts of "the" rhetorical tradition. Carol Poster, for instance, argues that silence played a key role in Neoplatonic and early Christian adaptations of Plato's teachings: Plato, Alcinous, and Augustine believed speech was potentially misleading to students of philosophy and, later, to the followers of Jesus. In this view, worthy disciples could ascertain proofs through things and (silent) demonstrations, as in Jesus' miracles. Where silence in this view "spoke" of transcendence more powerfully than speech could, the silences that many women have been mandated to keep have also carried powerful meanings for them and their dedicated listeners. Scholars such as Julie A. Bokser, Glenn, Nan Johnson, and Krista Ratcliffe not only have recovered examples of women who deployed their silences under oppressive conditions but also have rethought the stakes of such silences for rhetorical research more broadly. After all, as Glenn argues, recovery work itself is unsustainable without considerations of how such work can and should inform rhetorical theory going forward: "though we have made some headway, we have yet to seriously probe our own disciplinary silences and silencings, the *unspoken*" (151, emphasis in original).

As generative as specific recovery has been, then, it is the historiographical and theoretical work that is potentially most heuristic and disruptive because of the changes it can pose for how rhetoric is done, both in large-scale research projects and in everyday communicative projects. Glenn challenges interlocutors to consider silence an opportunity to change rhetorical tactics rather than "considering such silence to be static, empty, annoying, or even threatening" (6). Many teachers can recount at least one instance of posing a question to a class only to be met with silence—prompting the very responses Glenn mentions or prompting attempts to fill the gap. In his review of Paul Kameen's *Writing/Teaching*, Byron Hawk notes Kameen's insistence on honoring the inventional moment that such silence represents. Instructional silence can just mean a teacher's impatient pause while waiting for (or while waiting to give) a pre-scripted response, but it can also give rise to a heuristic moment of unpredictability: "possibilities lie in that moment between the placing of a question in the air and the occurrence of some muddled and/or insightful response" (380).

What can make the difference—to the teacher, especially—between "muddled and/or insightful" is rhetorical listening, which requires engagement between speakers and listeners, especially when such engagement is difficult. Rhetorical listening can differ markedly from the impatient practice of waiting for the supposedly right answer, while presuming that such an answer may never come. Michelle Ballif succinctly summarizes traditional notions of listening's passive function:

> The rhetorical act . . . has been traditionally theorized as something that a speaker "does" to an audience via dissemination; the message is *conveyed* to an audience—it is a post properly addressed to guarantee its arrival, its reception. The success of this rhetorical act, then, is dependent on whether the audience "gets" it and, without much resistance, "buys" the speaker's argument. (52, emphasis in original)

For Ballif, such a theory exonerates the speaker and reduces whatever complexity the title "speaker" might hold to the flat simplicity of "sender": one who "bind[s] an audience in a particular communicative situation" (53). So bound, the audience's potential role as an actual interlocutor is similarly reduced to "receiver," the logical partner in a relationship determined by still-prevalent conduit theories of communication. Ratcliffe observes a similar problem in her critique of "identification," a concept at the center of Kenneth Burke's influential rhetorical theory.

Ratcliffe finds that Burke's notion of identification is too grounded in presumed or desired sameness—a priori common ground that often too easily converts the possibility of shared rhetorical context and goals into an opportunity for straightforward incorporation and mastery or for outright rejection of the Other. In other words, for Ratcliffe, identification presents interlocutors with a polar choice: either there is common ground, in which case other differences are superfluous, or there is no commonality at all, in which case differences are not worth overcoming ("Rhetorical").

But differences—whether of knowledge in a teaching situation, of language, of culturally informed rhetorical repertoires—are legion across communicative situations, and rhetorical listening can provide a middle-way alternative to both incorporation and rejection. In this middle, "a [listening] person must *choose* to stick with the work that needs to be done . . . realizing that such work may take patience, may not succeed, may even be misinterpreted" (Ratcliffe, *Rhetorical* 76). In the kinds of cross-cultural interactions in which I am primarily interested, this work entails, in Ratcliffe's words, "cultural/historical archaeological/ethnographic" (*Rhetorical* 62) effort—an everyday research methodology in which interlocutors sensitize themselves to "historically grounded cultural logics enveloping other people's claims" ("Rhetorical" 209). The cross-cultural rhetorical listener cannot stop at making snap judgments about silences or examples of speech/writing (for instance, that silence means misunderstanding or assent, or that an artifact of speech/writing is an error).

Most of the time, however, administrative, pedagogical, and other institutional responses to second-language English users do proceed from the assumption that English is a conduit and that people speaking/writing in English must share (or must be trying to acquire) standardized rhetorical competencies. One telling example plays out regularly in universities that have large numbers of international graduate students and instructors. Where international students become teaching assistants in large "gatekeeper" courses, especially in math and the sciences, their accents and (perceived or actual) unfamiliarity with U.S.-based teaching practices can combine with undergraduates' pressure to achieve to create tense interactions.[1] A 1997 exchange in the pages of Penn State University's student newspaper, the *Daily Collegian*, is typical. First, a columnist laments that many students "have trouble understanding" at least one of their instructors, which means that they are "being prevented from learning" (Lutz). At least one student writes a letter to the editor in agreement and relates a personal account of a frustrating/humorous encounter with an international teaching assistant (Feinman). A graduate student reminds the previous student-writers that college often means learning how to interact with and adapt to people who speak different varieties of English (Carvalho). Two undergraduates respond that, because they are "paying such a high price to obtain" their education, they should not have to shoulder the additional burden of translating their instructors' speech (Pohland and Eschenbaugh). In such an environment, arguing for the value of rhetorical listening runs up against the literal money value of tuition.

Assumptions about the competencies and trajectories of diverse English users are also prevalent in scholarly work—even in work that has historically opened opportunities for users of nonstandard varieties of English and of other native languages. Two well-known examples are the interlanguage hypothesis in the field of applied linguistics and the *Students' Right to Their Own Language* resolution passed by the Conference on College Composition and Communication in 1974. In one passage, the *Students' Right* resolution's authors note that "today's students will be tomorrow's employers. . . . English teachers who feel they are bound to accommodate the linguistic prejudices of current employers perpetuate a system that is unfair to both students who have job skills and to the employers who need them" (14). The document argues that teachers should immerse themselves in communities in which their dialect is *not* spoken in order to more closely identify with the difficulties their students face in most classrooms. It also notes that many editorial decisions about dialect and grapholect are often left to "secretaries and the technical writer" whose business it is to "standardize" the appearance of writing by executives, thus obviating the need for an "unreasonably restrictive" focus on standardization (13). But in the section titled "How Does Dialect Affect Employability?" the *Students' Right* authors recommend that teachers "stress the difference between the spoken forms of American English and EAE [Edited American English]" (14). On its face, this suggestion makes sense, given the often-wide disparities between spoken and written forms of any language and given the relatively conservative, formal nature of writing. But later in the same section, the document advises teachers that they should "begin [their] work in composition with [students with diverse "home" varieties] by making them feel confident that their writing, in whatever dialect, makes sense and is important to us. . . . Then students will be in a much stronger position to consider the rhetorical choices that lead to statements written in EAE" (14–15). "Interlanguage" rests on a similarly teleological assumption about standardized English. It posits that the difference between the expected utterance of a native speaker and the utterance of a language learner is evidence of a "separate linguistic system based on the observable output which results from the attempted production of a [target language] norm" (Selinker 214; also see Bardovi-Harlig; Bardovi-Harlig and Hartford; Kasper; Lakshmanan and Selinker; Makalela; Ohta; and Selinker and Douglas). That is, at the base of the hypothesis are two assumptions: that the native speaker arbitrates the norms of a target language and that the language learner is striving (and ought to strive) to acquire the same variety that native speakers purportedly use. Central to the hypothesis is the idea that certain linguistic forms "fossilize" as more or less unmodifiable target-language artifacts of first-language acquisition. While both the *Students' Right* and interlanguage traditions honor the languages students bring with them into classrooms—whether they are native English speakers or not—they often do so for the purpose of contrasting those languages with a preferred variety of English that requires less work on the part of students' interlocutors.

Listening to Puzzling Productions and Active Silences

But rhetorical listening—working harder to understand the possible meanings both of users' silences and utterances—can play a substantial role in an overall project of learning how English-language rhetorical practices are evolving by way of the hands and mouths of its widespread users. Travel is actually not necessary in this project, since local varieties of English proliferate in U.S. communities and since international varieties circulate in and out of the country continually. What *is* necessary, though, is patience—hearing not for immediate consumption or translation or evaluation but for ambivalence. Especially in the case of second-language users, both production (traditionally conceived) and silences can give rise to misunderstandings, snap judgments, and consternation on the part of native-speaking peers and instructors, as the student newspaper examples above attest. Such visceral responses can, however, be redirected. In an often-cited example, Min-Zhan Lu presents her students with a text in which a Malaysian English speaker uses the apparently incorrect verb collocation "can able to." Her students initially dismiss the usage, but Lu encourages them to think about the small but potentially significant difference between the definitions of "can" and "able": "can," according to the dictionary referenced, introduces a sense of external permission rather than just the individual ability that "able" denotes. In the ambiguous gap between "can" and "able," Lu is able to lead a discussion of cultural factors affecting the use of those two verbs interchangeably. She argues that, for U.S. students, the difference between being individually able and being *allowed* to do something by an external authority may be relatively small, given ideological elevations of individualism in America. Since this ideology is not as common in other cultures, English speakers from those cultures may see the gap between "can" and "able," where U.S. speakers cannot (451–52).

My own empirical research details other misunderstandings that are not necessarily linguistic in nature but that still present opportunities to listen. As part of a larger overall project, I observed at least two sections per semester of first-year composition at a large eastern university over the course of several semesters. These sections included at least one student each who self-identified as a nonnative English user. In an interview with me about her section, an experienced, full-time instructor related how one Arab student quickly changed the tenor of a discussion about government phone-tapping in the wake of the 9/11 attacks:

> One of the young men in class said he just didn't understand what the big deal was [about phone taps]—that we needed to get terrorists and whatever way we needed to get them, that was enough. . . . And finally [the student] from the [United Arab] Emirates said, "You can't understand how somebody else could feel [about phone taps], because you don't call your mother and your father on a daily basis the way I do." And then a native speaker in class who happened to have a Pakistani roommate . . . was like, none of this made any sense to her until she said she had a roommate who was an international student. She [the native speaker] said, "I identify with that—her parents call and she calls on a daily basis. Does that mean that her phone could be tapped?" And so all of a sudden, there was this personal level of conversation, and the young man who made the statement said, "Well, that couldn't happen to you—you have

nothing to hide. Only people that have things to hide should be concerned." He [the Arab student] goes, "How do you know I have nothing to hide?"[2]

On the surface, the question "How do you know I have nothing to hide?" shows that the student has no trouble articulating in English. And it does not, as in the case of Lu's student, demonstrate use of a syntactic construction that requires a re-hearing on the linguistic level. But it certainly calls for careful consideration: it invites a reappraisal of the student's position in his peers' preformed categories of "us" and "them." Certainty about where terrorists and nonterrorists are and about what they do gave way to unsettling ambivalence, which prompted more and different questions as the semester's in-class discussions proceeded:

> Students would check in with each other in their discussions, and they would say, "Well, I've never experienced that, but, well, what do you think" . . . so all of a sudden they began to recognize that, gee, maybe their worldview worked for them, but it may not necessarily work for someone else, so you know, I don't want to say it was like this vast change of "oh, everybody changed," no, but I would say that the benefit that came about was this willingness now to check in, this willingness to look at somebody else and say, "Well, I don't know, it doesn't seem like a big deal to me, but is that a big deal?"

As much as nonnative English users' speech and writing can elicit such foundational questions, their silences can also be loaded. And silence becomes particularly overdetermined in classrooms in the United States, in which speech ("class participation") is often so highly valued that it is difficult to think about silence except as a failure to engage academically. Applied linguists have often explained the silences of second-language users by offering culturally specific explanations that foreground "face." Much of their recent work raises questions about the argument, made by Penelope Brown and Stephen C. Levinson over twenty years ago, that politeness orientations are universal across cultures and that individuals more or less universally want to be liked by interlocutors ("positive face") at the same time that they want to preserve interlocutors' dignity ("negative face"). In a classroom with a native-English-speaking instructor and Chinese or Japanese students, then, an instructor familiar with the concept of face would tend to frame a student's nonresponse to his or her question as evidence of the student's desire to avoid appearing more intelligent than peers, to cover over perceived deficiencies in spoken English, or to avoid answering in a way that might challenge the instructor by way of reframing the question. This explanation is doubtless attractive for instructors looking for ways to manage increasing classroom diversity: it offers intuitively appealing explanations for silence, based on the assumption that students remain silent when they do not understand or when they are socially anxious in a foreign context.

But invoking culturally determined categories like "face" in increasingly diverse classroom contexts too easily glosses over differences among second-language users that result from their complex contacts with English. True, numerous international students arrive in the United States having learned English through formal grammar lessons and written translation exercises, which, according to Joy Reid, make them excellent "eye learners" of the language through written media but less-than-skilled "ear learners" who can comfortably and spontaneously speak. However, many others arrive with experiences and backgrounds that are revealed not through assumptions about a common set of educational experiences but through rhetorical listening. For example, participants in Jun Liu's study of Chinese students in the Midwest represent a range of experiences that complicate the stock image of American teacher and Chinese student. One student in Liu's study had earned a bachelor's degree and a master's degree in China, but he had also worked as a university lecturer during that time. A second student had worked as a visiting scholar in Germany before arriving here. A third worked as a doctor in China and then traveled with her husband to the United States, where she had been a homemaker for two years while her husband was enrolled in a PhD program. Liu does not expressly address the possible influences these diverse *individual* experiences may have added to students' *cultural* classroom behaviors, but it is worthwhile to ask questions about students' histories and motives, especially where their present behaviors do not map easily onto universalist notions of face.

In another example, which focuses on Turkish graduate students in the United States, Sibel Tatar reports that the students were often silent in class but that "they remained mentally active," responding nonverbally, keeping notes, and e-mailing the professor with questions and comments rather than saying them in large groups (289).[3] Some participants informed Tatar that they employed silence in order to listen to the comments of their native-English-speaking peers, whether to attend to linguistic considerations of how they phrased questions or whether to "protest against the perceived low quality of [peers'] contributions" (290).

In a third example, a Korean American undergraduate student I observed and interviewed related several different ways she gauges whether to use English or Korean around interlocutors who may use either. For this student, the choice of which language to use is more complicated than simply code-switching: the social stakes are high, and the immediate, short-term consequences of choosing incorrectly may be negative, since, as the student related, it is often important to address Korean-speaking elders using that language's system of honorific address—a system that is far less robust in English. This student may wait for someone in the group to take a turn at speaking (in one language or the other, as if to set the script and the stage) or may pretend that she doesn't know the language at first, resisting her own ability to communicate in favor of "try[ing] to get past the awkward moment."[4] A pedagogical situation in Liu's study reveals a similar strategy. One student reported having remained silent during a vocal interchange—a choice that allowed her to leverage what she apparently carefully listened to:

> In a recent mid-term written exam, I answered a question a class-mate raised in class. It seemed no one took notes when that question was answered in class, but I did and as a result I got two extra points in getting the answer straight in the mid-term exam. I was the only one who got the right answer. The professor later told me that I surprised him. The student who asked that question in class only got one point while I who listened carefully to the answer got two points. (46–47)

A linguistic framework might explain her performance as evidence of a lack of oral proficiency or as evidence of lag time in translating what could well have been a rapid exchange (at least to a nonnative speaker's ears). A face-oriented framework might suggest that she did not want to interrupt other speakers' interactions and/or that she wanted to avoid interjecting her own nonnative speech. But through interviewing the student and temporalizing her decision to remain silent, Liu is able to demonstrate that her silence is neither: rather, it shows evidence of rhetorical processing beyond the level of literal translation.

Conclusion

These few examples demonstrate students', teachers', and researchers' willingness to be puzzled—to set aside (at least temporarily) inherited categories of "us" and "them," "native" and "nonnative" in order to listen for emerging possibilities. Given the current flux of English as an international language and of associated rhetorical practices, the assumption that people who need to learn English will do so in predictable settings and that they will use it in predictable ways is untenable. In part, it is a matter of numbers: David Graddol repeats the British Council's estimate that, of the roughly 1.5 billion humans who use English in some capacity, 750 million—half of the global total—use it nonnatively. They may not use it on a day-to-day basis or use it with close friends and family, but they are puzzling through its utility as a lingua franca and as a marker of social status. In his study of Indonesian uses of English, for instance, Robert Holland found that English words appear in business communications and in advertising—among other venues—for reasons having as much to do with conveying economic privilege as with communicating idiomatically. It is dangerous to predict the roles that English will play in the future, especially in a moment of economic turmoil that affects the United States as much as it affects developing nations; it is conceivable that English itself could lose "market share" as other linguistic currencies, such as Mandarin, gain prestige. But this uncertainty about English is exactly the point: it is because no one can make firm predictions about its use that scholars, teachers, and students of the language need to attend (listen) carefully to the productive utterances and silences of its increasingly diverse users. Despite traditional attempts to keep second-language users and their uses at some distance, they are doing substantive work with and on the language my fellow native English speakers and I once thought was "ours." And rhetoricians and others interested in language use would do well to listen carefully, especially where we do not understand.

Notes

1. Approximately twenty states have laws mandating some assessment of international teaching assistants' English proficiency. Even institutions in less regulated states may encounter legal liability under tort or contract law for employing teaching assistants who are, arguably, sufficiently inarticulate to cause misunderstandings during the course of instruction (Oppenheim).

2. The instructor wished to remain anonymous.

3. Tatar's findings square with critical reassessments of the so-called silent period (Krashen)—an early stage of second-language learning in which learners may listen attentively to target language modeling but in which they do not speak. Studies by Priscilla Clarke, Ana Christina DaSilva Iddings and Eun-Young Jang, and Muriel Saville-Troike conclude that language learners are not merely passively silent during this putative period but are instead "extraordinarily psychologically active" (Iddings and Jang 587), silently rehearsing language forms and observing target-language social situations.

4. The student wished to remain anonymous.

Works Cited

Ballif, Michelle. "What Is It the Audience Wants? Or, Notes toward a Listening with a Transgendered Ear for (Mis)Understanding." *JAC* 19.1 (1999): 51–70. Print.

Bardovi-Harlig, Kathleen. "Exploring the Interlanguage of Interlanguage Pragmatics: A Research Agenda for Acquisitional Pragmatics." *Language Learning* 49.4 (1999): 677–713. Print.

Bardovi-Harlig, Kathleen, and Beverly S. Hartford, eds. *Interlanguage Pragmatics: Exploring Institutional Talk*. Mahwah, NJ: Erlbaum, 2004. Print.

Bokser, Julie A. "Sor Juana's Rhetoric of Silence." *Rhetoric Review* 25.1 (2006): 5–21. Print.

Brown, Penelope, and Stephen C. Levinson. *Politeness: Some Universals in Language Usage*. Cambridge: Cambridge UP, 1987. Print.

Canagarajah, A. Suresh. *Resisting Linguistic Imperialism in English Teaching*. Oxford: Oxford UP, 1999. Print.

Carvalho, M. D. "Instructors' Accents Not Problematic." *Daily Collegian*. Penn State University. Oct. 30, 1997. Web. Apr. 1, 2006.

Clarke, Priscilla. "Examining the Silent Period." *Australian Review of Applied Linguistics* 12 (1989): 122–37. Print.

Crystal, David. *English as a Global Language*. 2nd ed. New York: Cambridge UP, 2003. Print.

Ede, Lisa, Cheryl Glenn, and Andrea Lunsford. "Border Crossings: Intersections of Rhetoric and Feminism." *Rhetorica: A Journal of the History of Rhetoric* 13.4 (1995): 401–41. Print.

Feinman, Robin. "Students Frustrated with Language Barrier." *Daily Collegian*. Penn State University. Oct. 28, 1997. Web. Apr. 1, 2006.

Glenn, Cheryl. *Unspoken: A Rhetoric of Silence*. Carbondale: Southern Illinois UP, 2004. Print.

Graddol, David. *The Future of English?* London: British Council, 1997. Print.

Harklau, Linda. "From the 'Good Kids' to the 'Worst': Representations of English Language Learners across Educational Settings." *TESOL Quarterly* 34.1 (2000): 35–67. Print.

Hawk, Byron. "A Rhetoric/Pedagogy of Silences: Sub-version in Paul Kameen's *Writing/Teaching*." *Pedagogy* 3.3 (2003): 377–97. Print.

Holland, Robert. "Globospeak? Questioning Text on the Role of English as a Global Language." *Language and Intercultural Communication* 2.1 (2002): 5–24. Print.

Horner, Bruce. "Re-thinking the 'Sociality' of Error: Teaching Editing as Negotiation." *Representing the "Other": Basic Writers and the Teaching of Basic Writing.* Ed. Bruce Horner and Min-Zhan Lu. Urbana: NCTE, 1998. 139–65. Print.

Iddings, Ana, Christina DaSilva, and Eun-Young Jang. "The Mediational Role of Classroom Practices during the Silent Period: A New-Immigrant Student Learning the English Language in a Mainstream Classroom." *TESOL Quarterly* 42.4 (2008): 567–90. Print.

"International Students in the U.S." *Institute of International Education.* N.p. Nov. 18, 2008. Web. Nov. 1, 2009.

Johnson, Nan. "Reigning in the Court of Silence: Women and Rhetorical Space in Postbellum America." *Philosophy and Rhetoric* 33.3 (2000): 221–42. Print.

Kalamaras, George. *Reclaiming the Tacit Dimension: Symbolic Form in the Rhetoric of Silence.* Albany: State U of New York P, 1994. Print.

Kasper, Gabriele. "Introduction: Interlanguage Pragmatics in SLA." *Studies in Second Language Acquisition* 18.2 (1996): 145–48. Print.

Krashen, Stephen. *Second Language Acquisition and Second Language Learning.* London: Pergamon, 1981. Print.

Lakshmanan, Usha, and Larry Selinker. "Analysing Interlanguage: How Do We Know What Learners Know?" *Second Language Research* 17.4 (2001): 393–420. Print.

Leki, Ilona. "Coping Strategies of ESL Students in Writing Tasks across the Curriculum." *TESOL Quarterly* 29.2 (1995): 235–60. Print.

Liu, Jun. "Negotiating Silence in American Classrooms: Three Chinese Cases." *Language and Intercultural Communication* 2.1 (2002): 37–54. Print.

Logan, Shirley Wilson. *With Pen and Voice: A Critical Anthology of Nineteenth-Century African-American Women.* Carbondale: Southern Illinois UP, 1995. Print.

Lu, Min-Zhan. "Professing Multiculturalism: The Politics of Style in the Contact Zone." *College English* 45.4 (1994): 442–58. Print.

Lutz, Stephen. "Letter to Spanier: Language Barriers Make Learning Tough." *Daily Collegian.* Penn State University. Oct. 22, 1997. Web. Apr. 1, 2006.

Makalela, Leketi. "Differential Error Types in Second-Language Students' Written and Spoken Texts: Implications for Instruction in Writing." *Written Communication* 22.4 (2004): 368–85. Print.

Matsuda, Paul Kei. "Composition Studies and ESL Writing: A Disciplinary Division of Labor." *CCC* 50.4 (1999): 699–721. Print.

Ohta, Amy Snyder. "Interlanguage Pragmatics in the Zone of Proximal Development." *System* 33.3 (2005): 503–17. Print.

Oppenheim, Nancy. *How International Teaching Assistant Programs Can Prevent Lawsuits.* ERIC Document Reproduction Service. 1997. ED 408886. Web. Oct. 30, 2009.

Pohland, Erin, and Susan Eschenbaugh. "Not TA Translators." *Daily Collegian*. Penn State University. Nov. 12, 1997. Web. Apr. 1, 2006.

Poster, Carol. "Silence as a Rhetorical Strategy in Neoplatonic Mysticism." *Mystics Quarterly* 24.2 (1998): 48–73. Print.

Ratcliffe, Krista. "Rhetorical Listening: A Trope for Interpretive Invention and a 'Code of Cross-Cultural Conduct.'" *CCC* 51 (1999): 195–224. Print.

———. *Rhetorical Listening: Identification, Gender, Whiteness*. Carbondale: Southern Illinois UP, 2005. Print.

Reid, Joy. "'Eye' Learners and 'Ear' Learners: Identifying the Language Needs of International Students and U.S. Resident Writers." *Grammar in the Composition Classroom: Essays on Teaching ESL for College-Bound Students*. Ed. Patricia Byrd and Joy M. Reid. New York: Heinle, 1998. 3–17. Print.

Royster, Jacqueline Jones, ed. *Southern Horrors and Other Writings: The Anti-lynching Campaign of Ida B. Wells, 1892–1900*. Boston: Bedford, 1997. Print.

Saville-Troike, Muriel. "Private Speech: Evidence for Second Language Learning Strategies during the 'Silent Period.'" *Journal of Child Language* 15 (1988): 567–90. Print.

Selinker, Larry. "Interlanguage." *International Review of Applied Linguistics in Language Teaching* 10.3 (1972): 209–31. Print.

Selinker, Larry, and Dan Douglas. "LSP and Interlanguage: Some Empirical Studies." *English for Specific Purposes* 6.2 (1987): 75–85. Print.

Students' Right to Their Own Language. Spec. issue of *CCC* 25.3 (1974). Print.

Tatar, Sibel. "Why Keep Silent? The Classroom Participation Experiences of Non-Native-English-Speaking Students." *Language and Intercultural Communication* 5.3/4 (2005): 284–93. Print.

"United States—Fact Sheet—American FactFinder." *Census.gov*. N.p. June 20, 2006. Web. Jan. 17, 2007.

Student Silences in the Deep South: Hearing Unfamiliar Dialects

Suellynn Duffey

ong into my adult life, when I first moved below the Mason-Dixon Line, I went deep into the Old South. I did not gently dip my toes into waters along the shoreline by merely crossing the Ohio River into northern Kentucky, nor did I dock in Atlanta, where the influx of non-southerners and other forces has remade southern identity into that of the New South. Instead, I moved far into the heart of the South's very old regional identity, to the rural southeast corner of Georgia, where traces of the South's historical identities are still very much alive: cotton fields, longleaf pines, and dirt roads; boiled peanuts, plantations, and homes painted blue to ward off evil; Confederate flags, "Miss" attached to first names as a sign of respect, and nearly endless summer. There I heard speech I came to love and miss, once I left. I even occasionally heard the language of my family, none of whom were southerners but whose speech nonetheless carried similar vocabulary: we too (Scots-Irish in Ohio) had called wishbones "pulley bones." The South was both strange and familiar to me.

As enigmatic as the South remained, no matter how hard I studied it, it also gave me riches, including my insights here about silence and listening, but for many reasons, I do not claim that the student behaviors I write about are *essentially* southern. While I am not constructing a singular, regional, southern identity around student silences, region is nonetheless an important part of my discussion. Even if the silences and listening are not essentially southern, I am fairly certain that *place* shaped the behavior I saw because the behavior was so prevalent and I'd not seen it in the other regions where I'd taught. Thus, even if the behaviors may not be *place-specific*, they are certainly *place-generated* (Duffey). Emphasizing a literally grounded sense of place, I follow to some extent Nedra Reynolds in *Geographies of Writing: Inhabiting Places and Encountering Difference*, where she writes:

> What do bodies, city walls, pathways, streams, or . . . trees have to do with rhetoric, writing, or an intellectual discussion? . . . While race, class, and gender have long been viewed as the most significant markers of identity, geographic identity is often ignored or taken for granted. However, identities take root from particular sociogeographical intersections, reflecting where a person comes from. . . . Geographical locations influence our habits, speech patterns, style, and values—all of which make it a rhetorical concept or important to rhetoric. (11)

Place, then, is important to the rhetoric of silence and listening.

To some extent, my emphasis on place and region aligns also with Kristie S. Fleckenstein's goals to invent a "biorhetoric," one that "position[s] us within the ambiguous interplay of materiality and semiosis" (761). Biorhetoric, Fleckenstein argues, "emphasizes the inextricability of materiality and semiosis . . . [and their] entanglement in a nonlinear weave" (762). She goes on to say that "we cannot escape place, although we can deny it and redefine it" (766). Instead of denying it, of course, my aim is to foreground it, to illustrate how a particular geographic location both shaped and was reflected in the rhetorical and epistemological interactions during student-teacher conferences and how geographic region intersected with silences and listening.

In foregrounding geographic location, I need also to point out that as much as place or region is literal and grounded, identities defined by place are also shifting and ephemeral. For example, when I lived in the South, I was identified as a northerner, although when I lived in northern Wisconsin, I was considered by at least one colleague to be southern in my speech and my manners, a very startling revelation to me. I am midwestern by virtue of where I've lived most of my life (Ohio). But not even all Midwests are alike: Wisconsin and Oklahoma (by some accounts) are also midwestern states, but their Midwests (and mine) are vastly different. Similarly, there is not a singular "South," as TV commercials on Turner South (broadcast in the South in 2006) openly assert. In these, a diverse range of individuals mark one or another version of what they call "My South," and the composite, from Cajun to Carolina, is all "South" and proud of it! This composite South is both grounded in material, demonstrable, visual realities and also ephemeral—partly because it is so varied. Similarly, I point to a rural, southeast Georgia, the place of my observations, that is both grounded and ephemeral and, as Reynolds points out, a place of "particular sociogeographical intersections, influenc[ing a person's] . . . habits, speech patterns, style, and values" (11).

The "southern" silences I write about are primarily my students', although their silences occasioned mine, too. At unexpected moments and in two particular and different ways (which I lay out below), certain students went silent in conferences with me. These very small moments might have been insignificant had they not sometimes jarred me and unsettled behaviors I had developed and honed over thirty years of classroom teaching and conferencing. These repeated moments created disjunctures for me and urged me to investigate the sound waves I did not hear, to listen heuristically and rhetorically.

My observations about student listening and either the silence or the coded verbal behavior that accompanied it in the South demonstrate aspects of silence and listening to be complex rhetorical arts, ones this volume aims to explore. Importantly, students' silences can be powerful instantiations of listening as a heuristic, an assertion that should be so obvious it need not be stated. Because, however, of the way student silences have been constructed in the last several decades of composition scholarship, the point needs to be made. In this, I join Mary M. Reda, who in her book *Between Speaking and Silence: A Study of Quiet Students* challenges our discipline to radically revise how we interpret student silences. When, Reda argues, the lecture mode of instruction dominated, student silence was evidence of good behavior, but as student-centered instruction has replaced lecture, silence has been constructed negatively, to indicate in students a deficit, an absence (for example, of attentiveness or engagement). Interested in how students themselves interpret their silence, Reda discovered that they constructed it in multiple ways, not singularly negative, and she argues that scholars need to attend much differently to student silences than we have so far. The small study I offer here concentrates on silence and listening through the lens of place, which is not one of Reda's concerns, but my observations are entirely in keeping with her claim that we reconstruct our interpretations of student silence, particularly that we unseat the perception of student silence as deficit or absence or failure.

Her Body Made Me Listen
A Scene

Her body is the color of latte. Mine is white. Hers faces the desk at which we sit, and one of her arms stretches across the desktop and supports her head, adorned with intricately braided designs. She appropriates the space for herself.

She makes no eye contact with me. She makes no perceptible movement but rests, still. I do not think her asleep, as she may seem.

I sit beside her, my chair angled toward her, my body half facing her and half facing her essay on the desk between us.

I speak. She listens.

The Backstory

A few weeks into my first semester at Georgia Southern University, I was holding conferences with each student over rough drafts of their first formal assignment. When Ashley's turn came, she walked in prepared: she pulled out her papers, arranged them in front of us, sat erect beside me, listened as I discussed her draft, made a few comments, and took notes. She was businesslike, apparently in control and ready to receive help, in some ways a model student. But the conference was short, shorter than I expected: I gave a few comments on the very short piece of writing we had before us; Ashley acknowledged that she understood, with perhaps a question or two; and then she packed up and left.

Because of the brevity of Ashley's first draft, she and I might well have worked considerably longer on it. But when Ashley signaled she was finished, our conference ended, and I wondered what good, if any, would come of it. Ashley had given me very few verbal signals that she was "with me" in our discussion, and because our conference was also short, I could not feel much confidence that the meeting had been effective or had helped her understand, more than her brief essay demonstrated, what the assignment was asking of her. I didn't, however, press too much for more time or attention than Ashley seemed willing to give. It was early in the semester, and one of my primary goals for each conference was to quell the fear students often have of meeting with their professor. I knew that Ashley would have more than one chance to revise her essay, and so our short conference might have accomplished enough for the time being. Because I wasn't sure we'd done enough in conference to help her essay much, I was surprised when it improved—in length and in her conception of the topic. I always expect students to surprise me—because I've learned that they so often do—but I hadn't received many clues that Ashley might.

Ashley and I continued to meet throughout the semester, often at her request, and sometimes we chatted more informally than we had on that first day. In this way, as well as through the results I saw in her writing, I had evidence that the conferences helped her and that she thought so, too. One day, when Ashley was in my office, we got ready to talk, and very soon, her long, slender brown arm stretched out on my desk and her head of ornate braids lay down upon it, her eyes closed. I continued talking, but to all appearances, Ashley, with her face turned away from me, could have been asleep, or at least resting. I could easily have thought she was disengaged, but I wasn't wary because even though Ashley gave me none of the usual signals that she was attentive, I had learned to recognize that her ways of listening—and of showing that she was listening—were different from those of students I was accustomed to. Like in our first conference, she said nothing, or almost nothing, but the informality in Ashley's body posture and language contrasted with the businesslike formality of our first conference. Like then, she surely heard my comments but gave very few verbal or nonverbal signals that she had. Since Ashley's silence and body at rest are ways I behave in communicative situations in which I am very close to the person I'm in dialogue with—someone I love, a family member, a trusted colleague—I had to look beyond my own experience to listen to what Ashley's silence was telling me. In this particular conference, the one in which she was most dramatically silent, Ashley listened in ways that seemed to require her to shut out other stimuli (visual ones, oral responses to me, body movement). And she did so without any apparent self-consciousness.

Interpreting the Story, Hearing Its Silence

Ashley's silences invited me to hear them differently from how such silences might well be interpreted and certainly differently from how they have been constructed in much composition scholarship. Her silence invited me into a kind of silence, as well, one in which I had to put aside any early preconceptions about Ashley as a student that I might have formed as well as preconceptions encultured by discourse in our profession and listen to and reinterpret the evidence before me. I might easily have interpreted Ashley's silence as something besides listening, for example, as a way of ignoring me, of resisting our work together, or, at the very least, of behaving outside the accepted mores of student-teacher conference. While Ashley might seem to have ignored me, once I listened to her, I came to believe that she was listening, probably very intently. I had to listen with acute awareness to hear the unfamiliar dialect of her silence fairly and accurately.

It was unmistakably clear to me that the picture of Ashley at rest, "appropriating" my desk, carried none of the defiance or disregard of space or authority that the term "appropriating" might suggest. Nor was it evidence of a lazy student, nor a disengaged one, I am certain. The history that Ashley and I had created demonstrated to me that whatever her silence signaled, it did not entail any of these interpretations of silence that our pedagogical discussions would offer.

If I concentrate only on the absence of Ashley's oral response to me, I could read her actions as part of a "southern" code of politeness different from mine: "Be quiet and listen; show respect" (to parents, educators, elders). And while it is probable that Ashley's listening was a coded, learned behavior, I've partly discounted any of the ready explanations I've come up with about which aspects of her life taught such listening to her: long church services in which she learned to listen to adults speaking? A culture in which children are schooled to be silent as a sign of respect for authority? A hierarchical family or social culture? None of these is much more than an offshoot of stereotyping southern culture. Such ready explanations might obscure the important listening Ashley did. They would also redirect my teacher's attention *away from* the actual learning situation, one in which Ashley listened to my voice and I listened to the dialect of her silence, what I believe to be evidence of her way of processing information, of learning. For this and other reasons, I search for more than what any of those first speculations explains.

For Ashley, silence was "productive," a term Cynthia Ryan uses. And even though Ashley was silent, she was not silenced. Paradoxically, then, Ashley's silence—which, if it were read as part of the regional code of politeness, a code that honors hierarchy, authority, clearly codified and non-egalitarian roles of speaker and listener, a code that seems to me to impose distances between people—functioned in her interactions with me in a way that crossed a distance. It is important to remember that silence itself is a complex rhetorical phenomenon. As Cheryl Glenn has shown, it can be as "powerful as speech"; it is a mode of knowing that "complements language"; although not always strategic, especially when it is imposed, silence "as a rhetoric . . . [is] a constellation of symbolic strategies that (like spoken language) . . . serves many functions" (xi).

As is clear, one of the many things that interest me about Ashley is how much she truly listened as we conferenced. Supporting this observation is something I learned years ago: during class discussions, participating vocally is far from the only way students demonstrate engagement. The most silent students may be highly engaged and speak little or not at all—out of shyness or out of a learning style that requires the learner to process internally for a long while before speaking or writing. Students like this demonstrate their engagement in other ways—in what they write, in what they say during conferences, or in a rare comment that offers a penetrating insight. As Glenn points out, the "function of silence—that is, its effects upon people—varies according to the social context in which it occurs" (xii), and, I would add, its functions vary according to the users' habits, preferences, mental processing patterns, and so forth.

For Ashley, silence seems very much to have served a heuristic function, a "symbolic strategy" (Glenn xi). Part of that function may have been cognitive, for example, allowing her to process the oral comments I made on her draft essay. But part of it may well have drawn on what George Kalamaras calls the "tacit dimension." Kalamaras writes, "Because I am arguing for a more expansive perception of rationality . . . , I will refer to two particular modes of understanding: *conceptual* and *nonconceptual*. . . . [C]onceptual understanding or awareness . . . mean[s] those perceptions formed through process of thoughts. Nonconceptual . . . mean[s] those perceptions that are not bound by the categorizing capacity of intellect or thought" (8). Since we may typically think cognitive understanding functions through more Western, logo-centric epistemological processes, it is useful to include Kalamaras's nonconceptual yet rational way of knowing, a way that seems perfectly (though not necessarily) aligned with silence, with Ashley's kind of listening.

Some composition scholars, such as the contributors to *Minding the Light: Essays in Friendly Pedagogy* edited by Anne Dalke and Barbara Dixson, locate this nonconceptual epistemology in spiritual, religious realms, particularly in the Quaker religion. It certainly exists in spiritual realms, but I think not only there. Nonconceptual thought can be, I believe, a meditative way of knowing in other realms besides the spiritual and religious, a way of knowing that may well be outside of *logos* while it is at the same time rational. (Our Western vocabulary, however, makes understanding this kind of nonconceptual, non-religious thought difficult to understand, drawing boundary lines where it does.) As Krista Ratcliffe asserts, rhetorical listening leads us "to question [the dominance] of *logos* as we know it" ("Rhetorical Listening" 204). Ashley's listening certainly does. Even though her response to our conferences may have resulted in discursive and conceptual changes in her writing, her means of arriving at these changes were not necessarily logo-centric.

Ashley's listening was not characterized by only the absence of speaking. Ashley, though silent, was neither "silenced" nor passive; she enacted a kind of agency through her silence and the subsequent revisions to her writing, at least insofar as we stipulate that my judgment of improvement to her writing is reliable. Ratcliffe posits a possible explanation of Ashley's agency when she draws on Jacqueline Jones Royster's "model of critical readerly agency . . . [one that] offers the possibilities of both . . . readerly and authorial [agencies], functioning as subject positions, with everyone rotating in and out of each position, assuming respect for the process, the people, and each other's subject positions" ("Eavesdropping" 109). That Ashley "appropriated" my desk space, closed her eyes as I spoke, and created more elaborate, well-formed essays afterward are strong indicators that she "assumed a subject position" during her interaction with me.

Their Words Made Me Speechless

Just as interesting but more difficult for me to understand were the ways my enculturations affected my reactions to students' various listening behaviors. I reacted negatively to some but not to Ashley's. Many times, in conferences over draft writing, students—of both African and European descent, both female and male, both rural Georgian and Atlanta urban—stopped me in my tracks with their responses to me.

When the energy was high in a conference, seemingly productive—when dialogue had been a back-and-forth exchange—I'd hear a sudden "Yes, ma'am" that was accompanied by an almost expressionless face, much silence, and a very still body posture. The moments always felt to me out of synch with the momentum I felt, outside the character of the interaction prior to it. Stopped short like this, I felt the progress of our conversation derailed, and as a means of recovering our momentum, I would ask questions of the student to confirm where we were in the conference: "Do you really understand what I'm saying? I don't want to go on talking if I'm confusing you." Often, the student would indicate and later convince me through his or her revisions (as Ashley had) that the conference talk was "working," even though I'd had those moments of doubt. I learned quickly that a "Yes, ma'am" did not mean what I felt it might have: a signal of politeness, a signal that the student was ready to finish and leave and wanted me to stop talking, a signal that the student didn't have a clue what I was talking about but was too uncomfortable to ask. I puzzled over such moments, over my reaction to them as much as to the student behavior that was outside the realm of my experience to date, and I eventually learned that none of my first explanations was right. But I doubt that I ever got through a conference punctuated by this kind of "Yes, ma'am" without momentarily being thrown.

These unfamiliar speaking/listening experiences in the regionally defined space of the Old South invited me to puzzle out such small moments and to inflect my puzzling out with the region in which I first encountered them. To help me through my puzzlement, I asked an undergraduate student, who herself was often silent during our conferences, to explore these moments with me. A student who had taken several classes with me over four years, she often visited my office, brought me honey from her uncle, and told me long stories of her very conservative, religious upbringing in a family where none of the women (except one) ever wore slacks of any kind (they all wore dresses), where her grandfather ministered to a church, the congregants of which were all her extended family, and where the congregants mixed old practices of spell-casting and talking in tongues with Christian religion. When I told Alisha that I always felt, in these "Yes, ma'am" conference moments, as if the forward progress of the conference had been derailed, she was completely amused at how *wrong* I was, and she was unafraid to tell me. She said that her "Yes, ma'am"s (and those of the other students) meant "I'm with you; keep going. This conversation is working!"

And yet every signal I heard meant just the opposite of what she and the other students intended. It seems, then, that "Yes, ma'am" in these moments is much closer to a tradition of call and response than simply a code of politeness or respect or a stop-gap measure to disguise some intention the speaker wants to keep hidden. The silence that followed "Yes, ma'am," both verbal and nonverbal (as I interpreted the facial expressions that accompanied the refrain), may well have been what Glenn calls "expressive." "[S]ilence," Glenn writes, "is too often read as simple passivity in situations where it has actually an expressive power." It can either "deploy power" or it can "defer to power" (xi). "Yes, ma'am," when used as my students did in these conference moments, however, is not best characterized by the dichotomy, deferring to or deploying power. Instead, it seems to be expressive of participation, a third stance somewhere outside of this dichotomy.

These instances in which encoded identities exhibited themselves demonstrate patterns of student listening that were (always) unfamiliar to me, no matter how well I could identify them, as I eventually did. But the student silence I often heard beside me during conferences has forced me to *listen heuristically* and *rhetorically*—because the students' behavior in my office and their performance in revising essays afterward seemed, again and again, incongruent with my expectations, shaped as my expectations were to read such student silence as inattentiveness, resistance, unwillingness to hear me.

Much as error analysis (for example, Mina P. Shaughnessy's) is a window into observing rhetorical processes previously unobserved, so is my moving to the South a window into these particular varieties of listening and silence, what may be an intricate double helix, one strand of which is students' listening to my voice, another strand of which is my listening to the dialects of their silences. Again, in *Unspoken*, Glenn writes that she is "hopeful that further research on the rhetorics of silence will be rooted in the classroom" (159). This beginning research shows, I think, how much work there is yet to do on the rhetorical concepts of silence and listening and, equally, how much *place* can contribute to our knowledge in rhetoric and composition.

Works Cited

Dalke, Anne, and Barbara Dixson, eds. *Minding the Light: Essays in Friendly Pedagogy*. New York: Peter Lang, 2004. Print.

Duffey, Suellynn. "Place, Culture, Memory." *The Writing Program Interrupted: Making Space for Critical Discourse*. Ed. Jeanne Gunner and Donna Strickland. Portsmouth, NH: Boynton/Cook/Heinemann, 2009. 186–93. Print.

Fleckenstein, Kristie S. "Bodysigns: A Biorhetoric for Change." *JAC* 24.1 (2001): 761–90. Print.

Glenn, Cheryl. *Unspoken: A Rhetoric of Silence*. Carbondale: Southern Illinois UP, 2004. Print.

Kalamaras, George. *Reclaiming the Tacit Dimension: Symbolic Form in the Rhetoric of Silence*. Albany: State U of New York P, 1994. Print.

Ratcliffe, Krista. "Eavesdropping as Rhetorical Tactic: History, Whiteness, and Rhetoric." *JAC* 20 (2000): 87–119. Print.

———. "Rhetorical Listening: A Trope for Interpretive Invention and a 'Code of Cross-Cultural Conduct.'" *CCC* 51 (1999): 195–224. Print.

Reda, Mary M. *Between Speaking and Silence: A Study of Quiet Students*. Albany: State U of New York P, 2009. Print.

Reynolds, Nedra. *Geographies of Writing: Inhabiting Places and Encountering Difference*. Carbondale: Southern Illinois UP, 2004. Print.

Ryan, Cynthia. "Unquiet Gestures: Thoughts on a Productive Rhetoric(s) of Silence." *JAC* 22 (2002): 667–78. Print.

Shaughnessy, Mina P. *Errors and Expectations: A Guide for the Teacher of Basic Writing*. New York: Oxford UP, 1977. Print.

Contributors

Index

Contributors

Joy Arbor is assistant professor of communication at Kettering University where she teaches professional communication and listening across difference. Having presented on Compassionate Listening at the Rhetoric Society of America Conference and the Conference on College Composition and Communication, she continues to study five citizen delegates in terms of the rhetorical effects of listening to stories of suffering. She is also working on a book developing a rhetorical theory and practice that promotes intervention in the suffering of others. She has received awards and fellowships for her human rights research and service, public writing, and poetry. Earning her PhD from the University of Nebraska–Lincoln, she has taught writing and rhetoric at that school, the College of the Canyons, and the American University in Cairo. For more information on the Compassionate Listening Project, please see www.compassionatelistening.org.

Suellyn Duffey, associate professor and writing program administrator, University of Missouri–St. Louis, lived in the rural southeast for five years while she taught in the writing and linguistics department at Georgia Southern University. Her experiences there, as a non-southerner, prompted the investigation she undertakes in this volume and extends her interest in the widely varying (institutional) cultures in which she has taught and directed writing programs. She has published chapters in several book as well as articles in *CCC*, the *Journal of the Council of Writing Program Administrators*, *Writing on the Edge*, and *Across the Disciplines* on topics ranging from writing program administration (ethics, collaborative program structures, and the junior WPA) to basic writing (pedagogy and tracking) and the seductive power of technology.

Frank Farmer is associate professor of English at the University of Kansas, where he teaches courses in writing and rhetorical theory. He is the author of *Saying and Silence: Listening to Composition with Bakhtin* and editor of *Landmark Essays on Bakhtin, Rhetoric, and Writing*. His work has appeared in *CCC, College English, JAC, Rhetoric Review*, and several other leading journals. His current interests center on public writing, public culture, style, and theories of everyday life. He is currently a Conger-Gable Teaching Professor of English.

Kennan Ferguson is associate professor of political science at the University of Wisconsin–Milwaukee, where he teaches political theory. He is the author of *Politics of Judgment, William James: Politics and the Pluriverse*, and *All in the Family: On Community and Incommensurability*. His current research concerns the politics of sensoria, primarily through the form of cookbooks.

Kristie S. Fleckenstein is professor of English at Florida State University, where she teaches undergraduate courses for the department's editing, writing, and media major and graduate courses in visual rhetoric, modern rhetorical theory, and feminist rhetoric for the rhetoric and composition program. She is the author of *Vision, Rhetoric, and Social Action in the Composition Classroom*, which received the 2009 W. Ross Winterowd Award for Best Book in Composition Theory, as well as *Embodied Literacies: Imageword and a Poetics of Teaching*, recipient of the 2005 CCCC Outstanding Book of the Year Award. She has published articles and book chapters on issues related to materiality, feminist theory, visual rhetoric, and pedagogy. Currently, she is at work on a book-length study of the intersections of photography and rhetoric in the nineteenth century.

Cheryl Glenn is Liberal Arts Research Professor of English and Women's Studies and codirector of the Center for Democratic Deliberation at The Pennsylvania State University. She has been visiting professor at the University of New Mexico, the University of Cape Town, and the University of Alberta and has lectured widely throughout the United States, Canada, Europe, and Africa. In the summers, she teaches at the Bread Loaf Graduate School of English. In 2008, Glenn served as chair of the

Conference on College Composition and Communication. Her publications include *Rhetoric Retold: Regendering the Tradition from Antiquity through the Renaissance, Unspoken: A Rhetoric of Silence, Rhetorical Education in America, The St. Martin's Guide to Teaching Writing, The Writer's Harbrace Handbook, Making Sense,* and *The Harbrace Guide for Writers.* Glenn's rhetorical scholarship has earned her National Endowment for the Humanities and Mellon fellowships, the Richard Braddock Award from *CCC,* and the Outstanding Article Award from *Rhetoric Review.* She has received four teaching awards.

Wendy Wolters Hinshaw is a doctoral candidate in rhetoric and composition at Ohio State University, where she teaches in the Department of English and Department of Women's Studies. Her articles on the rhetoric of trauma, teaching testimonial literature, and pedagogical approaches to student resistance have appeared in *JAC* and *Transformations.* Her dissertation, "Incarcerating Rhetorics, Publics, and Pedagogies," investigates how art and writing empower prisoners to counter reductive representations of criminality and how activists mobilize prisoners' creative work to both humanize the incarcerated and reeducate the public about incarceration practices in the United States.

Melissa Ianetta is associate professor and director of writing at the University of Delaware, where she teaches courses in writing and literature. Currently, she serves on the executive board of the Council of Writing Program Administrators and, with Lauren Fitzgerald, edits the *Writing Center Journal.* Her work on the history of rhetoric has appeared in *College English, PMLA, Rhetoric Review,* and the *Writing Center Journal.* She is currently working on a project that examines the belletristic traditions of women's improvisational rhetoric.

Jay Jordan is assistant professor of English in the University Writing Program at the University of Utah. His research focuses on current and historical interactions between native and nonnative users of privileged language varieties, especially at scenes of writing. He teaches undergraduate and graduate courses in rhetoric and composition, and he coordinates Utah's first-year writing course. He has published in *CCC, College English, Rhetoric Review,* and in several edited volumes, and he is coeditor of two collections on second-language writing.

Andrea A. Lunsford is the Louise Hewlett Nixon Professor of English and faculty director of the Program in Writing and Rhetoric at Stanford University. She has designed and taught undergraduate and graduate courses in writing history and theory, rhetoric, literacy studies, and women's writing and is the editor, author, or coauthor of several books, including *The Everyday Writer, Essays on Classical Rhetoric and Modern Discourse, Singular Texts/Plural Authors: Perspectives on Collaborative Writing, Reclaiming Rhetorica, Everything's an Argument, Writing Matters: Rhetoric in Private and Public Lives*, and *The Sage Handbook of Rhetorical Studies*.

Katherine Mack is assistant professor of rhetoric and writing at the University of Colorado, Colorado Springs. Her research and teaching interests include rhetorical theory and criticism, writing studies, South African cultural rhetorics, public memory, and visual rhetoric. She is currently at work on a monograph entitled "A Generative Failure: The Truth and Reconciliation Commission of South Africa." She has published in *Writing Program Administrators* and has an essay in a forthcoming collection, "The Global Memoryscape: Contesting Remembrance in a Transnational Age."

Joyce Irene Middleton is associate professor of English and director of ethnic studies at East Carolina University. She earned her PhD in English from the University of Maryland at College Park. She has published widely on Nobel laureate Toni Morrison as well as on film as visual rhetoric, orality and literacy, and race, whiteness, and feminism in such venues as *African American Rhetoric(s), Calling Cards: Theory and Practice in the Study of Race, Gender, and Culture*, and *The Sage Handbook of Rhetorical Studies*. She served as a guest coeditor for a special issue on whiteness studies in *Rhetoric Review*, and she currently edits a biweekly blog series called "CCCC Conversations on Diversity" for the Conference on College Composition and Communication. Currently, she is writing a book-length study on race, whiteness, and post–civil rights rhetoric(s) in film, writing, and the discourses of American identity and popular culture.

Nancy Myers is associate professor of English at the University of North Carolina at Greensboro (UNCG), where she teaches composition, linguistics, and the history of rhetoric. She received the UNCG Alumni Teaching Excellence Award in 2002 and, prior to that, received two teaching awards while at the University of Missouri at Kansas City. She is currently vice president (2008–10) of the Coalition of Women Scholars in the History of Rhetoric and Composition. At UNCG, she has served as director of English education and as director of English graduate studies. Along with Gary Tate and Edward P. J. Corbett, she is an editor of the third and fourth editions of *The Writing Teacher's Sourcebook*. Recent publications include essays in *Relations, Locations, Positions: Composition Theory for Writing Teachers; The Locations of Composition*; and *Stories of Mentoring: Theory and Praxis*.

Omedi Ochieng is assistant professor of communication studies at Westmont College. His research interests are in the study of the epistemology and ethics of rhetoric. Specifically, he researches how knowledge emerges and is articulated, legitimated, and disseminated institutionally, geographically, and historically. Toward this end, he has been engaged in the study of African theories of knowledge, specifically as these illuminate questions of authority and rationality, morality and ethics, power and politics, and judgment and aesthetics. A related line of study traces articulations of wisdom as a form of knowledge and ethics in the African American intellectual tradition.

Ashley Elliott Pryor is associate professor of women's and gender studies at the University of Toledo. Her primary area of research concerns Buddhist women (especially in Mongolia, Vietnam, and Taiwan) in transitional economic and political systems, with a special emphasis on what Buddhist teachings can contribute to increasing environmental sustainability in the face of rapid globalization. She is at work on a monograph on this topic and has presented papers and workshops in both Mongolia and Vietnam on these issues. Her past articles concern the role that the "non-human" voice has played in a variety of Western philosophic texts (Heidegger, Agamben, Plato, Cavarrero) as well as in meditative and contemplative traditions (especially in Mahayana Chan/Zen Buddhist lineages). She spent the summer of 2009 in Prescott, Arizona, as a NEH Summer Institute Fellow examining the work of American environmentalist Aldo Leopold.

Krista Ratcliffe is professor and chair of English at Marquette University in Milwaukee. There she has served as director of the first-year writing program, which won a 2006 CCCC Certificate of Excellence Award. Her teaching has earned her a university teaching award. She has served as president of NCTE's College Forum, as president of CCCC's Coalition of Women Scholars in the History of Rhetoric, and as president-elect of the Rhetoric Society of America. Her publications include *Anglo-American Feminist Challenges to the Rhetorical Tradition*, *Who's Having This Baby* (coauthored with Helen Sterk, Carla Hay, Alice Kehoe, and Leona Vande-Vusse), *Rhetorical Listening: Identification, Gender, Whiteness* (which won the 2006 *JAC* Gary Olson Award, the 2007 CCCC Outstanding Book Award, and the 2007 Rhetoric Society of America Book Award), and *Performing Feminist Administration in Rhetoric and Composition Studies* (coedited with Rebecca Rickly). Her work has appeared in edited collections, as well as in *CCC*, *JAC*, *Rhetoric Review*, and *College English*.

Adam Rosenblatt is a PhD candidate in modern thought and literature at Stanford. His dissertation, "Last Rights: Forensic Science, Human Rights, and the Victims of Atrocity," is a study of the international teams of forensic experts who investigate mass graves in the wake of human rights violations, identifying and returning bodies to their mourners and collecting evidence for war crimes tribunals. The dissertation focuses on the complex political landscape in which these investigations take place, their unique use of human rights concepts, and the ethical status of dead bodies that have suffered violence. Rosenblatt has occasionally published comics of his own, including the travel comic "Captain Heartbreak's Guide to Chile." He has taught classes on political and legal theory, the art and politics of silence, and graphic novels.

Shari Stenberg is associate professor at the University of Nebraska–Lincoln, where she teaches writing and rhetoric and coordinates the Faculty Leadership for Writing Initiative. She is author of *Professing and Pedagogy: Learning the Teaching of English*. Her writing on issues including teacher development, feminist rhetoric, and critical pedagogy appears in *College English*, *CCC*, *symploke*, and *Composition Studies*.

Margaret M. Strain is associate professor at the University of Dayton, where she teaches undergraduate and graduate courses in writing, composition theory, histories of rhetoric, and Irish drama. With Alexis Hart, she coedits the Interviews section of *Kairos: A Journal of Rhetoric, Technology, and Pedagogy.* She is also the cofounder of the Rhetoric and Composition Sound Archives with Brad E. Lucas. Her work on the disciplinary rise of composition studies, historiography, research methods, and oral narratives has appeared in *Rhetoric Society Quarterly, JAC, Writing on the Edge, Composition Forum,* and edited collections. Her current research focuses on the rhetorical role of the Gaelic language to mediate Catholic/Anglican relations in nineteenth-century Ireland.

Lisa Suter is assistant professor of English at the University of Tampa, where she currently specializes in the teaching of first-year writing. Lisa received her PhD from Miami University of Ohio, where her research focused on women's rhetorical education in the late nineteenth century. She is particularly concerned with the American Delsarte movement: a group of professional women taking charge of their own oratorical training (in unconventional ways) to become more effective public speakers on such subjects as suffrage, labor movements, racial equality, and more. She is at work on a book project.

Shevaun E. Watson is assistant professor of English and director of composition at the University of Wisconsin–Eau Claire. Her research focuses on the intersections of African American rhetoric and literacy, early American studies, transatlanticism, and historiography. Her work on this and other interests, including women's literacy, early American literature, writing program administration, and writing centers has appeared in *CCC, Writing Program Administration, Rhetoric Society Quarterly, Rhetorica, Early American Literature, Writing Center Journal, Composition Studies,* and several recent edited collections. Her teaching revolves around rhetoric and writing, particularly first-year composition, peer tutoring, composition studies, and topical seminars in rhetoric. She has served on the boards of the International and Southeastern Writing Center Associations. Watson is the winner of two dissertation awards and the 2010 Braddock Award.

Index

Italicized page numbers indicate illustrations.